Developing and Delivering
Practice-Based Evidence

This book provides a comprehensive account of everything a practitioner needs to know about the generation of practice-based evidence. It is just the book that is needed to inspire practitioners to engage with research through meeting with others in practitioner networks or influencing the agencies they work in, to start collecting data.

'It is a potentially historical text that captures in one volume the assembled knowledge of the vanguard who will lead essential changes in the way that knowledge is generated in the field of psychotherapy. It has the potential to be revolutionary as it becomes a recommended text for psychotherapy researchers and practitioners that will herald a shift in how research is conducted, who does it, how it is reported and the influence it will have on future services.'

Professor Sue Wheeler, Director of Counselling and Psychotherapy Programme, University of Leicester, UK

Developing and Delivering Practice-Based Evidence

A Guide for the Psychological Therapies

Edited by

Michael Barkham
Centre for Psychological Services Research
University of Sheffield

Gillian E. Hardy
Clinical Psychology Unit, Department of Psychology
University of Sheffield

John Mellor-Clark
CORE Information Management Systems
Rugby

A John Wiley & Sons, Ltd., Publication

This edition first published 2010
© 2010 John Wiley & Sons Ltd.

Wiley-Blackwell is an imprint of John Wiley & Sons, formed by the merger of Wiley's global
Scientific, Technical, and Medical business with Blackwell Publishing.

Registered Office
John Wiley & Sons Ltd, The Atrium, Southern Gate, Chichester, West Sussex, PO19 8SQ, UK

Editorial Offices
The Atrium, Southern Gate, Chichester, West Sussex, PO19 8SQ, UK
9600 Garsington Road, Oxford, OX4 2DQ, UK
350 Main Street, Malden, MA 02148-5020, USA

For details of our global editorial offices, for customer services, and for information about how to
apply for permission to reuse the copyright material in this book please see our website at
www.wiley.com/wiley-blackwell.

The right of the editors to be identified as the author of this work has been asserted in accordance
with the Copyright, Designs and Patents Act 1988.

Library of Congress Cataloging-in-Publication Data
    Developing and delivering practice-based evidence : a guide for the psychological therapies /
[edited by] Michael Barkham, Gillian E. Hardy, John Mellor-Clark.
        p. ; cm.
    Includes bibliographical references and index.
    ISBN 978-0-470-03234-3 (cloth)—ISBN 978-0-470-03235-0 (pbk.)   1. Evidence-based
psychotherapy.   I. Barkham, Michael.   II. Hardy, Gillian E.   III. Mellor-Clark, John.
    [DNLM: 1. Psychotherapy—methods.   2. Clinical Trials as Topic.   3. Evidence-Based
Practice.   4. Outcome Assessment (Health Care)—methods.   5. Quality Assurance, Health
Care—methods.   6. Research Design   WM 420 D4875 2010]
    RC455.2.E94D48 2010
    616.89′14—dc22   2009042886

A catalogue record for this book is available from the British Library.

Typeset in 10/12pt Minion by Aptara Inc., New Delhi, India.
Printed and bound in Singapore by Markono Print Media Pte Ltd

Impression   [2010]

Dedicated to the vision of
Ernest Amory Codman
and
Irene Elkin

Contents

List of Contributors		*xi*
Foreword		*xvii*
Preface		*xxi*
Acknowledgements		*xxv*

SECTION I: EVIDENCE-BASED PRACTICE AND PRACTICE-BASED EVIDENCE — 1

1 **The Current View of Evidence and Evidence-Based Practice** — 3
Peter Bower and Simon Gilbody

2 **Building a Rigorous and Relevant Knowledge Base for the Psychological Therapies** — 21
Michael Barkham, William B. Stiles, Michael J. Lambert and John Mellor-Clark

SECTION II: METHODOLOGICAL PLURALISM FOR INDIVIDUAL PRACTITIONERS — 63

3 **Scientific, Practical and Personal Decisions in Selecting Qualitative Methods** — 65
Nancy Pistrang and Chris Barker

4 **Theory-Building Case Studies as Practice-Based Evidence** — 91
William B. Stiles

5 **Single Case Quantitative Methods for Practice-Based Evidence** — 109
Dean McMillan and Stephen Morley

SECTION III: MEASUREMENT SYSTEMS FOR INDIVIDUAL
PRACTITIONERS AND SERVICES   139

6   Outcome Questionnaire System (The OQ System):
Development and Practical Applications in Healthcare Settings   141
Michael J. Lambert, Nathan B. Hansen and S. Cory Harmon

7   Treatment Outcome Package (TOP) – Development and use in
Naturalistic Settings   155
David Kraus and Louis G. Castonguay

8   Clinical Outcomes in Routine Evaluation (CORE) – The CORE
Measures and System: Measuring, Monitoring and Managing
Quality Evaluation in the Psychological Therapies   175
Michael Barkham, John Mellor-Clark, Janice Connell, Chris Evans,
Richard Evans and Frank Margison

SECTION IV: MONITORING STRATEGIES FOR INDIVIDUAL
PRACTITIONERS AND SERVICES   221

9   Using Benchmarks and Benchmarking to Improve Quality of
Practice and Services   223
Robert J. Lueger and Michael Barkham

10   Constructing and Disseminating Outcome Data at the Service
Level: Case Tracking and Benchmarking   257
Chris Leach and Wolfgang Lutz

SECTION V: MANAGING IMPROVEMENT VIA
ORGANIZATIONS AND PRACTICE NETWORKS   285

11   Organizational and Conceptual Framework for
Practice-Based Research on the Effectiveness of
Psychotherapy and Psychotherapy Training   287
Robert Elliott and Alberto Zucconi

12   Practice Research Networks and Psychological Services
Research in the UK and USA   311
Glenys Parry, Louis G. Castonguay, Tom D. Borkovec and
Abraham W. Wolf

SECTION VI: DEVELOPING AND DELIVERING PRACTICE-BASED EVIDENCE **327**

13 Improving Practice and Enhancing Evidence **329**
Michael Barkham, Gillian E. Hardy and John Mellor-Clark

Index *355*

List of Contributors

Chris Barker is Reader in Clinical Psychology at University College London. His research examines the communication of psychological help and support across a range of populations and settings, both professional and non-professional. He is an author of *Research Methods in Clinical Psychology* (Wiley, 2002) (with Nancy Pistrang and Robert Elliott). ✉ c.barker@ucl.ac.uk

Michael Barkham is Professor of Clinical Psychology and Director of the Centre for Psychological Services Research at the University of Sheffield. He has an abiding commitment to enhancing the methods and tools that underpin practice-based evidence. He was previously a member of the CORE System Trust and Joint Editor of the *British Journal of Clinical Psychology* (2004–10). ✉ m.barkham@sheffield.ac.uk

Tom D. Borkovec is a Distinguished Professor Emeritus of Psychology at the Pennsylvania State University. He has conducted basic and applied research on anxiety disorders, initiated practice research networks in the US, and contributed to the literature on the design and methodology of therapy outcome investigations. ✉ tdb@psu.edu

Peter Bower is a Reader at the National Primary Care Research and Development Centre and the NIHR School for Primary Care Research, University of Manchester. His area of expertise is the analysis of mental health services in primary care (including psychological therapies and self-help interventions), and the use of randomized controlled trials and systematic reviews in the development and testing of complex interventions. ✉ peter.bower@manchester.ac.uk

Louis G. Castonguay is Professor of Psychology at the Department of Psychology, Pennsylvania State University and President of the Society for Psychotherapy Research (2009–10). His research focuses primarily on the process of change in different forms of psychotherapy, the development of integrative treatments for anxiety and mood disorders, the conduct and effectiveness of psychological therapies in naturalistic settings, and the establishment of practice research networks. ✉ lgc3.psu.edu

Janice Connell is a Research Associate at the School of Health and Related Research (ScHARR), University of Sheffield. She has contributed to research utilizing large practice-based CORE data sets in the promotion of practice-based evidence within routine services. In particular, she has led on projects examining the effectiveness of student and trauma counselling. ✉ j.connell@sheffield.ac.uk

Robert Elliott is Professor of Counselling in the Counselling Unit at the University of Strathclyde, Glasgow and Professor Emeritus of Psychology at the University of Toledo. He has served as Co-editor of *Psychotherapy Research*, and *Person-Centered and Experiential Psychotherapies*, and also as President of the Society for Psychotherapy Research. ✉ fac0029@gmail.com

Chris Evans is a Consultant Psychiatrist in Psychotherapy in Nottinghamshire Healthcare NHS Trust and a Professor at the University of Nottingham. He is a group analyst as well as an analytic and systemic therapist who has worked clinically in mental health for 25 years. He was part of the team that developed the CORE-OM and CORE System and has particular expertise in psychometrics. He is involved in translating the CORE-OM into other languages and developing an adaptation for use with people with learning disabilities. ✉ chris@psyctc.org

Richard Evans is a Trustee of the CORE System Trust and a qualified counsellor and psychotherapist. He brings a wealth of experience of performance management and of IT to the field of outcome measurement and has worked closely with many services in helping them with their implementation of routine measurement for assessment, progress monitoring, case review and outcome, and the general task of service management. ✉ riche@btclick.com

Simon Gilbody is Professor of Psychological Medicine and Health Services Research at the University of York. He has first degrees in both psychology and medicine, and trained as a psychiatrist and cognitive behaviour therapist. His areas of expertise are in epidemiology, psychometrics and the analysis of clinical and cost-effectiveness using trials and evidence synthesis – including meta-analysis and decision modelling. ✉ sg519@york.ac.uk

Nathan B. Hansen is Assistant Professor in the Department of Psychiatry, Yale University School of Medicine. His clinical and research work focuses on HIV mental health, with a particular emphasis on the intersection of childhood abuse and interpersonal violence and HIV infection. He has worked to develop numerous individual and group-level interventions to prevent HIV infection among vulnerable and at-risk populations. ✉ nathan.hansen@yale.edu

Gillian E. Hardy is Professor of Clinical Psychology, Director of the Clinical Psychology Unit and the Doctorate in Clinical Psychology training programme at the University of Sheffield. She has published extensively on process and outcome psychotherapy research and for many years worked with a team of clinicians and researchers in a research clinic for the treatment of depression. She is Joint Editor of the *British Journal of Clinical Psychology* (2005–10). ✉ g.hardy@sheffield.ac.uk

S. Cory Harmon is at New York–Presbyterian Hospital, White Plains, New York. Her research interests include treatment deterioration and ruptures in therapeutic relationships. ✉ scoryharmon@hotmail.com

David Kraus is Chief Executive Officer of Behavioral Health Labs, Marlborough, Massachusetts. His research focuses on developing clinically meaningful outcome tools and processes for quality improvement. ✉ dkraus@bhealthlabs.com

Michael J. Lambert is Professor of Psychology and holds the Susa Young Gates University Professorship at Brigham Young University, Utah and is a past President of the Society for Psychotherapy Research. He has written extensively on the effects of psychotherapy especially as it relates to spontaneous remission, placebo effects, common healing factors and deterioration. The work published in this book represents the culmination of his 35 years as a provider and researcher. ✉ michael_lambert@byu.edu

Chris Leach is Consultant Clinical Psychologist at South West Yorkshire Partnership NHS Foundation Trust and Visiting Professor at the University of Huddersfield. His main research interest is in evaluating effectiveness of psychological therapies in routine practice. He is also a statistician and a former Editor of the *British Journal of Mathematical and Statistical Psychology*. ✉ Chris.Leach@swyt.nhs.uk

Robert J. Lueger is the Dean of the College of Arts and Sciences and Professor of Psychology at Creighton University in Omaha, Nebraska. He conducts research on psychotherapy and counselling outcomes in mental health service delivery systems. The goal of this research is to identify case-relevant models of treatment response that can be used to inform clinicians about the progress of an individual client currently receiving treatment. ✉ RobertLueger@creighton.edu

Wolfgang Lutz is Professor and Head of the Department of Clinical Psychology and Psychotherapy, University of Trier. His research on change in psychotherapy has the goal to support decision making in behavioural health based on empirical data. Current research efforts involve the assessment and modelling of individual change for patients diagnosed with anxiety or depressive disorders, as well as the identification of predictors and mediators of treatment outcome, sudden gains early in treatment and therapist differences. ✉ wolfgang.lutz@uni-trier.de

Frank Margison is Consultant Psychiatrist in Psychotherapy, Manchester Mental Health and Social Care Trust and a Fellow of the Royal College of Psychiatrists. His research interests have been in developing and teaching psychodynamic interpersonal therapy, outcome studies, and in using outcomes measures in routine practice. He was part of the team that developed the CORE-OM and CORE System and is a CORE System Trustee. ✉ frmargison@aol.com

Dean McMillan is a Senior Lecturer in Health Sciences at the University of York. He is interested in the use of single case designs in process and outcome research in cognitive behaviour therapy. ✉ dm645@york.ac.uk

John Mellor-Clark is Managing Director of CORE Information Management System Ltd. which resources and supports a large UK practice research network comprising over 250 services and 3,000 therapy practitioners. He has been engaged in the evaluation of UK psychological therapies and counselling for the past 20 years and regularly presents on topics such as best practice development, service quality benchmarking and introducing practitioner performance appraisal. ✉ john.mellor-clark@coreims.co.uk

Stephen Morley is Professor of Clinical Psychology and Director of the Programme in Clinical Psychology, Leeds Institute of Health Sciences, University of Leeds. He has a long-standing interest in single case methods and their application in clinical research settings. He has written several reviews on the application of statistical and graphical methods for analysing single case data. ✉ S.J.Morley@leeds.ac.uk

Glenys Parry is Professor of Applied Psychological Therapies at the University of Sheffield Centre for Psychological Services Research. She has a long-standing interest in applicable psychotherapy research, practice-based evidence and policy research on the delivery, organization and cost-effectiveness of psychological services. ✉ g.d.parry@sheffield.ac.uk

Nancy Pistrang is Reader in Clinical Psychology at University College London. Her research focuses on fundamental processes in psychological help, including that delivered by non-professionals as well as professionals. She is an author of *Research Methods in Clinical Psychology* (Wiley, 2002) (with Chris Barker and Robert Elliott). ✉ n.pistrang@ucl.ac.uk

William B. Stiles is Professor of Clinical Psychology at Miami University in Oxford, Ohio and he has held visiting positions at the Universities of Sheffield and Leeds in England, at Massey University in New Zealand, and at the University of Joensuu in Finland. He has been president of the Society for Psychotherapy Research and North American Editor of *Psychotherapy Research*. He is currently Co-editor of *Person-Centered and Experiential Psychotherapies* and Associate Editor of *British Journal of Clinical Psychology*. ✉ stileswb@muohio.edu

Abraham W. Wolf is Professor of Psychology in Psychiatry, School of Medicine, Case Western Reserve University and Associate Director of Adult Outpatient Services, Department of Psychiatry, MetroHealth Medical Center, Cleveland, Ohio. He has written and presented on the application of psychotherapy practice-based research networks. ✉ axw7@cwru.edu

Alberto Zucconi teaches person-centred psychotherapy at postgraduate level in the Faculty of Medicine at the University of Siena, and is President of the Istituto dell'Approccio Centrato sulla Persona (IACP). He also coordinates the association of Italian private psychotherapy training schools (CNSP). ✉ azucconi@iacp.it

Foreword

The field of psychotherapy historically has been fraught with disagreements, created by camps of individuals with strongly held views of what is correct – and what is not. Indeed, at the origins, Freud parted ways with several of his disciples over issues that, while seemingly arcane from our vantage, were central to psychoanalytic theory of the late nineteenth and early twentieth centuries. In many respects, the issues involved with the delivery of psychological therapies are no more resolved today than they were during Freud's lifetime, although certainly the topography has been altered.

The most polemical of the issues is arguable related to the 'correctness' of the various psychotherapy theories. Psychoanalytic theory, whose hegemony was unchallenged for decades, was by the mid-twentieth century finding itself under assault by behaviourists, who viewed psychoanalytic theory as unscientific and believed that treatments based on the theory were ineffective. But the behavioural force was not the only competitor – post-World War II witnessed the ascendance of humanistic approaches. The legacies of these three forces – psychoanalytic, behavioural and humanistic – remain entwined in modern development of psychological therapies, which now number several hundred (600 or more, according to some experts). The advocates of each approach adamantly emphasize the advantages of their respective approach and the disadvantages of others – it is a history as old as Freud and Jung.

Not surprisingly, the vast array of approaches motivated some to explain the benefits of psychotherapy by identifying the commonalities of the various therapies. Saul Rosenzweig, in 1936, noting that it appeared that all therapies worked about equally well, described what psychotherapies had it common and how these commonalities led to therapeutic change. But the common factor models of Rosenzweig and others were anything but unifying – they simply led to a new debate, with common factor models on one side and specific factor models on the other. That is to say, there is little agreement about how psychotherapy works.

Theoretical debates are closely related to disagreements about the benefits of psychological therapies. In the 1950s and 1960s, Hans Eysenck made the claim that psychotherapy was not effective and indeed might well be harmful. By psychotherapy, he meant therapies other than behavioural therapies; namely, psychoanalysis, psychodynamic therapies, humanistic therapies and eclectic therapies. On the other hand, Eysenck claimed that behavioural treatments were remarkably effective. To claim that most therapies were not useful was, not unexpectedly, distressing to psychotherapy professionals. In the late 1970s, Gene Glass and Mary Lee Smith used the emergent statistical method of meta-analysis to establish that indeed psychological therapies were remarkably effective – more effective than many widely accepted (and expensive!) medical treatments. But these and subsequent meta-analyses only led to the more fundamental debate – which treatment is most effective? Currently, the debate about the relative efficacy of various treatments is one that few in the field can avoid.

The relative efficacy of psychological therapies typically is investigated using randomized controlled trials (RCTs), a design in which patients are randomly assigned to one of two treatments. As one might expect, the use of RCTs is in itself controversial, with some claiming it is the 'gold standard' for acquiring knowledge about psychological therapies and others claiming that it provides a distorted view of how psychological therapies work.

A careful analysis of the issues in psychotherapy leads to the conclusion that there are philosophy of science differences among the various positions taken by academics and practitioners – differences that are fundamentally not reconcilable. The myriad of issues, the intensity of the debates and the nature of the fundamental differences leads to frustration, if not, for some, despair. Where is there some hope for common ground? Given a universal desire to improve the well-being of those experiencing psychological distress, the need to have a unifying theme is quite urgent.

Practice-based evidence, which involves measuring patient progress over the course of therapy, is in my view, a development that appeals to – or at least should appeal to – all researchers and practitioners. Practice-based evidence, as described by the authors contributing to *Developing and delivering practice-based evidence: A guide for the psychological therapies*, is a process that avoids the controversies discussed above and focuses rather on the fundamental question about whether a psychological therapy is benefiting the particular patient being treated. Of course, this is the evidence most vital to the patient sitting in the consulting room. Significantly, practice-based evidence is seen as important regardless of the approach used in therapy, whether one believes in common factors or specific ingredients, and whether one finds RCTs to be superior to other treatments.

As explained in this volume, the measurement of progress in psychotherapy is not only useful to the particular patient, but could play a central role in development of psychological therapies as a healing practice and as a science.

First, any professional has a duty to the public to establish that services delivered are worthwhile. Although RCTs have been used to establish the effectiveness of psychological therapies in an abstract sense, the public is most interested in whether psychological therapies work in the real world. Of course, accountability is not only due to patients. Those who financially pay for mental health services, whether they be governmental bodies, insurance organizations or the patient themselves, desire evidence about whether the services are working. Second, despite the effectiveness of psychological services, there is a desire to improve the quality of these services, for a particular patient and for a system of care. Practice-based evidence is critical for the therapist delivering the therapy and for managers of mental health systems – the results on the ground are the primary means to drive quality improvement. Third, the evidence that accumulates from practice should be central to understanding the nature of psychological therapies. Practice-based evidence has the potential to profoundly inform what is known about psychological therapies. Knowledge derived from practice-based evidence should not be antagonistic to those who conduct RCTs, but rather the top-down and bottom-up evidence will converge to create an amalgam that is richer and more useful than evidence from any one method.

Michael Barkham, Gillian Hardy and John Mellor-Clark have in *Developing and delivering practice-based evidence: A guide for the psychological therapies* created a comprehensive volume on practice-based evidence. Introductory chapters in this volume discuss the philosophy underlying these efforts and explain the role that practice-based evidence plays in the current practice of psychological therapies. Further chapters discuss how evidence can be used by individual practitioners and the scientific community. Then various chapters present existing systems for measuring patient progress and using that information to improve the quality of services. Finally, chapters explore how practice-based evidence can be used to manage services in systems of care.

Practice-based evidence is the Holy Grail for those who have sought a unifying approach to the practice and science of psychotherapy. My hope is that scientists and practitioners will quickly see the importance of this movement and understand how practice-based evidence can be a core process. This volume sets the stage for the future.

Bruce E. Wampold, PhD, ABPP
University of Wisconsin – Madison

July 2009

Preface

This book grew from our collective experience over the past 25 years of using a wide range of methods in order to build a robust evidence base for the processes and outcomes of the psychological therapies. In a context where the dominant research paradigm was drawn directly from evidence-based medicine – namely, evidence-based practice – we were increasingly drawn towards the development of a complementary paradigm that placed practitioners in routine practice using multiple methods in a central role to build a paradigm that became known as *practice-based evidence*. The term resonated with us as a way of shaping and harnessing the activities of everyday practitioners in building an evidence base driven by local questions but which also fed into national issues. Crucially, we did not view these two paradigms as dichotomies but rather as a chiasmus that yielded a more comprehensive and combined framework – namely that of *evidence-based practice and practice-based evidence*. Our vision was that these two complementary paradigms, working in harmony, could yield a more robust and relevant knowledge base for the psychological therapies that would be owned by practitioners and acknowledged by policy makers.

Part of this vision was drawn from our working with differing research methods and with differing models of psychological therapies. Hence, we have seen the potential and yield of both trials and observational data as well as from using qualitative approaches, case studies and, more recently, from mining very large naturalistic data sets. For us, adopting such an inclusive approach has the potential of yielding a more complete and thorough knowledge base for the psychological therapies, an approach akin to that of our becoming *teleoanalysts* whereby we consider the weight of total evidence from all sources and then make judgments as to its collective worth. Such an approach is premised on a valuing of all methods rather than the privileging of one method over another. No single method can develop or deliver a comprehensive science of the psychological therapies.

Accordingly, we sought like-minded colleagues from the UK, USA and continental Europe who have made major contributions to this collective effort of developing and delivering practice-based evidence. In so doing, we sought to bring together a broad range of authors who had their own particular approach that emphasized one component or level of practice-based evidence. The resulting text does not espouse a single approach, method or system. Rather, we sought a wide coverage of approaches and methods that build on existing research.

The resulting text complements the approach exemplified in Duncan, Miller and Sparks' *The Heroic Client* (Jossey-Bass, 2004). Although there are similarities and differences between the two texts, both argue the case for practice-based evidence. Our text will hopefully increase the coverage of practice-based methods available to practitioners and researchers for measuring, monitoring and managing the change process in the psychological therapies. Indeed, part of our vision concerns making long-standing techniques and approaches relevant to practice-based evidence, thereby ensuring we retain the richness of approaches that are naturally associated with psychological research. Hence, side-by-side, these two texts capture the pluralistic nature of practice-based evidence and convey the potential for a more inclusive approach to what is considered as evidence and how such evidence is used to deliver improved services.

The current text serves as an introduction – a guide – to practice-based evidence for the psychological therapies and attempts to show the range of methods available in developing and delivering this approach. We have structured the book into six sections, which, with the exception of the first and last sections, progress from the individual practitioner through to services and from themes of measurement, through monitoring, to management. The six sections are as follows:

- Section I introduces the paradigms of evidence-based practice and practice-based evidence and provide an overview of the strengths and vulnerabilities of current approaches to how we view the nature of evidence.
- Section II starts with the individual practitioner and presents a pluralistic approach to what are sometimes viewed as single case methods but framed here as a starting point for practitioners in routine practice settings to work within the practice-based paradigm.
- Section III presents accounts of three robust and rigorous measurement systems that have provided the basis for the systematic collection of very large data sets from routine practice. These systems can be used by individual practitioners, by groups of practitioners, and by services. In many ways, these – and other – systems lie at the heart of practice-based evidence because they provide the potential for the adoption of a common methodology and thereby help to construct shared databases drawn from routine practice.

- Section IV builds on previous descriptions of approaches to measurement and provides an overview of monitoring practice and quality improvement through the procedures of case tracking and benchmarking.
- Section V considers the need to adopt an organizational or networking approach in order to maximize the evidence yield from routine practice. Finally, we reflect on the attributes and limitations of practice-based evidence and some of the challenges for practitioners and researchers adopting this paradigm.
- Section VI concludes by summarizing the hallmarks of practice-based evidence and places the contributions from previous sections in the context of other work on practice-based evidence.

The book has been written with practitioners and researchers in the field of the psychological therapies, including counselling, in mind. However, in the title we only refer to the psychological therapies due to the developing profession of 'psychological therapist' in the UK that captures the activities of both professions. However, the relevance of practice-based evidence also has a crucial part to play in building a robust and relevant evidence base for other cognate disciplines.

Since beginning this book, there has – if anything – been an increased interest in practice-based evidence, derived from a range of factors including the greater potential of very large data sets, the increasing robustness of qualitative methodologies, and greater availability of IT systems – including networking – as well as political and institutional drivers which have sought to broaden the existing evidence base. We consider this book a starting point in providing a broader and more complete evidence base for the psychological therapies. Bringing together the breadth of pioneering work by leading academic practitioners in a single text is our contribution to this developing paradigm.

Michael Barkham
Gillian E. Hardy
John Mellor-Clark

Acknowledgements

We would like to express our gratitude to all the contributors to this text, for their patience, perseverance and responsiveness to the original brief and our repeated requests. They have all played key roles in fostering the development of a robust and relevant evidence base for practitioners, which we hope they will continue to do in the years to come.

Our thinking on the development and delivery of practice-based evidence reflects the influences of numerous practitioners and researchers and we thank them all. In particular, we wish to acknowledge the contributions of Barry Duncan, Ken Howard, Scott Miller and David A. Shapiro to our thinking. Each, in their own way, has laid down many of the foundation stones for the development and delivery of practice-based evidence.

Finally, we thank Karen Shield, Gill Whitley and all associated production staff at Wiley-Blackwell for their patience and support in the development and delivery of this project.

Section I

Evidence-Based Practice and Practice-Based Evidence

1

The Current View of Evidence and Evidence-Based Practice

Peter Bower[1] and Simon Gilbody[2]

[1] University of Manchester, UK, [2] University of York, UK

The nature of evidence-based practice

Decision making is fundamental to health services. Faced with a patient in distress, any mental health professional (such as a psychotherapist) will have to make a large number of decisions, relating to the overall nature of treatment that will be provided, through to specific decisions concerning particular therapeutic interventions made minute by minute in a psychological therapy session. Clearly, such decisions can have major implications for the course and eventual outcome of treatment.

What is the basis of these decisions? Psychological therapy has traditionally been viewed as a *profession*, and as such has a number of core attributes. First, it has a service orientation, making psychological expertise available to others. That expertise is based on a distinctive body of knowledge and skills, underpinned by abilities and values. There is a recognition among non-professionals of the authority of the professional, and with that recognition comes *autonomy*, at least when working within certain defined boundaries. Thus decisions about treatment are expected to be made on the basis of the practitioners' knowledge and skills, encapsulated in *clinical judgment*.

However, there are other pressures on the delivery of psychological therapy, which have challenged the autonomy of clinical judgment. Throughout its history, psychological therapy has been seen as having a relationship to science. The strength and nature of that relationship varies, but most forms of psychological therapy gain at least some of their authority and power from a supposed

Developing and Delivering Practice-Based Evidence   By Michael Barkham, Gillian E Hardy, and John Mellor-Clark   © 2010 John Wiley & Sons, Ltd

scientific basis, derived from theory and experiment concerning human psychology and mental processes. With scientific respectability comes a requirement for objectivity and transparency, which means that decisions must be justified on the basis of some codified form of knowledge, which is publicly available (at least in theory).

A second key influence is pressure on professionals from resource limited funding organizations, such as publicly funded health care systems and managed care organizations, which increasingly demonstrate a desire to limit spiralling costs (Parloff, 1982).

These pressures have led to a desire to modify the basis of decisions in healthcare, away from autonomous clinical judgments made by a professional, and towards the use of objective and transparent forms of knowledge. This has often been identified with a movement called 'evidence-based medicine' (EBM). Although the originators of the approach were generally medical staff, the philosophy is of potential relevance to all healthcare professionals, and because of this wider applicability it is generally labelled 'evidence-based practice' (EBP).

The nature of EBM was succinctly summarized by one of its originators, who defined it as 'the conscientious, explicit, and judicious use of current best evidence in making decisions about the care of individual patients' (Sackett et al. 1996). Box 1.1 presents a full description of EBM. In some ways, this statement is uncontroversial, because few might argue that 'evidence' about the effectiveness of treatments should guide decision making. The controversy derives from the focus on scientific evidence within EBP, and the rather limited range of scientific sources that meet the criteria for 'current best evidence'.

Box 1.1   Description of evidence-based medicine (Sackett et al., 1996)

Evidence-based medicine is the conscientious, explicit and judicious use of current best evidence in making decisions about the care of individual patients. The practice of evidence-based medicine means integrating individual clinical expertise with the best available external clinical evidence from systematic research. By individual clinical expertise we mean the proficiency and judgment that individual clinicians acquire through clinical experience and clinical practice. Increased expertise is reflected in many ways, but especially in more effective and efficient diagnosis and in the more thoughtful identification and compassionate use of individual patients' predicaments, rights and preferences in making clinical decisions about their care. By best available external clinical evidence we mean clinically relevant research, often from the basic sciences of medicine, but especially from patient-centred clinical research into the accuracy and precision of diagnostic tests (including the clinical examination), the power of prognostic markers, and the efficacy and safety of therapeutic, rehabilitative and preventive regimens. External clinical evidence both invalidates previously accepted diagnostic tests and treatments, and replaces them with new ones that are more powerful, more accurate, more efficacious and safer.

Source: Sackett, D. et al., Evidence-based medicine: what it is and what it is not, *British Medical Journal, 312,* 71–72. BMJ Publishing Group, 1996

'Evidence' in evidence-based practice

What is evidence? Simply put, it is the basis for a belief, such as the belief that a particular treatment will work for a patient. Beliefs may arise from a number of sources. Two major sources of relevance to health services are personal experience and scientific research. The philosophy of EBP readily accepts that several forms of evidence exist, ranging from the most rigorous scientific research, through less rigorous forms of research, personal clinical experience and the opinions of experts. However, EBP imposes a hierarchy of *trustworthiness*, with those forms of evidence lower in the hierarchy only to be used when higher forms of evidence are unavailable. Where higher forms exist, they trump lower forms.

If evidence is about the basis of beliefs, then what are the beliefs of relevance? The scope of evidence-based practice is actually fairly limited, and is focused on two questions. The first is the causal question: 'does psychological therapy work?' That is, can psychological therapy be said to *cause* beneficial effects in those who receive it (Basham, 1986). The second is the comparative question: 'which works best?' (Basham, 1986). If psychological therapies are responsible for beneficial effects, a key question is which of the many alternative therapies achieves the best outcomes.

Does psychological therapy work? Making sense of cause

To the uninitiated, determining whether a treatment works simply requires the delivery of that treatment and measurement of outcome after it has been received. If benefits follow application, then it might seem a reasonable conjecture that the treatment is responsible. However, to the scientific mind, such a conjecture remains unproven, because there are so many other variables that might have also been responsible for change. For example, changes might be due to the treatment, personal development, or life events outside of psychological therapy. These are known as *confounding variables*, which make it unclear whether any single factor (such as treatment) can be held responsible for any observed changes (Davey Smith & Phillips, 1992). For example, some mental health problems improve without any treatment. This is known as 'spontaneous remission', and it is possible that the mere passage of time might be responsible for the changes observed. Therefore, time is said to be *confounded* with treatment. Examining patients before and after a treatment cannot determine whether time or the treatment is actually responsible for the observed changes.

Making sense of causal relations cannot rely on simple observation, but requires *experiment*. This involves active intervention to vary some parameters, and hold others constant, which means confounds can be removed and causal relationships established. One key type of experiment (the randomized controlled trial (RCT)) is one of the key technologies of EBP.

The technology of evidence-based practice

The randomized controlled trial

In an experiment, the researcher actively manipulates some parameters (called *independent variables*) and then examines the effect of this manipulation on other parameters (called *dependent variables*). This is designed to exclude the possibility that confounders are responsible for the observed findings.

Experiments are designed to improve our confidence that a relationship between an independent and dependent variable is 'causal', i.e. the treatment causes outcomes and can be said to 'work'. The confidence with which a researcher can conclude that an experiment has demonstrated a causal relationship is described as the *internal validity*. The function of the RCT is to provide the optimal safeguards against key threats to internal validity through three interrelated mechanisms (Mahoney, 1978; Spector, 1981): control; comparison; and randomization. Each of these key aspects of RCTs is described briefly below.

Control

Control is the basis of experiment, and involves holding variables constant or varying them systematically so that their effect can be examined. For example, treatment length may be controlled in a comparison of two psychological therapies, which means that differences in outcome cannot be due to differences in treatment length. Another common form of control is the restriction of patient entry to the trial, so that patients with particular disorders or co-morbidities are excluded. This ensures that the natural history of the disorders cannot be responsible for any differences in outcome.

Comparison

Comparison involves setting the independent variable at different levels (e.g. giving patients different amounts of treatment), allocating patients to these different levels and examining the differences in outcome that result. If some patients do not receive any treatment, it is called a control group: when they receive an alternative treatment, they are called a *comparison group*. Control and comparison groups protect against key threats to internal validity. One key threat is *history*, i.e. changes over time outside the research context that account for patient outcome (Campbell & Stanley, 1966). It is well known that a significant proportion of psychological problems will improve over time through *spontaneous remission*. Control and comparison groups provide protection against such a threat by ensuring that it affects both groups. Another threat to validity in psychological therapy trials are non-specific treatment effects (i.e. the time spent with a caring professional may be beneficial, whether that professional has any psychological therapy skills at all). If both comparison groups are treated by caring professionals, then any benefits from this will cancel out when the groups are compared. Any differences in outcome between the groups will reflect real differences in the therapies, rather than the benefits of spending time with a caring person.

Randomization

Control groups provide protection against confounders and other sources of bias with one all-important proviso: 'all other things being equal' (Latin *ceteris paribus*). If the patients making up the groups differ significantly in characteristics that may relate to outcome (e.g. the severity of their disorders), then any conclusions made about them will be vulnerable because these differences could very well account for any observed differences in outcome rather than the treatment provided. This validity threat is called *selection bias* (Campbell & Stanley, 1966; Kleijnen et al., 1997). It is best countered by allocation of patients to treatment and control groups through a process of *randomization*.

Randomization ensures that the groups will both contain roughly equal levels of each patient variable, because every idiosyncratic value assigned to the first group will tend to be balanced later in the random process by assigning a similar variable to the other group or an opposite variable to the same group. With sufficient numbers of patients, randomization should ensure that there are no systematic differences in the average 'score' on any variable between the groups, meaning that any differences in outcome cannot reasonably be attributed to any pre-existing differences between the groups. Although this might be achieved by matching patients on variables before they are allocated, randomization has the advantage that the groups will be equal on *all* variables, both those known about and measured, and those that are unknown and unmeasured.

Reporting the use of randomization is not enough to avoid selection bias. It is necessary that the decision about whether a patient is eligible to participate in the study is separate from knowledge of the patient's allocation. For example, if a clinician is entering a patient in a RCT, it is important that the patient's eligibility is not altered because the clinician knows that the next treatment allocation is one that he or she views as unfavourable (e.g. a control group that involves no treatment). Research has shown that bias is less likely in those studies where allocation is adequately *concealed*, for example, where randomization is done centrally rather than by clinicians, or through the use of numbered, sealed and opaque envelopes that can be checked by a trial administrator (Chalmers et al., 1983; Schulz et al., 1995). Other methods in which the allocation is transparent are more vulnerable to selection bias.

Control, comparison and randomization are key aspects of trials, but there are many other issues to consider in their design, analysis and interpretation (Bower & King, 2000).

Although a well-conducted RCT provides the best test of casual and comparative questions, each RCT generally provides only a single test. A key scientific principle is the need for replication of research studies by other researchers, which highlights the need for additional studies to increase confidence that particular results are not due to chance. A key type of scientific publication is the *review*, which brings together published information on a topic. Given that finding and appraising all the research evidence on many areas can be a daunting task, review articles are always popular among those who conduct and use research.

However, it has been suggested that traditional review articles are open to bias and lack transparency (Mulrow, 1987). For example, individual pieces of primary research might use different methods and differ in their rigour. How are different sorts of evidence and different results to be reconciled? Authors of reviews can either consciously or unconsciously be selective in the research they include. To avoid these sources of bias requires the second major technology of EBP: the systematic review.

The systematic review

Systematic reviews seek to draw together individual primary research studies in order to provide an overview that is more comprehensive, accurate and generalizable than the results of individual studies. The aim of systematic reviews is to ensure that all sources of bias are made explicit and, where possible, minimized. The ways in which this is achieved are briefly described below.

Explicit research question

Firstly, a systematic review starts with an explicit research question. These questions are often formulated according to the PICO algorithm (Population,

Intervention, Comparison, Outcome). For example, in patients with major depression (population), is cognitive behaviour therapy (intervention) more effective than experiential psychological therapy (comparison) in reducing depressive symptoms and avoiding relapse (outcome)?

Systematic reviews also make explicit the types of evidence that are needed in order to answer the question. This is often restricted to RCTs, but can include almost any type of study in principle.

Comprehensive searches for studies

Reviews need to have a comprehensive overview of the evidence, rather than reviewing only a selected part. The rise of EBP has led to significant advances in the technology of searching for literature, mainly though harnessing the power of electronic bibliographical databases such as MEDLINE (Haynes et al., 2005). There is increasing knowledge about which databases need to be searched, how to search them and the different biases that emerge from reliance on bibliographic databases of published research, such as *publication bias* (Gilbody et al., 2000).

Quality appraisal

Systematic reviews seek to sort good quality evidence from biased and misleading evidence by introducing the idea of *quality appraisal*. The previous section on the methods of RCTs discussed the key methodological issue of concealment of allocation. Quality issues such as these can be appraised using a standardized checklist, to assess the overall quality of the evidence, and examine whether there is a consistent relationship between the quality of studies and their eventual outcomes.

Synthesis

Systematic reviews synthesize primary research literature in order to highlight consistencies and differences between individual studies, and to provide a more accurate and precise estimate of relationships between treatments and their effects. Sometimes this synthesis is narrative. In this case, important areas of consistency and disagreement between individual studies are described and explained, and the reviewer will attempt to summarize the totality of the evidence.

The most common mathematical tool used for quantitative synthesis of multiple studies is *meta-analysis* (Sutton et al., 1999). Although the terms systematic review and meta-analysis are sometimes used interchangeably, they are not identical, as meta-analysis is not necessary for a systematic review, nor is it sufficient to make a review systematic. In meta-analysis, primary studies deemed sufficiently similar in terms of setting, population, intervention and outcome are statistically summarized to get an overall estimate of effectiveness.

Research studies such as RCTs and systematic reviews are published in academic journals, and as such have a limited effect on practitioners who generally do not (and indeed cannot) keep abreast of all available evidence. To bridge the gap between research and practice requires the third key technology of EBP, the clinical guideline.

Clinical guidelines

Clinical guidelines are 'systematically developed statements to assist practitioner and patient decisions about appropriate healthcare for specific clinical circumstances' (Field & Lohr, 1990). They may offer concise instructions on many aspects of healthcare practice, including screening, diagnosis, management and prevention. Mental healthcare is not exempt from the guideline process: one of the earliest 'evidence-based' guidelines produced in the US was on depression (Agency for Health Care Policy Research, 1993). In England and Wales the National Institute for Health and Clinical Excellence (NICE) has developed a portfolio of guidelines in mental health.

In the same way that EBP has helped introduce and codify what is good research and what is unreliable research, there is now an emerging consensus about what constitutes a 'good guideline'. This recognizes the difference between consensus-based guidelines developed by panels of experts and guidelines developed within the analytical framework of EBP. Well-developed evidence-based guidelines pay reference to the explicit evidence hierarchy to grade the strength of research in a particular area of practice. From this, they interpret the strength of evidence in making a recommendation. Well-constituted guideline development groups include individuals with the technical skills to synthesize and grade the evidence in a rigorous manner, together with key stakeholders (practitioners, policy makers and service users) who are able to interpret and contextualize evidence with reference to the realities of clinical practice and service delivery. This process can be time consuming and difficult to achieve in areas where the evidence is not clear-cut.

The principles of EBP have been applied in the evaluation of effectiveness of guidelines themselves as a technology; in their ability to influence clinical practice and to improve patient outcomes (Grimshaw et al., 2004). Research tends to support the superiority of evidence-based guidelines over consensus-based guidelines, and suggests that the involvement of key stakeholders is worth the time and effort. In addition, the most influential guidelines tend to be those that are developed nationally, but interpreted locally, with due reference to local aspects of clinical practice and service delivery, and with a realistic appraisal of the local resource constraints that will be involved in local implementation strategies. In addition, the way in which guidelines are disseminated is central in determining whether they influence local clinical practice. Passive dissemination methods (such as awareness campaigns and mailshots from national bodies) are generally much less effective than guidelines that have an active dissemination programme through the use of local champions and educational outreach.

Key organizations involved in evidence-based practice

EBP and its technologies are best exemplified by the Cochrane Collaboration (www.cochrane.org/). The Cochrane Collaboration is an international non-profit and independent organization, which seeks to provide up-to-date, accurate information about the effects of healthcare and ensure that it is accessible to all. It produces and disseminates systematic reviews and promotes the search for RCT evidence.

Two major products of the Collaboration are the Cochrane Database of Systematic Reviews and the Central Register of Controlled Trials. Both are published quarterly as part of *The Cochrane Library*. The Library currently holds details of 564,387 trials, 5,676 Cochrane systematic reviews and 9,403 other reviews of various treatments (as of early 2009).

As noted earlier, NICE (www.nice.org.uk/) is an organization responsible for providing guidance on healthcare interventions in England and Wales (Rawlins, 2004). NICE guidelines are developed using a complex process of evidence synthesis and consensus among clinicians, patients and managers. NICE evaluates both the clinical *and* cost effectiveness of a range of healthcare interventions, including drugs (new and existing), medical devices, and procedures (usually operations). It has also provided guidance on individual conditions such as depression (NICE, 2004) and different ways of delivering psychological therapies such as computerized cognitive behaviour therapy (CCBT) (Kaltenthaler, Parry & Beverley, 2006).

A good exemplar of the impact of EBP is the NICE guidelines for depression, which 'make recommendations for the identification, treatment and management of depression for adults aged 18 years and over, in primary and secondary care'.

The guidelines themselves are based on a comprehensive evidence review, focusing on RCTs that have been identified, assessed and summarized using systematic review techniques. The end result is a description of the best evidence concerning the treatment of various types of depression (differing according to severity). The guidelines provide a blueprint for service delivery that in theory provides the most effective and efficient model available.

The benefits of evidence-based practice

Many of the advantages of EBP are evident from clinical guidelines. These represent a clear, explicit statement of the totality of the scientific evidence concerning a particular clinical area, which is transparent to professionals and clients, updated regularly, and holds out the promise of effective and efficient service delivery in the pursuit of maximum health gain from available healthcare resources.

As a profession, psychological therapists stand to gain from the use of EBP in a number of ways. It provides the necessary methodological underpinning to the 'scientist-practitioner' model adopted by some within the profession (Barlow, Hayes & Nelson, 1984). The technologies of EBP can indicate when therapies are actually doing more harm than good (Rose et al., 2002; Roth & Fonagy, 2004), and can also provide protection for professionals in terms of legal challenges (Persons & Silberschatz, 1998). Finally, EBP can provide support for the continued provision of effective therapies that might otherwise be under threat (either in general, or from alternatives such as pharmacological treatments).

Despite these advantages, EBP is contentious, perceived as having less to do with the scientific basis of health services and more as a method of ensuring that health professionals follow the dictates of managers and policy makers (Graham-Smith, 1995; Roth & Fonagy, 2004). The following section considers the main scientific and professional tensions that exist.

Tensions in evidence-based practice

Scientific issues

'No evidence of effectiveness' versus 'evidence of no effectiveness'

RCTs are expensive, and it is doubtful that any health service could afford to conduct enough RCTs and replications for every relevant treatment and patient group to meet the requirements of EBP. Some therapies are not evaluated because there is insufficient economic or professional impetus to fund expensive research. Currently, the evidence base for psychological therapy is dominated by CBT, partly because of the effectiveness of the therapy, and partly because very few alternatives have been subjected to randomized evaluations. Theoretically, 'no evidence of effectiveness' is a very different state from 'evidence of no effectiveness' (Altman & Bland, 1995; Persons & Silberschatz, 1998), as the latter suggests a treatment should not be used, whereas the former suggests that it should be used, but only in the context of a RCT to develop the necessary evidence base. If this distinction is not understood, potentially effective therapies may be discarded, and the choice of therapies limited so that service delivery may become excessively homogenous.

Internal and external validity

Earlier, the concept of internal validity was discussed. However, another type of validity is also of great importance. This is *external validity*, which refers to the confidence with which a researcher can expect relationships found in the context of one particular experiment to *generalize* to other contexts (Cook & Campbell, 1979). For example, if a treatment is found to be efficacious in a managed care setting in the United States, will the same results be found in the United Kingdom, or a developing country, where there are differences in context, therapists and patients? Generally, judgments of external validity are made on the basis of similarity, where results can be generalized 'with most confidence where treatment, setting, population, desired outcome and year are closest in some overall way to the original program treatment' (Campbell, 1986).

Unfortunately, characteristics of treatment, setting and population are routinely controlled in RCT, which means there is often a gap between what goes on in RCT, and what happens in routine healthcare settings. In the latter, patients may self-refer, may present with multiple, complex problems, and also receive other treatments at the same time. Such patients may not be included in RCT because of these other factors, but therapists in routine care cannot afford to be so selective. Therapists in routine settings may have a wide variety of experience and skill, and may routinely change their therapeutic strategies rather than adhering to a single approach. Again, such behaviour may not be tolerated in the rigorous confines of a research study.

Because of this, there is a large inferential gap between the results found in an RCT and the *application* of those results to other settings. There is a genuine tension between internal and external validity. To maximize internal validity, the researcher must maximize control, such as control over the type of treatment provided, therapy quality and the types of patients who enter the RCT. If treatment was provided by a range of therapists of differing skill, then internal validity is threatened. If the results of the RCT suggested that the treatment was ineffective, critics may point out that the treatment provided may have been of low quality, and that the study was not a fair test of the treatment as it was designed to be delivered.

Although external validity remains a key weakness of RCTs, it is an issue that can be examined empirically (Shadish et al., 1997). The tension between internal and external validity is one which is germane to many areas of healthcare where the ascendancy of the RCT has raised concerns about the limited evaluation of real world clinical practice (Naylor, 1995). The most robust response has been to maximize external validity, within the context of RCTs – using so-called 'pragmatic RCTs' (Hotopf, Churchill & Lewis, 1999). Such RCTs are conventionally larger than traditional tightly controlled RCTs, and the inclusion criteria are very broad such that they reflect the type of participant upon whom the intervention will eventually be used in the real world (involving co-morbidities – such as mixed depression and anxiety, or the presence of alcohol problems – both common exclusion criteria in traditional RCTs). Such RCTs are few and far between in psychological therapy, but have been successfully used in primary care mental health trials (Simon, Wagner & Von Korff, 1995), addressing the concerns that trials do not reflect real world practice or effectiveness (Gilbody, Wahlbeck & Adams, 2002b).

Experiment versus observation

The reliance on RCTs within EBP may lead to a denial of the utility of other research paradigms. There are many situations where RCTs may be inappropriate (Black, 1996; Jadad, 1998). Trials may be inappropriate where significant outcome events (such as suicide) are very rare, or where treatments are strongly influenced by patient preferences.

The forgoing discussion about the limited applicability of RCTs has led some researchers to reject the very notion of randomization. This too chimes with many cultural barriers that exist within psychological therapy to participation in RCTs where patients (and clinicians) must be willing to undergo randomization and to receive a particular treatment according to the play of chance. The effectiveness of interventions is instead examined within large groups of patients using observational (rather than experimental) designs (Gilbody, House & Sheldon, 2002a). In order to recapture the power of causal inference inherent in randomized designs, several sophisticated statistical techniques have emerged with which to 'mimic' the process of randomization and to exclude the effect of confounding factors. These techniques are known as instrumental variables or 'propensity scores', and are more commonly used in the United States in examining the effectiveness of interventions from routinely collected data (Rubin, 1997). The major limitation of these techniques is the ability to only match for known confounding factors, where the effects of unknown confounding factors might still produce spurious results (Iezzoni, 1990).

Clinical versus cost-effectiveness

The notion of clinical effectiveness (such as that within NICE recommendations) is one that is central to EBP, but the focus on cost-effectiveness is more controversial. A cost-effectiveness perspective is sometimes at odds with the central tenets of EBP. For example, cost-effectiveness is a theoretical perspective used to maximize the efficiency of healthcare, such that the maximum healthcare gain is achieved within finite healthcare resources

(Drummond et al., 2005). This sometimes conflicts with EBP where a demonstration of health benefits or effectiveness of an intervention is a necessary and sufficient condition in deciding whether to adopt a treatment. When some interventions deliver only marginal health gain at high cost, then evidence-based practice does not provide an explicit method within which to decide whether it should be adopted (Maynard, 1997). Within structures such as NICE guidelines, the cost-effectiveness of an intervention is considered at all times.

Quantitative versus qualitative research

RCTs are not appropriate methodologies for understanding the processes by which psychological therapies achieve change. This may require in-depth qualitative analysis of individual cases of therapy (so-called *process research*) (Persons & Silberschatz, 1998; Rice & Greenberg, 1984) or studies of patient experience in the therapeutic encounter. To claim that EBP does not address these factors is probably a misconception, based on the major uses to which EBP has been put – focusing largely on the effectiveness of interventions. There is an emerging consensus on the role and importance of qualitative research in answering the 'how' and 'why' questions inherent in clinical practice. These are questions that will not be answered using RCTs, and there is a recognition that a specific question needs the best and most appropriate research design with which to answer it. This will often be a qualitative research design (Mays & Pope, 1995), which are now commonly used alongside quantitative designs in judging the effectiveness, role and value of healthcare interventions (Mays & Pope, 2000). As with quantitative designs (such as RCTs) there is also an emerging consensus on what constitutes good and poor qualitative research (Mays & Pope, 1995).

Specific versus common factors

EBP tends to focus on the evaluation of specific therapy 'brands' such as CBT, interpersonal psychotherapy (IPT) and suchlike. The history of psychological therapy is replete with significant 'turf wars' around effectiveness, and there is much contention about the current dominance of CBT within clinical guidelines in the UK.

There is evidence that suggests that specific aspects of therapy account for a relatively small amount of variation in outcome, and that so called common factors (i.e. aspects of the relationship between professional and client, and the way in which they interact, often described as the *therapeutic alliance*) are probably more important. However, common factors are not easily understood within the paradigm of EBP. Where EBP is dominant, crucial ingredients of therapy such as common factors may be undervalued. However, a therapist ostensibly using an 'evidence-based' therapy may be ineffective if he or she does not attend to common factors (Roth & Fonagy, 2004).

Empirically supported treatments versus processes of change

There is another downside to the identification of certain therapies as 'evidence-based' or 'empirically supported' (Chambless & Hollon, 1998). This labelling tends to encourage distinctions between therapies that may not have any basis in clinical reality. The critics suggest that it is less important to identify 'brand name' therapies that meet arbitrary criteria in RCTs, and instead focus on the identification of psychological principles of change that are supported by evidence from RCTs, clinical practice and experimental studies. For example, the 'hourglass' model of treatment development has been described (Salkovskis, 1995), in which highly controlled studies are relevant for only one portion of the development cycle, while less controlled methods (such as case studies and effectiveness studies) have crucial roles early and late in the development of the therapy respectively.

Professional issues

Statistical versus clinical judgment

As noted earlier, one of the key aspects of a profession relates to the importance placed on professional clinical judgment. However, an inevitable consequence of EBP is a downplaying of the role of clinical judgment processes (Tanenbaum, 1993). Critics suggest that this leads to a 'cookbook' approach to therapy, where the complexity of patient presentation and professional response is reduced to a few broad guidelines. Although the very definition of EBP described above indicates that clinical judgment is a necessary complement to RCT-based evidence (Sackett et al., 1996), the processes by which the two are to be integrated are far less clear (Dowie, 1996). EBP is in line with the large number of research studies that have demonstrated multiple flaws in human judgment (Dawes, 1988; Meehl, 1954; Tversky & Kahneman, 1974).

Assisting decision-making versus threatening legitimacy

Downplaying clinical judgment is a crucial restriction to professional autonomy, but many psychological therapists face a greater threat from EBP. Within medicine, treatments that are tested with EBP are not themselves closely tied to the profession of medicine, and thus the results of RCTs of particular interventions do not challenge the legitimacy of the profession of medicine per se. The situation is different for psychological therapists, because most practitioners are more firmly wedded to particular theoretical orientations. A medic can easily swap one medication for another, but this option is not open to psychological therapy practitioners, given the time required to retrain in an entirely new model of therapy. EBP thus represents not just a threat to professional autonomy, but a more fundamental threat to legitimacy.

Conclusions – evidence-based practice in perspective

One of the key impacts of RCTs and EBP is not in the detail of the scientific methods, but in the broad aim of encouraging an openness to scientific evaluation in healthcare. These are not ideas that will go away, and there is a broad consensus that these ideas have changed healthcare for the better, increasing the scientific basis of healthcare and improving the quality of care that is offered. Less predictable, but equally important changes have been in the *culture* of healthcare and in increasing the *accountability* and *transparency* of healthcare decision making – at an individual and at a population level. The power imbalance between patient and practitioner has been lessened and the powers of custom and professional self-interest (in the face of empirical evidence) have become less easy to justify. A measured response by psychological therapy to EBP should reflect the strengths and limitations of this approach that we have highlighted in this chapter.

References

Agency for Health Care Policy Research (1993). *Depression in primary care.* Washington, DC: US Department of Health and Human Services.

Altman, D. and Bland, M. (1995). Absence of evidence is not evidence of absence. *British Medical Journal, 311,* 485.

Barlow, D., Hayes, S. & Nelson, R. (1984). *The Scientist-Practitioner: Research and accountability in clinical and educational settings.* New York: Pergamon Press.

Basham, R. (1986). Scientific and practical advantages of comparative design in psychotherapy outcome research. *Journal of Consulting and Clinical Psychology, 54,* 88–94.

Black, N. (1996). Why we need observational studies to evaluate the effectiveness of health care. *British Medical Journal, 312,* 1215–1218.

Bower, P. & King, M. (2000). Randomised controlled trials and the evaluation of psychological therapy. In N. Rowland & S. Goss (eds.), *Evidence-based counselling and psychological therapies* (pp. 79–110). London: Routledge.

Campbell, D. (1986). Relabeling internal and external validity for applied social scientists. In W. Trochim (ed.), *Advances in quasi-experimental design and analysis* (pp. 67–77). San Francisco: Jossey-Bass.

Campbell, D. & Stanley, J. (1966). *Experimental and quasi-experimental designs for research*. Chicago: Rand McNally.

Chalmers, T., Celano, P., Sacks, H. & Smith, H. (1983). Bias in treatment assignment in controlled clinical trials. *New England Journal of Medicine*, *309*, 1358–1361.

Chambless, D. & Hollon, S. (1998). Defining empirically supported therapies. *Journal of Consulting and Clinical Psychology*, *66*, 7–18.

Cook, T. & Campbell, D. (1979). *Quasi-experimentation – Design and analysis issues for field settings*. Chicago: Rand McNally.

Davey Smith, G. & Phillips, A.N. (1992). Confounding in epidemiological studies: why 'independent' effects may not be all they seem. *British Medical Journal*, *305*, 757–759.

Dawes, R. (1988). You can't systematize human judgement: dyslexia. In J. Dowie & A. Elstein (eds.), *Professional judgment: a reader in clinical decision making* (pp. 150–162). New York: Cambridge University Press.

Dowie, J. (1996). The research-practice gap and the role of decision analysis in closing it. *Health Care Analysis*, *4*, 5–18.

Drummond, M.F., Sculpher, M., Stoddard, G.L., O'Brien, B. & Torrance, G.W. (2005). *Methods for the economic evaluation of health care*. Oxford: Oxford University Press.

Field, M. & Lohr, K. (1990). *Clinical practice guidelines: directions for a new program*. Washington: National Academy Press.

Gilbody, S.M., House, A.O. & Sheldon, T.A. (2002a). Outcomes research in mental health – A systematic review. *British Journal of Psychiatry*, *181*, 8–16.

Gilbody, S.M., Wahlbeck, K. & Adams, C.E. (2002b). Randomised controlled trials in schizophrenia: a critical review of the literature. *Acta Psychiatrica Scandinavica*, *105*, 243–251.

Gilbody, S., Song, F., Eastwood, A. & Sutton, A. (2000). The causes, consequences and detection of publication bias in psychiatry. *Acta Psychiatrica Scandinavica*, *102*, 241–249.

Graham-Smith, D. (1995). Evidence-based medicine: Socratic dissent. *British Medical Journal*, *310*, 1126–1127.

Grimshaw, J.M., Thomas, R.E., MacLennan, G., Fraser, C., Ramsay, C.R. et al. (2004). Effectiveness and efficiency of guideline dissemination and implementation strategies. *Health Technology Assessment*, *8*, 1–72.

Haynes, B., McKibbon, K., Wilczynski, N., Walter, S., Werre, S. et al. (2005). Optimal search strategies for retrieving scientifically strong studies of treatment from Medline: analytical survey. *British Medical Journal*, *330*, 1162–1163.

Hotopf, M., Churchill, R. & Lewis, G. (1999). Pragmatic randomised trials in psychiatry. *British Journal of Psychiatry, 175,* 217–223.

Iezzoni, L.I. (1990). Using administrative diagnostic data to assess the quality of medical care: pitfalls and potential of ICD-9-CM. *International Journal of Technology Assessment in Health Care, 6,* 81–94.

Jadad, A. (1998). *Randomised controlled trials: A user's guide.* London: BMJ Publishing.

Kaltenthaler, E., Parry, G. & Beverley, C. (2006). The clinical and cost-effectiveness of computerised cognitive behaviour therapy (CCBT) for anxiety and depression. *Health Technology Assessment, 10,* 1–186.

Kleijnen, J., Gotzsche, P., Kunz, R., Oxman, A. & Chalmers, I. (1997). So what's so special about randomisation? In A. Maynard & I. Chalmers (eds.), *Nonrandom reflections on Health Services Research* (pp. 93–106). London: BMJ Publishing.

Mahoney, M. (1978). Experimental methods and outcome evaluation. *Journal of Consulting and Clinical Psychology, 46,* 660–672.

Maynard, A. (1997). Evidence-based medicine: an incomplete method for informing treatment choices. *The Lancet, 349,* 126–128.

Mays, N. & Pope, C. (1995). Rigour and qualitative research. *British Medical Journal, 311,* 109–112.

Mays, N. & Pope, C. (2000). *Qualitative research in health care.* London: BMJ Publishing.

Meehl, P. (1954). *Clinical versus statistical prediction: A theoretical analysis and review of the evidence.* Minneapolis: University of Minnesota Press.

Mulrow, C. (1987). The medical review article: state of the science. *Annals of Internal Medicine, 106,* 485–488.

National Institute for Clinical Excellence (NICE) (2004). *Depression: core interventions in the management of depression in primary and secondary care.* London: HMSO.

Naylor, C.D. (1995). Grey zones of clinical practice: some limits to evidence based medicine. *The Lancet, 345,* 840–842.

Parloff, M. (1982). Psychotherapy research evidence and reimbursement decisions: Bambi meets Godzilla. *American Journal of Psychiatry, 139,* 718–727.

Persons, J. & Silberschatz, G. (1998). Are results of randomised controlled trials useful to psychotherapists? *Journal of Consulting and Clinical Psychology, 66,* 126–135.

Rawlins, M.D. (2004) NICE work – providing guidance to the British National Health Service. *New England Journal of Medicine, 351,* 1383–1385.

Rice, L. & Greenberg, L. (1984). *Patterns of change.* New York: Guilford Press.

Rose, S.C., Bisson, J., Churchill, R. & Wessely, S. (2002). Psychological debriefing for preventing post traumatic stress disorder (PTSD). *Cochrane*

Database of Systematic Reviews 2002, Issue 2. Art. No.: CD000560. DOI: 10.1002/14651858.CD000560.

Roth, A. & Fonagy, P. (2004). *What works for whom? A critical review of psychotherapy research* (2nd edn). London: Guilford Press.

Rubin, D.B. (1997). Estimating causal effects from large data sets using propensity scores. *Annals of Internal Medicine, 127,* 757–763.

Sackett, D., Rosenberg, W., Gray, J., Haynes, B. & Richardson, W. (1996). Evidence-based medicine: what it is and what it is not. *British Medical Journal, 312,* 71–72.

Salkovskis, P. (1995). Demonstrating specific effects in cognitive and behavioural therapy. In M. Aveline & D. Shapiro (eds.), *Research foundations for psychotherapy practice* (pp. 191–228). Chichester: John Wiley & Sons, Ltd.

Schulz, K., Chalmers, I., Hayes, R. & Altman, D. (1995). Empirical evidence of bias: dimensions of methodological quality associated with estimates of treatment effects in controlled trials. *Journal of the American Medical Association, 273,* 408–412.

Shadish, W., Navarro, A., Crits-Christoph, P., Jorm, A., Nietzel, M. et al. (1997). Evidence that therapy works in clinically representative populations. *Journal of Consulting and Clinical Psychology, 65,* 355–365.

Simon, G., Wagner, E. & Von Korff, M. (1995). Cost-effectiveness comparisons using 'real world' randomized trials: The case of new antidepressant drugs. *Journal of Clinical Epidemiology, 48,* 363–373.

Spector, E. (1981). *Research designs.* London: Sage Publications.

Sutton, A., Jones, D., Abrams, K., Sheldon, T. & Song, F. (1999). Systematic reviews and meta-analysis: a structured review of the methodological literature. *Journal of Health Services Research and Policy, 4,* 49–55.

Tanenbaum, S. (1993). What physicians know. *New England Journal of Medicine, 329,* 1268–1270.

Tversky, A. & Kahneman, D. (1974). Judgement under uncertainty: heuristics and biases. *Science, 185,* 1124–1131.

2

Building a Rigorous and Relevant Knowledge Base for the Psychological Therapies

Michael Barkham[1], William B. Stiles[2], Michael J. Lambert[3] and John Mellor-Clark[4]

[1]Centre for Psychological Services Research, University of Sheffield, UK, [2]Miami University, Ohio, USA, [3]Brigham Young University, Utah, USA, [4]CORE IMS, Rugby, UK

Introduction

The paradigm of evidence-based practice is now shaping the format and delivery of the psychological therapies. The achievements and the substantial yield of this movement have been well summarized (see Bower & Gilbody, Chapter 1). In the current chapter, we reflect on the assumptions underlying evidence-based practice and consider the benefits of broadening this paradigm to include a wider constituency of evidence, particularly in relation to what we call *practice-based evidence*. Our aim is to argue that although trials methodology has contributed much to the evidence base on effective treatments, questions remain concerning the underlying assumptions of evidence-based practice. Our proposition is that there is an alternative, broader foundation for deciding the relevance of research to practice that, combined with trials methodology, can yield a more robust knowledge base for practitioners and services.

We first set out a vision of a broader research perspective as documented in several key strategic texts. Second, we consider the randomized controlled trial (RCT) together with a range of design and methodological issues associated with it. Third, we present a résumé of practice-based research together with its virtues and vulnerabilities. And finally, we suggest models for bringing together,

Developing and Delivering Practice-Based Evidence   By Michael Barkham, Gillian E Hardy, and John Mellor-Clark   © 2010 John Wiley & Sons, Ltd

in differing ways, the strengths of trials methodology and practice-based studies. Throughout the chapter we make links, where appropriate, to other chapters in this text which, in themselves, are premised on the basis of complementing and strengthening currently accepted approaches to gathering evidence.

Towards an inclusive research strategy for building an evidence base

Definitions

The evidence from trials methodology is continually building and feeding meta-analytic and systematic reviews of specific literatures. However, the relevance of such evidence for specific practices has been an increasing focus of attention. Green and Glasgow (2006) have drawn attention to this issue as being one of disparity between trial data and what they term the *weight of evidence*. By this term they mean 'indirect evidence including non-experimental data, practitioner experiences, and the cumulative wisdom derived from systematic analysis of these and an understanding of the situations and populations in which they would be applied' (p. 127). They argue that trials, because they are strong on the criterion of internal validity, support the weight of evidence for Type 1 translational research – that is, from laboratory settings to policy implementation. However, trials are invariably weak in relation to external validity and thereby do not add to the weight of evidence regarding Type 2 translational research – that is, from studies of efficacy to adoption in community and routine settings (for a full exposition, see Sussman et al., 2006). Crucially, Green and Glasgow argue that decision-making bodies need to consider the *totality of evidence* because no single study can yield a definitive answer. Hence, we need to appreciate what each of these types of studies can yield.

So, what is meant by evidence-based practice and practice-based evidence? Evidence-based medicine has been defined as

> the conscientious, explicit, and judicious use of current best evidence in making decisions about the care of individual patients. The practice of evidence-based medicine means integrating individual clinical expertise with the best available external clinical evidence from systematic research (Sackett et al., 1996, p. 71).

The issue then becomes one of defining what is the best external clinical evidence. We suggest that evidence-based practice needs to be informed by practice-based evidence as well as controlled studies. In their definition of practice-based research, Barkham and Margison (2007) modified the above definition to read as follows:

> Practice-based evidence is the conscientious, explicit, and judicious use of current evidence drawn from practice settings in making decisions about the care of individual patients. Practice-based evidence means integrating both individual clinical expertise and service-level parameters with the best available evidence drawn from rigorous research activity carried out in routine clinical settings (Barkham & Margison, 2007, p. 446).

Accordingly, the emphasis is on acquiring evidence via rigorous research carried out in routine clinical practice. This chapter and this book argue for the adoption of a complementary paradigm with the potential for a combined knowledge base arising from the contribution of both these approaches.

Towards an inclusive research strategy

The aspiration of a broader based approach has been documented in several key articles. *Bridging science and service*, a report by the US National Advisory Mental Health Council's (NAMHC) Clinical Treatment and Services Research Workgroup (1999) and written under the auspices of both the National Institute of Health and the National Institute of Mental Health, sets out a vision of the role and kinds of research paradigms most likely to deliver a relevant evidence base for mental health services. Although some specifics of the US managed care system differ significantly from those in the UK and continental Europe, this does not lessen the relevance of arguments for a strategic shift in the focus and orientation of research.

The NAMHC report distinguished four key domains of research activity: efficacy, effectiveness, practice and service systems. The primary aims of each activity were stated as follows:

- *Efficacy research* aims to examine whether a particular intervention has a specific, measurable effect and also to address questions concerning the safety, feasibility, side effects and appropriate dose levels;
- *Effectiveness research* aims to identify whether efficacious treatments can have a measurable, beneficial effect when implemented across broad populations and in other service settings;
- *Practice research* examines how and which treatments or services are provided to individuals within service systems and evaluates how to improve treatment or service delivery. The aim is not so much to isolate or generalize

the effect of an intervention, but to examine variations in care and ways to disseminate and implement research-based treatments;

- *Service systems research* addresses large-scale organizational, financing and policy questions. This includes the cost of various care options to an entire system; the use of incentives to promote optimal access to care; the effect of legislation, regulation and other public policies on the organization and delivery of services; and the effect that changes in a system (e.g. cost-shifting) have on the delivery of services.

All four types of research describe the domains of activity that are needed in order to provide a comprehensive approach to the accumulation of evidence. Substantive reviews exist of efficacy and effectiveness studies (e.g. see Lambert & Ogles, 2004). This has a major focus on the area of practice research with the aim of building an interface between this activity and those of efficacy and effectiveness research in service of a more inclusive research strategy (Margison et al., 2000).

More recently, an article entitled *Evidence-based practice in psychology* (APA, 2006) considered alternative forms of evidence with a particular focus on the psychological therapies. The report defined evidence-based practice in psychology as *'the integration of the best available research with clinical expertise in the context of patient characteristics, culture, and preferences'* (APA, 2006). Hence, their use of the term *evidence-based* was broad and inclusive and they espoused multiple types of research evidence including: clinical observation, qualitative research, systematic case studies, single-case experimental designs, public health and ethnographic research, process-outcome studies, studies of interventions as delivered in naturalistic settings (effectiveness research), RCTs and their logical equivalents, and meta-analytic approaches. In relation to specific interventions, the APA policy identified two principal approaches: *treatment efficacy* and *clinical utility* (APA) (2002). The former is synonymous with efficacy research and the latter relates to *'the applicability, feasibility, and usefulness of the intervention in the local or specific setting where it is to be offered'* (APA, 2002, p. 1053). Minimally this comprises

> attention to generality of effects across varying and diverse patients, therapists, settings, and the interaction of these factors; the robustness of treatments across various modes of delivery; the feasibility with which treatments can be delivered to patients in real-world settings; and the costs associated with treatments (APA, 2006, p. 275).

In the broader context of establishing a robust and relevant evidence base for the psychological therapies, the APA report thus emphasizes two points. First, it makes it clear that research relating to clinical utility is complex and methodologically challenging. Indeed, it probably requires huge investment and collective resources. But second, this class of research is necessary as part of a knowledge base for delivering quality care within national health service delivery systems. As examples of future work to be carried out, the APA (2006) article identified 17 priority areas. In addition to identifying the need for efficacy and effectiveness of psychological treatments with older adults, children and with under-represented groups, it included a focus on the effectiveness of widely practiced treatments that have not yet been the focus of controlled research (e.g. integrative therapy). Crucially, it also espoused building treatment models based on the identification and observation of those practitioners in the community who obtained the best outcomes. Accordingly, about a third of the areas focused on components more associated with clinical utility including models of treatment based on practitioners yielding the best outcomes, criteria for discontinuing treatments, accessibility and utilization of psychological services, the cost-effectiveness and cost-benefits of psychological interventions, the building and testing of practice research networks, and the effects of feedback systems and procedures to practitioner or client.

Targeting research to investigate what makes for an effective practitioner is a crucial component of practice-based evidence because it shifts the focus of attention onto the practitioner as much as on the treatment. It is further supported by the APA report which considers the role of clinical expertise and patient characteristics, culture and preferences. In relation to the former, the report made clear that the 'individual therapist has a substantial impact on outcomes, both in clinical trials and in practice settings' (p. 276) and cited a range of supporting research concerning the contribution of therapists themselves (e.g. Crits-Cristoph et al., 1991; Huppert et al., 2001; Wampold & Brown, 2005). The importance of focusing on clinical expertise (i.e. practice) is premised on the fact that *'treatment outcomes are systematically related to the provider of the treatment (above and beyond the type of treatment)'* (APA, 2006, p. 276).

Finally, with respect to patient characteristics, culture and preferences, the key issue can be summarized as follows:

> Underlying all . . . questions is the issue of how best to approach the treatment of patients whose characteristics (e.g. gender, gender identity, ethnicity, race, social class, disability status, sexual orientation) and problems (e.g. comorbidity) may differ from those of samples studied in research (APA, 2006, p. 279).

In an age where societies are becoming increasingly multicultural and diverse, it becomes increasingly crucial to ensure that adopted research strategies relate to and reflect the current societal make-up.

In summary, both the NAMHC and APA reports suggest the need for a broader approach to evidence-based practice. A conclusion from the APA (2006) report was that '. . . EBPP requires an appreciation of the value of multiple sources of scientific evidence' (p. 280). The report moves to redress the balance from focusing predominantly on evidence via RCTs to including, as equally important, designs targeted at clinical utility and based in real-world settings. Our view is that these are complementary approaches and that a more robust knowledge base will derive from the use of both practice-based and trials-based approaches. Before considering practice-based approaches in more detail, we will first revisit the principles and procedures which underpin trials methodology.

Trials and tribulations

There is a wealth of literature attesting to both the robustness of trials methodology within the field of the psychological therapies (e.g. Jacobson & Christensen, 1996) as well as informed and lively debates between proponents and admonishers of RCTs (e.g. Persons & Silberschatz, 1998). Wessely (2007) notes that following the 1948 Medical Research Council (MRC) trial of streptomycin for tuberculosis – generally recognized as the first true RCT due to the role played by the statistician Austin Bradford Hill – the 1965 MRC trial of depression is broadly considered the forerunner of the modern RCT within the field of psychiatry. The crucial component in this design arose out of implementing a procedure of randomization. The centrality of randomization rests on the principle that the potential for bias is reduced because the only systematic way in which participants differ in, for example, the two groups in a trial relates to the interventions they receive. Accordingly, meaningful differences are a result of the different interventions rather than any other variable or unwitting bias. This is a powerful logic and the RCT design has yielded important developments in the nature of medical and psychological interventions.

Within the field of the psychological therapies, there has been a history of utilizing trials methodology to determine the efficacy of treatments. Landmark trials include the 1975 Temple study (Sloane et al., 1975) comparing two active treatments (psychotherapy and behaviour therapy) with a control condition (waiting list), and the 1989 National Institute for Mental Health's Treatment of Depression Collaborative Research Program (Elkin et al., 1989) which compared two active psychological therapies (cognitive behaviour therapy (CBT) and interpersonal psychotherapy (IPT)) with Imipramine plus clinical management and also with a placebo plus clinical management condition. The former trial is noteworthy both for its relative simplicity and clarity of design but also because it yielded considerable overlap in techniques used by the different theoretical orientations. The latter trial is noteworthy as being one of the most expensive psychological therapy trials in the field to date, delivering findings suggesting no clear advantage to either active psychological treatment, and with the placebo arm showing rates of client improvement approaching those of the active psychological treatments. However, even though the principal investigator – Irene Elkin – is held in high esteem and acknowledged as having no allegiance to either of the psychologically active approaches, the results of this study have led to considerable debate and criticism, not least because the findings appeared to challenge the superiority of one specific psychological approach (cf. Jacobson & Hollon, 1996a, 1996b).

Moving beyond the contribution of single trials, a higher-order level of analysing this particular class of studies was used by Smith and Glass (1977) who employed meta-analysis in the first application of this statistical approach to trials in the psychological therapies. The results showed the broad range of psychological therapies to be effective. The yield of such work has, however, brought with it diverse views. On the one hand meta-analytic reviews have tended to suggest the broad equivalence of differing treatment approaches, known as the Dodo verdict from Alice in Wonderland: '*Everybody* has won and *all* must have prizes' (e.g. Ahn & Wampold, 2001; Gloaguen et al., 1998; Wampold et al., 1997) together with accompanying explanations for such a finding (see Stiles, Shapiro & Elliott, 1986). Cuijpers et al. (2008), in a recent meta-analysis of depression, concluded that CBT did modestly better than other treatments and person-centred did moderately less well, but that the differences between these two treatment approaches and the remainder of treatments were small. The authors' conclusion was a slight modification of the Dodo verdict, altering it to 'They all should have prizes, but not all should have the same prize'.

By contrast, the empirically supported treatments (EST) approach in the US and the UK has developed lists based on evaluations of the evidence designating particular psychological therapies as empirically supported treatments for specific disorders and used these as the basis for clinical practice guidelines (utilizing a minimum requirement of two RCTs showing superiority to pill or psychological placebo or by equivalence to an already established treatment). Examples of UK National Institute for Health and Clinical Excellence (NICE) practice guidelines can be found at www.nice.org.uk/Guidance/ while US equivalents can be found at www.guideline.gov/.

What is puzzling, however, is to find such a dichotomy of positions resulting from meta-analytic and EST traditions given that the proponents of each position would consider themselves to be basing results on high-quality evidence. While there are probably multiple reasons for this situation (e.g. see Joyce et al., 2006), it does highlight the potential problem arising from defining evidence in a very specific or singular way. Indeed, the fact that evidence from successive meta-analytic reviews and from the EST tradition delivers apparently discrepant results, or at least is being interpreted as different, may, in itself, be sufficient reason to question whether our current model of evidence is best serving our collective needs in terms of the psychological therapies. Even where there are differences between treatments for disorders, meta-analytic reviews and lists of effective psychotherapies cannot hope to keep pace with the evolution and innovations in therapies that bear the same name but have been significantly modified and continuously change over time.

A related issue is that there is a relative paucity of evidence linking theoretically mutative ingredients to outcomes within specific psychological therapies (i.e. lack of specific efficaciousness). Indeed, some commentators have argued that results of RCTs have been slightly misinterpreted by inferring that 'observed improvements are a direct result of interventions that characterize the approach' (Joyce et al., 2006). By contrast, a contextual model places an emphasis on factors which are common across therapeutic approaches and includes the therapeutic alliance, placebo effects, adherence effects in addition to the effects and variability introduced via therapists (Lambert & Ogles, 2004). Wampold (2001) sets out the relative effect sizes attributable to treatments and specific ingredients (i.e. apropos a medical model) as compared with common factors and therapist effects (i.e. apropos a contextual model). While his purpose was to promote the place of common factors, a conservative interpretation of the data would at least argue for an equivalent consideration of such factors as has been afforded by research funders and agencies to the search for treatment specificity.

Accordingly, it is important to consider the RCT in the context of the psychological therapies where, for many, it is considered the gold standard but where there are also countervailing views which propose there to be no *single* gold standard – no universal best method (e.g. Cartwright, 2007). Rather, such a position proposes that gold standard methods are those approaches which yield reliable information relating to the existing or potential knowledge base. In addition, there are increasing challenges to certain statistical and procedural aspects of trials from biostatisticians who have concerns about how some statistical procedures have become accepted as standard (e.g. see Berger, Matthews & Grosch, 2008). Further, a review of 193 RCTs of psychological therapies published between 1999 and 2003 yielded results showing that study authors considered statistical power in less than half (46%) of the studies, interpreted effect sizes in less than one-third (31%) of studies, and in only 2% of studies were confidence intervals reported (Faulkner, Fidler & Cumming, 2008). The authors concluded that the value of RCT evidence depends, to a large extent, on statistical analysis. Hence, issues relating to the design, implementation and analysis of RCTs in the psychological therapies, as well as in other areas of psychosocial interventions (e.g. see Bottomley, 1997), are not without distinct problems. In the following section we review some sceptical questions regarding RCTs and their contribution to the evidence base as currently construed.

The randomized control trial

The RCT places a priority on internal validity to draw inferences about cause and effect. RCTs, which address statistical differences between groups of people in alternative treatment conditions, have been a powerful tool in medical research. Crucially, the RCT is one specific design in which a key strength is the random allocation of patients to treatment conditions which is carried out by an independent procedure. Indeed, the ability of the RCT to balance unknown contributory factors at intake is its major strength. However, random allocation does not protect RCTs against any other forms of bias (for a detailed account, see Jadad & Enkin, 2007). A key issue in moving towards an acceptance of a broader range of evidence is the need to be mindful that trials methodology, whilst helpful and necessary, is not a panacea. Essentially, randomized trials were designed for drug comparisons where the adoption of double-blind procedures can balance placebo and allegiance effects and where individual patient differences are addressed by randomization, and patient participation is limited to adherence to the particular medication regime. In trials of psychological therapies, double-blind designs are all but impossible and single-blind trials also virtually impossible. The practitioner must know what treatment is being implemented and the patient, ethically, must know the range of interventions to which they might have been randomized. In this respect, a key plank underpinning the integrity of the RCT method is removed. That is, what is feasible and acceptable in drug trials is not so in trials of psychological therapies. The authors are aware of only one double-blind study in the field – one in which both therapists and patients were led to believe they were offering and receiving an effective treatment which was in fact a placebo (Wojciechowski, 1984). This does not mean that they have any lesser role in building an evidence base for the psychological therapies, but it does mean that their integrity cannot be directly assumed from the field of drug trials and that, ironically, they are even more challenging to implement because the context, setting and demands differ.

Importantly, RCTs are not always a necessary precursor to the adoption of efficacious interventions. This point has been made humorously in an article published in the *British Medical Journal* entitled 'Parachute use to prevent death and major trauma related to gravitational challenge: systematic review of randomised controlled trials' (Smith & Pell, 2003). The authors argued that the adoption of parachutes as policy lacked any evidence from RCTs in which parachutes had been evaluated against a control group! However, as one considers situations in which the effectiveness is not self-evident, then it becomes more relevant to consider the evidence. Difficulties arise when the effects of an intervention may be small or negligible, or less than another intervention. These difficulties multiply when such effects carry considerable economic costs – the very situation in which the psychological therapies exist. However, it is self-evident that there are substantive areas relating to practice where the psychological therapies are not amenable to trials methodology. For example, the importance of a positive therapeutic alliance rests largely on correlational studies rather than RCTs. It would not be credible – or ethical – to conduct an RCT to evaluate the alliance, contrasting therapies that maximize the alliance with others in which patients are treated disrespectfully, demeaned, ridiculed and intentionally misunderstood at every turn (Norcross & Lambert, 2006). One does not need an experiment to understand that mistreating vulnerable people would be damaging to their mental health. The crux of the issue here is the need to identify the key issues and factors which affect quality of care and adopt the most appropriate methodology to address that issue. In other words, it is a matter of fit between question and method that is paramount rather than the espousal of the superiority of a single method in and of itself.

This view is echoed in the 2008 Harveian Oration, *De Testimonio: On the evidence for decisions about the use of therapeutic interventions,* by Sir Michael Rawlins, Chairman of the National Institute for Health and Clinical Excellence (NICE) – the body in the UK which sets standards for the acceptability of drug and psychological treatments. Rawlins, whilst seeing an absolutely crucial role for trials evidence, argues for abandoning the hierarchy of evidence that places one form of evidence above another:

> Hierarchies attempt to replace judgement with an oversimplistic, pseudo-quantitative, assessment of the quality of the available evidence. Decision makers have to incorporate judgements, as part of their appraisal of the evidence in reaching their conclusions. Such judgements relate to the extent to which each of the components of the evidence base is 'fit for purpose'. Is it reliable? Does it appear to be generalizable? Do the intervention's benefits outweigh its harms? And so on. Decision makers have to be teleoanalysts. Although techniques such as Bayesian statistics will undoubtedly assist they will not be a substitute for judgement. As William Blake (1757–1827) observed: "God forbid that truth should be confined to mathematical demonstration" (Rawlins, 2008, p. 34).

His notion of decision makers becoming teleoanalysts – that is, as people considering more thorough, complete evidence which cannot be summarized within a single methodological tradition – accords closely with the need for developing an evidence base that combines differing forms of evidence. He concluded that there is a need for

> investigators to continue to develop and improve their methodologies; for decision makers to avoid adopting entrenched positions about the nature of evidence; and for both to accept that the interpretation of evidence requires judgement (Rawlins, 2008, p. 34).

What is so crucial about this oration is that it comes from the head of the main UK independent body whose purpose is the evaluation of scientific evidence in relation to all healthcare interventions.

Randomized controlled trials and responsiveness

The controlled experiment is the closest science has come to a basis for infer-ring causation. If everything is held constant (i.e. controlled) except for one variable that is independently varied, then any distinctive consequences can be attributed to that independent variable. If one client receives an intervention and an identical client does not but is treated identically in all other respects, then any differences in their outcomes must have been caused by the inter-vention. Difficulties arise because no two people are identical and because it is impossible to treat – psychologically – two people identically in all respects ex-cept one. The RCT is an adaptation of the experimental method that addresses differences among clients statistically. Rather than comparing single clients, in-vestigators randomly assign clients to different treatment groups, assuming that relevant individual differences will be more-or-less evenly distributed across the groups. Even though outcomes may vary within groups (because clients are not identical), mean differences between groups beyond those due to chance should be attributable to the different treatments.

As detailed elsewhere (Haaga & Stiles, 2000; Stiles, 2005), many of the diffi-culties in conducting RCTs in counselling and the psychological therapies can be understood as manifestations of *responsiveness* (Stiles, Honos-Webb & Surko, 1998). Responsiveness refers to behaviour that is affected by emerging context, including others' behaviour. For example, therapists are being responsive when they make a treatment assignment based on a client's presenting problems or design homework assignments taking into account a client's abilities or rephrase an explanation that a client seemed not to understand the first time. Therapists and clients are responsive to each other on timescales that range from months to milliseconds. Though far from perfect, their responsiveness usually aims to be appropriate; they try to promote desired outcomes in ways consistent with their approach. In effect, then, the anticipated outcome (the dependent variable) feeds back to influence the delivery of the treatment (the independent variable) on all timescales. This, in turn, confounds the causal logic of the experiment.

As an example of how responsiveness impairs RCTs, treatment- and control-group clients may seek help outside a research protocol, responding appropri-ately to their own requirements. To the extent that they are successful, both groups may manage to find the help they need, diluting the experimental manipulation. Within treatment protocols, therapists and clients tend to com-pensate for protocol-imposed restrictions by responsively making different or more extensive use of the tools they are allowed. For example, a therapist told to decrease question-asking may compensate with more evocative reflections or remaining silent, giving clients more space to talk (Cox, Holbrook & Rutter, 1981; Cox, Rutter & Holbrook, 1981).

Even within treatment groups, no two clients receive the same treatment. Therapist competence demands systematically responding to emerging client differences. Hardy et al. (1998) found that therapists tended to use more affective and relationship-oriented interventions with clients who had an over-involved interpersonal style, but more cognitive and behavioural interventions with clients who had an under-involved interpersonal style. Although, or perhaps because, they received different mixes of interventions, clients with these different interpersonal styles had equivalent positive outcomes. Issues of responsiveness may be even greater in effectiveness research, insofar as the latitude for responsiveness is arguably greater in ordinary practice. Outside of formal research protocols, therapists are relatively free to devise a customized intervention plan and to deviate from or amend the plan in response to emerging information.

Importantly, the correlational strategy for identifying active ingredients is also blocked by responsiveness. One might think the helpfulness of a process component (interpretations, 'mm-hms', homework, relaxation training) could be assessed by correlating its frequency or intensity with outcome. But correlations assume independent observations, implying that the component is delivered ballistically, or at least randomly with respect to client requirements. Such a treatment would be absurd. If therapists are responsive to clients' requirements, clients will get the optimum amount of the component. If the level is always optimum, then outcome will tend to be the same across clients insofar as it depended on that component. Therapists are not perfectly responsive, of course, but any appropriate responsiveness tends to defeat the process-outcome correlation logic and may even reverse it. And, consistently, most common interventions are uncorrelated with outcome (Stiles, 1988; Stiles et al., 1998; Stiles & Shapiro, 1994). The few process components that empirically correlate with outcome, such as the alliance, group cohesion, empathy and goal consensus (Norcross, 2002), are not discretionary actions, but *achievements* (Stiles & Wolfe, 2006). That is, they are products of responsive action, of doing the right thing at the right time.

Overall, trials methodology has contributed a body of evidence demonstrating the benefits of a range of psychological therapies. However, as much as it is important to be aware of the strengths of this approach, it is also important for practitioners, researcher and policy makers to be aware of the potential vulnerabilities and limitations of RCTs. Ardent proponents of trials methodology readily acknowledge limitations. For example, Jacobson and Christensen (1996), in an article advancing the benefits of clinical trials, state:

> Clinical trials are not panaceas. They cannot and should not be the sole designs used for investigating psychotherapy. . . . If psychotherapy research is designed to advance knowledge in the broadest sense, and not simply to test hypotheses about the efficacy and clinical utility of psychotherapy, no one design or paradigm of research will be sufficient (p. 1038).

However, even in the general area of effectiveness, a more robust approach would see RCT designs as one component of an evidence base wherein other methodologies could then be used to elucidate and detail findings arising from trials. Given that manualized treatments in trials, delineating core skills and specific competencies, are delivered by individual practitioners to individual patients who respond to each other and thus add variability in the intervention within broad contextual therapeutic factors, and given there is still good evidence from these trials that therapy is effective, this is a real demonstration that therapy works. However, we need to use other methodologies to help determine the efficacious factors.

Tribulations

In addition to the issues discussed above, there are further specific problems regarding RCT evidence for the psychological therapies that are important to raise in line with the view that the RCT is not a panacea. One primary concern is the *researcher allegiance effect*. Evidence from meta-analytic studies suggests that allegiance effects may account for a greater proportion of the outcome variance than that accounted for by differences between treatments (see Haaga & Stiles, 2000). It is invariably the case that research attesting to the benefits of a candidate therapy is typically carried out by researchers with an allegiance to that specific therapy and this allegiance can be gleaned from such sources as self-descriptions and previous publications (Luborsky et al., 1999). Although this is an issue that has been apparent for a long time, it has not been seriously tackled at the level of research design although Leykin and DeRubeis (2009) have provided a very thoughtful commentary on the issues. The implications are important. For example, a thorough review of contrasting treatments for depression found that when researcher allegiance was partialled out of the analyses, the superiority of CBT over a range of comparator treatments reduced to become a small effect difference (Robinson, Berman & Neimeyer, 1990). That is, apparent differences between treatments could be accounted for by researcher allegiance.

Trials are often unwittingly set up to give the candidate intervention the best – or a better – chance of yielding a positive or advantageous outcome over the comparator intervention. Wampold (2007) compared specific trials where person-centred therapy was initially framed as supportive therapy and used as a control condition with no manual and then, in a further trial, framed as an active treatment with a manual. In the former it did poorly while in the latter the outcomes were broadly equivalent with the candidate treatment. His point was that the form of person-centred therapy in both studies was largely the same leading him to conclude that outcomes of treatments can be influenced by how they are framed and supported within any trial. A position of equipoise is all too rare in trials and there may be an argument for any research evidence which might be used in the service of building an approved basis for treatment recommendations to ensure that health service researchers, whose focus is on healthcare systems rather than aligned to specific psychological interventions, are equal partners in designing any investigation so as to minimize potential biases. Such a move would also position such trials more within the relevant health service system together with its accompanying complexities.

A further major issue relates to *therapist effects and statistical power*. RCTs are primarily powered to evaluate main effects but are often inadequately powered to investigate interaction effects. It is important to consider statistical power in relation to particular tests within a study rather than to the study as a whole. Because they are more vulnerable to failure of randomization, smaller N studies are more likely to carry some bias between the two groups on some variable that might be an alternative explanatory variable for any differences in outcomes. However, statistical power has almost always ignored the therapist as a factor in design and analyses issues. Because a single therapist will see more than one client in a study, the clients are not independent of each other, a situation that violates the assumption of non-independence of data. So, while the criticism of under-powered trials is pervasive in the literature, the more interesting and relevant perspective on this issue relates to the place of therapists as a component in the design and analyses of trials.

The characteristics, skills, experience and qualities of the therapists are likely to be important factors influencing patient outcomes (Elkin, 1999). Because therapists may vary in their effectiveness, the outcomes for patients treated by the same therapist may be similar (clustered) to some degree, that is, outcomes for patients treated by the same therapist may differ less than patients treated by different therapists. Therefore, therapist variability is of prime concern in the study of patient outcomes and needs to be addressed by the use of appropriate statistical analysis such as hierarchical (multilevel) linear modelling (e.g. Kim, Wampold & Bolt, 2006; Wampold & Brown, 2005). Studies have suggested that where clustering is present but ignored in analysis, assumptions about the independence of patient outcomes are violated, standard errors will be inflated, p-values will be exaggerated, and the power of the trial reduced (for more details, see Lee & Thompson, 2005; Roberts & Roberts, 2005). The importance of clustering has been recognized by its inclusion in the extended CONSORT guidelines for non-pharmaceutical trials. These recommend that the effects of any clustering, for example, patients within therapists and therapists within sites or services, should be reported and the modelling of treatment effects should allow for patient characteristics while controlling for this clustering (Boutron et al., 2008).

Most trials focus on contrasts between treatments and are powered by the number (N) of clients. All-too-often, the selection of therapists is a matter of pragmatics determined either by how many available therapists there are, how many could reasonably see the required N of clients in the allocated time frame, or cost/time allocation. There is an interesting anecdote about Sir Ronald Fisher, one of the founders of modern statistical methods, who developed procedures in relation to agriculture and ways of obtaining the best yield. Of all the factors he considered, the one variable he omitted was that of the farmer. In a direct parallel, much of the current evidence base for the psychological therapies derives from trials which are open to the same criticism: failure to design by and analyse for the therapist as a factor. Within a trial having a low N of practitioners, one or two practitioners could introduce significant bias. As an example, in a high-quality RCT comparing CBT and non-directive counselling for depression and anxiety, two practitioners accounted for approximately 40% of patients seen in the trial (King et al., 2000). Conceptually, the variance accounted for by therapists becomes attributed to treatments and could work either for or against the therapy. However, attributing portions of outcome variance inappropriately to treatments undermines the gold standard of RCTs. Further, however many therapists are selected, they are unlikely to be selected at random from the population of therapists in routine settings. Hence there are serious issues regarding the extent to which findings attributable to therapists within a trials methodology can be generalized to the population of therapists in the community.

Interestingly, practitioner effects may be masked by the logic of the explanatory trial. To test the effect of the target intervention, investigators seek to reduce practitioner variation via treatment manuals, training, adherence checks and supervision. Hence, explanatory trials that reported on therapist effects have, unsurprisingly, generally reported small effects (e.g. Clark et al., 2006; Elkin et al., 2006). Importantly, however, the number of therapists is usually so small that significant differences between them would be difficult to detect because such studies are underpowered and not designed to address this question. In contrast, data from routine care suggests just the opposite trend. Okiishi et al. (2006) examined outcomes between therapists who saw anywhere from 30 to hundreds of clients and found substantial differences in recovery and deterioration rates between the top and bottom 10% of therapists, but no differences in outcome as a function of the type of psychotherapy offered to clients.

As specific problems of methodology, these issues are not insurmountable but they do require considerable adjustment to the way in which RCTs in the psychological therapies are designed, implemented and interpreted. Indeed, a standard design is more likely to comprise many therapists each seeing a few clients (rather than vice versa). As such, traditional methods of analysing data are not well suited to dealing with the reality that clients are, effectively, nested within therapists. Analyses of data need to move towards adopting multilevel modelling techniques utilizing large Ns of therapists. The need for such studies takes trials into health service settings with the purpose of better reflecting the everyday realities of service delivery and decision making – practical clinical trials.

Practical clinical trials

An important distinction exists between *explanatory* clinical trials and *practical* clinical trials (Tunis, Stryer & Clancy, 2003). Explanatory trials further our knowledge of how and why a particular intervention works. In the psychological therapies, such trials address some psychological phenomenon that underpins a particular intervention. By contrast, *practical* – or *pragmatic* – *trials* focus on information needed to make healthcare decisions within routine practice settings, and it is this design that we will explicate here as it takes us one step towards broadening the evidence base. The distinctive features of practice trials are as follows:

- selection of clinically relevant interventions for comparison
- inclusion of a diverse population of participants
- recruitment of participants from a variety of settings
- collection of data on a broad range of health outcomes.

The *selection of clinically relevant interventions* is crucial insofar as comparisons must be between viable and plausible alternative treatments to inform healthcare decision making. For example, the use of a placebo as a treatment condition is a feature of explanatory trials as it helps us to understand the added value of a formal intervention. However, delivering a placebo intervention in a healthcare setting is rarely an option and so does not help inform decision making. Treatment as usual (TAU) is often used as a treatment condition and, providing it is known what constitutes TAU, then whether a targeted treatment performs better than TAU will help decision making. Often, trials select a comparator as a minimum treatment (e.g. applied relaxation) with the aim of testing whether the targeted treatment performs better than the comparator. This may provide evidence that, for example, more psychologically informed treatments yield larger benefits but is relatively poor in informing decision makers as to what treatment to deliver because the minimum intervention is rarely a viable treatment option. Indeed, in general we do not really know enough about TAU when used as a comparison.

The *inclusion of a diverse population of participants* is important for generalizability similar to the logic of *technology transfer studies* (see Lueger & Barkham, Chapter 9) in which the intervention is drawn from an efficacy trial but the population parameters to which it is applied are relaxed. A practical trial may take this slightly further, for example, by not requiring a diagnosis, thereby informing decision makers about whether the intervention would be applicable in the absence of a formal diagnosis.

The *recruitment from a range of settings* leads to a better approximation to real-world clinical settings in relation to both practice settings and practitioners. The former are crucial in order to test the tolerance of specific interventions while the latter addresses the possibility of practitioner effects. In practice research, the diversity of practitioners and settings needs to be designed into studies in order to test their effects.

Finally, *measuring a broad range of relevant health outcomes* can provide information on the most relevant outcomes to different decision makers. In addition to specific and theoretically oriented outcomes, studies should assess quality of life, functioning, satisfaction and costs. Also long-term follow-up needs to be considered in research designs as there is evidence that results can vary as a function of follow-up period.

The shift reflected in practice trials more towards health and psychological services research is a welcome move and goes a considerably way to incorporating the complexities of real-world practice. However, they are firmly rooted in the paradigm of trials methodology which, as we have shown, is not without its problems. In pursuit of a knowledge base that complements trials, the next section considers how the evidence base of the psychological therapies can be enhanced by practice-based research.

Practice-based studies

Beyond explanatory and practical clinical trials, there is the field of effectiveness research. This is a wide-ranging term that incorporates technology transfer studies testing the transportability of trials evidence into practice settings. As such, effectiveness studies might include randomization procedures within clinical settings or, if not, would certainly follow protocol-driven treatment procedures. In such cases, there are design and/or procedural impositions introduced into the delivery of the service. Such studies differ from what we call practice-based studies that utilize data from treatments *as routinely delivered in practice settings* – that is, they evaluate the delivery of the service as it occurs naturally within the health service setting (for other accounts, see Barkham & Margison, 2007; Margison, 2001).

Features of practice-based studies

In the same way that traditional RCTs, as described above, have certain specific components, so do practice-based studies. However, while RCTs can be construed as applying multiple layers of filters to ensure a very precise target data set, practice-based studies relax these filters with the specific purpose of trying to reflect the activity of routine practice. Table 2.1 summarizes the contrasting hallmarks of practice-based studies and trials methodologies. Here we summarize some of the key features.

Table 2.1   Hallmarks of randomized controlled trials and practice-based studies

Trial/study feature	*Randomized controlled trials*	*Practice-based studies*
Design	• Formal: design provides the overarching rationale and framework for the trial/research • Control and/or contrast components of design are crucial	• Informal: design is placed 'over' already existing routinely collected data collection • Focus can be on translational work (i.e. testing efficacy findings in practice settings), investigation of quality or safety components, or process issues
Philosophy and policy	• Top-down approach: Invariably initiated by policy makers, funding agencies and researchers	• Bottom-up approach: Driven and owned by practitioners in service of quality agenda
Hypotheses	• Usually focused on a single 'main' scientific question	• Can focus on single or complex questions
Investigator allegiance	• Researcher usually an expert in candidate treatment being investigated	• More focused on delivery and service issues
Sample	• Highly selected: targeted according to specific hypotheses • Stringent inclusion and exclusion criteria applied to protect internal validity construct	• Unselected: initial sampling frame comprises all clients or practitioners • Study sample can comprise total pool of data or a selected subsample to focus on specific issues or subgroup
Treatment(s)	• Single/specific treatment(s) • Manualized • Additional training for therapists usual prior to study • Adherence ratings/checks	• All treatments as delivered in practice • Not manualized • No additional training other than would occur in fulfilment of continuing professional development • Adherence checks only as naturally adopted procedures within the service (i.e. not imposed by study requirements)

Table 2.1 (*Continued*)

Trial/study feature	Randomized controlled trials	Practice-based studies
Location	• Not usually associated with specific service/delivery locations because focus is 'science' rather than 'practice' • Increasingly multisite implementation in order to yield required N of clients	• Often associated with local service(s) in order for feedback to be utilized • Can be single or multiple services depending on common methodology and question(s) being asked
Measurement	• Single primary outcome measure usually the standard with additional secondary outcomes	• Outcome and service parameters defined by common methodology
Ethics	• Ethics approval always required incorporating informed consent	• Ethics approval is usually best secured but use of routinely collected aggregated data should not raise concerns for review boards
Relation of measurement to sample	• Rich data on focused (small?) N of clients	• Rich data on large N of clients and practitioners although any study can be selective about what data to include

Rooted in routine practice

Practice-based studies need to place near-zero limitations on included data. That is, rather than controlling variables as in an RCT, they aim to capture data drawn from routine practice such that the subsequent research endeavour is moulded to reflect everyday clinical activity. Accordingly, practice-based studies can be viewed as meeting all inclusion criteria as specified by Shadish et al. (1997) in Table 2.2. Shadish and colleagues grouped inclusion criteria into three stages or levels with each successive stage characterized by the relaxation of additional inclusion criteria. Hence, any study meeting all nine criteria as listed in Table 2.2 would be a strong exemplar of a practice-based study. However, it is certainly not the case that all criteria need to be met. Crucial, however, is the absence of randomization which is, de facto, not a characteristic of routine practice. But this is not to infer that features of practice-based studies and trials methodology cannot be combined at some meta-level and we discuss such possibilities at the end of this chapter.

Table 2.2   Criteria for client selection in practice-based studies

Features of client samples in practice-based studies

Stage 1 criteria	• Carried out in community mental health centres, primary care settings • Involving clients referred through normal clinical routes • Involving experienced, professional practitioners with regular caseloads rather than therapists in training or therapists receiving training specifically for the research study
Stage 2 criteria	• Do not use treatment manual • Do not monitor implementation of treatment
Stage 3 criteria	• Clients heterogeneous in personal characteristics • Clients heterogeneous in focal presenting problems • Practitioners not trained immediately before study in the specific treatment focus being studied • Therapists free to choose a variety of treatment models rather than limited to a single model

Adapted from Shadish, W.R. et al., Evidence that therapy works in clinically representative conditions, *Journal of Consulting and Clinical Psychology*, 65, 355–365. American Psychological Association, 1997

Measurement systems

Although there may be no restrictions on data inclusion, there are clear requirements relating to the basic tenets of measurement – namely, the use of well designed, valid and reliable measurement systems and procedures. Importantly, experimental control and establishing causal relationships are not the primary concerns. Instead, logic, feasibility and plausibility govern the planning, data collection and perhaps most crucially, interpretation of the results. Hence, data can be used not only to investigate the application of results from RCTs to routine practice, but also to considering questions of service quality and delivery. One of the key roles of measurement systems is to deliver large data sets using common measures. Quality measurement systems have been developed in the US and the UK and are documented in subsequent chapters (e.g. Barkham et al., Chapter 8; Kraus & Castonguay, Chapter 7; Lambert, Hansen & Harmon, Chapter 6).

Large data sets and practice research networks

The adoption of a common methodology provides the basis for the collection of large N data sets from health organizations, insurance companies and collaborating services. The latter have led to the growth of practice research networks (PRNs; for details, see Parry et al., Chapter 12). In contrast to trials, PRNs utilize data gathered in real-world practice settings rather than specifically orchestrated clinical trials. They have been described as naturalistic laboratories for large-scale data collection (Hickner, 1993). The rise of PRNs has been in response to two major concerns: the first relates to constraints placed upon the generalizability of efficacy research, and the second focuses on the issue of the lack of robustness of some effectiveness research whereby the possible explanatory accounts for results are sufficiently numerous as to undermine the activity (Borkovec et al., 2001). Importantly, however, PRNs are not a critical component for the delivery of practice-based evidence but rather provide one route for yielding such evidence. Indeed, bar a few exceptions, the research output from PRNs has been less than might have been hoped (see Parry et al., Chapter 12).

In the UK there are a growing number of large databases relating to the psychological therapies. These include the CORE National Practice-based Evidence Datasets (Mellor-Clark & Barkham, 2006) and the government's initiative on Improving Access to Psychological Therapies (IAPT; Layard, 2006). Both these initiatives are yielding information and knowledge about the delivery of psychological therapies (e.g. Barkham et al., 2008; Clark et al., 2009; Richards & Suckling, 2009; Stiles et al., 2008a). The former has been a standard bearer for espousing the philosophy and delivery of practice-based evidence in the UK along with the work of like-minded practitioner-scientists in the US (e.g. Kraus & Castonguay, Chapter 7; Lambert et al., Chapter 6) and continental Europe (e.g. Lutz, 2002; Lutz et al., 2005). By contrast, the IAPT initiative is an interesting example of a hybrid where a common measurement standard has been imposed in order to obtain national data on psychological interventions approved by the UK's National Institute for Health and Clinical Excellence. Hence, the ways in which these datasets have been developed differ considerably in terms of the contrasting philosophical drivers behind each initiative.

Ownership by practitioners

The concept of practice-based evidence is crucial in one central respect. That is, it provides the foundations for generating research questions that are grounded in the practice context and, for this reason, need to be relevant to practitioners and the delivery of routine services. Such questions may be pragmatic or theory driven but have in common a fundamental relevance to practice. Within this context, the overarching aspiration within practice-based evidence is to build an approach to the collection of evidence within which all practitioners and all *bona fide* research approaches can contribute. In this regard, practice-based research is inclusive of a range of research methodologies and is consistent with the axiom that trials methodology alone cannot build a science of the psychological therapies. In practice-based evidence, practitioners have ownership of the questions and the evidence. Moreover, *practice* is the core driver of the process – driven by practitioners' and managers' desires to provide a quality service to their clients. At this level, the issue of *ownership* of the research activity by practitioners becomes crucial as they strive to innovate and generate solutions to local issues within a national context.

Research questions and designs

A distinctive feature of practice-based evidence is its ability to generate data at multiple levels from a single case through to many thousands of cases. Because data is collected routinely, designs are overlaid onto data rather than it being generated in response to a specific design as occurs in trials methodology. Hence, a data set can be interrogated as a whole for such topics as client safety or to sample a subgroup of clients who are under-represented in more standard-sized data sets. Or, a data set can be used as the sampling frame from which design components can be specified so as to extract a subset of data meeting precisely stated criteria (e.g. clients aged 25–35 with two dependants) that would be either extremely difficult to collect within a trial design – or, if it were collected, would entail a very extended timescale. Ultimately, however, questions best suited to practice-based studies are those that trials cannot address (i.e. conditions to which people cannot be randomized), or that sample under-represented groups or clinical presentations, which test the transportability of trial findings in routine settings, and perhaps more than anything else, aim to improve the overall quality of service delivery for clients.

Quality and practice improvement

A key aspiration of practice-based measurement systems is the exploration of relationships between the inputs, processes and outputs of the service delivery system with the aim of improving practice. This is well exemplified by methodologies utilized in services other than the psychological therapies. For example, in the field of stroke and rehabilitation Horn and Gassaway (2007) have adopted a distinctive approach in order to build a *practice-based evidence for clinical practice improvement* (PBE-CPI) methodology. Horn and colleagues have argued that it is impossible for a randomized clinical trial to test all possible interactions among interventions encountered in routine practice. By contrast, the large and natural variation encountered in current practice within and between services provides the opportunity for evaluating the relative effectiveness of differing treatment combinations: 'PBE-CPI methodology identifies . . . interventions that are associated with better outcomes for specific types of patients in real-world practice' (p. S56).

People seeking psychological help are entitled to receive a quality service and this aim becomes a prime focus of practice-based evidence. The components enabling a quality evaluation of a service have been summarized as comprising five activities: (1) the adoption and use of an IT system to store, organize, filter and undertake performance appraisals using the collected data; (2) the central role of preparatory training for service staff to ensure best use of the data; (3) the adoption of a common reporting framework; (4) the co-development and use of national service indicators from anonymized and aggregated data; and (5) the development of networks to support the interpretation and utilization of the data for enhancing service quality (Mellor-Clark et al., 2006).

Benchmarks and case tracking

Two examples of quality procedures in practice-based evidence are the use of benchmarks and case tracking (see Leach & Lutz, Chapter 10; also Lueger & Barkham, Chapter 9). Within practice-based research, the aim is to *locate* the processes and outcomes of targeted services against a standard – a benchmark – that is, against evidence outside the targeted settings but within a similar delivery service or configuration at a single point in time (e.g. Evans et al., 2003) or by comparing across years (e.g. Barkham et al., 2001). Such benchmarks become standards that are indicators of quality and lead to the activity of benchmarking. Examples of benchmarks for a range of service parameters can be found in a special issue of *Counselling & Psychotherapy Research* (2006) in relation to, amongst others, completion rates for measures (Bewick et al., 2006), initial contact (Cahill, Potter & Mullin, 2006), unilateral termination (Connell, Grant & Mullin, 2006), recovery and improvement rates (Mullin et al., 2006) and waiting times (Trusler et al., 2006). Benchmarking can also take the form of comparing effectiveness in a particular clinical setting against the outcomes obtained in efficacy studies (e.g. Barkham et al., 2008; Merrill et al., 2003; Minami et al., 2007).

A conceptually related procedure, which is increasingly coming to the fore, is that of case tracking (for details, see Leach & Lutz, Chapter 10). In the same way that benchmarking locates a treatment outcome in the context of outcomes derived from different studies (or some other feature of a service against data on the feature from a wider source), case tracking locates a client's ongoing data against a trajectory derived from a larger base of similar clients. Hence, the procedures of benchmarking and case tracking aim to locate data from a specific situation, setting or session against a larger pool of data for which the parameters are known and understood. Case-tracking methodology has been promoted by the work of Lambert and colleagues and most crucially enhanced by using feedback procedures (see Lambert, 2001; Lambert et al., 2001, 2003, 2005, Chapter 6).

A framework for practice-based evidence

In order to capture the purpose and process of practice-based research, we present a generic five-stage model that would encompass the diversity of approaches within practice-based research. We emphasize that this is illustrative of *a* model of practice-based evidence and other models and stages may be equally appropriate within the overarching philosophy.

1. *Quantification of process or outcome*: Crucially, the processes and outcomes within counselling and the psychological therapies need to be quantifiable. This requires initial inquiries such as focus groups with consumers (e.g. patients, clinicians, administrators) and scholarly efforts to understand existing knowledge, theory and methodological procedures, which help identify what needs to be quantified and how best to proceed. By this we mean that domains of interest are operational to the extent that they can be defined and captured via data. Hence, this includes the application of both quantitative and qualitative procedures until an understanding of the strengths and limitations of measurement procedures are well in hand.
2. *Development and adoption of routine measurement*: This requires several elements including the development or identification of a measurement system and then its widespread adoption in practice settings (see Chapters 6–8). In effect, this is the health technology at the heart of practice-based research. Crucially, in this approach the use of a measurement system precedes the identification of any question and, hence, differs from traditional stand-alone trials methodology in which the question of interest is identified first, which then determines specific measurement tools and procedures selected for that purpose.
3. *Identification of a practical question of interest*: A key element in progressing practice-based research is the identification of an issue either of interest to practitioners and/or service managers, or an issue that has been identified as problematic.
4. *Utilization of routinely collected data via analyses to address the question of interest*: This stage comprises the analysis of data, equivalent to the results section of a standard experiment or trial. Importantly, the analyses and procedures employed are likely to be broader in scope than those used in traditional trials.
5. *Developing a feedback loop*: In this stage new information leads to change in practice and the collection of further data following the change.

An example shows these five generic stages. After a psychological test was developed and its validity was established, Nielsen et al. (2009) used test scores to examine the value of ongoing intake procedures at a university clinic. Existing assessment data over an 11-year period were examined to see if keeping a client after performing the intake versus referring the client to another therapist had an effect on client outcome. The study began as a result of differences of opinion between practitioners over the value of intake. The data essentially led to the conclusion that rather than enhancing outcomes for clients (based on matching client with therapist following intake), intake had no detectable positive effect and in fact slowed client recovery and therefore was costly. The information was used to abandon the intake procedure because it was not cost-effective. Wait-list time was therefore reduced and both wait-list and treated clients could be expected to suffer for shorter periods of time as a result. Although practice-based evidence was used to eliminate intake, the same information could have led to a decision to modify the current intake procedure and continued assessment used to modifying intake practices until the beneficial consequences of an intake could be detected.

Vulnerabilities of practice-based evidence

It is a fundamental principle that no research method is without threats to its validity and practice-based studies are no exception. However, the nature of the threats differs from those that apply to RCTs and in this section we outline a number of such threats to practice-based evidence and suggest ways in which they might be addressed.

Data quality

The first requirement that should become a mantra for services is the aspiration to collect data that passes a specified standard criterion for quality. Although it can be argued that data from efficacy research is selective prior to inclusion in a study, practice-based data is vulnerable if it is selective in some other sense. Incompleteness of data might be at the level of the data itself (i.e. missing data points), practitioners' caseload (i.e. self-selecting their clients), or the inclusion, or not, of all practitioners.

At the level of data, the aspiration is to ensure that all measures or in-struments (and their respective items) are completed. Hence, services should encourage clients – and practitioners – not to omit items. However, even with such encouragement, some clients will omit items. Within both efficacy and practice-based research, there are many ways of dealing statistically with miss-ing data and adopting such a strategy is invariably the approach taken within efficacy trials. However, within practice-based research, as long as appropriate encouragement and support have been given, there is an alternative, although not mutually exclusive, approach: namely, to consider the *value* of missing data as additional information. That is, clients omit specific items for a reason that may yield more clinical information for the practitioner than had they com-pleted the item. Missing items can still be addressed or corrected statistically but the recognition that deliberately missed items are providing information is a crucial difference between efficacy and practice-based studies because the latter works on common methodology yielding very large data sets. Hence, it becomes possible to drill down and investigate small groups of clients who omit certain items in a way that is not feasible within efficacy trials because the N of such examples would be minimal.

In terms of client data, it is unrealistic to expect all clients to provide data in the same way that it is unrealistic to expect all trains to arrive on time. The expectation needs to be realistic and achievable. The initial sampling frame should be the service as a whole or whatever overarching system unit is being employed (e.g. specific site within a service). Importantly, the sampling frame is not directly associated with the N of clients – that is, it does not necessarily mean that the N has to be large. It is quite appropriate to carry out a practice-based study on a small service but the crucial component would be that all consecutive clients referred to the service were included in the data set. Of course, if a common measurement system to that used in similar services at other sites is employed, then this smaller data set can contribute to a larger data set which might yield more robust findings.

Assuming that the sampling frame can be defined, one standard to aspire to might be an 80% completion rate as most people might agree that this is a clear majority and it is likely that results derived from this level of return would be regarded as acceptable to most stakeholders. It should also be remembered that clients cannot be forced to complete measures – their willingness to do so is voluntary and the service they receive can never be affected by their refusal to complete a measurement package. Of course, it may be that treatment assignment is enhanced or better matched with information arising from completion of assessment measures. However, the final call will always remain with the client. A portion of clients referred for psychological therapies do not take part in providing data other than as part of the entry into treatment. In this respect, the failure to capture data from such clients undermines all research methodologies. A key challenge for building the evidence base for the psychological therapies is accessing those clients – and potential clients – who are reluctant to engage with services.

A related concern regards client or practitioner data that are not collected. There is always the concern that unless all of a practitioner's clients submit data, then the practitioner is, what is often termed, *cherry picking* (i.e. they are selecting those clients who have – or the practitioner thinks have – a better outcome). The issue here focuses on the system of data collection and the organizational climate within which such data is collected. With the development of easy-to-use information technology, there is the very real potential for data to be collected via computer at each session providing the data serves a clinical purpose – that is, it is not burdensome to either clients or practitioners and meets a clinical need. The notion of using very short measures or single items that enable the client to check-in regarding their current state, recent events and concerns provides a way of ensuring that data reflects the temporal course of any intervention and is a safeguard against there being no data subsequent to the initial assessment. The issue of practitioners not returning data or contributing data to practice-based studies probably raises different issues from those addressed above and might relate more to organizational climate and management issues.

Treatment delivery

A second issue in practice-based studies relates to knowledge regarding the actual interventions being delivered. The methodology of RCTs is built on treatment protocols and manuals such that what treatment is being delivered is known and that it is being delivered by practitioners who have been specifically trained and whose delivery of the treatment is tested for its adherence to the specific manual detailing the intervention. Testing involves the collection of adherence ratings to show that the practitioners are delivering the components of the treatment as specified and also that they are not delivering components of alternative treatments that might be active ingredients of change. Being able to implement a similar level of evaluation within routine practice would seem to be challenging to say the least and in this context there are a number of points to address.

First, it is important to start from the premise that all study procedures and processes need to be fit for a given purpose and transporting a procedure from one methodology to another without consideration of its aims would, itself, be a questionable action. The principle is that different paradigms use different methods in order to address different questions. We stated earlier that practice-based studies reflect practice as it is carried out in routine settings without imposition of additional tiers or data collection. Recall that of the nine criteria presented in Table 2.2, two of them refer explicitly to treatment implementation in terms of not using treatment manuals and not monitoring implementation of treatment. If it becomes national policy to collect data on treatment adherence and this becomes part of routine practice then, de facto, it becomes a part of practice-based studies. Second, current measurement systems – for example, the CORE System – collect practitioners' assignments of what type of psychological therapy they are practicing. Corroboration from supervisors might be a possibility but, again, this would be the responsibility of services to implement. And third, the agenda for practice-based studies focuses on quality of outcomes within the overall service delivery system rather than as a function of any specific type of psychological therapy per se.

Finally, it is important to ensure that the level of evidence is appropriate to the question being asked. For example, if the question is one of overall effectiveness, then it may not be a crucial issue as to whether the treatments as stated are delivered in pure form. That is, being unable to specify the components of the treatments as delivered beyond their brand name (e.g. CBT or person-centred therapy) is not a fatal flaw. In relation to this latter issue, Stiles and colleagues reported two studies in which treatment as delivered was determined from a practitioner-completed form in which they ticked from a range of orientations to reflect the delivery in any given client's treatment (Stiles et al., 2006, 2008a). Hence, a client's treatment could be rated as comprising only CBT-focused therapy, or CBT and another brand, or a combination of more orientations. The overall outcome from the Stiles et al. (2008a) study was reported as an uncontrolled effect size of 1.34. This report received criticism in the form that pre-post data was only available on 39% of clients and there was no independent evidence to support practitioners' accounts and no evidence of the quality of delivery (see Clark, Fairburn & Wessely, 2008 for criticisms; and Stiles et al., 2008b for rebuttal). However, in a large study as part of the IAPT initiative and drawing on similar clients (i.e. from primary care), Richards and Suckling (2009) achieved a 97% pre-post completion rate which yielded an uncontrolled effect size of 1.38 – remarkably similar to the findings of Stiles and colleagues.

Delivering change agency support and developing quality feedback

In setting out the aims of practice-based evidence, there is a crucial component relating to helping deliver the appropriate organizational climate whereby the collection and use of data is maximized and shown to be a sustainable venture. Developing the appropriate climate is, in many ways, the starting point of practice-based evidence. That is, to deliver practice-based evidence requires the development of a culture in which the effort and yield is valued by participants. In this respect, engaging with practice-based evidence in a genuine way involves being part of a change agency approach wherein the hopes and fears arising from the adoption of measurement, monitoring and management are addressed. At this level, adopting practice-based evidence becomes an organizational intervention: it is not about using a standard outcome measure just because it exists any more than it is about having clinical supervision just because it's expected of a practitioner. Indeed, some of the generic principles of supervision provide a starting point.

The generic aims of clinical supervision are manifold but include, amongst others, ensuring appropriate governance and safe practice, developing a learning experience for the practitioner within a supervisory relationship, being able to place their clients in the context of their overall caseload, recognizing limitations and identifying training needs. From the perspective of practice-based evidence, the culture of openness to data is evident with case study methods (see Stiles, Chapter 4) that, in themselves, most closely approximate clinical supervision. That is, they involve close investigation of a clinical case from a perspective other than that of the practitioner. Hence, case study methods, like supervision, have the potential for challenging existing views on case material, a feature shared by many qualitative methods (see Pistrang & Barker, Chapter 3) and further informed by the use of quantitative methods (see McMillan & Morley, Chapter 5).

The adoption of a common measurement system extends practice-based evidence beyond the privacy of a supervisory relationship to wider service settings comprising multiple clients and/or practitioners. However, although the nature of the data differs, the generic principles of supervision apply in pursuit of improving quality. But the potential challenges at this level for practitioners and service managers are considerable where evaluation can be viewed with suspicion. At this juncture, there is a clear role for delivering change agency support to facilitate the changing philosophy. For example, the implementation of the CORE System in services was facilitated by a clear commitment to change agency support in the form of workshops and tutoring informed by work on organizational leadership. In particular, Kotter's stage model of change was used which set out clear stages of change drawn from organizations (Kotter, 1995; Kotter & Cohen, 2002). Importantly, the model is about drawing out leadership potential rather than implementing management systems to ensure completion of the task (see Evans et al., 2006).

Practice-based evidence can be used as a systematic approach to building and maintaining an effective service whether at the level of, for example, a UK NHS Trust (e.g. Lucock et al., 2003) or US state (e.g. Brower, 2003). To the extent that results are fed back into the service system, the process might be considered to be a topic closely linked to audit. Conventionally, audit deals with the details of inputs, activities and outputs, setting desired standards and examining the potential steps that might lead to change. The whole process forms an iterative loop with the standards against which the service is to be assessed being, themselves, continually revised.

Although the evidence derived from this practice approach is of value in and of itself, it carries with it the crucial component of situated generalization – the process whereby practitioners accept evidence for change to practice if there is a clear connection with the situation in which the improvement takes place. Hence, it contains great potential for building reflective practice whereby practitioners can be the consumers of their – and other practitioners' – research. Lucock et al. (2003) described building a service delivery system on a model of practice-based evidence and identified key components and reflections on this process. They deemed seven factors to be important in bringing about a change management consistent with practice-based evidence: (1) ownership, especially in being party to decision making; (2) training sessions to disseminate revised ways of working; (3) clarity of written documentation to explain procedures; (4) a range of venues for voicing and sharing concerns; (5) clear lines of accountability; (6) providing staff with a background – and context – to national policy drivers; and (7) feedback of results to clinicians as a standard procedure. While these factors are very closely related to organizational, leadership and management procedures that embed practice-based evidence within a service setting, the key product of this cycle lies in the feedback provided to clients, practitioners, the service and all other stakeholders.

Building better designs for evidence-based practice and practice-based evidence

The danger of multiple paradigms is that they are seen as competitive or mutually exclusive: one paradigm is right and the other wrong. A move away from such a dichotomous position would be to construe each paradigm as occupying a space along a continuum. However, one component of a continuum is its linearity and this fuels the argument that a research question is first tested under one condition and then tested under the other. The usual direction is from efficacy to effectiveness and several models have been proposed accordingly: for example, a developmental model (Linehan, 1999) or an hour-glass model (Salkovskis, 1995). Notwithstanding the value of these particular models, the key issue is to present a model, or models, in which each approach is equally valued – that is, there is a position of equipoise. Here we briefly outline two such models. The first model, termed *complementary*, assumes that each paradigm remains independent but that we consider the 'weight' of evidence from a position of being a teleoanalyst – attempting to combine information from differing classes of evidence. The second model, termed *combined*, considers incorporating components of both designs into a hybrid design with the aim of yielding information bridging rigour and relevance criteria.

Complementary model

The paradigm of practice-based evidence has previously been presented as complementary to evidence-based practice (e.g. Barkham & Mellor-Clark, 2000, 2003). As a consequence, this complementarity generates an evidence cycle between the rigours of evidence-based practice and the relevance of practice-based evidence. The two paradigms have the potential for feeding into each other to generate a model for the knowledge base of the psychological therapies that is both rigorous and relevant. This cyclical model is presented in Figure 2.1 to demonstrate the practical products, yields and activities arising from each paradigm.

A key principle in this cyclical model is that each component is equally valued in helping to deliver best practice and this, in turn, has important implications for the relationship between policy, practice and research. The traditional linear direction is of RCTs informing policy which, in turn, directs practice. The complement to this process is of practitioners developing and building an evidence base rooted in practice. This can then feed into and inform issues that can be shaped into more finely tuned tests of specific hypotheses through efficacy research. The yield of both these evidence bases can then better inform policy. Hence, in this cyclical and chiastic model, policy per se is not the driver for practice. Rather, policy is a product of knowledge informed by a combined evidence base. Hence, any specific policy will have a provenance that

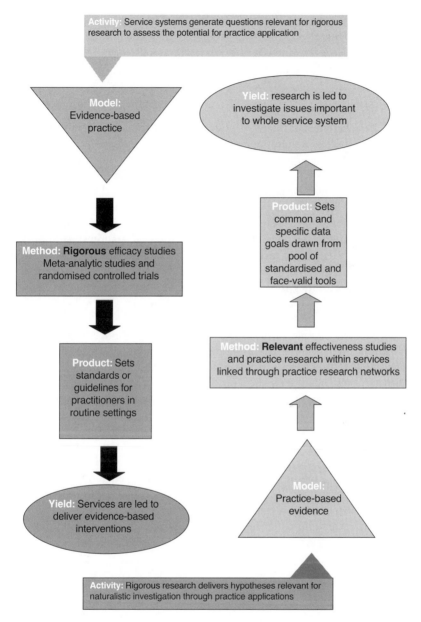

Figure 2.1   The interrelationship between evidence-based practice and practice-based evidence. *Source*: Barkham, M. & Mellor-Clark, J., Bridging evidence-based practice and practice-based evidence: Developing a rigorous and relevant knowledge for the psychological therapies, *Clinical Psychology & Psychotherapy, 10*, 319–327. John Wiley & Sons Ltd., 2003

is grounded in both paradigms. The openness of researchers and practitioners to cycle through these differing paradigms may provide us with a more robust knowledge base about the process and outcomes of psychological interventions.

Combined model

Given the inherent limitations of both controlled trials and observational or naturalistic studies, it becomes a priority to identify research designs that are better able to display both the rigour required to meet criteria for guidelines and the relevance demanded by routine practitioners and healthcare decision makers (Barkham & Parry, 2008). While such designs as the comprehensive cohort trial – also referred to as the comprehensive cohort study – go some way towards building a bridge between efficacy and practice-based evidence, they do not address the need for designing a new generation of studies that integrate the strengths of each approach. An example of the need to invest in new designs arises not only from the arguments already put forward, but also from the opportunities afforded by, for example, the existence of increasingly large data sets. These have implications for how we design, fund and analyse future studies.

At one level, it would be possible to work with existing hybrid designs and, for example, nest a multisite comprehensive cohort design within the UK national IAPT roll-out (where people either select to be randomized to CBT or an alternative bona fide intervention or follow a cohort in which they select their treatment of choice); this would yield information pertinent to clinical decision making in relation to treatment choice and effectiveness as well as other service parameters relating to, for example, waiting times and risk of deterioration, which occur naturally within service settings and are not manipulated within trial designs. However, the more challenging and creative path is one of establishing common ground between such initiatives and generating a combined agenda and design, not least because – as stated earlier – the experience of differing evidence bases (i.e. meta-analytic reviews and empirically supported treatments) generating differing views is, ultimately, confusing and unhelpful to practitioners.

Conclusions

The purpose of this chapter has been to outline distinctive approaches to the collection of evidence relating to the psychological therapies. Green and Glasgow (2006), in considering issues of translation methodology, concluded that if government bodies aspire to securing more encompassing and consistent evidence-based practice, then they need to invest in and promote more practice-based evidence whereby effort is made to address issues of external validity as well as the realities and diversity of routine practice. As Veerman and van Yperen (2007) state, there needs to be a collective effort between practitioners and researchers in order to yield 'the practice-based evidence needed to establish solid evidence-based practices' (p. 219).

In a similar vein, we have argued that a model of evidence premised on the chiasmus of the term *evidence-based practice*, namely *evidence-based practice and practice-based evidence*, might yield a richer and more collaborative knowledge base for the psychological therapies that, in turn, might deliver guidance which can be owned and implemented by practitioners. Fundamental to this proposition is the view that while RCTs provide valuable evidence, they are not the only source of evidence and have intrinsic scientific vulnerabilities in the field of the psychological therapies. Equally, practice-based studies require enhanced methodologies and more comprehensive implementation. However, this can only be achieved by adopting a position of equipoise in which each approach is equally valued. If we value differing approaches equally, then this moves us towards being teleoanalysts – that is, people and professionals who are able to combine differing information from different paradigms into a collective whole in order to make healthcare decisions based on the overall weight of evidence rather than on any single definition, model or hierarchy of evidence.

Acknowledgements

We would like to thank Nancy Rowland for her careful reading of and comments on an earlier version of this chapter.

References

Ahn, H. & Wampold, B. (2001). Where oh where are the specific ingredients? A meta-analysis of component studies in counseling and psychotherapy. *Journal of Consulting and Clinical Psychology, 48,* 251–257.

American Psychological Association (APA) (2002). Criteria for evaluating treatment guidelines. *American Psychologist, 57,* 1052–1059.

American Psychological Association (APA) (2006). Evidence-based practice in psychology: APA Presidential task force on evidence-based practice. *American Psychologist, 61,* 271–285.

Barkham, M. & Margison, F. (2007). Practice-based evidence as a complement to evidence-based practice: From dichotomy to chiasmus. In C. Freeman & M. Power (eds.), *Handbook of evidence-based psychotherapies: A guide for research and practice* (pp. 443–476). Chichester: John Wiley & Sons, Ltd.

Barkham, M. & Mellor-Clark, J. (2000). Rigour and relevance: Practice-based evidence in the psychological therapies. In N. Rowland & S. Goss (eds.), *Evidence-based counselling and psychological therapies: Research and applications* (pp. 127–144). London: Routledge.

Barkham M. & Mellor-Clark J. (2003). Bridging evidence-based practice and practice-based evidence: Developing a rigorous and relevant knowledge for the psychological therapies. *Clinical Psychology & Psychotherapy, 10,* 319–327.

Barkham, M. & Parry, G. (2008). Balancing rigour and relevance in guideline development for depression: The case for comprehensive cohort studies. *Psychology and Psychotherapy: Theory, Research and Practice, 81,* 399–417.

Barkham, M., Margison, F., Leach, C., Lucock, M., Mellor-Clark, J. et al. (2001). Service profiling and outcomes benchmarking using the CORE-OM: Towards practice-based evidence in the psychological therapies. *Journal of Consulting and Clinical Psychology, 69,* 184–196.

Barkham, M., Stiles, W.B., Connell, J., Twigg, E., Leach, C. et al. (2008). Effects of psychological therapies in randomized trials and practice-based studies. *British Journal of Clinical Psychology, 47,* 397–415.

Berger, V.W., Matthews, J.R. & Grosch, E.N. (2008). On improving research methodology in clinical trials. *Statistical Methods in Medical Research, 17,* 231–242.

Bewick, B.M., Trusler, K., Mullin, T., Grant, S. & Mothersole, G. (2006). Routine outcome measurement completion rates of the CORE-OM in primary care psychological therapies and counselling. *Counselling & Psychotherapy Research, 6,* 50–59.

Borkovec, T.D., Echemendia, R.J., Ragusea, S.A. & Ruiz, M. (2001). The Pennsylvania Practice Research Network and future possibilities for clinically meaningful and scientifically rigorous psychotherapy effectiveness research. *Clinical Psychology: Science and Practice, 8,* 155–167.

Bottomley, A. (1997). To randomise or not to randomise: Methodological pitfalls of the RCT design in psychosocial intervention studies. *European Journal of Cancer Care, 6,* 222–230.

Boutron, I., Moher, D., Altman, D.G., Schulz, K.F. & Ravaud, P. (2008). Extending the CONSORT statement to randomized trials of nonpharmacologic treatment: Explanation and elaboration. *Annals of Internal Medicine, 148,* 295–309.

Brower, L.A. (2003). The Ohio mental health consumer outcomes system: Reflections on a major policy initiative in the US. *Clinical Psychology & Psychotherapy, 10,* 400–406.

Cahill, J., Potter, S. & Mullin, T. (2006). First contact session outcomes in primary care psychological therapy and counselling services. *Counselling & Psychotherapy Research, 6,* 41–49.

Cartwright, N. (2007). Are RCTs the gold standard? *BioSocieties, 2,* 11–20.

Clark, D.M., Fairburn C.G. & Wessely, S. (2008). Psychological treatment outcomes in routine NHS services: a commentary on Stiles et al. (2007). *Psychological Medicine, 38,* 629–634.

Clark, D.M., Ehlers, A., Hackmann, A., McManus, F., Fennell, M. et al. (2006). Cognitive therapy versus exposure and applied relaxation in social phobia: A randomised controlled trial. *Journal of Consulting and Clinical Psychology, 74,* 568–578.

Clark, D.M., Layard, R., Smithies, R., Richards, R.A., Suckling, R. et al. (2009). Improving access to psychological therapy: Initial evaluation of two UK demonstration sites. *Behaviour Research and Therapy, 47,* 910–920.

Connell, J., Grant, S. & Mullin, T. (2006). Client initiated termination of therapy at NHS primary care counselling services. *Counselling & Psychotherapy Research, 6,* 60–67.

Cox, A., Holbrook, D. & Rutter, M. (1981). Psychiatric interviewing techniques VI. Experimental study: Eliciting feelings. *British Journal of Psychiatry, 139,* 144–152.

Cox, A., Rutter, M. & Holbrook, D. (1981). Psychiatric interviewing techniques V. Experimental study: Eliciting factual information. *British Journal of Psychiatry, 139,* 29–37.

Crits-Christoph, P., Baranackie, K., Kurcias, J.S., Carroll, K., Luborsky, L. et al. (1991). Meta-analysis of therapist effects in psychotherapy outcome studies. *Psychotherapy Research, 1,* 81–91.

Cuijpers, P., van Straten, A., Anderson, G. & van Oppen, G. (2008). Psychotherapy for depression in adults: A meta-analysis of comparative outcome studies. *Journal of Consulting and Clinical Psychology, 76,* 909–922.

Elkin, I. (1999). A major dilemma in psychotherapy outcome research: Disentangling therapist from therapies. *Clinical Psychology: Science and Practice, 6,* 10–32.

Elkin, I., Falconnier, L., Martinovitch, Z. & Mahoney, C. (2006). Therapist effects in the NIMH Treatment of Depression Collaborative Research Program. *Psychotherapy Research, 16,* 144–160.

Elkin, I., Shea, M.T., Watkins, J.T., Imber, S.D., Sotsky, S.M. et al. (1989). National Institute of Mental Health Treatment of Depression Collaborative

Research Program: general effectiveness of treatments. *Archives of General Psychiatry, 46,* 971–982.

Evans, R., Mellor-Clark, J., Barkham, M. & Mothersole, G. (2006). Developing the resources and management support for routine evaluation in counselling and psychological therapy service provision: Reflections on a decade of CORE development. *European Journal of Psychotherapy and Counselling, 8,* 141–161.

Evans, C., Connell, J., Barkham, M., Marshall, C. & Mellor-Clark, J. (2003). Practice-based evidence: Benchmarking NHS primary care counselling services at national and local levels. *Clinical Psychology & Psychotherapy, 10,* 374–388.

Faulkner, C., Fidler, F. & Cumming, G. (2008). The value of RCT evidence depends on the quality of statistical analysis. *Behaviour Research and Therapy, 46,* 270–281.

Gloaguen, V., Cottraux, J., Cacherat, M. & Blackburn, I. (1998). A meta-analysis of the effects of cognitive therapy in depressed patients. *Journal of Affective Disorders, 49,* 59–72.

Green, L.W. & Glasgow, R.E. (2006). Evaluating the relevance, generalization, and applicability of research: Issues in external validation and translation methodology, *Evaluation and the Health Professions, 29,* 126–153.

Haaga, D.A.F. & Stiles, W.B. (2000). Randomized clinical trials in psychotherapy research: Methodology, design, and evaluation. In C.R. Snyder & R.E. Ingram (eds.), *Handbook of psychological change: Psychotherapy processes and practices for the 21st century* (pp. 14–39). New York: John Wiley & Sons, Inc.

Hardy, G.E., Stiles, W.B., Barkham, M. & Startup, M. (1998). Therapist responsiveness to client interpersonal styles during time-limited treatments for depression. *Journal of Consulting and Clinical Psychology, 66,* 304–312.

Hickner, J. (1993). Practice-based network research. In M.J. Bass, E.V. Dunn, P.G. Norton, M. Stewart & F. Tudiver (eds.), *Conducting research in the practice setting.* London: Sage Publications.

Horn, S.D. & Gassaway, J. (2007). Practice-based evidence study design for comparative effectiveness research. *Medical Care, 45,* S50–S57.

Huppert, J.D., Bufka, L.F., Barlow, D.H., Gorman, J.M., Shear, M.K. et al. (2001). Therapists, therapist variables, and cognitive–behavioral therapy outcome in a multicenter trial for panic disorder. *Journal of Consulting and Clinical Psychology, 69,* 747–755.

Jacobson, N.S. & Christensen, A. (1996). Studying the effectiveness of psychotherapy: How well can clinical trials do the job? *American Psychologist, 51,* 1031–1039.

Jacobson, N.S. & Hollon, S.D. (1996a). Prospects for future comparisons between drugs and psychotherapy: Lessons from the CBT-versus-pharmacotherapy exchange. *Journal of Consulting and Clinical Psychology*, *64*, 104–108.

Jacobson, N.S. & Hollon, S.D. (1996b). Cognitive-behavior therapy versus pharmacotherapy: Now that the jury's returned its verdict, it's time to present the rest of the evidence. *Journal of Consulting and Clinical Psychology*, *64*, 74–80.

Jadad, A.R. & Enkin, M.W. (2007). *Randomized controlled trials: Questions, answers and musings* (2nd edn.). Oxford: Blackwell Publishing.

Joyce, A.S., Wolfaardt, U., Scribney, C. & Aylwin, A.S. (2006). Psychotherapy research at the start of the 21st century: The persistence of the art versus science controversy. *Canadian Journal of Psychiatry*, *51*, 797–809.

Kim, D-M., Wampold, B.E. & Bolt, D.M. (2006). Therapist effects in psychotherapy: A random-effects modeling of the National Institute of Mental Health Treatment of Depression Collaborative Research Program data. *Psychotherapy Research*, *16*, 161–172.

King, M., Sibbald, B., Ward, E., Bower, P., Lloyd, M. et al. (2000). Randomised controlled trial of non-directive counselling, cognitive-behaviour therapy and usual general practitioner care in the management of depression as well as mixed anxiety and depression in primary care. *Health Technology Assessment*, *4*, 9.

Kotter, J.P. (1995). *Leading change*. Cambridge, MA: Harvard Business School Press.

Kotter, J.P. & Cohen, D.S. (2002). *The heart of change: Real live stories of how people change their organizations*. Cambridge, MA: Harvard Business School Press.

Lambert, M. (2001). Psychotherapy outcome and quality improvement: Introduction to the special section on patient-focused research. *Journal of Consulting and Clinical Psychology*, *69*, 147–149.

Lambert M.J. & Ogles, B. (2004). The efficacy and effectiveness of psychotherapy. In M.J. Lambert (ed.), *Bergin & Garfield's handbook of psychotherapy and behavior change* (5th edn., pp. 139–193). New York: John Wiley & Sons, Inc.

Lambert, M.J., Harmon, C., Slade, K., Whipple, J.L. & Hawkins, E.J. (2005). Providing feedback to psychotherapists on their patients' progress: Clinical results and practice suggestions. *Journal of Clinical Psychology*, *61*, 165–174.

Lambert, M.J., Whipple, J.L., Hawkins, E.J., Vermeersch, D.A., Nielsen, S.L. et al. (2003). Is it time for clinicians to routinely track patient outcome? A meta-analysis. *Clinical Psychology: Science and Practice*, *10*, 288–301.

Lambert, M.J., Whipple, J.L., Smart, D.W., Vermeersch, D.A., Nielsen, S.L. et al. (2001). The effects of providing therapists with feedback on patient progress during psychotherapy: Are outcomes enhanced? *Psychotherapy Research, 11,* 49–68.

Layard, R. (2006). The case for psychological treatment centres. *British Medical Journal, 332,* 1030–1032.

Lee, K.J. & Thompson, S.G. (2005). Clustering by health professional in individually randomized trials. *British Medical Journal, 330,* 142–144.

Leykin, Y. & DeRubeis R.J. (2009). Allegiance in psychotherapy outcome research: Separating association from bias. *Clinical Psychology: Science and Practice, 16,* 54–65.

Linehan, M.M. (1999). Development, evaluation, and dissemination of effective psychosocial treatments: Levels of disorder, stages of care, and stages of treatment research. In M.D. Glantz & C.R. Harte (eds.), *Drug abuse: Origins and interventions* (pp. 367–394). Washington, DC: American Psychological Association.

Luborsky, L., Diguer, L., Seligman, D.A., Rosenthal, R., Krause, E.D. et al. (1999). The researcher's own therapy allegiances: A "wild card" in comparisons of treatment efficacy. *Clinical Psychology: Science and Practice, 6,* 95–106.

Lucock, M., Leach, C., Iveson, S., Lynch, K., Horsefield, C. et al. (2003). A systematic approach to practice-based evidence in a psychological therapies service. *Journal of Clinical Psychology and Psychotherapy, 10,* 389–399.

Lutz, W. (2002). Patient-focused psychotherapy research and individual treatment progress as scientific groundwork for an empirically based clinical practice. *Psychotherapy Research, 12,* 251–272.

Lutz, W., Leach, C., Barkham, M., Lucock, M., Stiles, W.B. et al. (2005). Predicting rate and shape of change for individual clients receiving psychological therapy: Using growth curve modeling and nearest neighbor technologies. *Journal of Consulting and Clinical Psychology, 73,* 904–913.

Margison, F. (2001). Practice-based evidence in psychotherapy. In C. Mace, S. Moorey & B. Roberts (eds.), *Evidence in the psychological therapies: A critical guide for practitioners* (pp. 174–198) London: Brunner-Routledge.

Margison, F., Barkham, M., Evans, C., McGrath, G., Mellor-Clark, J. et al. (2000). Measurement and psychotherapy: Evidence-based practice and practice-based evidence. *British Journal of Psychiatry, 177,* 123–130.

Mellor-Clark, J. & Barkham, M. (2006). The CORE system: Developing and delivering practice-based evidence through quality evaluation. In C. Feltham & I. Horton (eds.), *Handbook of counselling and psychotherapy* (2nd edn., pp. 207–224). London: Sage Publications.

Mellor-Clark, J., Curtis Jenkins, A., Evans, R., Mothersole, G. & McInnes, B. (2006). Resourcing a CORE Network to develop a National Research

Database to help enhance psychological therapy and counselling service provision. *Counselling & Psychotherapy Research, 6,* 16–22.

Merrill, K.A., Tolbert, V.E. & Wade, W.A. (2003). Effectiveness of cognitive therapy for depression in a community mental health center: A benchmarking study. *Journal of Consulting and Clinical Psychology, 71,* 404–409.

Minami, T., Wampold, B.E., Serlin, R.C., Kircher, J.C. & Brown, G.S. (2007). Benchmarks for psychotherapy efficacy in adult major depression. *Journal of Consulting and Clinical Psychology, 75,* 232–243.

Mullin, T., Barkham, M., Mothersole, G., Bewick, B.M. & Kinder, A. (2006). Recovery and improvement benchmarks in routine primary care mental health settings. *Counselling & Psychotherapy Research, 6,* 68–80.

National Advisory Mental Health Council (NAMHC) (1999). *Bridging science and service: A report by the National Advisory Mental Health Council's clinical treatment and services research workgroup* (NIH Publication No. 99-4353). Washington, DC.

Nielsen, S.L., Okiishi, J., Nielsen, D.L., Hawkins, E.J., Harmon, S.C. et al. (2009). Termination, appointment use, and outcome patterns associated with intake therapist discontinuity. *Professional Psychology: Research and Practice, 40,* 272–278.

Norcross, J.C. (ed.) (2002). *Psychotherapy relationships that work: Therapist contributions and responsiveness to patient needs.* New York: Oxford University Press.

Norcross, J.C. & Lambert, W.G. (2006). The therapy relationship. In J.C. Norcross, L.E. Butler & R.F. Levant (eds.), *Evidence-based practices in mental health: debate and dialogue on the fundamental questions* (pp. 208–218). Washington, DC: American Psychological Association.

Okiishi, J.C., Lambert, M.J., Eggett, D., Nielsen, S.L., Dayton, D.D. et al. (2006). An analysis of therapist treatment effects: Towards providing feedback to individual therapists on their patients' psychotherapy outcome. *Journal of Clinical Psychology, 62,* 1157–1172.

Persons, J.B. & Silberschatz, G. (1998). Are the results of randomized trials useful to psychotherapists? *Journal of Consulting and Clinical Psychology, 66,* 126–135.

Rawlins, M.D. (2008). *De Testimonio: On the evidence for decisions about the use of therapeutic interventions.* The Harveian Oration of 2008. Royal College of Physicians.

Richards, D.A. & Suckling, R. (2009). Improving access to psychological therapies (IAPT): Phase IV prospective cohort study. *British Journal of Clinical Psychology, 48,* 377–396.

Roberts, C. & Roberts, S.A. (2005). Design and analysis of clinical trials with clustering effects due to treatment. *Clinical Trials, 2,* 152–162.

Robinson, L.A., Berman, J.S. & Neimeyer, R.A. (1990). Psychotherapy for the treatment of depression: A comprehensive review of controlled outcome research. *Psychological Bulletin, 108,* 30–49.

Sackett, D., Rosenberg, W., Gray, J., Haynes, B. & Richardson, W. (1996). Evidence-based medicine: what it is and what it is not. *British Medical Journal, 312,* 71–72.

Salkovskis, P.M. (1995). Demonstrating specific effects in cognitive and behavioural therapy. In M. Aveline & D.A. Shapiro (eds.), *Research foundations for psychotherapy research* (pp. 191–228). Chichester: John Wiley & Sons, Ltd.

Shadish, W.R., Matt, G.E., Nararro, A.M., Siegle, G., Crits-Cristoph, P. et al. (1997). Evidence that therapy works in clinically representative conditions. *Journal of Consulting and Clinical Psychology, 65,* 355–365.

Sloane, R.B., Staples, F.R., Cristol, A.H., Yorkston, N.J. & Whipple, K. (1975). *Psychotherapy versus behavior therapy.* Cambridge, MA: Harvard University Press.

Smith, G.C.S. & Pell, J.P. (2003). Parachute use to prevent death and major trauma related to gravitational challenge: systematic review of randomised controlled trials. *British Medical Journal, 327,* 1459–1461.

Smith, M.L. & Glass, G.V. (1977). Meta-analysis of psychotherapy outcome studies. *American Psychologist, 32,* 752–760.

Stiles, W.B. (1988). Psychotherapy process-outcome correlations may be misleading. *Psychotherapy, 25,* 27–35.

Stiles, W.B. (2005). Dialogue: Convergence and contention. In J.C. Norcross, L.E. Beutler & R.F. Levant (eds.), *Evidence-based practices in mental health: Debate and dialogue on the fundamental questions* (pp. 105–107). Washington, DC: American Psychological Association.

Stiles, W.B. & Shapiro, D.A. (1994). Disabuse of the drug metaphor: Psychotherapy process-outcome correlations. *Journal of Consulting and Clinical Psychology, 62,* 942–948.

Stiles, W.B. & Wolfe, B.E. (2006). Relationship factors in treating anxiety disorders. In L.G. Castonguay & L.E. Beutler (eds.), *Principles of therapeutic change that work* (pp. 155–165). New York: Oxford University Press.

Stiles, W.B., Honos-Webb, L. & Surko, M. (1998). Responsiveness in psychotherapy. *Clinical Psychology: Science & Practice, 5,* 439–458.

Stiles, W.B., Shapiro, D.A. & Elliott, R. (1986). 'Are all psychotherapies equivalent?' *American Psychologist, 41,* 165–180.

Stiles, W.B., Barkham, M., Mellor-Clark, J. & Connell, J. (2008a). Effectiveness of cognitive-behavioural, person-centred, and psychodynamic therapies in UK primary care routine practice: Replication in a larger sample. *Psychological Medicine, 38,* 677–688.

Stiles, W.B., Barkham, M., Mellor-Clark, J. & Connell, J. (2008b). Routine psychological treatment and the Dodo Verdict: A rejoinder to Clark et al. (2007). *Psychological Medicine, 38,* 905–910.

Stiles, W.B., Barkham, M., Twigg, E., Mellor-Clark, J. & Cooper, M. (2006). Effectiveness of cognitive-behavioural, person-centred, and psychodynamic therapies as practiced in UK National Health Service settings. *Psychological Medicine, 36,* 555–566.

Sussman, S., Valente, T.W., Rohrbach, L.A., Skara, S. & Pentz, M.A. (2006). Translation in the health professions: Converting science into action. *Evaluation and the Health Professions, 29,* 7–32.

Trusler, K., Doherty, C., Grant, S., Mullin, T. & McBride, J. (2006). Waiting times for primary care counselling services. *Counselling & Psychotherapy Research, 6,* 23–32.

Tunis, S.R., Stryer, D.B. & Clancy, C.M. (2003). Practical clinical trials: Increasing the value of clinical research for decision making in clinical and health policy. *Journal of the America Medical Association, 290,* 1624–1632.

Veerman, J.W. & van Yperen, T.A. (2007). Degrees of freedom and degrees of certainty: A developmental model for the establishment of evidence-based youth care. *Evaluation and Program Planning, 30,* 212–221.

Walwyn, R. & Roberts, C. (in press). Therapist variation within randomised trials of psychotherapy: Implications for precision, internal and external validity. *Statistical Methods in Medical Research.*

Wampold, B.E. (2001). *The great psychotherapy debate: Models, methods, and findings* (5th edn., pp. 767–804). Mahwah, NJ: Erlbaum.

Wampold, B.E. (2007). Psychotherapy: The humanistic (and effective) treatment. *American Psychologist, 62,* 857–873.

Wampold, B.E. & Brown, G. (2005). Estimating therapist variability in outcomes attributable to therapists: A naturalistic study of outcomes in managed care. *Journal of Consulting and Clinical Psychology, 73,* 914–923.

Wampold, B., Mondlin, G., Moody, M., Stich, F, Benson, K. et al. (1997). A meta-analysis of outcome studies comparing bona fide psychotherapies: Empirically 'All must have prizes.' *Psychological Bulletin, 122,* 203–215.

Wessely, S. (2007). A defence of the randomized controlled trial in mental health. *BioSocieties, 2,* 115–127.

Wojciechowski, F.L. (1984). *Double blind research in psychotherapy.* Lisse, Netherlands: Swets & Zeitlinger.

Section II

Methodological Pluralism for Individual Practitioners

3

Scientific, Practical and Personal Decisions in Selecting Qualitative Methods

Nancy Pistrang and Chris Barker

Department of Clinical, Educational and Health Psychology, University College London, UK

Introduction

As the interesting variety of chapters in this volume demonstrates, there are many different ways to go about the task of researching the process and outcome of psychological therapy and counselling, and all of these ways have their own particular strengths and limitations. This chapter focuses on qualitative approaches, aiming firstly to delineate the unique contributions that they can make to the corpus of practice-based evidence for the psychological therapies, and secondly to guide researchers and practitioners who wish to undertake a qualitative study in making their choice of method from amongst the sometimes bewildering menu of possibilities.

It is worth saying at the outset that we have written this chapter in a pluralistic spirit. Qualitative methods have many attractions, but they also have their characteristic drawbacks and limitations, as in our opinion do all other methods of researching psychotherapy and counselling. We strongly agree with the editors of the present volume that the way that the field will progress is by integrating data from several complementary sources of evidence.

This introductory section examines some background issues, looking briefly at the history, characteristics and underlying philosophy of qualitative methods. The second section outlines the characteristics of some of the most popular varieties of qualitative research within the therapy and counselling field. The third section discusses how one goes about choosing between all of these different approaches, a choice which, as our title says, involves balancing scientific, practical

Developing and Delivering Practice-Based Evidence   By Michael Barkham, Gillian E Hardy, and John Mellor-Clark   © 2010 John Wiley & Sons, Ltd

and personal considerations. Finally, we will look at some special issues raised by doing qualitative research, such as possible risks and benefits to participants and how qualitative and quantitative approaches can be combined.

With regards to terminology, we intend this chapter to address qualitative research methods in the area of psychological therapy and counselling generally, as well as research on other less formal types of psychological helping relationships, such as social support, peer support or befriending. Our general position (Barker & Pistrang, 2002) is that all these forms of relationships share important properties and are best studied together under the label of psychological helping relationships. However, as the present volume focuses on professional helping, we will use the terms psychological therapy and counselling, together or separately, interchangeably throughout the chapter. The chapter is principally aimed at those new to qualitative research, in order to give them the fundamental grounding necessary to conduct their own projects. However, qualitative research is best thought of as a craft, and it is hard to learn in isolation just by reading. By far the best way to become skilled is to obtain the guidance of an experienced supervisor or colleague.

Qualitative methods in psychology and related areas

Systematic qualitative methods are of course not new to the social sciences, having been pioneered in anthropology and sociology during the last century (under headings such as ethnography, participant observation, ethnomethodology and conversational analysis). However, their acceptance into psychology, medical research and related areas has been relatively recent, and, within psychotherapy research, they have come a long way in the last couple of decades. In the early 1990s, when we were preparing the first edition of our clinical and counselling psychology research methods text (Barker, Pistrang & Elliott, 1994), qualitative methods were seen as a rather novel, daring and risky enterprise, and their contribution was looked upon sceptically by many established researchers. However, eight years later, when we were preparing the second edition (Barker, Pistrang & Elliott, 2002) the climate had changed markedly, and qualitative methods seemed to have gained much greater acceptance.

There now seem to be signs of a wider, although by no means complete, incorporation of qualitative methods within the field. Articles using qualitative methods are now increasingly published in mainstream journals (at least in British ones; the US remains more traditional in this respect). There have been recent authoritative volumes, both British (e.g. McLeod, 2001; Smith, 2008; Willig, 2008; Willig & Stainton-Rogers, 2008) and American (e.g. Camic, Rhodes & Yardley, 2003; Creswell, 1998; Denzin & Lincoln, 2005), surveying a range of qualitative approaches. Volumes such as the present one are evidence of a healthy pluralistic outlook. On UK clinical psychology training programmes, many more qualitative theses are being produced than 15 years ago (Harper, 2008). However, most mainstream journals still publish far more quantitative than qualitative papers, and qualitative evidence is not greatly valued in reviews of the literature, so although qualitative approaches have definitely been granted citizenship, that citizenship still seems second class. It will be interesting to see how the picture will look 10 years from now.

What is qualitative research?

Perhaps reflecting our view that qualitative methods are now more widely accepted and understood, we have been making the tacit assumption that readers are familiar with the nature and advantages of qualitative research. However, some brief recapitulation might be in order. In a nutshell, their central advantage is that they can provide what the ethnographer Clifford Geertz (1973) labelled 'thick description'. In other words they can use the richness and complexity of natural language to go beyond some of the simplifications imposed by a purely numerical approach. They are particularly valuable for investigating the personal meanings that people attach to their experiences.

For instance, a client's score of 23 on the Beck Depression Inventory tells you something about the general quality of their mood state. However, if you were to ask them 'How are you feeling right now?' they would possibly respond with something along the lines of 'Well, I haven't been right since I lost my job at the bank last month. I just seem to be stuck in a rut and can't get going any more. I keep crying for no reason at all, I don't see any point in life, and I'm ashamed to talk to any of my friends. On the other hand, my partner has tried to be supportive, though I haven't made it easy for him . . .'.

This little snippet of speech points to the potential richness of qualitative research: the data are vivid and easy to understand, you feel that you know the person and their world much better than you would from just being told their simple BDI score, and all the complexities in the person's account are preserved. On the other hand, it does raise the question of how does one go about collecting and analysing such free-response data in a systematic manner. What can it tell you? Or as Bill Stiles, another contributor to the present volume, once put it in a conference paper (Stiles, 1994), 'When you've heard a story, what do you know?'

Qualitative methods thus enable one to get the 'insider's view', and they are especially valuable when working with disadvantaged populations, such as psychiatric inpatients or people with intellectual disabilities. Some qualitative researchers talk about 'giving voice' to such individuals. The presentation of a qualitative paper, which usually will include direct quotations from participants, is a way for participants to have their speech and ideas directly conveyed to the reader. There is a parallel with the act of empathy in psychotherapy. The qualitative researcher is listening carefully to the participant's underlying meaning, but instead of reflecting it back (as a therapist might), the researcher enables the participant's experience to be communicated to a wider audience. The empathy must be accurate, in the sense that it should represent fairly what the participant is attempting to say or do. However, rather like interpretation in psychotherapy, it may also be the case that the researcher will comment on the participant's meanings or use of language – it is the interplay between the participant's own words and the intellectual commentary of the researcher that gives qualitative research its interesting flavour.

Thus the central advantage of qualitative studies is that they are able to represent the richness, complexity and variety of clients' and therapists' 'lived experiences'. They are, however, less good at addressing questions of comparison and causality. They can examine people's own perceptions of causality and difference, for example by asking 'Do you feel that the therapy has improved your psychological well-being?', but post-hoc personal testimonials are not a very trustworthy guide to the efficacy of an intervention. Questions of what change has occurred and what has caused it are better addressed, at least partly, within experimental or quasi-experimental research designs.

Some philosophical background

There are two schools of thought about the differences between qualitative and quantitative approaches. The first regards each approach as being fundamentally different and incompatible, in terms of the assumptions that each makes about epistemology (a branch of philosophy dealing with how knowledge is arrived at). The second position regards the choice of approach as a pragmatic one, that is, simply as a choice between words and numbers.

We regard ourselves as belonging more to the pragmatic camp, and, as we will explain below, see no contradiction in adopting a pluralist stance and engaging in both types of research. However, it is worth saying a word or two about what the underlying epistemological issues are, to place them in context.

Some qualitative authors see a fundamental dichotomy between the philosophy behind quantitative approaches (often subsumed under the label of 'positivism'), and qualitative approaches, often labelled as naturalistic enquiry. Up until recently it was not unusual for papers, particularly student theses, reporting on qualitative research to begin with a long denunciation of the positivist, quantitative approach. The sense was that one had to sign up to one or the other of two mutually exclusive sets of philosophical values, which then led you to be either an exclusively quantitative researcher or an exclusively qualitative researcher.

There is in fact a range of epistemological positions underpinning qualitative (and quantitative) research. Willig (2008) describes a continuum ranging from the 'radical constructionist' to the 'naive realist'. They vary on the position they take about the nature of reality. On the one hand, radical constructionists (e.g. Gergen, 1985; Lincoln & Guba, 1985) argue that there is no such thing as an objective reality – that there are many realities varying according to different people in different places, times and cultures. On the other hand, realists view reality as having an essentially independent existence, and attempt to employ research methods to more accurately represent its nature. However, this constructionist-realist distinction is something of a simplification, and it does not map neatly onto the qualitative-quantitative dichotomy. On the one hand, some qualitative researchers are interested in people's phenomenological worlds, that is how they view reality, without necessarily regarding the external world as being socially constructed. On the other hand, some quantitative researchers, for example those using the method of repertory grids derived from personal construct theory (Winter, 1992), take a constructivist perspective, that is they are interested in the mental categories people use to make sense of the world. Where these epistemological distinctions are important is in the consideration of how one evaluates a piece of research. Realists use concepts such as accuracy and bias, which social constructionists avoid.

Qualitative and quantitative approaches also differ in their position on what is the central approach to gaining knowledge. Qualitative researchers often see their aim as achieving in-depth understanding of a phenomenon, usually by studying a small number of participants. The research could possibly culminate in generating new theory. Quantitative researchers, on the other hand, are often more concerned about testing theories or hypotheses, using the so-called hypothetico-deductive methods, and the issue of generalization of their findings to a wider population is a central concern.

Ten or fifteen years ago, these conflicts between proponents of different paradigms were quite heated, but these so-called 'paradigm wars' now appear to be subsiding. Papers exploring the possibilities of pluralistic approaches are appearing (Barker & Pistrang, 2005) and there is a growing literature on 'mixed methods' approaches (Tashakkori & Teddlie, 2002; Yardley & Bishop, 2008). The methodological pluralist position, which we espouse, is that no single research method is best overall: all have their individual strengths and weaknesses, and it is the task of the researcher to fit the research method to the questions being posed. Of course different researchers will also have their own personal leanings and cognitive styles, and these will also play a role in the choice of a method, both between qualitative and quantitative approaches overall, and within the various different qualitative approaches. Furthermore, practical considerations such as the amount of resources available and the context in which researchers work will also influence their choices. The rest of this chapter will attempt to elucidate these issues.

Some popular approaches to qualitative research

Main features of qualitative research

Having reviewed the general background to qualitative approaches, we will now look at the main features of some of the different variants of qualitative research. As we hope to have already made clear, qualitative research is not a unitary entity in itself. There are many different varieties, and, as in any academic area, there are disagreements between qualitative researchers about how best to approach the research enterprise. Our aim in this section is to outline some of the approaches that are most commonly used within psychotherapy and counselling research. We cannot go into great depth or detail, but hope that our thumbnail sketches will give readers enough of a flavour of what each involves. We will also point readers towards specialist references giving additional detail on each approach. Apart from these, there are several helpful texts addressing a range of different orientations (e.g. Camic et al., 2003; McLeod, 2001; Smith, 2008; Willig, 2008). This second section of the chapter is intended to give the background context for each approach; the third section will focus on how researchers might choose between them.

'Brand name' versus generic approaches

Although the state of the field compels us to address the various 'brand name' orientations, we do not wish to imply that researchers must always work within a specific qualitative research orientation. In our view, there is often considerable overlap between many of the approaches, and, as we will discuss below, they can partially be clustered into families of similar approaches. Furthermore, there are also a number of texts expounding more generic approaches to qualitative research (e.g. Miles & Huberman, 1994; Silverman, 2000; Taylor & Bogdan, 1998).

However, it is easy for novice researchers to feel insecure about not working within a named approach. This might arise because people who evaluate research, such as journal reviewers and editors, and thesis supervisors and examiners, tend to require that qualitative research be done using a recognized 'brand name'. This breeds the unfortunate tendency for researchers to give their method a label, merely in order to protect themselves against such criticism. We would argue that the important thing is that the research be carried out in a systematic and rigorous way, and that its procedures be clearly described, whatever the label under which it is conducted.

Data collection methods

Qualitative data can be obtained by a number of different methods. Probably the most common is self-report, in which the researcher interviews the client or therapist (or possibly a third party such as a family member of the client) in order to obtain that person's direct perspective. There are various types of interviews, but the vast majority of studies use the semi-structured interview, in which the researcher develops an interview guide (often referred to as an interview protocol or schedule) to ensure that the important topics are covered (Smith, 1995). However, the questions do not have to be asked in a fixed order and not all questions are asked in all interviews. The interviews are recorded, but researchers nearly always work from transcripts rather than the primary recordings.

The second possibility is to study therapy process directly, via audio or video recordings of the client-therapist interaction. This gives the advantage of being able to study what was actually said in the interaction, rather than relying on verbal reports. Some researchers combine the two approaches. The method of tape-assisted recall (e.g. Elliott & Shapiro, 1988) uses recordings of sessions, but then participants listen to the recordings and are interviewed about what they thought and felt at significant moments of the interaction.

Families of qualitative approaches

The various different qualitative methods can be grouped into two main families that share some key characteristics. In our research methods text (Barker et al., 2002), we grouped methods according to their underlying philosophical position, that is according to whether they were derived from a phenomenological or a social constructionist epistemology. This was a useful heuristic classification, but it was an oversimplification and the distinction between the two approaches was not always clear-cut. It also placed a primary emphasis on epistemological issues. Here we will group methods according to what each is attempting to do and what kinds of questions it can answer. This seems a useful division in the context of the present application to psychological therapy. The two families of approaches are:

1. *Thematic analysis* approaches, which are concerned with identifying the main themes or categories in the data.
2. *Language-focused* approaches, which look in close detail at how language is used in an interaction or a piece of text.

This is not intended to be a complete classification of qualitative approaches. We have omitted some families completely (e.g. ethnographic approaches), which are important in the context of qualitative research generally, but are of lesser interest in the study of the psychological therapies.

This classification has considerable overlap with that of Rennie (2004), who divides approaches according to the type of data collection method, that is either verbal reports or therapy transcripts. Most thematic analysis approaches are concerned with analysing self-report data, and most language-focused approaches look at therapy transcripts. However, there are some notable exceptions, for example, content analysis studies of therapy sessions or discourse analysis studies of interview data. Furthermore, the focus on fitting the method to the research question is central to this chapter. However, Rennie's focus on the source of data is important and easy to lose sight of, and the overlap between his classification and ours is high.

We will now examine each of these families in turn, attempting to outline its characteristics as a whole, and then of the major orientations within it. We are aiming to give a thumbnail sketch of the essence of each approach, in terms of what types of research questions it is good for and what kinds of output it generates. For each approach, we will give an illustrative application to research on psychological therapy.

Thematic analysis approaches

The family of thematic analysis methods is both the largest in terms of the number of members and also probably the most commonly used in this application area. The defining feature of thematic approaches is their common aim, which is to characterize the important ideas (usually referred to as themes or categories) that occur in the data. This can be within a single individual or, more usually, across a number of participants. The typical output from such an analysis is a list of key themes, possibly with subthemes, sometimes arranged in a hierarchical structure. Approaches within this family range from the more structured methods such as framework analysis and content analysis, to the more in-depth and more explicitly psychological methods of the phenomenological approaches. In addition to the approaches described below, there are many useful expositions of specific procedures for systematically conducting thematic analysis (e.g. Boyatzis, 1998; Braun & Clarke, 2006; Bryman, 2004; Dey, 1993; Hill, Thompson & Williams, 1997; Joffe & Yardley, 2003).

Content analysis

It may seem odd to begin with content analysis, as it is more a quantitative than a qualitative method. However, we are including it because it does share several common features with other thematic analysis methods, and it also illustrates some issues about how the fuzzy boundary between quantitative and qualitative approaches is drawn. It is a hybrid approach, in that its input is qualitative but its output is quantitative. The essence of content analysis is that the researcher uses a structured coding scheme to label ideas or categories in the data, and then goes through the data set systematically identifying the occurrences of each content category (Bryman, 2004; Joffe & Yardley, 2003). There is usually more than one rater in order to allow for inter-rater reliability to be calculated.

The coding scheme, which includes a definition for each category, can either be derived from theory or previous research, or it can be empirically derived from the data obtained.

As an example, content analysis was used in Lane and Viney's (2005) study of short-term group therapy, based on personal construct theory, for breast cancer survivors. One goal of the therapy group was to reduce the women's sense of existential threat that comes from having had a life-threatening illness. Threat was assessed using categories from Gottschalk and Gleser's (1969) content analysis system, including various types of anxiety such as death anxiety, mutilation anxiety, separation anxiety, etc. The qualitative data were generated by a writing task, in which the women responded to the following request: 'I would like you to write about your life right now, both the good and the bad. Write as much as you can in about 15 min.' This was done before and after the therapy. The results of the content analysis showed that women in the therapy group improved more than those in a control group on the categories of anxiety, depression and hope.

Framework analysis

Framework analysis (Ritchie & Spencer, 1994) was developed within the context of social policy research. It is useful for research questions that concern people's understanding of concepts; Ritchie and Spencer give the example of understanding how different categories of workers in employment training schemes understood the term 'disability'. Framework analysis has become particularly popular in medical research, having been featured in Pope, Ziebland & Mays' (2000) influential *British Medical Journal* paper on qualitative data analysis.

The main aspect of framework analysis is, as its name suggests, a systematic approach to the analysis of the data. The analyst develops a structured index of themes (the framework), which is then applied to the data. Various types of charts and tables are used as visual aids in order to display the data and to enable multiple researchers to work on and cross-check the analysis. It is based on technique rather than epistemology, seeking to be a helpful way of analysing the data and communicating the findings for applied qualitative research. It is similar to the pragmatic approach taken by Miles and Huberman (1994) in their influential book on qualitative data analysis.

As an example, Bennett and Parry (2004) used framework analysis as part of a larger study that aimed to develop a way of measuring therapist competence in cognitive analytic therapy. They took a pool of 96 statements about therapist competencies, for example, 'Hypotheses are formulated and offered to the client in an appropriate and useful form'. Using the framework approach, the two researchers were able to independently code these 96 items and come to a consensus on a grouping into 12 overall thematic domains.

Grounded theory

Grounded theory was, historically, one of the first organized approaches to qualitative research. Interest in it initially arose from Glaser and Strauss's (1967) book entitled *The discovery of grounded theory* in which they aimed to provide a systematic way of conducting qualitative research in sociology, which was at that time, at least in the USA, dominated by quantitative approaches.

The grounded theory method has subsequently been widely adopted in the social sciences, particularly in health-related applications: Charmaz's (1991) book on coping with chronic illness is an influential example of a study using the method. Strauss and Corbin's (1998) popular text provides an elaborate set of procedures for conducting grounded theory studies. In the UK, Henwood and Pidgeon's (1992) paper, which drew on grounded theory, was an important landmark in the acceptance of qualitative methods generally. However, as Willig (2008) describes, grounded theory is no longer a unified approach; it has become fractured due to an unfortunate falling-out between its two original proponents.

The output of a grounded theory analysis is ideally the generation of theory about the phenomenon of interest. In common with other thematic approaches, the analyst will attempt to articulate a set of key themes or categories in the data, as a means of identifying the central aspects of the phenomenon, which will then lead to the generation of theory. Some grounded theory analysts aim to reduce the set of themes to one single superordinate theme (a 'core category'), although whether this is possible depends on the complexity of the data.

A study by Bolger (1999) provides a good example of practice-based qualitative research using grounded theory. The research question was how clients experience emotional pain. The participants were clients in a therapy group for adult children of alcoholic parents (and interestingly, the researcher disclosed that she was herself an adult child of alcoholic parents). Data were collected via a semi-structured interview. In accordance with the aims of grounded theory, the analysis yielded a core category, 'the broken self', characterized by features such as 'woundedness' and 'disconnection'.

Interpretive phenomenological analysis

Phenomenological psychology in general is a school of psychology concerned with understanding an individual's inner world and experiences (Spinelli, 2005): their 'life world', in the phenomenological jargon. This has an obvious overlap with clinicians' empathic engagement with their clients, and for this reason the phenomenological approach is often very popular with clinicians. There is a particularly high overlap with the assumptions and approaches of person-centred and existential therapy and counselling, within which empathizing with the client's idiosyncratic world-view is central to the therapeutic enterprise; indeed some of the more interesting writings on phenomenology have come from therapists identified with those orientations (e.g. Laing, 1959; Shlein,

1963). However, all schools of therapy, including cognitive and psychodynamic, clearly engage in the activity of understanding and making sense of the client's frame of reference, and to that extent they are all phenomenological.

From a research point of view, there are several varieties of phenomenological research. One particularly user-friendly version is Interpretive Phenomenological Analysis (IPA), which was developed by Jonathan Smith and his colleagues in the 1990s (Smith & Osborn, 2008). Its initial applications were within health and social psychology, but in the last few years it has been increasingly adopted within mental health research. One attraction of IPA is that it is psychologically oriented, in that it is concerned with cognitions and emotions (in contrast to, for example, discourse analysis, for which such constructs are not relevant). It is the most psychological of the thematic approaches: even grounded theory does not necessarily focus on cognitions and emotions. A further attraction is that it is a clearly set out, well-structured approach, requiring a minimum of philosophical baggage, and thus is relatively easy to learn for newcomers to the method (although it still requires supervision from an experienced researcher).

As an example, Macran, Stiles and Smith (1999) were interested in how therapists' experience of receiving their own personal therapy had affected their clinical work. Seven therapists who worked mostly from a psychodynamic or client-centred orientation were interviewed. Their accounts yielded twelve themes organized into three domains. For instance, the second domain 'Orienting to the client' had two related themes 'Giving the client space' and 'Holding back from jumping in to help'. Macran et al. concluded that when therapists experienced helpful conditions in their own therapy, they were better able to provide these conditions for their clients.

Narrative analysis

There is a compelling argument that the activity of telling stories is central to human existence (Sarbin, 1986). We use stories to make sense of our world, including making sense of who we are ourselves; indeed, several authors (e.g. McLeod, 1997) have argued that psychotherapy can be conceptualized in narrative terms. Narrative analysis attempts to understand the nature of these stories, as they are told within the topic area of the particular piece of research. The data are sometimes gathered in a 'narrative interview' (Murray, 2003), which focuses on eliciting a chronological account of the participant's experiences.

Several versions of narrative analysis exist (Avdi & Georgaca, 2007; Murray, 2003); although we are considering narrative analysis here, within the section on thematic analysis, some of these versions arguably belong in the family of language-focused approaches (see next section). Thematic versions of narrative analysis focus on the meaning of individuals' stories, classifying them into thematic clusters. Structural versions, which are closer in spirit to language-focused approaches, pay more attention to how a story is told rather than what the story says, for example, by examining the use of narrative mechanisms for conveying a persuasive and coherent story. However, a central aspect of all of these versions is that they examine accounts as a whole, looking at stories as a complete entity. This is in contrast to other thematic analysis approaches, which break down the material into categories, sometimes thereby losing a coherent sense of the person who gave the account or the thread running through the themes.

An example of a thematic narrative analysis is Humphreys' (2000) study of the stories told by members of Alcoholics Anonymous during group meetings. He identified five different story types – which he labelled the 'drunk-a-log', the serial story, the apologue, legends and humorous stories – and examined the characteristics and therapeutic functions of each story type both in enhancing group members' identification with the core principles of Alcoholics Anonymous and also in maintaining their continued abstinence from alcohol.

Language-focused approaches

Language-focused methods aim to examine in detail how language is used, from a functional point of view, in an interaction or piece of text. Their intellectual origins are in linguistics and sociology, and reflect those disciplines' concerns with examining social and linguistic rules at a micro-level of analysis. They can be seen as part of the 'linguistic turn' that manifested itself in several different intellectual disciplines in the late twentieth century. Important areas of common ground in other disciplines are speech act theory in philosophy (Searle, 1969) and pragmatics in linguistics (e.g. Grundy, 1995).

Here we will focus on the family's two main members, conversation analysis and discourse analysis. These are not distinct terms, and some disparity of usage exists in the literature, particularly in that some pieces of research which are labelled as discourse analysis seem closer to what is usually understood as conversation analysis. The two approaches also share many common features, although they do each have a distinct emphasis, and each also has a number of variants (Wooffitt, 2005). We will address them in turn.

Conversation analysis

Conversation analysis arose within sociology and still retains a sociological flavour (Drew, 2003). Its central concern was to understand the social rules underlying the management of spoken discourse. It took a seemingly obvious phenomenon, for example that speakers typically speak in talking turns, one at a time, and questioned how such a form of social orderliness is achieved. When one tries to unpick the mechanisms involved in turn-taking in discourse, it turns out (no pun intended) that they involve complex social regulatory processes between the two speakers (Sacks, Schegloff & Jefferson, 1974).

Conversation analysis has recently been advocated as a method for studying psychotherapeutic interactions (Madill, Widdicombe & Barkham, 2001), although there are as yet not many examples in the literature. One fascinating early example, although described by its authors as discourse analysis, is Labov and Fanshel's (1977) book-length study of a single hour-long therapy session of a client with an eating disorder. They attempt to elucidate, through an exhaustive and detailed analysis of each party's speech patterns, the subtleties of how client and therapist respond to and influence each other.

Conversation analysis is closely related to other procedures that attempt to study the psychotherapeutic process in a moment-by-moment way. Task analysis (Greenberg, 1984) examines how particular actions in therapy are accomplished. One example used by Greenberg is how therapists go about helping clients resolve problematic reactions, that is when the client describes times when their reaction to an event was inappropriate or excessive. Comprehensive process analysis (Elliott, 1984) uses tape-assisted recall methods to study significant events in the therapy, for example, those moments which the client designates in a recall session as having been particularly helpful or unhelpful. As its name suggests, this is a mixed-method approach, including some quantitative measures as well as qualitative analysis.

One interesting application of conversation analysis is McCabe, Heath, Burns and Priebe's (2002) study of consultations between patients with psychosis and their psychiatrists in outpatient settings. By examining transcripts of the interactions, they found that many of the patients actively attempted to initiate discussion about their psychotic symptoms, but that their psychiatrists seemed reluctant to engage with this material.

Discourse analysis

Discourse analysis is yet another label covering a wide variety of approaches. Like conversation analysis, it pays close attention to how language is used within a piece of discourse. However, the emphasis is often on understanding the linguistic repertoires that the speakers draw upon to accomplish their apparent goals in the interaction, and how common understandings of definitions and meanings between the speakers are arrived at. In comparison with conversation analysis, discourse analysis is less focused on the mechanics of how conversations are accomplished and more focused on the social and cultural resources that speakers draw upon. Discourse analysis can also be applied to a wide range of materials, both interactions and written texts, whereas conversation analysis is predominately used to study two-person spoken interactions.

Within the UK, especially within social psychology, discourse analysis has been strongly influenced by Potter and Wetherell's (1987) book *Discourse and social psychology*, in which they argue that discourse is not simply a device for conveying meaning, but that people use language (either spoken or written) to accomplish things. Thus discourse analysis is action-oriented in that it aims to understand the strategies that people employ in creating certain kinds of outcomes.

An example of discourse analysis within the therapy process research tradition is provided by Madill and Barkham's (1997) single case study of how a client presented herself over several sessions of brief psychodynamic therapy. The analysis showed how the client, at various times in the therapy, seemed to adopt three definable 'subject positions' drawn from historical and cultural influences – the dutiful daughter, the daughter of a bad mother and the damaged child – and how positive psychological change was achieved in a pivotal session by a resolution of issues arising from these three positions.

A note on computer-assisted analysis

Some computer programs have been developed to assist researchers with conducting qualitative analysis. These include Atlas.ti, Ethnograph, NVivo and NUD*IST. Their advantages are that they are good for data management: they allow easy indexing and retrieval of segments of text, and coding categories can easily be changed or merged. This all becomes more important with larger data sets and when several researchers are working as a team. However, it is important to remember that, while computer programs can be useful mechanical aids, they cannot replace the human activity of thinking about the meaning of the data. Unfortunately, we have come across research projects where the use of computer-assisted analysis seems to have led to over-elaborated and undigested presentations of the findings. The decision about whether to use a computer program ultimately will depend not only on the nature of the data set but also on personal preference: some researchers may feel they can get a better feel for, and overview of, their data by using traditional paper-and-pencil methods.

How do you choose a method?

As we have indicated in the title of this chapter, the choice of qualitative method depends on a combination of scientific, practical and personal factors. This applies both to the choice of doing qualitative research in the first place, and then, once the decision has been taken to adopt a qualitative approach, also to the choice of the particular qualitative method. The latter issue will be the main focus here, but we will briefly recapitulate the issues involved in choosing a qualitative approach overall.

Our central message is that the principal determinant of the choice of method is the research question that you are attempting to answer, and most of our attention will be given to looking at how different qualitative methods are designed to answer different questions. However, other factors certainly do play a role, particularly the researcher's own personal preferences and cognitive style, and it is important to be aware of what kind of influence these each have, especially if you are in the first stages of planning your own research.

The choice to adopt a qualitative approach generally

Why would a researcher adopt a qualitative approach in the first place? From a scientific point of view, as we have stated earlier, the unique advantage of qualitative research is that it can provide a detailed, in-depth examination of the phenomenon of interest. It is also usually inductive, so it is valuable for the generation of theory. It is less good, however, at research questions involving comparison or causality. Therefore the main scientific reason for doing qualitative research is if you are interested in gaining an in-depth understanding, possibly with the goal of generating theory.

However, personal factors certainly enter into this overall choice of approach. In our experience of working with clinical psychology doctoral students, the personal preference for a particular method often precedes the consideration of the appropriateness of the method for the study. Many students will say 'I want to do a qualitative project' without having really thought about whether it is most appropriate for the research questions that they intend to investigate. There are often both push and pull factors operating. On the one hand, some people enjoy the complexity of qualitative data and the sense of human contact that comes from interviewing participants in depth or carrying out a close reading of texts. On the other hand, some people feel that they are not competent at, or have an aversion to, statistical methods. Some may even seek out qualitative approaches because they are perceived as being an easier option. We always give a clear health warning at this point. Qualitative approaches are far from being an easy option: they involve much painstaking work, carefully reading and re-reading voluminous data sets. Compared with the hours of labour entailed in transcribing interviews and carrying out qualitative analysis, doing quantitative analysis, which involves entering data into to a spreadsheet and analysing it with a statistical package, does not seem so daunting.

Practical factors also enter into the overall decision to adopt a qualitative approach. Qualitative projects usually have smaller sample sizes, and so they are more feasible with a hard-to-obtain population, which applies to many clinical samples. Also certain qualitative approaches, for example those that involve analysing the process of therapy sessions, are compatible with everyday clinical work, so can be undertaken by practitioners with limited resources available. Such process investigations are often especially suited to qualitative research.

Choosing between qualitative methods

Once the overall decision to adopt a qualitative approach has been taken, the researcher must then decide upon the specific qualitative method. The first step is to decide which of the two broad families of approaches (thematic analysis or language-focused approaches) best fits the overall aims of the research. The second step is then to choose the specific method from within that particular family. The first step is usually the easier one, as the different families are quite distinctive in their aims and approaches; the second is often less clear-cut, as there is considerable overlap between the approaches. This second choice is also more dependent on personal factors, that is whether the language and procedures of the particular approach fit with your own way of working.

We will illustrate these choices using a running example. We will suppose that the researcher is interested in studying the topic of therapist self-disclosure during therapy. This topic can, of course, be studied both quantitatively and qualitatively. There is an existing quantitative literature on how therapist disclosure affects the process and outcome of therapy (Farber, 2006), including an interesting randomized experiment (Barrett & Berman, 2001) showing that it had a positive impact on both. There is also a small body of qualitative research; for example, Knox, Hess, Petersen and Hill (1997) examined clients' experiences of helpful therapist disclosures. However, for the present purposes, we will generate some hypothetical research questions within this topic to illustrate how they might best be answered using particular qualitative approaches.

Thematic analysis approaches

Research questions concerning therapists' thoughts and feelings about using disclosure, and the types of disclosure they use, would lend themselves to thematic analysis approaches, using semi-structured interviews in order to obtain therapists' opinions and experiences, and to analyse their accounts.

Let us suppose that the researcher is interested in the question of how therapists understand the concept of self-disclosure and how they view its use in therapy. More specifically, a research question might be: 'What are therapists' views about when, and what type of, disclosure is appropriate or inappropriate?' Generic thematic analysis approaches (e.g. Boyatzis, 1998; Braun & Clarke, 2006; Hill et al., 1997) could then be used to address this systematically by coding various aspects of the respondents' accounts, for example, how they understand and define self-disclosure, whether there are different subtypes, in what contexts it is used, and what the perceived positive or negative impact is. For researchers who feel more comfortable with a highly structured approach, *framework analysis* would enable a detailed mapping of the themes within and across respondents by use of charts or tables or other visual displays. If the research question were focused primarily on identifying the different subtypes and their frequency of occurrence (e.g. the number of therapists who report using each subtype), then *content analysis* could be used.

Grounded theory could also be used to address the above question, though the emphasis would be more on developing an overarching set of ideas that bring coherence to the data set. For example, themes or categories identified in the interviews might indicate that therapist self-disclosure is particularly important in the ways in which it affects the therapeutic alliance, such as enhancing the client-therapist bond. Using the grounded theory approach, the researcher might identify a central or 'core' category (Strauss & Corbin, 1998) of therapist disclosure as a facilitator of the therapeutic alliance, and illustrate the various ways in which this occurs. Thus, this approach would result in the generation of a tentative theory of effective therapist self-disclosure.

If, on the other hand, the research question were 'What are therapists' experiences of using self-disclosure in therapy sessions?', then *phenomenological approaches*, such as IPA, would be more appropriate. The focus here would be more on respondents' personal experiences, for example., their feelings and thoughts about, and meanings they attach to, using disclosure in their therapeutic repertoire. While this overlaps to some extent with the areas addressed by other thematic approaches, a phenomenological approach would place a greater emphasis on understanding the respondent's personal world, and would probably appeal to researchers who like a more interpretative approach. So, for example, the interview and the data analysis might focus in detail on therapists' personal experiences of using self-disclosure, how they decide to disclose or not, what makes them feel more or less comfortable about using self-disclosure, and how they have experienced the process of the therapy session after using self-disclosure.

A *narrative* approach could also be used to address the question of therapists' experiences of using self-disclosure, but the focus would be on identifying the central features of participants' accounts (or 'stories') at a more macro-level. The researcher would aim in the interview to obtain more of a chronological account of therapists' experiences, for example, a description of the therapy session, or episode within a session, in which self-disclosure occurred, starting with the context, what the client had said, what went through the therapist's mind, what the self-disclosure was, how the client appeared to react, and what the therapist felt or thought afterwards. Using narrative analysis, prototypical stories could be identified; two stories, for example, might be the 'premeditated disclosure' and the 'spontaneous disclosure'.

Language-focused approaches

Research questions focusing on how therapist self-disclosure is used within actual therapy sessions would lend themselves more to the language-focused approaches. For example, the researcher might be primarily interested in when, how and in what ways self-disclosure occurs within the therapeutic process. In this case, it would make sense to use recordings of client-therapist interactions (or transcriptions of these recordings) as the source of data. This would allow a detailed analysis of self-disclosure in action. In contrast to thematic analysis approaches, the focus would not be on participants' feelings and cognitions, but rather on the speech and interaction itself – what, when and how things are said.

Conversation analysis could be used to address questions concerning the immediate precursors of and consequences of therapist disclosures in the interaction. For example, are there any types of client talk that seem to increase the likelihood of therapist disclosures? Are there any noticeable impacts of therapist disclosure on the subsequent speech of either party in the interaction? Thus, conversation analysis might shed light on the nitty-gritty of how therapist disclosure influences and is influenced by statements made by the client. (Tape-assisted recall could be used as an additional method here, if the researcher wanted to obtain therapists' or clients' reactions to specific disclosure events.)

Discourse analysis might be used to answer slightly different questions concerning the functions of therapist disclosure, that is what it accomplishes within the therapeutic interaction. More specifically, how do therapist disclosures function in terms of the power differentials in the therapeutic relationship? Or how does the therapist seek to portray herself in her disclosures? Focusing on the latter question, the researcher might use discourse analysis to identify different types of self-portrayals (e.g. as an 'error-prone fellow being', a 'role model', a 'victim'), each serving a particular function within the relationship.

Summary

We hope that the above extended example of how different methods could be used to study therapist disclosure has given the reader a sense of the issues that are involved in making a choice of qualitative methods in any given topic area. The central point is that there are many ways to approach any given area of research, and the choice of method is determined largely by the question that one is attempting to answer. The first question that researchers should ask themselves is 'What do I want to find out, and which methods will help me do that?' Once that question has been addressed, the researcher can then decide whether the indicated methods seem congenial in terms of philosophy and general approach, and also whether practical considerations might narrow the available options.

Some additional questions

The main body of this chapter has attempted to address two central and frequently asked questions about qualitative research: 'Why would I want to use a qualitative approach?' and 'How do I choose the particular qualitative method?' In this concluding section we will briefly address some other frequently asked questions, concerning conducting qualitative research in clinical practice, the use of qualitative methods in combination with quantitative approaches, and quality standards in qualitative research.

Can qualitative research possibly have therapeutic benefits (or possibly cause harm)?

One often overlooked aspect of qualitative research, at least that using in-depth interviews, is that being in the study often seems to benefit the participants. We are not aware of any systematic research that has addressed this interesting issue, but it is certainly borne out by anecdotal evidence from our own studies. For example, in two studies of helping processes within couple relationships, one using conjoint, in-depth interviews (Harris, Pistrang & Barker, 2006) and the other using the tape-assisted recall method (Pistrang, Picciotto & Barker, 2001), participants often spontaneously commented on how valuable it was to have someone listen to them attentively and empathically for an extended period of time, which was a rare event in their lives. This is consistent with Rogers' (1975) ideas about the positive effects of empathic relationships, and also with research showing that assessment interviews given as part of a pre-post measurement in outcome studies can be therapeutic (Svartberg et al., 2001).

The other side of the coin is that semi-structured interviews with clinical populations entail potential risks. Participants may disclose material that is highly distressing, or material that the researcher suspects may indicate a potential for harm to self or others (e.g. if they talk about abuse or domestic violence). This is an issue particular to qualitative research: due to the open-ended nature of interviews, participants may divulge information that neither they nor the researcher anticipated. Researchers must ensure that they have robust systems in place to exercise their duty of care to the participants in such instances.

Can I do qualitative research with my own clients?

Given what we have said about the appeal of qualitative research to clinicians, one might assume that a potential way of carrying out practice-based research is for therapists to conduct qualitative research with their own clients. We would, however, advise against this on ethical grounds. Combining the roles of therapist and researcher raises irresolvable conflicts of interest. It is not possible for clients to consent freely to participate in their own therapist's research, as they may fear negative consequences if they disappoint him or her by refusing. Furthermore, if the client were being interviewed by their own therapist about their reactions to the therapy, they would find it difficult to respond honestly. A solution to this is to invite someone from outside the service who is interested in gathering practice-based qualitative evidence, for example, a colleague or a research student, so that clients' confidentiality and freedom of choice can be preserved.

Can qualitative and quantitative methods be combined?

This chapter's pragmatic stance, of fitting the method to the research question, extends to the issue of combining qualitative and quantitative methods. Some studies ask several different kinds of research questions, and a different type of research method may be appropriate for addressing each of them. For example, a comparative treatment trial may be designed both to measure the clinical outcome of the therapies being tested and also to understand clients' experience of receiving each type of therapy. The quantitative component will use methods appropriate for conducting a randomized trial; the qualitative component may use in-depth interviews with a subset of clients in order to understand which components of the therapy are experienced as more and less helpful or what the mechanisms of change are. The researchers may also conduct conversation or discourse analyses of the therapy sessions, in order to elucidate the processes of therapeutic delivery (e.g. Madill et al., 2001).

Qualitative and quantitative methods can be combined within the same study, within different studies in a research programme, or at the level of the field as whole (Barker & Pistrang, 2005). This means that individual researchers should feel free to pursue the questions that interest them, using the methods that are most appropriate for the questions, subject to their own personal preferences and the constraints of the setting in which they are working.

How do I know whether a piece of qualitative research is done well?

Finally, we have not addressed the issue of how qualitative studies are to be evaluated, or what are 'good practice' guidelines for conducting qualitative studies. There is now a substantial literature on this topic, setting out principles for carrying out rigorous studies and procedures for enhancing the credibility of the conclusions that are drawn (e.g. Elliott, Fischer & Rennie, 1999; Mays & Pope, 2000; Yardley, 2000). It is essential that researchers who are planning to embark on qualitative research consult this literature at the start. However, there is also some debate about whether quality control checklists are appropriate for, or can be universally applied to, all genres of qualitative research (e.g. Reicher, 2000). Such checklists need to be tailored to fit the aims and methods of the particular study. As Barbour (2001) argues, if used uncritically, checklists can reduce qualitative research to a set of technical procedures that can result in 'the tail wagging the dog'.

Conclusion

This chapter has attempted to give an overview of the issues and choices for would-be qualitative researchers in psychotherapy and counselling. We hope that it has helped readers understand the nature of some of the various approaches, and the considerations that need to be taken into account when choosing between them. Qualitative research is an intriguing blend of art and science. There are definite skills that can be acquired, but it also requires the researcher to be able go beyond the mechanical aspects of the research to see the central ideas behind the words and to represent them to the readers and consumers of the research. It is a challenging, but ultimately highly rewarding endeavour.

References

Avdi, E. & Georgaca, E. (2007). Narrative research in psychotherapy. *Psychology and Psychotherapy: Theory, Research and Practice, 80*, 407–419.

Barbour, R.S. (2001). Checklists for improving rigour in qualitative research: a case of the tail wagging the dog? *British Medical Journal, 322*, 1115–1117.

Barker, C. & Pistrang, N. (2002). Psychotherapy and social support: integrating research on psychological helping. *Clinical Psychology Review, 22*, 361–379.

Barker, C. & Pistrang, N. (2005). Quality criteria under methodological pluralism: implications for doing and evaluating research. *American Journal of Community Psychology, 35*, 201–212.

Barker, C., Pistrang, N. & Elliott, R. (1994). *Research methods in clinical and counselling psychology.* Chichester: John Wiley & Sons, Ltd.

Barker, C., Pistrang, N. & Elliott, R. (2002). *Research methods in clinical psychology: An introduction for students and practitioners* (2nd edn.) Chichester: John Wiley & Sons, Ltd.

Barrett, M.S. & Berman, J.S. (2001). Is psychotherapy more effective when therapists disclose information about themselves? *Journal of Consulting and Clinical Psychology, 69*, 597–603.

Bennett, D. & Parry, G. (2004). A measure of therapist competence derived from cognitive analytic therapy. *Psychotherapy Research, 14*, 176–192.

Bolger, E.A. (1999). Grounded theory analysis of emotional pain. *Psychotherapy Research, 9*, 342–362.

Boyatzis, R.E. (1998). *Transforming qualitative information: Thematic analysis and code development.* London: Sage Publications.

Braun, V. & Clarke, V. (2006). Using thematic analysis in psychology. *Qualitative Research in Psychology, 3*, 77–101.

Bryman, A. (2004) *Social research methods* (2nd edn.). Oxford: Oxford University Press.

Camic, P.M., Rhodes, J.E. & Yardley, L. (eds.) (2003). *Qualitative research in psychology: Expanding perspectives in methodology and design.* Washington, DC: American Psychological Association.

Charmaz, K. (1991). *Good days, bad days: The self in chronic illness and time.* New Brunswick, NJ: Rutgers University Press.

Creswell, J.W. (1998). *Qualitative inquiry and research design: Choosing among five traditions.* Thousand Oaks, CA: Sage Publications.

Denzin, N. & Lincoln, Y.S. (eds.) (2005). *The Sage handbook of qualitative research.* Thousand Oaks, CA: Sage Publications.

Dey, I. (1993). *Qualitative data analysis: A user-friendly guide for social scientists.* London: Routledge.

Drew, P. (2003). Conversation analysis. In J.A. Smith (ed.), *Qualitative psychology: A practical guide to research methods* (pp. 51–80) London: Sage Publications.

Elliott, R. (1984). A discovery-oriented approach to significant change events in psychotherapy: Interpersonal Process Recall and Comprehensive Process Analysis. In L.N. Rice & L.S. Greenberg (eds.), *Patterns of change: Intensive analysis of psychotherapy process.* New York: Guilford Press.

Elliott, R. & Shapiro, D.A. (1988). Brief structured recall: A more efficient method for studying significant therapy events. *British Journal of Medical Psychology, 61*, 141–153.

Elliott, R., Fischer, C.T. & Rennie, D.L. (1999). Evolving guidelines for publication of qualitative research studies in psychology and related fields. *British Journal of Clinical Psychology, 38*, 215–229.

Farber, B.A. (2006). *Self-disclosure in psychotherapy.* New York: Guilford Press.

Geertz, C. (1973). *The interpretation of cultures.* New York: Basic Books.

Gergen, K.J. (1985). The social constructionist movement in modern psychology. *American Psychologist, 40*, 266–275.

Glaser, B.G. & Strauss, A.L. (1967). *The discovery of grounded theory: Strategies for qualitative research.* Chicago: Aldine.

Gottschalk, L.A. & Gleser, G.C. (1969). *The measurement of psychological states through the content analysis of verbal behavior.* Berkeley: University of California Press.

Greenberg, L.S. (1984). Task analysis: the general approach. In L.N. Rice & L.S. Greenberg (eds.), *Patterns of change: Intensive analysis of psychotherapy process.* New York: Guilford Press.

Grundy, P. (1995). *Doing pragmatics.* London: Arnold.

Harper, D. (2008). Clinical psychology. In C. Willig & W. Stainton-Rogers (eds.), *The Sage handbook of qualitative research in psychology.* London: Sage Publications.

Harris, T.J.R., Pistrang, N. & Barker, C. (2006). Couples' experiences of the support process in depression. *Psychology and Psychotherapy: Theory, Research and Practice, 79*, 1–21.

Henwood, K.L. & Pidgeon, N. (1992). Qualitative research and psychological theorising. *British Journal of Psychology, 83*, 97–111.

Hill, C.E., Thompson, B.J. & Williams, E.N. (1997). A guide to conducting consensual qualitative research. *The Counseling Psychologist, 25*, 517–572.

Humphreys, K. (2000). Community narratives and personal stories in Alcoholics Anonymous. *Journal of Community Psychology, 28*, 495–506.

Joffe, H. & Yardley, L. (2003). Content and thematic analysis. In D.F. Marks & L. Yardley (eds.), *Research methods for clinical and health psychology.* London: Sage Publications.

Knox, S., Hess, S.A., Petersen, D.A. & Hill, C.E. (1997). A qualitative analysis of client perceptions of the effects of helpful therapist self-disclosure in long-term therapy. *Journal of Counseling Psychology, 44*, 274–283.

Labov, W. & Fanshel, D. (1977). *Therapeutic discourse.* New York: Academic Press.

Laing, R.D. (1959). *The divided self: An existential study in sanity and madness.* London: Tavistock Publications.

Lane, L.G. & Viney, L.L. (2005). The effects of personal construct group therapy on breast cancer survivors. *Journal of Consulting and Clinical Psychology, 73*, 284–292.

Lincoln, Y. & Guba, E.G. (1985). *Naturalistic inquiry.* Beverly Hills, CA: Sage Publications.

Macran, S., Stiles, W.B. & Smith, J.A. (1999). How does personal therapy affect therapists' practice? *Journal of Counseling Psychology, 46*, 419–431.

Madill, A. & Barkham, M. (1997). Discourse analysis of a theme in one successful case of psychodynamic-interpersonal psychotherapy. *Journal of Counseling Psychology, 44*, 232–244.

Madill, A., Widdicombe, S. & Barkham, M. (2001). The potential of conversation analysis for psychotherapy research. *The Counseling Psychologist, 29*, 413–434.

Mays, N. & Pope, C. (2000). Assessing quality in qualitative research. *British Medical Journal, 320*, 50–52.

McCabe, R., Heath, C., Burns, T. & Priebe, S. (2002). Engagement of patients with psychosis in the consultation: conversation analytic study. *British Medical Journal, 325*, 1148–1151.

McLeod, J. (1997). *Narrative and psychotherapy*. London: Sage Publications.

McLeod, J. (2001). *Qualitative research in counselling and psychotherapy*. London: Sage Publications.

Miles, M.B. & Huberman, A.M. (1994). *Qualitative data analysis: An expanded sourcebook* (2nd edn.). Thousand Oaks, CA: Sage Publications.

Murray, M. (2003). Narrative analysis and narrative psychology. In P.M. Camic, J.E. Rhodes & L. Yardley (eds.), *Qualitative research in psychology: Expanding perspectives in methodology and design*. Washington, DC: American Psychological Association.

Pistrang, N., Picciotto, A. & Barker, C. (2001). The communication of empathy in couples during the transition to parenthood. *Journal of Community Psychology, 29*, 615–636.

Pope, C., Ziebland, S. & Mays, N. (2000). Analysing qualitative data. *British Medical Journal, 320*, 114–117.

Potter, J. & Wetherell, M. (1987). *Discourse and social psychology*. London: Sage Publications.

Reicher, S. (2000). Against methodolatry: Some comments on Elliott, Fischer, and Rennie. *British Journal of Clinical Psychology, 39*, 1–6.

Rennie, D. (2004). Anglo-North American qualitative counseling and psychotherapy research. *Psychotherapy Research, 14*, 37–55.

Ritchie, J. & Spencer, L. (1994). Qualitative data analysis for applied policy research. In A. Bryman & R.G. Burgess (eds.), *Analysing qualitative data*. London: Routledge.

Rogers, C.R. (1975). Empathic: An unappreciated way of being. *The Counseling Psychologist, 5*, 2–10.

Sacks, H., Schegloff, E.A. & Jefferson, G. (1974). A simplest systematics for the organisation of turn taking in conversation. *Language, 50*, 696–735.

Sarbin, T.R. (ed.) (1986). *Narrative psychology: The storied nature of human conduct*. New York: Praeger.

Searle, J.R. (1969). *Speech acts: An essay in the philosophy of language*. Cambridge: Cambridge University Press.

Shlein, J.M. (1963). Phenomenology and personality. In J.T. Hart & T.M. Tomlinson (eds.), *New directions in client-centered therapy.* Boston, MA: Houghton-Mifflin.

Silverman, D. (2000). *Doing qualitative research: A practical handbook.* London: Sage Publications.

Smith, J.A. (1995). Semi-structured interviewing and qualitative analysis. In J.A. Smith, R. Harré & L. Van Langenhove (eds.), *Rethinking methods in psychology.* London: Sage Publications.

Smith, J.A. (ed.) (2008). *Qualitative psychology: A practical guide to research methods* (2nd edn.). London: Sage Publications.

Smith, J.A. & Osborn, M. (2008). Interpretative phenomenological analysis. In J.A. Smith (ed.), *Qualitative psychology: A practical guide to research methods* (2nd edn.). (pp. 53–80). London: Sage Publications.

Spinelli, E. (2005). *The interpreted world: An introduction to phenomenological psychology* (2nd edn.). London: Sage Publications.

Stiles, W.B. (1994). 'When you've heard a story, what do you know?' Paper presented at the Society for Psychotherapy Research meeting, York, England.

Strauss, A. & Corbin, J. (1998). *Basics of qualitative research: Techniques and procedures for developing grounded theory* (2nd edn.). Newbury Park, CA: Sage Publications.

Svartberg, M., Seltzer, M.H., Choi, K. & Stiles, T.C. (2001). Cognitive change before, during, and after short-term dynamic and nondirective psychother-apies: a preliminary growth modeling study. *Psychotherapy Research, 11,* 201–219.

Tashakkori, C. & Teddlie, C. (eds.) (2002). *Handbook of mixed methods in social and behavioral research.* Thousand Oaks, CA: Sage Publications.

Taylor, S.J. & Bogdan, R. (1998). *Introduction to qualitative research methods: A guidebook and resource* (3rd edn.) New York: John Wiley & Sons, Inc.

Willig, C. (2008). *Introducing qualitative research in psychology: Adventures in theory and method* (2nd edn.). Buckingham: Open University Press.

Willig, C. & Stainton-Rogers, W. (2008). *The Sage handbook of qualitative re-search in psychology.* London: Sage Publications.

Winter, D.A. (1992). *Personal construct psychology in clinical practice.* London: Routledge.

Wooffitt, R. (2005). *Conversation analysis and discourse analysis: A comparative and critical introduction.* London: Sage Publications.

Yardley, L. (2000). Dilemmas in qualitative health research. *Psychology and Health, 15,* 215–228.

Yardley, L. & Bishop, F. (2008). Mixing qualitative and quantitative methods: a pragmatic approach. In C. Willig & W. Stainton-Rogers (eds.), *The Sage handbook of qualitative research in psychology.* London: Sage Publications.

4

Theory-Building Case Studies as Practice-Based Evidence

William B. Stiles
Miami University, Ohio, USA

Introduction

In addition to its potential for healing, psychotherapy offers an extraordinary opportunity to observe human experience and behaviour. Practitioners have expertise in and daily access to precisely the sorts of phenomena that theories of counselling and psychotherapy seek to explain. These include aspects of people that others seldom or never see. Practitioners may gain new and useful understandings about human feeling, thinking, communication and relationships that could, if shared, improve theory and practice. This chapter, which is an edited and expanded version of an article published previously (Stiles, 2007), describes one way that practitioners' clinical experience can be converted into practice-based evidence. I call it *theory-building case study research.*

Theory is important

Theories are ideas about the world conveyed in words, numbers, diagrams or other signs. The theories that practitioners use in treating clients (e.g. person-centred, psychoanalytic, cognitive-behavioural) offer distinct sets of assumptions and principles about the nature and sources of psychological problems and about approaches and interventions to address them. These principles are the intellectual tools that guide practitioners' day-to-day and minute-to-minute clinical decisions.

Developing and Delivering Practice-Based Evidence   By Michael Barkham, Gillian E Hardy, and John Mellor-Clark   © 2010 John Wiley & Sons, Ltd

Theories need work

Theories of counselling and psychotherapy do not provide complete descriptions or exact specifications for moment-to-moment interventions. Practitioners who use them have to interpret what is happening and adapt what they do to emerging circumstances, the state of the client, and the relationship (Stiles, Honos-Webb & Surko, 1998). Some practitioners identify themselves with one theory, while others combine theories, but most find themselves modifying or extending the theories they use at least some of the time. Rather than adhering precisely to something they have read, they are privately engaging in theory building. These practitioners have made empirical observations on relevant case material that have led to modifications or elaborations of theory. Their observations could be incorporated into the explicit theory to improve others' understanding.

Unique features of cases can inform theory

Theories of counselling and psychotherapy are meant to encompass more than is ever encountered in a single case. Each case includes details not shared with other cases, and a good clinical theory helps practitioners understand the variations as well as the common features.

Turning this around, unique features of cases can show where theories need to grow. Unlike statistical hypothesis testing, where unique features are often regarded as error, case studies can use them to inform theory (Rosenwald, 1988; Stiles, 2003, 2005, 2007, 2009).

I think this point is the one made by the parable of the six blind men and the elephant. The man who felt its side said the elephant was like a wall; the man who felt its tusk, like a spear; the man who felt its trunk, like a snake, and so forth. Each inference was different, but all were at least partly justified and all described the same animal. Although the blind men in the parable failed to listen to each other, the point is that the elephant (like counselling and psychotherapy) has many aspects. An adequate theory has to incorporate the distinct features of each case as well as the common features. Restricting attention to the themes that are common across cases will miss the most interesting parts. Each case tells us something new, and new observations are always valuable, whether they confirm previous theory or add something unexpected.

Research provides quality control on theory

The researcher's task is making systematic observations and describing them in ways that are accurate and relevant to the theory. The goal is that theory should correspond to observation and practice; the theory should describe the world accurately.

If the theoretical description and the clinical observation do not match, then something needs adjusting. Either the observations were somehow misleading or inaccurately described or the theory needs to be modified. So the researcher's task is making and checking observations (and re-checking observations) and, when necessary, adjusting the theory so that it corresponds better with the observations. In this process, failures are as important as successes. Observations that show where the theory does not work can be scientifically as important as observations that show where the theory does work.

Statistical hypothesis testing versus case study

Both hypothesis testing and case study research can be used to build theories, and both can provide scientific quality control on theory. In contrast to hypothesis testing, however, case studies address many theoretical issues in the same study rather than focusing on only one or a few.

The familiar statistical hypothesis testing strategy is to derive one statement from a theory and compare that statement with many observations. That is, we test a hypothesis by seeing if it holds across cases. If the observations tend to correspond to the statement, then our confidence in the statement is substantially increased. We say that the hypothesis was confirmed, or at least that the null hypothesis was rejected. This yields a *small* increment of confidence in the theory as a whole.

The case study strategy is to compare each of many theoretically-based statements with one or a few observations. It does this by describing the case in theoretical terms. Each case is different and may address different aspects of the theory. At issue is the correspondence of theory and observation – how well the theory describes details of the case. Because each detail may be observed only once in each case, the change in confidence in any one theoretical statement is small. However, there are many details, and each can be described in theoretical terms. Because many statements are examined, the gain in confidence in the theory as a whole may be as large as from a statistical hypothesis-testing study (Campbell, 1979). The key is multiple points of contact between the case and the theory; this is accomplished through rich case descriptions and detailed links between theory and case observations.

Observations permeate theories

In any scientific research, observations change theories. They may confirm or disconfirm or strengthen or weaken the theory. More constructively, the changes may involve extending, elaborating, refining, modifying, or qualifying the theory. The theoretical ideas change to fit the observations.

To describe how observations change theories, I like to say that the observations *permeate* the theory (Stiles, 1993, 2003, 2009). This is a diffusion metaphor; I picture particles of observation spreading through the theoretical interstices. Aspects of the new observations actually enter and become part of the theory. For example, the theory may be explained differently, using words that accommodate the new observations along with the previous ones. Or the new observations may be used as illustrations.

The American philosopher Charles Sanders Peirce used the name *abduction* for the logical operation of making up theoretical tenets to accommodate observations. This was meant to complement and parallel the terms induction and deduction. Abduction is what theorists do when they modify a theory to encompass some new or unexpected observation. The logic is that if the newly abduced theoretical tenet were true, then the observation would be expected (Peirce, 1965; Rennie, 2000). This is one way that new observations may permeate theories.

Through research, then, observations accumulate in theories. New observations permeate the theory while earlier thinking and results are retained. The diffusion metaphor offers an alternative to the brick wall metaphor for how science is cumulative. That is, understanding grows not by stacking fact upon fact, but by infusing observations that expand the theory.

Thus, a theory is not a fixed formula but a growing and changing way of understanding. This is a view of theory from the perspective of theorists who may change it and practitioners who must adapt it, rather than from the perspective of students who have to read and memorize a static version of what other people have said.

Theory-building research versus enriching research and clinical case studies

Not all research is theory-building research. Some research has a different goal, which has been called *enriching* or *deepening* or *hermeneutic*. Enriching research involves considering multiple perspectives and alternative interpretations and unpacking the history of textual meanings. Its product is not an internally consistent theory but a deeper, broader, more profound appreciation of the phenomenon (Stiles, 2003, 2006).

Because it has different purposes, enriching research involves different methods and is evaluated by different standards. For example, whereas theory-building research seeks *generality* (the theory accurately describes many cases or circumstances), enriching research seeks *transferability* (people who read the research can extend it for their own purposes; the research illuminates understanding of their own experiences; Lincoln & Guba, 1985).

Clinical case studies – those aimed at understanding a particular case rather than building theory or contributing to a more general understanding – may also use methods and standards different from theory-building case study research. As in enriching research, theories may suggest alternative perspectives, offering insights into the case. Such case studies may be important for clinical decision making or training.

How to do theory-building case studies

There is no one correct method for doing case studies. If the procedures were fully prescribed, the activity would be a laboratory exercise, not research. The point of any research is to find new ways to examine an idea, new ways to make observations that check the accuracy of a theory. In this section, I do not give step-by-step instructions but advance some broader considerations and suggestions for readers who are conducting theory-building case studies.

Familiarity with the theory and courage to change it

For your new observations to permeate a theory, you need to know the theory. You must be able to put your observations in the context of what has gone before. You must know what is new and what converges with others' observations. What are the logical implications of making the changes you want to make? What aspects of the theory do your clinical observations agree or disagree with?

In addition to familiarity with the theory and research, you will need the courage to change the theory and make adjustments in light of your own observations. You must be confident enough to comment on which aspects of the theory seem to fit your observations and which must be amended. Simultaneously, however, you must be humble enough to accept the possibility that your own observations and thinking may be mistaken.

Selecting a case

Good cases are ones that show something new or interesting or theoretically relevant. Probably every case can teach something, though you may not know what it will teach until you have finished the study. In contrast to statistical hypothesis-testing studies, case studies do not require representative sampling. An unusual case can be as informative as a typical case (if any case is typical).

The main requirement is to be explicit in reporting the reasons for deciding to write about a particular case.

Rich case record

A prerequisite for a case study of a counselling or psychotherapy client is a rich collection of information about the client and the treatment. Elliott (2002) has provided a valuable list of such sources, which I have borrowed from:

1. Basic facts about client and practitioner, including demographic information, diagnoses, presenting problems, treatment approach or orientation.
2. Recordings of treatment sessions. Verbatim transcriptions of audio or video recordings are a particularly strong source for grounding your inferences. Practitioners' process notes may also be useful, though these have been filtered through the practitioner's attention and memory and so may be less trustworthy.
3. Session-by-session assessments. Repeated measurement of the client's problems (e.g. Phillips, 1986), goals, symptoms (e.g. Barkham et al., 2006; Lambert et al., 2004), evaluations of sessions (e.g. Elliott & Wexler, 1994; Stiles et al., 1994), strength of the client-practitioner relationship (e.g. Agnew-Davies et al., 1998; Horvath & Greenberg, 1989), and client perceptions of significant treatment events (e.g. Llewelyn, 1988) can help track process and progress. Other chapters in this volume offer additional suggestions for such measures.
4. Outcome assessments. Treatment outcome has both descriptive qualitative (how the client changed) and quantitative (how much the client changed) aspects, and measures of both are helpful. There are many measures of outcome reviewed in other chapters in this volume.
5. Post-treatment interviews. Sometimes clients can be interviewed after they have finished treatment, to gather their impressions (e.g. Elliott, Slatick & Urman, 2001).
6. Other personal documents, such as personal journals or diaries, poetry, artwork, letters or e-mail messages can be useful.

There are no firm rules about what information must be used. Useful studies may sometimes be based on only one or a few of the sources listed here. The point of a rich case record is to permit multiple links to theory, facilitate trustworthy inferences, and provide a source of evidence for presentation to your readers.

Analyzing case study materials

There are many ways to go about qualitative analysis of case materials, but it may be useful to think of the work in three phases:

1. Gaining familiarity. This includes listening to or watching recordings, reading transcripts, and reviewing other available materials. Typically, researchers review case materials many times, perhaps taking different perspectives or asking different questions and making notes about the case and their thoughts. There is value in systematically attending to each item (e.g. each passage in a transcript) and temporarily suspending judgment about whether it is important.
2. Selecting and focusing. The goal of this phase is deciding what the focus of the study will be. It also includes selecting materials (e.g. passages in a transcript) that are relevant to the focal theoretical topic or theme.
3. Interpreting. This conceptual analysis phase requires explicit linking of observations to theoretical concepts and ideas and making sense of what has happened in terms of the theory.

Throughout this process, the goal is to establish points of contact between theory and observation. This can involve, for example, making many explicit links between particular theoretical concepts and specific passages of therapeutic dialogue. At issue is whether the observed phenomena and events recognizably correspond to the theoretical concepts and posited relations among them. The points of contact may be observations that fit the theory, observations that are contrary to theory, or observations that the theory should account for but does not (yet). In the interpretation phase, these alternatives can be reconciled; investigators may need to abduce new tenets – to modify or elaborate the theory in order to encompass the new observations.

Much research in counselling and psychotherapy is collaborative. It is valuable – some would say essential – to involve multiple people in observing and reporting. Each can independently read transcripts, listen to recordings and generally become familiar with case materials. Having more than one person considering the material can inject new ideas into your understanding of the case and smooth the rough edges of your interpretations. Consensus among multiple observers can help make the product more convincing to others. It may also be more fun to have collaborators.

Apply the case to the theory rather than (just) the theory to the case

Theory-building case studies are meant to change the theory, not just to understand the case. Of course, applying the theory to the case is an essential first step in theory-building – seeing how the theory corresponds to the new observations. But investigators then must turn the observations back on the theory in order to improve it. This is a major difference between clinical case studies and theory-building case studies. This is why investigators must have familiarity with the theory and the confidence to modify it – to extend its scope, to change its expression, and so forth.

I think many case studies miss this distinction. They may adhere to previous theory and ignore observations that fail to fit. They may cite authority rather than observation –what Freud thought, for example, rather than what actually happened.

Of course, a respectful attitude toward theory has a place in clinical applications. We often fail to appreciate phenomena the theories point to, so crediting the theory or esteemed theorists above our own initial impressions may open us to things we had overlooked. But case studies that merely apply theories, without putting them at risk of alteration, do not make a scientific contribution.

How to report theory-building case studies

A first step in learning to report case studies is to see how others have done it. Some journals that publish case studies include: *Counselling and Psychotherapy Research; Clinical Case Studies; Person-Centered and Experiential Psychotherapies; Counselling Psychology Quarterly, Psychology and Psychotherapy: Theory, Research, and Practice; Psychotherapy Research; Journal of Clinical Psychology: In Session*; and the online journal, *Pragmatic Case Studies in Psychotherapy*. For some recent case studies that I have been involved in, building a developmental theory of psychological change that we call the *assimilation model*, see Brinegar et al., 2006; Humphreys et al., 2005; Osatuke et al., 2005; and Stiles et al., 2006.

Some writing tips

In this section, I have listed a few suggestions for writing journal articles about theory-building case studies. For another list, focused mainly on accumulating a database of cases with standard information, rather than on theory building, see the instructions to authors on the website of the online journal *Pragmatic Case Studies in Psychotherapy*.

1. Pick the one or two most interesting things you have learned from the case and write about those. Do not attempt to say everything you know about the case.
2. Begin with the main point of the study, stating the main theoretical topic, the fact that it is a theory-building case study, and a phrase about the nature of the case.

3. Very early in the introduction, summarize the relevant parts of the theory (not the whole theory!). Incorporate (and explain that you are incorporating) any changes you have made to the theory as a result of this case study. The point of this introduction is to quickly provide your readers with the best possible conceptual framework for understanding what you did and what you observed, including your additions to the framework. Do not make readers start back where you started.

4. Selectively review other research about your main topic, linking what others have said with your current understanding. How would you explain their observations?

5. Depending on the journal you intend to submit your report to, you may need to explain briefly what is meant by a theory-building case study.

6. At the end of the Introduction, summarize the purpose and design of your study and your reasons for writing about this case.

7. In the Method, describe the client, the therapist, the treatment, the co-investigators (including yourself), any measures you used, and your procedures (including how you gathered the data and how you and your co-investigators dealt with the material and came to your interpretations), in that order.

8. Case studies require particular sensitivity to ethical issues of anonymity and informed consent (see discussion of research ethics by Bond, 2004). This can be briefly described in your description of the client or the procedure.

9. In the Results section, the central goal is to link observations with theoretical concepts. Make multiple points of contact between observation and theory! Clinical theories are rich and detailed, and the case material should be compared to the theory in many ways, not just in one way. Interpretations – the theoretical points you make – should be *grounded* in observations. This can be accomplished by presenting verbatim passages from sessions or interviews or other sorts of records. Such presentations should be considered as evidence, not merely as illustrations. Show readers why you made your interpretations, and explain how the theory links with and explains what you observed.

10. In reporting results, state your theoretical interpretation first and then describe the evidence that led you to it. For example, state the conceptual conclusion of your paragraph in the initial topic sentence. Begin each section with the main point of that section. Do not ask readers to keep all the pieces of evidence in mind, waiting until the end of the paragraph or the section to learn your conclusion.

11. In your Discussion, focus on the theoretical contribution – what you have learned, how you have supported or changed the theory. Acknowledge limitations. Note that criteria for evaluating qualitative work are somewhat different from criteria for evaluating statistical hypothesis-testing studies (e.g. Elliott, Fischer & Rennie, 1999; Stiles, 1993, 2003).

Case studies do not yield conclusions: generality is carried by the theory

As discussed earlier, a case study cannot yield much confidence in any one sentence. Another way to say this is: case studies do not yield one-sentence conclusions. By the same token, case studies typically do not test hypotheses or answer simple research questions. Hypotheses and questions narrow the study to a single statement, and case studies typically do not change confidence in single statements very much.

This lack of hypotheses and conclusions can make case studies profoundly puzzling to people used to hypothesis-testing research. There is no one-sentence generalization that captures your results. When someone asks what you found, there is no sentence to summarize it. You may have to explain how to generalize from case-study research when you talk to researchers.

In theory-building case studies, the only way to generalize is through the theory. The theory typically includes a description of what it applies to. To the extent that the theory has a logical structure, observations on one part of the theory affect other parts of the theory too. If the theory does a good job explaining the many details of your case, this lends confidence that it will explain other people's cases as well. Observations on different cases and different aspects of cases strengthen the whole theory because the theory says how different aspects of counselling and psychotherapy are related to each other. The logical internal consistency and generality are some of the main reasons for having a theory in the first place. For this reason, it is important to make the logical structure of the theory explicit.

Theory-building in the case of Karen

To illustrate theory-building case study research, I will review some contributions of the case of Karen (Stiles et al., 2006) to the *assimilation model* (Stiles, 2002; Stiles et al., 1990), a theory of psychological change in psychotherapy. Karen was a 36-year-old woman treated for mild depression in two weekly sessions of psychodynamic-interpersonal therapy plus a three-month follow-up session as part of a research project on very brief therapy (Barkham et al., 1999). Because Karen was seen within a research project, there was more information on her therapy than might typically be available in practice. Nevertheless, the main sources were audio recordings (subsequently transcribed) and clinical notes (used as a memory aid by Karen's therapist, who was a co-author). Thus, similar research could be done by many practitioners.

The assimilation model suggests that personality can be construed as a community of voices. Each voice is constructed from traces of interrelated experiences, such as those surrounding a significant person. The voice metaphor emphasizes the theoretical tenet that traces of experiences are active in people; when circumstances address the voice (e.g. because they are similar to the original experiences), the voice may speak and act. The community may include voices of parents, friends, skills, or life episodes that have been assimilated and hence are smoothly accessible as resources in daily life.

Problematic voices (e.g. representing traumatic events or discrepant action patterns), on the other hand, are unassimilated or incompletely assimilated, but may also emerge when addressed by circumstances, leading to emotional distress or maladaptive behaviours. The model describes the process by which problematic voices may be assimilated into the community during successful psychotherapy as a series of stages called the Assimilation of Problematic Experiences Sequence (APES; Stiles, 2002), which has been constructed and refined in a series of case studies. The stage names characterize the relation of the problematic voice to the community as (0) warded off/dissociated, (1) unwanted thoughts/avoidance, (2) vague, painful awareness/emergence, (3) problem statement/clarification, (4) understanding/insight, (5) application/working through, (6) problem solution/resource, or (7) mastery/integration, which are understood as points along a continuum. Clients may enter therapy with problems at any stage, and any movement along the continuum could be considered as progress.

As summarized in the report of the Karen case study:

> This study's contributions to the assimilation model included an elaboration of the concept of position as a manifestation of voice and a demonstration of how DSA [*Dialogical Sequence Analysis*] methodology can expose problematic patterns of interaction in very brief segments of therapeutic dialogue. This study showed how unassimilated problems may be enacted in microcosm from the very first moments of treatment. It also directed attention to a way a skillful therapist may work responsively in the ZPD [*zone of proximal development*], pressing ahead (in APES terms) on both process and content while monitoring the client and modulating when the client was not following. And it demonstrated the possibility of productive assimilation in very brief psychotherapy (Stiles et al., 2006, p. 419).

Position, voice, and the use of Dialogical Sequence Analysis

The case was chosen to explore the use of DSA (Leiman, 2002, 2004; Leiman & Stiles, 2001) for studying therapeutic assimilation. DSA is a set of theoretical concepts used for making sense of patterns embedded in sequences of utterances. It focuses on identifying and describing problematic positions and patterns as they emerge in therapeutic dialogue. These positions can be inferred from a client's words, intonation, and timing within relatively small segments of therapy dialogue, making it possible to study assimilation in smaller samples of dialogue than previously.

This integration of DSA with the assimilation model in the Karen case contributed several useful concepts, including the understanding that voices are manifested as momentary *positions*, that is stances that the person adopts in relation to events, things, other people, and aspects of self. Conversely, the positions a person takes may be understood as the observable manifestations of internal voices. This distinction between the observable momentary stance (position) and the underlying continuity (voice), which had not been explicit previously, makes possible more precise theoretical descriptions, for example,

> When people encounter the circumstances that trigger problematic voices, they may suddenly re-enact the problematic patterns, adopting positions that resemble those they were forced into during the prior, problematic events or adopted as an immediate response to such events. Unlike normal, appropriate changes of personal stance to things and events, which are accomplished smoothly, comfortably and voluntarily, shifts to problematic positions and patterns tend to be sudden, unexpected and involuntary. Attempts to integrate the problematic positions with the currently acceptable self, which is also positioned, can be acutely distressing (Stiles et al., 2006, p. 409).

Enactment of problems in microcosm

The very first exchange in Karen's therapy (four speaking turns each by client and therapist) enacted a dialogical pattern in which Karen (C) responded to her own potential vulnerability by adopting a controlling caretaker position in relation to the therapist (T):

C1: My voice is a bit croaky at the moment.
T2: Have you got a bug or something?
C3: I don't know what it is actually, if it's the change in the climate since I've been back from holiday, it might just be that I've picked something up.
T4: Oh right.
C5: Hope it's short-lived anyway.
T6: Mm. Yes, we're into the season now where we give people fans because it's . . .
C7: Yeah, do you want that off actually?
T8: No, it's fine, it's fine, it's up to you, it's comfortable.

In her first three turns (C1–C5), Karen seemed to take a position of apologizing for her croaky voice, calling the therapist into an understanding, considerate counter-position. At T6, the therapist responded to Karen's vulnerability and discomfort by referring to the electric fan and the season (it was summer, and the room could get hot). That is, he adopted a somewhat concerned, caring position.

Karen's response was surprising. At C7, she briefly acknowledged the therapist's concern ('yeah') and then expressed her concern about the therapist's comfort, in effect reversing roles to adopt a considerate position toward him. That is, she seemed to make an abrupt shift from her potentially vulnerable position (as a client and as slightly ill) to a stronger, more controlling caretaker position.

During the rest of the session Karen offered at least 16 instances, in various domains of her life, past and present, illustrating elements of a sequence in which she normally took a strong caretaker position towards her family, friends and co-workers, whereas if she allowed herself to become vulnerable, she was dismissed.

Therapeutic work in the Zone of Proximal Development

The ZPD is a concept proposed by Vygotsky (1978) and used in developmental psychology to refer to the region between what a child can achieve alone and what the child can achieve with adult assistance. It describes the child's capacity for intellectual growth and change. As applied to psychotherapy, the therapeutic ZPD can be understood as a region between the client's present APES level and the level the client can manifest in collaboration with the therapist (Leiman & Stiles, 2001). Thus, the therapeutic ZPD links the joint work by therapist and client with the client's internal development as formulated by the assimilation model.

Therapeutic work during Karen's first session explored component positions in the recurrent and maladaptive pattern, in which Karen stepped in to become a caretaker rather than allowing herself to become vulnerable. In the following early passage, the therapist tentatively suggested that Karen might be responding to something not yet directly available to her. In effect, he was testing the limits of Karen's ZPD and moving along the APES continuum from stating the problem towards an understanding of it (stage 3 to stage 4).

T42: Yes, sure. Let's, let's try and get into what it feels like to be taking someone's problems on board. What's that like?
C43: I feel a bit like initially, always initially, "oh don't worry, it's [T: "don't worry, I can . . ."] help you.
T44: "I can help you." There's a kind of feeling inside that you want to reach out and help. You want to?
C45: Oh yeah, I mean, I'm a very . . . I think 'cos I always feel strong, that when somebody else is feeling that they can't cope, I feel I've got enough strength for them to lean on me. And I allow them to lean and sometimes too far, to the point that I start to topple.

T46: So this business about being strong feels like it's something that you, you're not sure about. You're not sure how strong you really are inside, underneath.

C47: I think I've discovered I'm probably not as strong as I'd like to be, unfortunately [T: mhm].

At T44, the therapist introduced the term 'inside'. He used it again in combination with 'underneath' at T46. Karen accepted his suggestion of vulnerability as the underlying alternative to strength but emphasized that she was not happy about it. Her constructive use of this intervention suggests that this was within her ZPD.

During the second session, Karen reached a new understanding that could be characterized as an insight (APES stage 4). The therapist formulated Karen's caring position as exercising control through giving, which prevented Karen from meeting her own dependent needs. Karen responded by describing her wish to be able to relax control and be more dependent in her close relationships. The therapist's interventions seemed to stay slightly ahead of Karen, in APES terms, while remaining in the ZPD. This led shortly into a joint formulation that seemed to resonate deeply for Karen:

T97: Mm. Mm. There's, you've got other ways of, yeah, you've got, you've got a very well-developed repertoire of controlling, dominant, quite a pattern, which you can always fall back on in moments of frustration.

C98: But I don't like the results that come.

T99: No, no, you don't want to do that, but you can't help it.

C100: No, and that's what I'm trying, you've hit the nail on the head probably there. Not realizing it myself it probably is, it's, it's trying to be a partnership [T: mm-hm], trying to be a relationship, and yet for a lifetime I've been fighting that [T: mm-hm, mm-hm].

The expression 'you've hit the nail on the head' in C100 appeared to mark an insight centred on Karen's recognizing that her strong, controlling caretaker position was triggered maladaptively by her own feelings of neediness and vulnerability. Interestingly, this precisely described the pattern that was enacted in the very first exchange.

The therapist then repeated and elaborated Karen's conclusion, apparently seeking to consolidate the gain. He next advanced the topic within the ZPD, prompting Karen to link the pattern to her history and her hopes. In APES terms, this was work on moving from stage 4 (understanding/insight) to stage 5 (application/working through):

T103: So you're hoping, you're hoping for a different sort of relationship?

C104: Mm.

T105: [omitted text] So it's coming to terms with your own power, your own forcefulness and your own, your own history. And the fights, the battles that you're fighting, you know, that forceful you is fighting earlier battles I guess.

C106: Oh yeah definitely!

T107: It's going back to the story of your life.

C108: Yeah, yeah, from as long, well as long as I can remember.

T109: How awful that you need to be in control, you need to be . . .

C110: And I think that's why I've been very singular-minded, even though I have been in a marriage, I've been very independent [T: mm] and very self-centred I suppose, without even knowing that that's what I was.

From Karen's subsequent report in the follow-up session, it appeared that she used her new understanding to assimilate her problematic controlling side, giving her greater flexibility in her relationships and greater scope for meeting her own needs for care.

Assimilation in brief therapy

Karen's progress in therapy illustrated – and hence strengthened – the model's account of therapeutic progress across three of the eight APES stages: (3) problem statement/clarification, (4) understanding/insight, and (5) application/working through. There were suggestions that Karen was well prepared for therapy and that she had made APES progress between her assessment session (not studied) and her first therapy session. Karen's progress showed how substantive psychological change can occur in a small number of sessions and, conversely, how the assimilation model can contribute to an understanding of the process of change in such cases.

The observations in the Karen case offer only slight support to any one tenet of the assimilation model considered in isolation. The evidence for the usefulness of the DSA method and position/voice distinction, the enactment of core problems in microcosm, the nature of work in the ZPD, the systematic progression through parts of the APES, and the possibility of substantive assimilation in two sessions were all illustrated, but one could not claim any of these as solidly demonstrated as isolated conclusions on the basis of this one case. However, because these (and other) observations fit or expand the assimilation model, the study does, I suggest, yield an increment of confidence in the theory as a whole.

Conclusion

Theories are tools that practitioners use in their practice. Practitioners routinely witness people's pain, struggle, courage and joy in a depth and detail rarely possible in psychological laboratories or daily life. Theory-building case study research, I think, offers a way that these rich and valuable observations can be used as practice-based evidence and shared to improve future practice.

References

Agnew-Davies, R., Stiles, W.B., Hardy, G.E., Barkham, M. & Shapiro, D.A. (1998). Alliance structure assessed by the Agnew Relationship Measure (ARM). *British Journal of Clinical Psychology, 37*, 155–172.

Barkham, M., Mellor-Clark, J., Connell, J. & Cahill, J. (2006). A core approach to practice-based evidence: A brief history of the origins and applications of the CORE-OM and CORE System. *Counselling and Psychotherapy Research, 6*, 3–15.

Barkham, M., Shapiro, D.A., Hardy, G.E. & Rees, A. (1999). Psychotherapy in two-plus-one sessions: Outcomes of a randomized controlled trial of cognitive-behavioral and psychodynamic-interpersonal therapy for sub-syndromal depression. *Journal of Consulting and Clinical Psychology, 67*, 201–211.

Bond, T. (2004). *Ethical guidelines for researching counselling and psychotherapy.* Rugby, UK: British Association for Counselling and Psychotherapy.

Brinegar, M.G., Salvi, L.M., Stiles, W.B. & Greenberg, L.S. (2006). Building a meaning bridge: Therapeutic progress from problem formulation to understanding. *Journal of Counseling Psychology, 53*, 165–180.

Campbell, D.T. (1979). 'Degrees of freedom' and the case study. In T.D. Cook & C.S. Reichardt (eds.), *Qualitative and quantitative methods in evaluation research* (pp. 49–67). Beverley Hills, CA: Sage Publications.

Elliott, R. (2002). Hermeneutic single-case efficacy design. *Psychotherapy Research, 12*, 1–21.

Elliott, R. & Wexler, M.M. (1994). Measuring the impact of treatment sessions: The Session Impacts Scale. *Journal of Counseling Psychology, 41*, 166–174.

Elliott, R., Fischer, C. & Rennie, D. (1999). Evolving guidelines for publication of qualitative research studies in psychology and related fields. *British Journal of Clinical Psychology, 38*, 215–229.

Elliott, R., Slatick, E. & Urman, M. (2001). Qualitative change process research on psychotherapy: Alternative strategies. In J. Frommer & D.L. Rennie (eds.), *Qualitative psychotherapy research: Methods and methodology* (pp. 69–111). Lengerich, Germany: Pabst Science Publishers.

Horvath, A.O. & Greenberg, L.S. (1989). Development and validation of the Working Alliance Inventory. *Journal of Counseling Psychology, 36*, 223–233.

Humphreys, C.L., Rubin, J.S., Knudson, R.M. & Stiles, W.B. (2005). The assimilation of anger in a case of dissociative identity disorder. *Counselling Psychology Quarterly, 18*, 121–132.

Lambert, M.J., Morton, J.J., Hatfield, D., Harmon, C., Hamilton, S. et al. (2004). *Administration and scoring manual for the Outcome Questionnaire (OQ-45.2)*. Orem, UT: American Professional Credentialing Services.

Leiman, M. (2002). Toward semiotic dialogism. *Theory and Psychology, 12*, 221–235.

Leiman, M., (2004). Dialogical sequence analysis. In H.H. Hermans & G. Dimaggio (eds.), *The Dialogical Self in Psychotherapy* (pp. 255–269). London: Brunner-Routledge.

Leiman, M. & Stiles, W.B. (2001). Dialogical sequence analysis and the zone of proximal development as conceptual enhancements to the assimilation model: The case of Jan revisited. *Psychotherapy Research, 11*, 311–330.

Lincoln, Y.S. & Guba, E.G. (1985). *Naturalistic inquiry*. Beverly Hills, CA: Sage Publications.

Llewelyn, S.P. (1988). Psychological therapy as viewed by clients and therapists. *British Journal of Clinical Psychology, 27*, 223–237.

Osatuke, K., Glick, M.J., Stiles, W.B., Greenberg, L.S., Shapiro, D.A. et al. (2005). Temporal patterns of improvement in client-centred therapy and cognitive-behaviour therapy. *Counselling Psychology Quarterly, 18*, 95–108.

Peirce, C.S. (1965). *Collected papers of Charles Sanders Peirce*. Cambridge, MA: The Belknap Press of Harvard University Press.

Phillips, J.P.N. (1986). Shapiro Personal Questionnaire and generalized personal questionnaire techniques: A repeated measures individualized outcome measurement. In L.S. Greenberg & W.M. Pinsof (eds.), *The psychotherapeutic process: A research handbook* (pp. 557–589). New York: Guilford Press.

Rennie, D.L. (2000). Grounded theory methodology as methodological hermeneutics: Reconciling realism and relativism. *Theory & Psychology, 10*, 481–502.

Rosenwald, G.C. (1988). A theory of multiple case research. *Journal of Personality, 56*, 239–264.

Stiles, W.B. (1993). Quality control in qualitative research. *Clinical Psychology Review, 13*, 593–618.

Stiles, W.B. (2002). Assimilation of problematic experiences. In J.C. Norcross (ed.), *Psychotherapy relationships that work: Therapist contributions and responsiveness to patients* (pp. 357–365). New York: Oxford University Press.

Stiles, W.B. (2003). Qualitative research: Evaluating the process and the product. In S.P. Llewelyn & P. Kennedy (eds.), *Handbook of Clinical Health Psychology* (pp. 477–499). Chichester: John Wiley & Sons, Ltd.

Stiles, W.B. (2005). Case studies. In J.C. Norcross, L.E. Beutler & R.F. Levant (eds.), *Evidence-based practices in mental health: Debate and dialogue on the fundamental questions* (pp. 57–64). Washington, DC: American Psychological Association.

Stiles, W.B. (2006). Numbers can be enriching. *New Ideas in Psychology*, *24*, 252–262.

Stiles, W.B. (2007). Theory-building case studies of counselling and psychotherapy. *Counselling and Psychotherapy Research*, *7*, 122–127.

Stiles, W.B. (2009). Logical operations in theory-building case studies. *Pragmatic Case Studies in Psychotherapy*, *5*, 9–22. Available at: http://jrul.libraries.rutgers.edu/index.php/pcsp/article/view/973/2384

Stiles, W.B., Honos-Webb, L. & Surko, M. (1998). Responsiveness in psychotherapy. *Clinical Psychology: Science and Practice*, *5*, 439–458.

Stiles, W.B., Elliott, R., Llewelyn, S.P., Firth-Cozens, J.A., Margison, F.R. et al. (1990). Assimilation of problematic experiences by clients in psychotherapy. *Psychotherapy*, *27*, 411–420.

Stiles, W.B., Leiman, M., Shapiro, D.A., Hardy, G.E., Barkham, M. et al. (2006). What does the first exchange tell? Dialogical sequence analysis and assimilation in very brief therapy. *Psychotherapy Research*, *16*, 408–421.

Stiles, W.B., Reynolds, S., Hardy, G.E., Rees, A., Barkham, M. et al. (1994). Evaluation and description of psychotherapy sessions by clients using the Session Evaluation Questionnaire and the Session Impacts Scale. *Journal of Counseling Psychology*, *41*, 175–185.

Vygotsky, L. (1978). *Mind in society: The development of higher psychological processes.* Edited by M. Cole, V. John-Steiner, S. Scribner & E. Souberman. Cambridge, Mass: Harvard University Press.

5

Single Case Quantitative Methods for Practice-Based Evidence

Dean McMillan[1] and Stephen Morley[2]

[1] *Department of Health Sciences, University of York, UK,* [2] *Academic Unit of Psychiatry and Behavioural Sciences, University of Leeds, UK*

Introduction

Clinicians, clients and services need data that are both *rigorous* and *relevant* (Barkham & Mellor-Clark, 2000). Studies should be rigorous enough to be trustworthy; at the same time research must provide answers to questions that are relevant to each of these groups. Together these 'two Rs' are the defining features of practice-based evidence (Barkham & Mellor-Clark, 2000). The two, however, are often thought to be – perhaps often are – in a state of conflict (Parry, 2000). Evidence-based practice has a set of procedures designed to protect the methodological integrity of a study, which helps to ensure that the rigorousness criterion is met. Doubts persist, however, about the applicability of such research to routine clinical practice (Westen, Novotny & Thompson-Brenner, 2004). The very features of the research that protect the rigorousness criterion, such as the use of diagnostically pure samples, treatment manuals, and so on, are the same features that distance it from routine practice and, arguably, clinical relevance. Conversely, real-life research is often criticized as being so methodologically flawed as to be worthless (Borkovec et al., 2001). If the conclusions of a study are not to be trusted they cannot, by definition, be relevant to anyone. There is, then, a seemingly intractable problem: methodologically robust research, by its nature, has within it the seeds of irrelevancy; research that attempts to be relevant often fails because it is not rigorous, and without rigour there can be no relevance. The point of this chapter is to argue that the quantitative single case design is well placed to resolve this tension and in so doing it can go some way to meeting the twin demands of practice-based evidence.

Developing and Delivering Practice-Based Evidence   By Michael Barkham, Gillian E Hardy, and John Mellor-Clark   © 2010 John Wiley & Sons, Ltd

One of the problems for single case research is that it suffers from a lack of a widely accepted terminology to describe the basic design and its variants (Hayes, 1981; Hilliard, 1993). Many terms have been used to describe exactly the same type of design, while the same term has also been used to describe markedly different approaches. It is important, therefore, that we provide a clear definition of what we mean by the design, and we shall do so in detail later on. For the moment, we can define it briefly as the *repeated* collection of *quantifiable* (*numerical*) data on a *single clinical case*, typically involving *repeated measurement* over a *baseline* period (Morley, 2007). *Experimental manipulation* through some form of *randomization procedure* may or may not take place (Hilliard, 1993). Each of these characteristics is intended to help the researcher *rule out alternative explanations* for a finding (Morley, 2007). The main strategy for doing this is to focus on *within-subject variability* and to seek to understand and explain the causes of that variation (Barlow et al., 2008). Such an approach may or may not include replicating the design over several cases to form a *single case series* (Hilliard, 1993). Although we shall focus on quantitative approaches here, qualitative approaches can also be profitably applied to the single case design. The collection of rich, detailed qualitative information throughout the course of treatment can prove useful in helping to rule out alternative hypotheses (Elliott, 2002; Hilliard, 1993).

There are a number of texts that describe the principles of single case research along with the major design and analysis considerations (e.g. Barlow et al., 2008; Kazdin, 1982; Morley, 1996). Although we shall cover some of these issues here, anyone who is interested in conducting this type of research should consult one or more of these, which discuss these principles in more detail than we are able to do. Instead, the aim of this chapter is to answer three questions. First, what makes the design potentially so useful for practice-based evidence? Secondly, why, given these advantages, is it not more widely used? Thirdly, what changes need to be made to the design to make it a useful strategy in practice-based evidence? We will suggest that changes do need to be made to the research ideal of the single case design, but with these in place the design can be simultaneously rigorous and relevant.

The relevance of single case designs for practice-based evidence

There is perhaps one main reason that the single case design is a useful tool for practice-based evidence. The reason is obvious, but nonetheless important: the level of analysis is primarily the individual client (Kazdin, 1982; Morley, 1996). This characteristic fits in with the natural focus and concern of the clinician (Morley, 1996). This is in contrast to the majority of commonly used research methods, which rely on a between-group design and inference at the group level. There are other advantages of the single case design, but many of these derive directly or indirectly from this simple fact.

The close match between what many clinicians spend much of their time doing (providing treatment to individual clients) and what the single case design involves (detailed analysis of a single case) means that the design has a better chance than many research methods of being carried out in standard clinical practice. Most clinical settings do not have the funding, infrastructure or technical assistance to conduct, for example, a randomized controlled trial (RCT). The funding and infrastructure needed to carry out single case research is much more modest, because what constitutes single case research is close to normal clinical practice. Although some degree of methodological knowledge is needed, most of the key principles are fairly straightforward and are well described in a number of texts (e.g. Barlow et al., 2008; Kazdin, 1982; Morley, 1996). With some trial-and-error learning, it is likely that any clinician could master the method. Furthermore, piloting can take place on single cases, so if changes need to be made then only one case of data is lost, rather than the substantially larger number in any between-group design that does not work first time around.

Aside from this practical advantage, the other strength of the design is the type of questions it can answer, questions that have a particular clinical relevance. Evidence-based practice is primarily concerned with establishing treatment efficacy. The question of efficacy is no doubt important, but is only one among several of relevance to clinicians. These include questions about processes (e.g. 'Why did the client improve?' 'What part of treatment was responsible for the change?') and theory, whether these are the mini-theories of a case formulation or predictions derived from large-scale psychological theories (e.g. the assimilation model, the cognitive formulation of panic) (Morley, 2007). Improving treatment and protecting the integrity of treatments offered to clients depends as much on answering these questions as it does on answering the global question of treatment efficacy (Greenberg & Watson, 2006). If we know why a treatment works rather than just that it works, we have information that may help the clinician to think through the questions that he or she faces every day in the clinic (e.g. 'How should I modify this treatment to make it better fit the needs of this client?', 'Why is this treatment not working for this client?'). These questions, particularly ones concerning therapy process, may be best answered by adopting a within-individual strategy (Hilliard, 1993), because such questions are intrinsically about behaviour within the individual dyad of therapist and client. In contrast, cross-sectional associations derived from group-level data can provide at best only indirect evidence of intrasubject variability (Hilliard, 1993). Single case research, with its focus on repeated measurement, within-individual variability and the causes of that variability, is well placed to answer these process questions.

This is not to say that single case research has little to offer research on efficacy and effectiveness. The design, if correctly conducted and replicated, is considered sufficiently rigorous to establish the criteria for an empirically validated treatment (Chambless et al., 1998). However, perhaps the most useful contribution the single case design can make to efficacy-effectiveness research is its ability to answer questions that are clinically relevant variants on those of evidence-based practice (e.g. 'Does this evidence-based treatment work for this particular type of client, who differs in some way from the sample characteristics of the evidence base?, 'Does this treatment, which as yet does not have an extensive evidence base, work?'). Clinicians and researchers alike often express concerns about the generalizability of findings based on an evidence-based practice model to routine settings. The single case design provides a feasible method by which the generalizability of evidence-based practice can be assessed. Perhaps more importantly, the design provides an ethical method for selecting a treatment other than the one suggested by the evidence base.

It remains unclear under what circumstances the clinician should decide to ignore a well-established evidence-based treatment for another option. It is clear, however, that generalizing from an evidence base, such as a series of randomized trials, to an individual client can be uniquely difficult in psychology. The logic of generalization rests on an inductive inference: if a group of clients with characteristics A, B, C and D (e.g. the diagnostic criteria for Generalized Anxiety Disorder) are effectively treated with intervention X in these trials, then on the basis of induction a client presenting in clinic with A, B, C and D also has a good chance of doing well with intervention X. The problem for this type of reasoning is that the client will also have characteristics E, F, G and so on, and it is unclear how these will moderate the relationship between a particular treatment and outcome.

While this is a problem for other life sciences such as medicine, it is particularly difficult for psychotherapy research. Psychology lacks a well-corroborated theory that specifies which variables out of the vast list of possibilities will alter treatment-outcome relationships and under what circumstances. This may well be because these relationships are as likely to be under the sway of idiographic as nomothetic laws (Meehl, 1978); so individual differences and combination of differences (the Es, Fs and Gs) may substantially moderate that relationship in ways that are hard to detail a priori. This suggests a need to regularly ignore the precepts of the evidence base. However, the lack of constraint imposed by a well-corroborated theory can combine dangerously with the ease of generating plausible-sounding explanations in psychology (Meehl, 1990). If a group of mental-health practitioners were to be given a pen portrait consisting of a handful of client characteristics (e.g. liking for structure, distant relationship with father, recent job loss), it would not take long to generate a half-dozen or so plausible reasons that intervention X would be inappropriate given these characteristics. However, with the same lack of effort a half-dozen counter-arguments could be generated suggesting that intervention X would be appropriate because the characteristic would make precisely no difference to the treatment outcome or even improve it.[1] The facility with which plausible-sounding arguments – especially contradictory ones – can be generated in psychology means that such reasons may not be a sufficient basis on which to reject the evidence base. The single case design provides a solution to these difficulties. We would argue that if a coherent, theoretically-framed argument can be offered suggesting that the alternative option should perform as well as or better than the evidence-based one, it is defensible to offer that treatment with one proviso: a detailed assessment of its effectiveness should be made. The single case design provides a rigorous method for making that assessment for the individual client. If the design was to be considered an ethical requirement of using a non-evidence-based treatment, our knowledge of what works under which circumstances and why would increase substantially. Fishman (2005) argues compellingly that a database of such evidence, accessible to clinicians, would constitute an important research innovation in psychotherapy.

Despite these advantages and the recurrent calls to make the single case design a bedrock of psychological research (e.g. Blampied, 2000; Hayes, 1981; Hilliard, 1993), the method still appears to be little used in clinical settings. There is, in fact, evidence that the publication of single case research has declined over the last quarter of a century (Peck, 2007). There are likely to be several reasons for this state of affairs (Hayes, 1981), but we suspect a main one is that the research ideal described in the classic texts on the design seems a far cry from what is possible in the real world. It may help, then, to provide an outline of this research ideal as a starting point for working out why the design is not more widely used.

The methodology of the single case design: the research ideal

Single case research and plausible alternative explanations

In terms of the research ideal, the single case design is a method of systematically dealing with alternative explanations to the research hypothesis that one variable (e.g. a therapeutic intervention) is responsible for change in another (e.g. symptoms) for an individual case (e.g. a client in therapy) (Morley, 2007). Put another way, the aim is to identify and rule out potential threats to validity. A useful framework for assessing the extent to which a design can deal with these threats is the one proposed by Cook and Campbell (1979). The framework

---

[1] This is a variation of Meehl's 'coffee and Danish problem' (see p. 228, Meehl, 1990).

identifies four broad categories of validity of which one, internal validity, is a particular focus of the single case design (Morley, 2007). All four, however, must typically be dealt with to meet the criteria of the research ideal. Table 5.1 summarizes the four types of validity along with examples of common threats. Tate et al. (2008) have produced a rating scale that can be used to evaluate how well a particular single case study deals with various threats to validity.

Basic features of the single case design

Over the 50 years of development of the single case method, researchers have sought to codify rules about how best to deal with plausible alternatives to the research hypothesis (Barlow et al., 2008). Three of the most important strategies for achieving this are repeated measurement, the baseline and the experimental manipulation of variables.

Repeated measurement

Repeated measurement is the defining feature of the single case design. It involves frequent measurement of key variables, including outcomes (e.g. anxiety, depression), process or theory variables (e.g. therapeutic alliance, beliefs about the uncontrollability of worry), and potential confounds (e.g. positive and negative life events unrelated to therapy). The frequency with which the measures are taken may differ from study to study and depends on the research aims. Measurement may take place on a weekly or daily basis and last several months; alternatively, an entire single case design could take place during a single session of treatment with measures taken every minute. The repeated measures provide data on the variation across time in the outcome. With this information the search can begin for the causes of that variation. In essence the researcher asks to what extent the variation is consistent with the hypothesis or one of the plausible alternatives.

Baseline

A baseline involves taking repeated measures of the outcome of interest before an intervention occurs so that the 'natural course' of the outcome is known (Barlow et al., 2008). For example, a client with Obsessive-Compulsive Disorder may be asked to keep a daily record of time spent engaged in rituals for a number of weeks before treatment begins. The reason for doing this is to help to establish that the intervention is responsible for a change in the outcome by providing a standard by which to judge any changes. In terms of the research ideal long baselines are considered helpful. The researcher wants to ensure that the judgment about a change in the outcome is as unambiguous as possible, and the best chance of doing so is to allow the pattern of the natural course

Table 5.1 Four types of validity (Cook & Campbell, 1979)

Type of validity	*Description*	*Examples of threats to validity*
Internal	Is there a causal relationship from one variable to another?	History: Events occurring in time other than treatment account for the change Maturation: Processes occurring within the individual, unconnected to treatment, account for the change Testing: The observed change is due to the number of times a measure is completed rather than a genuine change Instrumentation: The observed change is due to an alteration in the measurement instrument over time Regression to the mean: Reversion of scores towards the mean account for the observed change in the outcome
Statistical conclusion	Is the conclusion that there is or is not an association between the variables correct?	Use of an inappropriate statistical test Insufficient statistical power to detect an association Unreliable measures
Construct	To what extent are the operations in the study that are designed to index particular constructs (e.g. client completes a self-report measure of depression) accurate indexes of those constructs (e.g. depression)? To what extent can those operations be understood in terms of other confounding constructs?	The measure used to index a particular construct inadequately samples important features of that construct. Researcher or therapist expectancies bias the data obtained. The client completes a measure in a particular way to please the therapist or researcher.
External	Is the observed causal relationship generalizable across populations, settings and times?	Particular characteristics of the therapist (e.g. extremely experienced) limit generalizability to other therapists. Particular characteristics of the client (e.g. no co-morbidity) limit generalizability to other clients (e.g. presence of co-morbid problems).

to emerge before the intervention is introduced. If there is a marked change in that pattern after the intervention, we can begin to have some confidence that it was responsible for the change.

The type of pattern that emerges also determines the length of the baseline. As a general rule, a stable baseline can be shorter than a highly variable one. If during the baseline the outcome variable does not change substantially, but after the intervention a marked shift is seen, then this helps to build a case that the intervention was responsible for the change. In contrast, if the baseline is highly variable and lacks an obvious pattern, it may be difficult to detect a change in outcome that is due to the intervention. The rule here – at least in terms of the research ideal – would be to extend the baseline until a clearer pattern emerges.

Other patterns, such as a worsening or improving baseline, may occur and these also have implications for the length of this phase. If the outcome becomes worse during the baseline (e.g. a week on week increase in depressive symptoms), but after the intervention this trend reverses, then this helps establish the role of the intervention. However, even here there are complications. A sudden, dramatic worsening of symptoms may represent a temporary change that would dissipate regardless of any intervention (Morley, 2007). If an intervention were to be introduced at this point it leaves open the possibility that any improvement is due to this alternative rather than the treatment. The research ideal would caution against an introduction of treatment until the symptoms were stable. An improving baseline is also problematic, because any subsequent improvement during the intervention phase may have occurred whether or not the intervention was introduced. The recommendation here – again, for the research ideal – is to extend the baseline until the improvement levels off.

Experimental manipulation

Experimental manipulation involves the introduction or withdrawal at random of a variable (e.g. a particular treatment strategy) so that its effect on another variable (e.g. symptoms) can be assessed. As in an RCT, the play of chance introduced by randomization helps to reduce the number of plausible alternative explanations of any observed relationship between two variables, and, therefore, helps to increase our confidence that the intervention was responsible for the change in symptoms. The randomization strategy, however, often differs from that used in an RCT. Randomization in an RCT typically uses a between-group allocation: each participant is randomly allocated to one group (e.g. treatment) or another (e.g. wait list). In single case research randomization often occurs within a participant: for a single case, periods of time are randomly allocated to the presence or absence of treatment or to different types of treatment. Although the research ideal does not demand experimental manipulation, it is nevertheless considered an asset because of the effectiveness with which it rules out plausible alternatives. As in the between-group design, randomization in single case research is seen as the ultimate arbiter of causal claims.

Types of single case design

From these basic principles comes a remarkable variety of single case designs. We will limit our discussion to six main types, though it should be recognized that each of these can be elaborated and extended to produce further designs.

The AB design

The AB design is the most basic approach to single case research. It involves a baseline period (termed A), during which measures are taken repeatedly, and a subsequent intervention period (termed B), during which measurement continues. Figure 5.1 provides an example of such a design taken from a study that examined the effectiveness of cognitive analytic therapy for a client presenting with Dissociative Identity Disorder (Kellett, 2005). Six daily measures of key symptoms were taken over baseline (weeks 1 to 5), treatment (weeks 5 to 30)

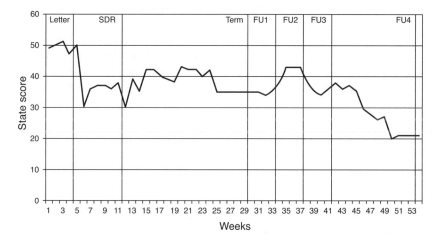

Figure 5.1 An AB design to examine the effectiveness of cognitive analytic therapy for Dissociative Identity Disorder

Note: Baseline data gathered during weeks 1 to 5. Therapeutic letter given at week 5. The sequential diagrammatic reformulation (SDR) took place between weeks 5 and 12. Therapy terminated (Term) at week 30. Follow-up appointments were offered at 1, 2, 3 and 6 months after the end of therapy (FU1, FU2, FU3, FU4). *Source*: Kellett, S., The treatment of Dissociative Identity Disorder with Cognitive Analytic Therapy: Experimental evidence of sudden gains, *Journal of Trauma and Dissociation*, 6, 55–81. Taylor & Francis Group, 2005.

and follow-up (weeks 30 to 53), of which one, depersonalization, is graphed in Figure 5.1.

The AB design differs from the simple pre-post design, in which the clinician takes a measure of the outcome variables (e.g. dissociative symptoms) once before an intervention and then repeats the measures at the end of treatment. In the pre-post design it is possible that factors other than treatment were responsible for any observed improvement in symptoms. The client, for instance, may have been on an improving trajectory and would have improved regardless of the intervention (maturation). Alternatively, an event external to therapy may have occurred during treatment and this may account for the improvement in symptoms (history). The addition of repeated measurements during phases A and B can help to rule out some of these alternatives, at least to some extent. For example, a steady baseline would cast doubt on the alternative explanation that the client was already on an improving trajectory. If an external, positive event occurs during therapy (e.g. meeting a new partner) and the timing of that event is known, the repeated measures taken across treatment can be examined to assess the relationship between the intervention, the external event and the change in symptoms. If a substantial improvement in symptoms occurred after the start of treatment, but before the event, then this rules out the possibility that the positive event is entirely responsible for improvement seen by the end of treatment.

Although the AB design is an advance on the pre-post design, it is in terms of the research ideal the weakest strategy, because it leaves open so many alternative explanations for any observed improvement in symptoms. For example, were a positive event to have occurred at the same time as the introduction of treatment, this may account for symptom change. Furthermore, even with a lengthy baseline, it remains possible that the natural course of the symptoms would have improved at some point and that point may, by chance, be during the treatment period.

The withdrawal design

An extension of the AB design is to withdraw the intervention so that there is a return to a baseline condition (i.e. ABA), a strategy that can be further elaborated to include one or more additional withdrawals (e.g. ABABAB). If the outcome variable improves each time condition B is introduced, but returns to baseline levels during the A phase, then this strengthens the leverage on any causal claims we want to make about the treatment. For example, it helps to rule out the alternative explanation that improvement was taking place anyway, regardless of the introduction of treatment, because the design establishes that improvement occurs only when the intervention is in place. Randomization may be introduced in this design by randomly varying the lengths of each phase. This helps to rule out certain threats to validity, such as the possibility

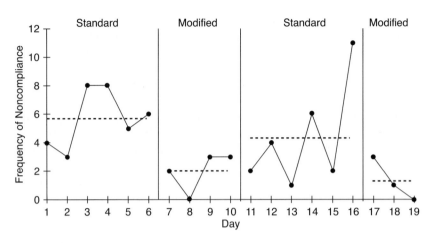

Figure 5.2 A withdrawal design (ABAB) comparing standard and modified treatment for a 12-year-old boy showing disruptive behaviour in a residential setting. *Source*: Field, C.E. et al., Using functional assessment and experimental functional analysis to individualize treatment for adolescents in a residential care setting, *Clinical Case Studies*, 3, 25–36. Sage Publications, 2004

that variation in symptoms shows a consistent cyclical effect that co-occurs with but is independent of the introduction and withdrawal of treatment.

Field, Nash, Handwerk and Friman (2004) provide an example of such a design in a single case study of a 12-year-old boy in residential care with a history of disruptive behaviour, including non-compliance, self-injury and altercations with peers. A functional analysis of the non-compliance behaviour led the authors to hypothesize that staff members and peers were inadvertently reinforcing it by providing increased attention subsequent to the behaviour. The authors used an ABAB design to compare the standard programme that was in place at the time with a modified programme designed to provide an increase in positive attention for compliant behaviour, which was operationalized as a minimum of 12 positive interactions for every 1 negative interaction. Figure 5.2 summarizes the results of the study. The mean daily rates of non-compliance, indicated by the dotted lines, provide some evidence that when the modified programme was in place the rates of the behaviour decreased.

The ABC design with counterbalancing

A further variation of the AB design is to introduce a different intervention in a C phase of treatment, so that the two interventions can be compared. A counterbalancing procedure is also used: half of the participants are randomly assigned to receive B then C; the other participants receive C then B. The strategy of counterbalancing the order of the two treatments helps to rule out several plausible alternative explanations. For example, greater improvement may occur at certain points in the treatment regardless of which treatment technique is used. Another possibility is that the second intervention may be more effective than the first one only because it is preceded by the first. Counterbalancing allows the researcher to examine these possibilities.

Vlaeyen et al. (2001) used a counterbalanced ABC design to compare the effectiveness of two different treatment techniques in altering pain-related fears in people with chronic back pain. One strategy, graded exposure in vivo, involved a series of behavioural tests in which irrational expectations were challenged. The second, graded activity, involved the client increasing activity levels according to a pre-arranged quota. The results of the study are summarized in Figure 5.3

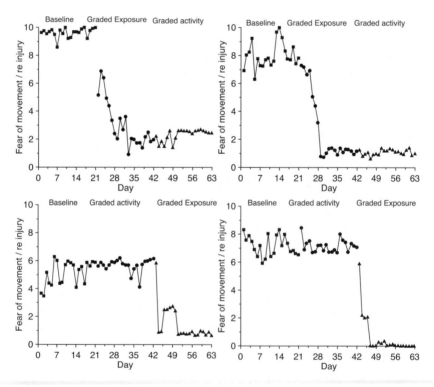

Figure 5.3 A counterbalanced ABC design comparing the effects of two treatment strategies on fear of movement/re-injury (0–10 visual analogue scale) measured on a daily basis (baseline = 0–21 days; first condition = 22–42 days; second condition = 43–63 days). *Source:* Vlaeyen, J.W.S. et al., Graded exposure in vivo in the treatment of pain-related fears: A replicated single-case experimental design in four patients with chronic low back pain, *Behaviour Research and Therapy*, *39*, 151–166. Elsevier, 2001

which illustrates that changes in the fear of movement/re-injury occurred only when graded exposure was introduced.

The multiple-baseline design

This design involves the use of several baselines. Each baseline is extended for varying lengths of time so that each intervention starts at different points. In some designs the baselines all apply to one person. There may, for instance, be four interventions for four separate target behaviours. All of the targets behaviours would be repeatedly measured for a period of time and then the interventions would be introduced one at a time. Alternatively, there may be a single target behaviour for a client, but the intervention would be introduced sequentially in different settings (e.g. different classes in school). The use of multiple baselines can also be applied across several clients. Here the same outcome is examined for each client, but the length of baseline differs. Multiple baseline designs are useful strategies for making inferences about the effects of an intervention when it may be difficult or impossible to withdraw the treatment. If change in the outcome is seen when the intervention is introduced, but the other baselines remain stable, this reduces the number of plausible alternatives that could account for the observed changes in outcome.

Different randomization strategies can be used with the multiple-baseline design. One possibility is for the researcher to pre-determine the length of each baseline and then randomly assign the target behaviours, settings or participants to them. For example, three participants could be randomly assigned to baselines of 4, 6 or 8 weeks. The alternative is to randomly determine the length of each baseline separately for each target behaviour, setting or participant. Three participants, for instance, could each have a minimum of a two-week baseline, with measures taken daily, after which the starting point for the intervention would be determined separately and at random for each participant.

Figure 5.4 gives an example of a multiple-baseline design across three clients in a study that sought to evaluate a version of cognitive behaviour therapy for Post-traumatic Stress Disorder with Cambodian refugees (Hinton et al., 2006). The treatment was designed to be culturally sensitive and included a specific target on neck-focused panic attacks, which the authors suggest is a common form of presentation for this refugee community. Weekly measures included the Neck-Focused Flashback Severity Scale (N-FFS) and the Neck-Focused Panic Attack Severity Scale (N-PASS). Treatment was introduced sequentially for the three clients at weeks 8, 14 and 20.

The changing criterion design

Another strategy that reduces the number of plausible alternative explanations without the need to withdraw treatment is the changing criterion design.

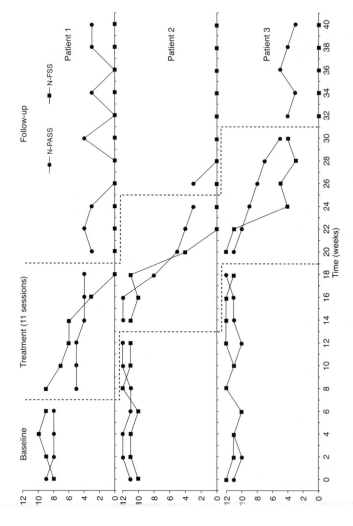

Figure 5.4 A multiple-baseline design examining the effectiveness of cognitive behaviour therapy for Cambodian refugees with Post-traumatic Stress Disorder

Note: N-PASS = Neck-Focused Panic-Attack Severity Scale; N-FSS = Neck-Focused Flashback Severity Scale. *Source:* Hinton, D.E. et al., Somatic-focused therapy for traumatized refugees: Treating Post-traumatic Stress Disorder and comorbid neck-focused panic attacks among Cambodian refugees, *Psychotherapy: Theory, Research, Practice, Training, 43*, 491–505. American Psychological Association, 2006

In this approach after a baseline phase several levels of an intervention are introduced in a stepwise fashion. The design comes from an operant paradigm in which the occurrence of a reinforcer is contingent on behaviour occurring at a pre-specified frequency. Once the behaviour meets the target and has shown sufficient stability, a new target is set and the sequence repeated.

Although the criterion is usually linked to a reinforcer, the design could be used outside of a behavioural approach. Morley (1996) gives the hypothetical example of varying the amounts of accurate empathy in session with a client and examining the relationship to depth of self-exploration. A study by Freeston (2001) used a changing criterion design that was not explicitly linked to a reinforcement schedule in the treatment of a 14-year-old male with Obsessive-Compulsive Disorder. The client had a variety of cleaning rituals, including brushing his teeth in the evening for over 11 minutes. Cleaning during the morning was not excessive, but in the evening the client felt compelled to continue brushing until he had a sensation of perfectly clean teeth. The changing criterion design involved gradually decreasing the length of time that the client brushed his teeth in the evening with the aid of a timer. Figure 5.5 summarizes the results of the intervention and indicates the final target of four minutes was

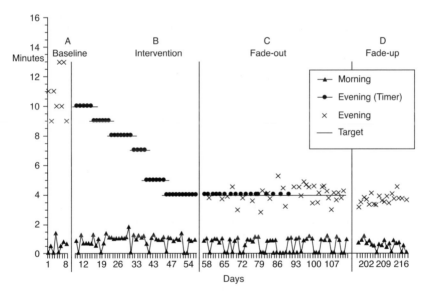

Figure 5.5   A changing criterion design to reduce the duration of evening teeth-brushing in a 14-year-old male with Obsessive-Compulsive Disorder. *Source:* Freeston, M.H., Cognitive-behavioural treatment of a 14-year-old teenager with Obsessive-Compulsive Disorder, *Behavioural and Cognitive Psychotherapy, 29,* 71–84. Cambridge University Press, 2001

maintained during a phase in which the timer was gradually withdrawn and subsequently during a follow-up period.

Morley (1996) provides a number of guidelines for the use of the design. The more steps that are used the less likely it is that an apparent link between changes in behaviour and changes in criterion are related by chance alone. It also helps to vary the length of the phases and the magnitude of changes in criterion for the same reason. Finally, it may also be worthwhile considering whether the direction of the criterion can be reversed to provide additional evidence of the controlling effect of the criterion on the behaviour. This may, of course, be ethically problematic if the behaviour is considered undesirable.

The alternating treatment design

The alternating treatment design (ATD) compares two or more treatments in the same person by alternating between those interventions at random. Masuda et al. (2004) used an ATD to compare the effects of a cognitive-defusion strategy and a thought-control strategy on measures of discomfort and believability in a negative thought. Each one of four clients received three 30-second phases of the two conditions, with the order of the phases decided at random. Figure 5.6 summarizes the results of this study. The act of randomly switching between treatments is a potentially powerful method of limiting alternative explanations, but careful planning is needed. The length of each phase must be sufficient to ensure that the effect of the treatment during the phase can be detected. It may also be necessary to introduce strategies to reduce carry-over effects of one treatment on a subsequent treatment phase such as the use of gaps to separate the different treatments.

Measurement and analysis in single case designs

As a consequence of the focus on the single client and the use of repeated measurement for that client, the type of measurement in single case research differs from that in traditional between-group designs (Morley, 2007). While between-group approaches rely on standardized instruments, in single case research a combination of standardized and non-standardized measures is used. There are practical and theoretical reasons for this. The essence of single case research, repeated measurement, may make it impossible to use many common standardized instruments, because they are not validated for use with such frequency. However, the use of non-standardized measures also allows the clinician to develop a tailor-made method assessing the particular symptoms and so forth of the individual client, which is in keeping with the general ethos of single case research. Standardized measures are also used in single case research to provide

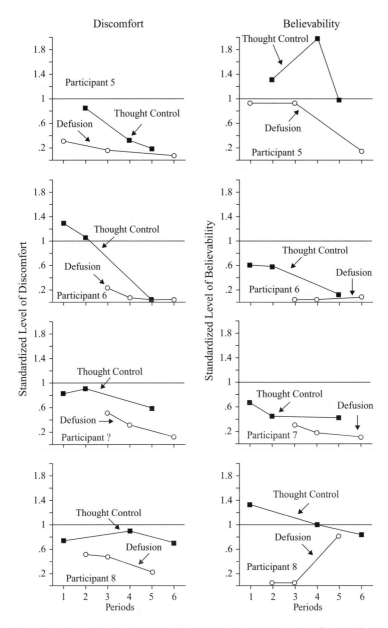

Figure 5.6 An alternating treatment design comparing cognitive-defusion (three 30-second phases) and thought-control strategies (three 30-second phases) on discomfort and believability of negative thoughts. *Source:* Masuda, A. et al., Cognitive defusion and self-relevant negative thoughts: Examining the impact of a ninety year old technique, *Behaviour Research and Therapy*, *42*, 477–485. Elsevier, 2004

corroborative evidence for changes detected by the non-standardized measures and to provide a 'common language' (Fishman, 2005) for communication of findings across studies, but the frequency of measurement will be substantially less (e.g. pre-treatment, mid-treatment, post-treatment, follow-up). There may also be reasons to add an extra layer of measurement: uniform non-standardized measures that, rather than being tailor-made measures for a particular client, ask the same questions of different clients. These can be given to different clients on a repeated basis, so that a comparison of the repeated-measures data can be made across clients.

Historically single case researchers have tended to eschew statistical analysis in favour of visual analysis of graphed data (Kratochwill & Brody, 1978). The argument of the proponents of this approach is straightforward: if you cannot see an effect with your eyes when you plot the data, it is not there. A statistically significant effect in the absence of a clear visual one only proves the adage that statistical and clinical significance are different beasts. There are, however, a number of limitations of visual analysis, such as an increased risk of type I errors, characteristics of the data and presentation distorting the judgment of raters, and poor inter-rater reliability (Onghena & Edgington, 2005). This suggests a need to supplement graphical analysis with some form of statistical approach, but many familiar statistical techniques, such as t-tests, are inappropriate for repeated-measures data because of the problem of serial dependency (Onghena & Edgington, 2005). Alternatives are available, however, such as interrupted time-series analysis or other modelling techniques (Onghena & Edgington, 2005).

Problems in applying the research ideal to standard clinical practice

The research ideal that we have described may not immediately seem to hold the answer to the tension between rigour and relevance in psychotherapeutic research. The design is certainly rigorous, but it may seem applicable to only a narrow range of interventions, mainly, perhaps exclusively, behavioural ones. The design undoubtedly bears the imprimatur of its behavioural heritage, which has led some to question whether the approach has applicability to other therapeutic approaches (Hill, 2006). This problem aside, any real-world clinician reading the description of the research ideal may spot a number of pragmatic problems that may substantially limit the applicability of the design. If we are to generate a single case methodology that is both rigorous and relevant, we need to identify the reasons that endanger the relevance of the strategy to the real world of clinical practice.

Applying a behavioural methodology to non-behavioural interventions

The characteristics of behavioural treatments

There are several features of behavioural treatments that make them suitable candidates for single case research, many of which are lacking from other therapeutic approaches (Hilliard, 1993). A behavioural model locates the independent variable in environmental contingencies. Changes in these contingencies can bring about a rapid shift in behaviour. A sudden and dramatic alteration in an outcome variable shortly after the introduction of the intervention helps build a case that the intervention rather than some alternative was responsible for the observed change.

Behavioural interventions are often also capable of being withdrawn. If environmental contingencies control a particular behaviour, then reversing the contingencies back to the original state should also reverse the behaviour back to its original state. As discussed above, the withdrawal design is a particularly powerful method of establishing a causal relationship between one variable and the other. In addition, both the environmental contingencies and the outcome of interest are often fairly easy to observe. For example, in the ABAB study discussed above (Field et al., 2004; see Figure 5.2) it would be a straightforward matter to establish whether the modified treatment strategy was in place, because it was clearly operationalized in behavioural terms (12 positive interactions for every 1 negative interaction). The definition of the outcome, the adolescent's non-compliance, is also reasonably easy to operationalize as particular instances of behaviour. This makes it reasonably straightforward to establish whether the intended manipulation occurred and whether it brought about a shift in the outcome variable. Finally, with behavioural interventions it is often possible to identify a discrete treatment strategy and to examine its relationship to an outcome in isolation. This fits neatly with the logic of experimentation, in which one variable and one variable only is manipulated while all others are held constant. Many non-behavioural treatments lack these characteristics. This leads to some difficulties when clinicians and researchers want to apply the design outside of the traditional behavioural field.

The characteristics of non-behavioural treatments

One of the most striking features of many psychological treatments is their complexity. A treatment is likely to consist of several components, all of which are presumed to be active in some way. Each of these active components may be hypothesized to operate on the outcome through more than one mechanism, and these components and their respective mechanisms may interact across time to influence the outcome. Furthermore, the effect of a particular therapeutic action may depend crucially on the context in which it occurs, and these relevant contextual variables are likely to be large in number: client or therapist characteristics, the history of the therapeutic relationship, what has occurred before in treatment, what is currently occurring outside treatment, and so on. Responsivity adds a further layer of complexity (Stiles, Honos-Webb & Surko, 1998). Therapist interventions are not shot 'ballistically' at a client, regardless of the client's response. Instead there is a moment-by-moment unfolding of interaction, in which both the therapist and client seek to adjust their behaviour on the basis of the other's response. These complex, context-dependent, responsive interventions do not fit neatly with the strictures of the single case research ideal. The manipulation of one variable in isolation typically means freeing it from the contextual variables that would hinder clear interpretation, but may be crucial to the observed relationship. The introduction of the variable would also be controlled, rather than responsive, to better ensure that it is clear exactly what it was that had the effect.

The nature of symptom change in many non-behavioural treatments leads to further difficulties. Change often takes place gradually and unsteadily. Some weeks symptoms may be worse and some better; only over the course of treatment, perhaps not until the end, can a pattern of improvement be discerned. Causal inferences under these circumstances can be difficult relative to a sudden and dramatic shift in the outcome variable. This also has implications for the analysis strategy. While reliance on visual analysis can be problematic for behavioural treatments, it will be even more so for non-behavioural ones, because of the likely absence of sudden and dramatic shifts and substantial within-phase variability. However, many of the statistical techniques that are appropriate for repeated-measures data, such as interrupted time-series analysis, are complex, require specialist statistical knowledge, and tend to be unfamiliar to clinicians. Furthermore, these analysis strategies typically require a large number of measurement points (greater than 50), which may be difficult to achieve in routine settings.

Although symptom change may be unsteady and variable in non-behavioural treatments, once change has taken place it tends not to be easily reversible. The aim of psychological treatment, after all, is to help the client to bring about a permanent or at least reasonably durable re-organization in some form of system (e.g. cognitive, interpersonal). The withdrawal design, one of the most powerful strategies for inferring a causal relationship, therefore becomes redundant for many psychological treatments.

Practical problems

Regardless of the difficulties of applying a behavioural method to non-behavioural treatments, any therapist working in a reasonably typical clinical setting is likely to identify a number of practical problems with the single case research ideal. A lengthy baseline, for instance, may help to rule out certain plausible alternative explanations, but may be difficult to organize in routine clinical practice, requiring, as it does, a further delay in treatment for someone who may have already spent several months on a waiting list. The clinician and client may also need to meet before the start of treatment so that baseline data can be collected. This may inconvenience the client while also decreasing the number of 'therapeutic hours' in the clinician's working week. The research ideal also requires a combination of measurement systems (e.g. standardized, individual non-standardized, uniform non-standardized), the measurement of several domains (e.g. outcomes, processes, potential confounds), and, crucially, repeated measurement. This may also place an unacceptable burden on the client and clinician. For example, the client must find time on a weekly or daily basis to complete the various measures. Experimental manipulation may also be difficult in standard clinical practice. Although one of the main strategies for ruling out plausible alternative explanations, it may interfere with the primary aim of clinical work – to help a client with his or her difficulties. For example, randomization in an alternating treatment design neatly rules out several threats to validity, but may be confusing for the client and, therefore, of questionable clinical utility.

Modifying the research ideal for practice-based evidence

It may not be feasible to make the research ideal work in routine practice for the types of complex interventions typically used in those settings. However, if some changes are made to the design, a workable compromise between rigour and relevance is possible. This requires some methodological concessions: some of the strongest designs, for example, will rarely be used, while other designs will need to be altered to fit clinical realities. With these changes in place the single case method can become a useful strategy for practice-based evidence.

Expanding the AB design

The AB design will often be the most appropriate choice for practice-based evidence, because it remains the closest to standard practice. Although in comparison to the other single case designs it may be the weakest, repeated measurement as part of an AB strategy can be combined with other sources of information to help build evidence for a treatment effect. This may be a particularly important strategy when the design is used to assess non-behavioural treatments, because many of the characteristics of these treatments, such as the lack of sudden and dramatic changes in symptoms, make the AB method difficult to interpret without additional corroborative evidence. Elliott (2002) in his description of the Hermeneutic Single Case Efficacy Design (HSCED) provides the most detailed exposition to date of such an approach. The HSCED retains the principle of the AB research ideal in that the aim is to rule out plausible alternative explanations for a finding, but differs in that sources of information in addition to quantitative measurement are drawn on to this end. In its full form the HSCED may place so many demands on the clinician and client as to become another research ideal. Elliott (2002), for instance, recommends an independent interview conducted every 8 to 10 sessions, at the end of therapy and at follow-up to provide data on the client's attributions for changes. Although such an approach may be unfeasible for standard practice, it may be possible to use a stripped-back version of the HSCED which uses sources of information that are routinely collected or would require minimal additional effort.

Therapists typically make contemporaneous notes about the content of each therapy session along with other potentially useful information, such as the client's update on life events. This and other sources of data, such as audiotapes of sessions, can be used to assess plausible alternatives. For example, if the therapist has a contemporaneous record made in session six that the client mentioned a change in the way he or she thought about and responded to one of the measures, this could indicate an instrumentation problem (Cook & Campbell, 1979). Any inference about treatment effectiveness would need to assess the extent to which changes in symptoms over the course of therapy could be accounted for by this alteration in the client's response to the measure.

Therapy, particularly during the final stages, often includes a discussion of what changes the client has made and what brought those about. The therapist can use this information to test out competing hypotheses, though to make best use of this it may require some planning on the therapist's part. Before such a session the therapist would need to review the change in process and outcome measures across the course of treatment as well as the other sources of information, such as case notes, to identify the major plausible alternative explanations that need consideration. These could then be discussed in the feedback session. It may also be useful to have a set of standard questions for use here; in particular, the therapist may want to probe for detailed, specific, appropriately balanced and experientially grounded examples of change brought about by therapy. As Elliott (2002) notes, general and overly positive feedback may indicate that reported changes are the result of a tendency to want to please the therapist rather than an indicator of genuine change.

An additional strategy, the natural extension of the feedback session, is to invite the client to act as a co-researcher throughout the course of treatment.

During treatment the clinician and client could put forward possible explanations for changes in symptoms and discuss their plausibility. The client may provide evidence that would help to rule out an alternative, but just as importantly he or she may provide other plausible alternatives that the clinician had failed to consider.

Obtaining suitable baseline information

The problem of providing a suitable baseline in routine clinical practice can be dealt with in a number of ways. With two assessment sessions spaced, for example, a week apart, it is possible to obtain three measures before the intervention. If measures are taken at the two assessments, and repeated on the day of the first treatment session, immediately before the start of that session, then there are three pre-intervention measurement points. An alternative is to identify a small number of target variables during the assessment and then generate a brief rating scale, which the client would complete daily in the time between assessment and treatment.

This approach to the baseline assumes that the assessment phase is not an intervention in itself, a potentially problematic assumption. By seeking help and attending an initial appointment, the client has begun the process of mobilizing resources to make changes. In addition, the therapist from the initial meeting onwards will be trying to convey hope and an expectation of improvement. Under these circumstances it is uncertain whether an assessment phase can be used as a baseline period. However, we would suggest that this is an empirical question that can be considered on a case-by-case basis. The degree of improvement during the assessment can be readily examined if repeated measures are taken during the course of this phase. If the baseline does not indicate pre-treatment improvement, then this threat to the interpretation of the results can be ruled out.

An additional strategy is to obtain a retrospective baseline (Elliott, 2002; Kazdin, 1981). Therapists routinely ask about the duration of a client's difficulties along with how the problem has varied over time and possible reasons for that variation. This information can be used to assess plausible alternatives. For example, a chronic, unremitting course decreases the likelihood that any change is due to maturation effects. Cognitive psychology provides some indications of how the accuracy of retrospective reports can be improved and these may be useful here (Schwarz & Sudman, 1994). One strategy is to use a timeline, which involves a graphical display of time in which key events, whether public or personal, are used as anchor points. Subjective information (e.g. mood state) tends to be recalled less well than objective information, so it may be useful to focus on symptoms that can be operationalized behaviourally, such as number of rituals each day in OCD or frequency of social contact in depression.

Mini-interventions as experimental manipulations

The experimental manipulation of variables can have a role to play in relevant and practicable research. This, however, is likely to require the use of brief manipulations, perhaps taking place within a single session or across a few days; at most it is likely to involve a small number of sessions. One option is the pre-treatment 'mini-intervention', which involves examining one component of the intervention before the start of the full treatment. For example, current cognitive treatment for social anxiety identifies a large number of maintaining factors, including the use of safety behaviours, the increased processing of somatic information, the generation of an inaccurate self-image based on that information, and narrow rules about acceptable social performance (Clark & Wells, 1995). Wells and Papageorgiou (1998) took one of these components, the processing of internal information, and examined its role in the maintenance of anxiety and negative beliefs in a brief pre-treatment intervention that used a single case method. The experimental manipulation consisted of asking clients who met diagnostic criteria for social phobia to focus attention internally and then externally in brief social interactions. The order of the two conditions was counterbalanced across participants. As predicted by the Clark and Wells (1995) model, anxiety and belief change were greater in the external-attention condition than the internal-attention one.

Such an approach goes some way to balancing the rigour and relevance criteria. The manipulation of a single variable, in this case attentional focus, brings with it the advantages of the experimental method for ruling out plausible alternative explanations. The design also remains feasible for standard clinical practice. It is, after all, just a more systematic method of carrying out a behavioural experiment, a commonly used strategy in cognitive therapy (Bennett-Levy et al., 2004). The research is also clinically relevant. It identifies a potential maintaining mechanism in this clinical problem and provides some initial evidence that altering attentional processing may be an active component of the treatment. As Borkovec and Castonguay (2006) point out, the use of mini-interventions in which circumscribed components of treatment are actively manipulated is an under-used research strategy, but one that offers the opportunity to increase our knowledge of basic change mechanisms in psychological treatments.

A second strategy is to embed a brief single case experimental design in the treatment phase. For example, the same within-session design that takes place pre-treatment could instead occur at some point during treatment. An alternative would be to use an experimental design as part of a between-session task. For example, a client with social anxiety could switch daily between an internal and external focus of attention during social interactions. The clinician could set this up as an alternating treatment design in which the decision about which strategy to use on a given day would be based on a randomized schedule.

Mini-interventions and treatment complexity

The use of pre-treatment and within-treatment mini-interventions alongside each other may be one method of dealing with treatment complexity. The pre-treatment mini-intervention examines a component of treatment outside of the context of therapy in which it usually occurs. This fits the logic of experimentation in which one variable is isolated and manipulated, but the removal of the component from the treatment context may alter the relationship between it and the outcome of interest. These advantages and disadvantages reverse for the within-treatment mini-intervention, and because of this the researcher can compare the results of the mini-intervention under these two conditions. This technique is analogous to the efficacy-effectiveness research strategy, in which a randomized trial is first performed under a methodologically strict procedure to protect internal validity and then in a more clinically representative sample and with a naturalistic treatment protocol. Just as in the efficacy-effectiveness paradigm, the researcher is looking for similar conclusions from the more and less controlled designs. If differences emerge, then this can be the start of another round of research in which possible reasons for the differences are explored. In fact, comparing the results of an experimental manipulation before and during treatment may be a profitable research strategy for increasing our understanding of how complex treatments work.

Replication and the strong-inference procedure

Even if we were able to use the research ideal in standard clinical practice, it would not be possible to design a study that effectively dealt with each and every plausible alternative. This will, of course, be even more the case in standard clinical practice, which involves abandoning some features of the research ideal. One strategy for practice-based evidence is to rely on replication across a series of single cases in which features of the design will be varied in an effort to rule out additional threats to validity not examined in the preceding designs. Rather than attempt the impossible – to rule out all threats with one case – the strategy aims to deal steadily with plausible alternatives across cases. This is, in effect, an example of the strong-inference procedure (Platt, 1964). The conclusion of a study (e.g. 'this new treatment worked') is met with the question 'what are the plausible alternatives?' or 'why shouldn't we believe the finding?'. Once these have been identified the researcher seeks to design a new study that will help to decide between the original conclusion and the plausible alternatives. The process is iterative: each new conclusion is exposed to the same question about alternative explanations and, if necessary, a further study is implemented. The single case design is particularly well suited to this strategy, because changes can be made quickly (Sidman, 1960).

Analysis of single case data for practice-based evidence

The analysis of single case data is potentially difficulty for practice-based evidence. Visual analysis alone may be insufficient but the analysis strategies for repeated-measures data may be too esoteric for many clinicians, who may be more familiar with between-group statistics. There are, however, a number of recommendations that may be of use. Careful examination of graphed data should still form the starting point of any analysis. It is also possible to enhance these graphs by calculating and visually displaying simple summary statistics (Morley & Adams, 1991). These statistics provide data on the central location of a particular phase (e.g. means, broadened medians), shifts in central location between phases (e.g. split-middle technique), and variability in data (e.g. trimmed-range method). Morley and Adams (1991) provide details of these methods, all of which require nothing more than a hand-held calculator.

Randomization tests are also likely to be suitable for practice-based evidence in some instances (Onghena & Edgington, 2005). The logic underlying these tests is straightforward and in simple cases the calculations can be made manually. Statistical packages are available for more complex calculations (for details, see Onghena & Edgington, 2005). These tests assume that some form of randomization is used in the assignment of treatment to time-points, which makes the Alternating Treatment Design an obvious candidate. However, other designs that may be more applicable in routine clinical settings may also be appropriate. For example, randomization tests can be used to analyse multiple-baseline designs as long as the length of each baseline is determined at random. The AB design is also suitable, if again the decision to introduce treatment is made at random.

Practical considerations

Our own experience of setting up a single case research group in Leeds, UK, has taught us that aside from these methodological changes, there are a number of practical issues that are needed to make single case research work in routine settings. Although one of the attractions of single case research is that it requires only one clinician, it may be more manageable to conduct it as part of a small network. This can reduce the workload of preparing measures and so on for any one clinician, allows much quicker research returns, and helps to establish one of the criteria for external validity (generalization across therapists). If a small research network is formed and the aim is to replicate results across clients, it will be necessary to agree on a protocol that will be used for the clients, including agreement about the standardized and uniform non-standardized measures that will be used. In Leeds, for instance, we have generated a brief protocol that states which measures to use and when for the main types of presenting problems that are seen. The protocol is designed to detail the minimum measures needed; additional measures can be added as the clinician sees fit.

It may also be necessary to obtain ethical approval, particularly if there is an intention to write up the research for publication. Single case research profits from its flexibility and its ability to quickly incorporate changes to the design to rule out plausible alternatives. We would suggest that rather than submit a new proposal for each variation and change to the design, a generic application is made in which the clinician-researcher outlines the types of designs that may be employed and the types of questions it may be used to answer.

The potential for publishing single case data has improved substantially over the last few years. While many of the leading cognitive-behavioural journals have always published single case research (e.g. *Behaviour Research and Therapy*, *Behavioural and Cognitive Psychotherapy*), there are now two electronic journals devoted entirely to the publication of case studies including single case research based on any treatment modality (*Clinical Case Studies*[2], *Pragmatic Case Studies in Psychotherapy*[3]).

Conclusion

The single case research design provides a set of elegant methodological strate-gies that help to rule out plausible alternatives for an observed finding. This helps the design to meet the rigour criterion demanded by practice-based ev-idence. The design does this while retaining a focus on the individual clinical case, a feature that helps to ensure the relevance of research, the second char-acteristic of practice-based evidence. As with any method, these two demands can conflict with one another, but with some changes a feasible balance can be achieved. We strongly recommend the methodology to clinicians and re-searchers interested in practice-based evidence. For researchers it promises the possibility of increasing the relevance of their work. At the same time it allows clinicians to make a methodologically robust contribution to research. It is at this meeting point that advances in our understanding of what works and why are most likely to occur.

---

[2] Available electronically at: http://ccs.sagepub.com/
[3] Available electronically at: http://pcsp.libraries.rutgers.edu/

Acknowledgements

We would like to thank David Broadbent, Gail Harrison, Maria Law and the other members of the Single Case Research and Practice Group in Leeds UK for their contribution to many of the ideas in this chapter.

References

Barkham, M. & Mellor-Clark, J. (2000). Rigour and relevance: The role of practice-based evidence in the psychological therapies. In N. Rowland & S. Goss (eds.), *Evidence-based counselling and psychological therapies: Research and applications.* (pp. 127–144). New York, NY: Routledge.

Barlow, D.H., Nock, M.K. & Hersen, M. (2008). *Single case experimental designs: Strategies for studying behavior change* (3rd edn.). Boston: Allyn & Bacon.

Bennett-Levy, J., Butler, G., Fennell, M., Hackman, A., Mueller, M. et al. (2004). *Oxford guide to behavioural experiments in cognitive therapy.* Oxford: Oxford University Press.

Blampied, N.M. (2000). Single case research designs: A neglected alternative. *American Psychologist, 55,* 960.

Borkovec, T.D. & Castonguay, L.G. (2006). Dialogue: Convergence and contention. In J.C. Norcross, L.E. Beutler & R.F. Levant (eds.), *Evidence-based practices in mental health: Debate and dialogue on the fundamental questions* (pp. 114–116). Washington, DC: American Psychological Association.

Borkovec, T.D., Echemendia, R.J., Ragusea, S.A. & Ruiz, A. (2001). The Pennsylvania Practice Research Network and future possibilities for clinically meaningful and scientifically rigorous psychotherapy effectiveness research. *Clinical Psychology: Science and Practice, 8,* 155–167.

Chambless, D.L., Baker, M., Baucom, D., Beutler, L., Calhoun, K. et al. (1998). Updates on empirically validated therapies, II. *The Clinical Psychologist, 51,* 3–16.

Clark, D.M. & Wells, A. (1995). A cognitive model of social phobia. In R.G. Heimberg, M.R. Liebowitz, D.A. Hope & F.R. Schneier (eds.), *Social phobia: Diagnosis, assessment, and treatment* (pp. 63–93). New York: Guilford Press.

Cook, T.D. & Campbell, D.T. (1979). *Quasi-experimentation: Design and analysis issues for field settings.* Boston: Houghton Mifflin.

Elliott, R. (2002). Hermeneutic single case efficacy design. *Psychotherapy Research, 12,* 1–21.

Field, C.E., Nash, H.M., Handwerk, M.L. & Friman, P.C. (2004). Using functional assessment and experimental functional analysis to individualize treatment for adolescents in a residential care setting. *Clinical Case Studies, 3,* 25–36.

Fishman, D.B. (2005). From single case to database: A new method for enhancing psychotherapy practice. *Pragmatic Case Studies in Psychotherapy, 1,* 1–50.

Freeston, M.H. (2001). Cognitive-behavioural treatment of a 14-year-old teenager with Obsessive-Compulsive Disorder. *Behavioural and Cognitive Psychotherapy, 29,* 71–84.

Greenberg, L.S. & Watson, J.C. (2006). Change process research. In J.C. Norcross, L.E. Beutler & R.F. Levant (eds.), *Evidence-based practices in mental health: Debate and dialogue on the fundamental questions* (pp. 81–89). Washington, DC: American Psychological Association.

Hayes, S.C. (1981). Single case experimental design and empirical clinical practice. *Journal of Consulting and Clinical Psychology, 49,* 193–211.

Hill, C.E. (2006). Dialogue: Convergence and contention. In J.C. Norcross, L.E. Beutler & R.F. Levant (eds.), *Evidence-based practices in mental health: Debate and dialogue on the fundamental questions* (pp. 110–112). Washington, DC: American Psychological Association.

Hilliard, R.B. (1993). Single case methodology in psychotherapy process and outcome research. *Journal of Consulting and Clinical Psychology, 61,* 373–380.

Hinton, D.E., Pich, V., Chhean, D., Safren, S.A. & Pollack, M.H. (2006). Somatic-focused therapy for traumatized refugees: Treating Post-traumatic Stress Disorder and comorbid neck-focused panic attacks among Cambodian refugees. *Psychotherapy: Theory, Research, Practice, Training, 43,* 491–505.

Kazdin, A.E. (1981). Drawing valid inferences from case studies. *Journal of Consulting and Clinical Psychology, 49,* 183–192.

Kazdin, A.E. (1982). *Single case research designs: Methods for clinical and applied settings.* New York: Oxford University Press.

Kellett, S. (2005). The treatment of Dissociative Identity Disorder with Cognitive Analytic Therapy: Experimental evidence of sudden gains. *Journal of Trauma and Dissociation, 6,* 55–81.

Kratochwill, T.R. & Brody, G.H. (1978). Single-subject designs: A perspective on the controversy over employing statistical inference and implications for research and training in behaviour modification. *Behavior Modification, 2,* 291–307.

Masuda, A., Hayes, S.C., Sackett, C.F. & Twohig, M.P. (2004). Cognitive defusion and self-relevant negative thoughts: Examining the impact of a ninety year old technique. *Behaviour Research and Therapy, 42,* 477–485.

Meehl, P.E. (1978). Theoretical risks and tabular asterisks: Sir Karl, Sir Ronald and the slow progress of soft psychology. *Journal of Consulting and Clinical Psychology, 46,* 806–834.

Meehl, P.E. (1990). Why summaries of research on psychological theories are often uninterpretable. *Psychological Reports, 66,* 195–244.

Morley, S. (1996). Single case research. In G. Parry & F.N. Watts (eds.), *Behavioural and mental health research: A handbook of skills and methods* (2nd edn., pp. 277–314). Hove: Lawrence Erlbaum.

Morley, S. (2007). Single case methodology in psychological therapy. In S.J.E. Lindsay & G.E. Powell (eds.), *The handbook of clinical adult psychology* (3rd edn., pp. 821–843). London: Routledge.

Morley, S. & Adams, M. (1991). Graphical analysis of single case time series data. *British Journal of Clinical Psychology, 30,* 97–115.

Onghena, P. & Edgington, E.S. (2005). Customization of pain treatments: Single case design and analysis. *Clinical Journal of Pain, 21,* 56–68.

Parry, G. (2000). Evidence-based counselling and psychological therapies: An overview. In N. Rowland & S. Goss (eds.), *Evidence-based counselling and psychological therapies: Research and applications* (pp. 57–75). London: Routledge.

Peck, D.F. (2007). Whither small N designs in cognitive behaviour therapy? *Clinical Psychology Forum, 184,* 24–26.

Platt, J.R. (1964). Strong inference. *Science, 146,* 347–353.

Schwarz, N. & Sudman, S. (1994). *Autobiographical memory and the validity of retrospective reports.* New York: Springer-Verlag.

Sidman, M. (1960). *Tactics of scientific research: Evaluating experimental data in psychology.* New York: Basic Books.

Stiles, W.B., Honos-Webb, L. & Surko, M. (1998). Responsiveness in psychotherapy. *Clinical Psychology: Science and Practice, 5,* 439–458.

Tate, R.L., McDonald, S., Perdices, M., Togher, L., Schultz, R. et al. (2008). Rating the methodological quality of single-subject designs and *n*-of-1 trials: Introducing the Single-Case Experimental Design (SCED) Scale. *Neuropsychological Rehabilitation, 18,* 385–401.

Vlaeyen, J.W.S., de Jong, J., Geilen, M., Heuts, P.H.T.G. & van Breukelen, G. (2001). Graded exposure in vivo in the treatment of pain-related fears: A replicated single case experimental design in four patients with chronic low back pain. *Behaviour Research and Therapy, 39,* 151–166.

Wells, A. & Papageorgiou, C. (1998). Social phobia: Effects of external attention on anxiety, negative beliefs, and perspective taking. *Behavior Therapy, 29,* 357–370.

Westen, D., Novotny, C. & Thompson-Brenner, H. (2004). The empirical status of empirically supported therapies: Assumptions, methods, and findings. *Psychological Bulletin, 130,* 631–663.

Section III

Measurement Systems for Individual Practitioners and Services

6

Outcome Questionnaire System (The OQ System): Development and Practical Applications in Healthcare Settings

Michael J. Lambert[1], Nathan B. Hansen[2] and S. Cory Harmon[3]

[1]Brigham Young University, Utah, USA, [2]Yale University School of Medicine, USA, [3]New York – Presbyterian Hospital, White Plains, NY, USA

Introduction

The aim of the OQ System is to provide measures and methods to enhance treatment outcomes for psychological disorders, especially for patients whose progress and eventual positive outcome is in doubt, by providing progress information directly to practitioners. This system is owned and distributed by OQMeasures (www.OQMeasures.com), and consists of several adult and youth measures contained in a software-OQ-Analyst. The central measure within the OQ-Analyst is the Outcome Questionnaire-45 (OQ-45), first developed and distributed in the United States in 1993. According to a survey conducted by Hatfield and Ogles (2004), it is the third most frequently used self-report instrument for measuring adult patient outcome in the USA. Unlike most psychological tests, it was developed specifically for use in monitoring patient well-being on a weekly basis during routine care. It was assumed that the measure would be taken prior to each treatment session, require about five minutes of patient time, and be composed of items that would reflect the consequences of receiving care, while remaining stable in untreated controls.

Developing and Delivering Practice-Based Evidence   By Michael Barkham, Gillian E Hardy, and John Mellor-Clark   © 2010 John Wiley & Sons, Ltd

OQ-45 respondents estimate frequencies of occurrence of 45 symptoms, emotional states, interpersonal relationships and social situations. Thirty-six negatively worded items (e.g. item 5, 'I blame myself for things') are scored *Never* = 0, *Rarely* = 1, *Sometimes* = 2, *Frequently* = 3, and *Almost Always* = 4; scoring is reversed (*Never* = 4, *Rarely* = 3, *Frequently* = 1, *Almost Always* = 0) for 9 positively worded items (e.g. item 13, 'I am a happy person'). This yields a total score ranging from 0 to 180. Higher scores reveal report of more frequent symptoms, distress, interpersonal problems and social dysfunction, and less frequent positive emotional states, pleasant experiences, successful social relationships and adaptive role functioning.

The OQ-45 manual (Lambert et al., 2004a) documents excellent internal consistency: Cronbach's $\alpha = 0.93$, good to excellent validity correlations between the OQ-45 and a wide variety of other instruments that are frequently used in psychotherapy outcome research, and the ability to distinguish between patient and psychologically healthy samples. The instrument has been normed on patient and non-patient samples across the USA and throughout much of the world through translations into 17+ non-English languages. Normative comparisons have been employed to provide markers for individual patient progress based on Jacobson and Truax's (1991) formulas for reliable and clinically significant change, fulfilling a necessary use of the instrument to inform clinician's about the degree of success a patient they are treating is having.

The Outcome Questionnaire-30 (OQ-30) is a derivative measure originally created for use by a behavioural health company managing the care of patients from a pool of 5,000,000 customers. The OQ-30 incorporated 30 items from the OQ-45 that had been found to be the most sensitive to the impact of treatment. It maintains the content interests of the OQ-45 (symptoms, interpersonal and social role functioning) without producing subscale scores.

The Severe Outcome Questionnaire (SOQ) is composed of the 30 items from the OQ-30 and an additional 15 items that capture symptoms and functioning of patients who have severe psychopathology such as bi-polar, schizophrenia and other psychotic illness. It was created with the intention of being especially appropriate for use in settings where highly impaired patients seek treatment, such as community mental health centres.

The Youth Outcome Questionnaire (YOQ) consists of 64 items that describe the symptoms and functioning of children from the ages of 4–17. It comes in formats suitable for parental/guardian report as well as self-report for children age 13 and older. The YOQ has six subscales that assess intrapersonal distress, somatic complaints, interpersonal relations, social problems, behaviour dysfunction and critical items. Like the OQ-45 it was created as a tracking measure rather than a diagnostic scale and has solid psychometric properties that make it suitable for this task.

The Youth Outcome Questionnaire-30 is a brief version of the YOQ that maintains the content areas of the YOQ, without providing subscale information. Like the OQ-30, it was originally developed for use by the same managed care company and has provided information about the progress of thousands of children throughout the United States.

The OQ-10 and YOQ-10 are derivative instruments intended for use in primary care medical settings as brief screening measures for the presence of psychological symptoms. The selection of items for these scales was based on their ability to discriminate between the physically ill and patients who have developed psychological symptoms and are in need of further screening and referral for treatment of their psychological difficulties. The scales were not developed for the purpose of tracking the outcome of treatments and are not considered treatment outcome measures.

Deviations from a positive course of treatment

The central feature of the OQ system family of measures is not the measures themselves, although they were specifically made for the purpose of quantifying the impacts of treatment, but the creation of decision-making tools (lab tests) based on comparing an individual patient's progress with that of similar patients who have undergone treatment. From both research and practice perspectives, identifying 'signal' cases, or cases at risk for poor outcome, is a critical component of enhancing treatment outcome. Additionally, from a healthcare management perspective, with a focus on containing costs and providing quality assurance in mental health services, identifying signal cases is essential for efficient allocation of resources. Quality assurance is 'fundamentally a case-based issue' (Lueger et al., 2001, p. 150) that should enhance 'problem-patient-therapy-therapist matches' (p. 157). Patient-focused research (Howard et al., 1996) emphasizes case-based approaches for optimizing treatment for the individual patient, and a number of actuarial methods have been developed for predicting the course of treatment and identifying 'signal' cases, with the goal of preventing treatment failures (Barkham et al., 2001; Kordy, Hannöver & Richard, 2001; Lambert et al., 2001; Lueger et al., 2000; Lutz et al., 2005; Lutz et al., 2006).

Traditionally, outcome prediction has utilized baseline characteristics of patients, therapists and the treatment context to predict treatment outcome. These variables are useful in creating models for case-mix adjustment and can guide the placement of patients into services (Brown et al., 2005; Hendryx et al., 1999). Many of the patient-focused research strategies, however, make use of ongoing treatment monitoring where patient progress (or lack thereof) is compared to data on the expected course of treatment from previously treated patients (Lambert et al., 2003; Lutz et al., 2005). Ongoing treatment-monitoring systems generally share a number of similar components. First, treatment monitoring requires routine assessment of patient functioning during the course of treatment. This assessment can be limited to pre-post measurement, though more commonly assessment occurs on a regular basis during the course of treatment, as frequently as every weekly session of therapy. Second, treatment monitoring requires the comparison of patient outcome to norms from similar patients receiving similar treatments. Third, treatment monitoring has the goal of feeding patient information back to the practice setting with the goal of informing treatment delivery to enhance outcomes. This feedback can range from reporting on the outcome of completed treatments to management, to ongoing feedback of session-by-session change to therapists and even patients.

While clinicians are confident in their ability to care adequately for patients in the absence of formal monitoring systems, as we shall point out shortly, therapists are highly reticent to predict that an ongoing case is showing progress consistent with final deterioration. In order to become more aware of pending treatment failure actuarial methods that take into account massive amounts of information about the treatment response of thousands of patients across thousands of therapists can be of considerable predictive benefit. For example, Finch, Lambert and Schaalje (2001) applied actuarial methods to a large data base consisting of 11,492 patients treated in a variety of settings including employee assistance programmes, university counselling centres, outpatient clinics and private practice settings, and were able to identify 50 separate courses of recovery based on OQ-45 scores. Similar methods have been applied using the OQ-30, YOQ and YOQ-30.

In fact, a variety of statistical procedures have been tested to determine if treatment failures could be accurately identified before they left treatment. We have found methods based on Hierarchical Linear Modeling (HLM) that model the shape and speed of change over time using session-by-session data produced by patients to be the most effective method (e.g. Lambert et al., 2002a; Spielmans et al., 2006). HLM is especially useful in analysing longitudinal data from routine care, a situation in which patients begin treatment at diverse levels of initial disturbance and have treatment lengths that are highly varied. The results of such modelling can be examined for subsets of patients who meet criteria for an event such as clinically significant or reliable change, (or deterioration), but are most valuable as a means for establishing session-by-session expectations for a course of psychotherapy in relation to unique levels of initial disturbance.

Research on ongoing treatment monitoring

Comparisons of individual patient response to session-by-session normative data have been employed in five large randomized controlled studies (RCTs) to evaluate the impact of using the OQ System (OQ-45) to assess and modify ongoing treatment response (Harmon et al., 2007; Hawkins et al., 2004; Lambert et al., 2001, 2002b; Whipple et al., 2003). These studies each required about one year of data collection and included session-by-session measurement of over 4,185 patients. All five of the studies assessed the effectiveness of providing therapists with session-by-session progress data as measured by the OQ-45, with particular focus on identifying patients who were not responding well to treatment (signal-alarm cases). Progress data was supplied in the form of a graph of OQ-45 scores detailing patient improvement and warning messages when improvement was not occurring or was not of the expected magnitude (see Figure 6.1 for an example of a feedback report). Additionally, two of the studies assessed the impact of providing both therapists *and patients* with OQ-45 progress information, and two of the studies assessed the impact of providing therapists with additional feedback regarding the patient's assessment of the therapeutic relationship, readiness for change and degree of social support (termed Clinical Support Tools Feedback or CST Feedback) (Lambert et al., 2004b). These latter three assessments were provided in concert with OQ-45 progress information when it was deemed that the patient was not progressing in treatment as well as expected and, in fact, predicted to leave treatment deteriorated.

The five studies summarized here include a number of commonalities. The most important of these include: (1) patients were randomly assigned into control (No feedback) or experimental (Feedback) groups at intake (one study employed an archival control); (2) the same therapists who saw control condition patients also saw experimental condition patients, thus minimizing the possibility that measured differences are attributable to therapist effects; (3) the therapists represented a variety of treatment orientations, with the majority ascribing to cognitive-behavioural or other eclectic orientations; (4) professional therapists represented about 50% to 100% of the clinicians participating in each study, with the balance comprised of graduate student or post-doctoral trainees. Characteristics of the five studies are presented in Table 6.1. As can be seen, four of the samples were essentially equivalent (and came from the same clinic), while participants in the fifth sample were older, more disturbed, and were treated in a hospital-based outpatient clinic.

In order to understand the meaning of the results it is essential to discuss particular details of the methodology used in the studies. First, outcome is defined and its operational definition is provided, along with rules for categorizing each client's treatment response (feedback). Next, the method for identifying likely treatment failures (signal-alarm cases) is highlighted in order to describe the feedback that is at the core of reducing treatment failure. Finally, the effects of feedback are summarized, and the implications of these results for research and practice are provided. We conclude with limitations of the research methodology and include an argument for routine utilization of formal feedback in clinical practice.

OQA: OQ Clinician Feedback Report   Page 1 of 1

Name:	12, case	**ID:**	12
Session Date:	12/21/2005	**Session:** 9	
Clinician:	Maristany, Mariana	**Clinic:**	Aigle
Diagnosis:	Unknown Diagnosis		
Algorithm:	Empirical ▓		

Alert Status:	**Red**
Most Recent Score:	79
Initial Score:	58
Change From Initial:	Reliably Worse
Current Distress Level:	Moderate

Most Recent Critical Item Status:

8. **Suicide** - I have thoughts of ending my life. **Never**

11. **Substance Abuse** - After heavy drinking, I need a drink the next morning to get going. **Never**

26. **Substance Abuse** - I feel annoyed by people who criticize my drinking. **Never**

32. **Substance Abuse** - I have trouble at work/school because of drinking or drug use. **Never**

44. **Work Violence** - I feel angry enough at work/school to do something I might regret. **Rarely**

Subscales	Current	Outpat. Norm	Comm. Norm
Symptom Distress:	45	49	25
Interpersonal Relations:	18	20	10
Social Role:	16	14	10
Total:	**79**	**83**	**45**

Total Score by Session Number

12/21/05	12/21/05	12/21/05	12/21/05	12/21/05

Score (y-axis): 50 to 120

Data points: 58.0 (session 1), 75 (R) (session 3), 81 (R) (session 5), 62 080 (session 7), 79 (R) (session 9)

Session Number (x-axis): 1, 3, 5, 7, 9

Graph Label Legend:

(R) = **Red:** High chance of negative outcome   (Y) = **Yellow:** Some chance of negative outcome
(G) = **Green:** Making expected progress   (W) = **White:** Functioning in normal range

Feedback Message:
The patient is deviating from the expected response to treatment. They are not on track to realize substantial benefit from treatment. Chances are they may drop out of treatment prematurely or have a negative treatment outcome. Steps should be taken to carefully review this case and identify reasons for poor progress. It is recommended that you be alert to the possible need to improve the therapeutic alliance, reconsider the client's readiness for change and the need to renegotiate the therapeutic contract, intervene to strengthen social supports, or possibly alter your treatment plan by intensifying treatment, shifting intervention strategies, or decide upon a new course of action, such as referral for medication. Continuous monitoring of future progress is highly recommended

http://localhost/OQA/OQ_ClinicianReport.aspx   9/26/2006

Figure 6.1   OQ System feedback report

Table 6.1   Summary of design characteristics of controlled outcome studies aimed at reducing deterioration and enhancing positive outcome

Study	Patients/ Therapists N	TAU	Therapist Feedback	Therapist/ Patient Feedback	Clinical Support Tools
Lambert et al. (2001)	609/31	X	X		
Lambert et al. (2002b)	1020/49	X	X		
Whipple et al. (2003)	981/48	X	X		X
Hawkins et al. (2004)	201/5	X	X	X	
Harmon et al. (2007)	1374/47		X	X	X

Prediction of treatment failure and description of the warning system

The essence of improving outcomes for poorly responding patients was the development of a signalling system that attempted to identify the failing patient before termination of services had occurred. Such a signalling system is at the core of the feedback used with therapists. It requires that the patient provide session-by-session OQ-45 data that is evaluated between sessions and judged to indicate a positive or negative sign for likely functioning at treatment termination. In patient-focused research, such a signalling system is based on the assumption that termination status can, in fact, be predicted prior to termination and that providing treatment progress information to the therapist will positively affect final outcome.

One way of assessing the meaningfulness of the feedback interventions is to classify final treatment response into categorizations based on Jacobson and Truax's (1991) criteria for reliable or clinically significant change. Based on their formulas for obtaining cut-off scores and reliable change, a score of 63/64 on the OQ-45 indicates that patients have equal probability of belonging to the functional and dysfunctional distributions. Therefore, a score of 64 or above on the OQ-45 is considered to be within the dysfunctional range, while scores below 64 are within the functional range. Additionally, Jacobson and Truax's formulas for computing the Reliable Change Index (RCI) indicate a change of 14 or more points signifies reliable change. Typically, patient change is presented categorically as *reliably deteriorated* (change greater than RCI in a negative direction), *no change* (change not greater than RCI), *reliably improved* (change equal to or greater than RCI in a positive direction), and *recovered* (change greater than RCI in a positive direction and crossing the cut-off score of 64, indicating that the patient has a higher likelihood of belonging to the functional distribution).

Table 6.2   Final outcome categorizations of not-on-track patients by treatment group

Outcome Classification	TAU (No Feedback)		OQ-45 Feedback		OQ-45 + CST Feedback	
	(n = 318)		(n = 582)		(n = 154)	
	n	%	n	%	n	%
Deteriorated/Reliable worsening	64	20.1	87	14.9	12	7.8
No reliable change	184	57.9	306	52.6	73	47.4
Reliable/Clinically significant change	70	22.0	189	32.5	69	44.8

Table 6.2 presents data for all patients in the five feedback studies who deviated significantly and negatively from their expected treatment course (i.e. not-on-track patients). Data are divided into three groups: Treatment as Usual (i.e. No Feedback), OQ-45 Feedback (Therapist Feedback and Therapist/Patient Feedback), and OQ-45 Feedback + Clinical Support Tools Feedback. Of particular note is the percentage of patients who deteriorated, or ended treatment with negative change. As can be seen, OQ-45 feedback resulted in a decrease in the percentage of not-on-track patients who ended treatment with reliable negative change (20.1% to 14.9%). Deterioration rates were further reduced when clinical support tools feedback was provided in addition to the OQ-45 feedback, with the percentage of deterioration falling to 7.8%. Additional benefits of feedback are seen in a comparison of not-on-track patients who meet criteria for reliable improvement and/or clinically significant change, with percentages increasing from 22.0% for treatment as usual, to 32.5% for OQ-45 feedback, and 44.8% for OQ-45 feedback + CST feedback. Taken together, results suggest that providing therapists with feedback on patient progress improves outcome for patients predicted to be treatment failures. Further, providing therapists with the patient's assessment of the therapeutic alliance, the patient's assessment of his or her own readiness for change, and assessment of the strength of social support networks further improves treatment outcome.

In addition to changes in final treatment outcome, results of the five studies indicate that session utilization may be affected by the provision of OQ-45 feedback. There were significant treatment length differences between experimental and control participants in four out of the five studies (Harmon et al., 2007; Lambert et al., 2001, 2002b; Whipple et al., 2003), with not-on-track patients in the feedback conditions receiving significantly more sessions than their treatment-as-usual counterparts. This result was not found in the study that was conducted at an outpatient hospital-based clinic where, in general, patients began treatment as more disturbed. This suggests that increases in treatment length may be just one mechanism of action by which feedback improves outcome. In two out of the five studies (Lambert et al., 2001; Whipple et al., 2003), patients who were on track for a positive outcome and in the experimental feedback condition received fewer sessions than on-track controls. This suggests the possibility that cost-effectiveness of psychotherapy can be positively impacted, with the most needy patients staying in treatment longer, and patients who recover quickly having fewer sessions when their therapist receives feedback on their progress.

Discussion of the OQ System in application to treatment monitoring

The studies summarized above clearly demonstrate the utility of the OQ-45 in assessing ongoing patient functioning during the course of treatment. Ongoing treatment monitoring shows great potential in improving the efficiency and effectiveness of psychotherapy. Additionally, monitoring treatment on a consistent basis has several advantages over more limited assessment (such as administering assessments at pre-treatment and post-treatment only). First, a central goal of quality assurance is the prevention of negative outcomes. Even under the best circumstances, such as in carefully crafted and controlled clinical trials research, roughly 10% of patients show negative outcome (deterioration), while another 25 to 40% will fail to improve and show no reliable change (Hansen, Lambert & Forman, 2002). Consistent ongoing assessment is the only way to get 'real-time' measurement of patient functioning that can be fed back to therapists in a timely fashion to impact the treatment for that patient. Intermittent or pre-/post-assessment alone limits or makes impossible the provision of feedback to therapists that can inform their treatment decisions regarding the actual patients who are completing questionnaires. While such data is useful to inform treatment expectations for future patients, and to inform management about the utilization and effectiveness of clinical services, the application of such data to individual cases is limited.

In fact, therapists have been shown to be poor judges when predicting who will not benefit from treatment. Hannan et al. (2005) conducted a study with 40 therapists, who, despite being aware of the purpose of the study, being familiar with the dependent measure (OQ-45) and its cut-offs for judging deterioration, and being informed that the base rate for deterioration was likely to be 8%, were only accurate in predicting deterioration in one case out of 550 patients (in fact, across all 40 therapists, only three patients were actually predicted to deteriorate). Therapists failed to identify 39 patients who actually deteriorated during treatment. While optimism and belief in the therapeutic enterprise are important characteristics for therapists to have, it is likely that without timely feedback about patient functioning, therapists will underestimate negative outcomes in therapy, even when they are aware that one in ten cases will deteriorate, and they will therefore be less likely to make appropriate adjustments to treatment plans that may prevent negative outcomes.

Second, from a practical perspective, the logistics of maintaining an ongoing treatment-monitoring system are easier to manage when assessment becomes a routine part of practice. A central question in such systems is 'who is responsible for data collection?', with the related questions of 'when are assessments administered?' and 'who keeps track of this?' Thus, if therapists administer questionnaires, do they do this before or after the session, and if assessment is intermittent, how does the therapist know to administer an assessment to patient A, but not to patient B? Is the therapist expected to keep track of this along with the patient case file, or is this handled on the management side and therapists are informed as needed? We have found that the most efficient system has been to simply make administration of assessments routine, with patients completing a questionnaire prior to each appointment in the clinic so there is no need to track who needs an assessment and who does not, and with assessments administered by clinic receptionists when patients check in for appointments. While there is a need for an employee who is responsible for gathering assessments, scoring them, managing the data, and preparing feedback for clinicians, this process has become increasingly automated, and can easily be handled as part of the routine tasks of administrative personnel using OQ-Analyst software. The National Registry of Evidence-based Programs and Practices (NREPP) recently rated the OQ-Analyst a 3.9 (out of 4) as meeting their criteria for 'readiness for dissemination' based on user guides and step-by-step instructions for implementation (www.nrepp.samhsa.gov/).

Third, any treatment-monitoring approach will be limited by patient dropout or premature termination of treatment. It is uncommon for therapists to know when treatment is going to end in such a way as to be ready with an assessment to obtain post-treatment data. Therefore data collection for post-treatment is frequently conducted at some point after termination, and typically requires mailing the questionnaire to patients or contacting them by phone to administer the questionnaire. These methods have drawbacks, such as potentially violating confidentiality in contacting former patients, having biased data as a result of patients who are unwilling to complete forms or who cannot be located, and administrative time in delivering these assessments. With routine ongoing treatment monitoring, missing data is less of a drawback, as statistical methods are able to fill gaps from incomplete data, and session-by-session assessment data should be available up to the last session a patient attends. This provides a much more complete and accurate estimate of treatment outcome.

There are several barriers to the implementation of ongoing treatment monitoring, including clinician resistance to monitoring, the logistics of establishing routine and ongoing assessment of treatment, issues of scoring assessments and data management, and developing procedures to provide useful and timely feedback to clinicians and patients. Additionally, to make use of these treatment-monitoring methods, normative data from similar patients and treatments are required to compute treatment expectations. While data to develop such norms are available for many patient categories and treatment approaches (e.g. cognitive and interpersonal therapies for affective and anxiety disorders), such data are not available for many more specific treatment situations.

Of course, treatment monitoring is only as good as the measurement tool used. In the feedback studies just summarized, the OQ-45 was the instrument used. This measure was specifically developed to be brief and quickly administered, thus being acceptable for routine use. It has been shown to have stable scores across time in non-treatment settings, as well as being sensitive to change over the course of treatment. Additionally, a large amount of data has been accumulated on the clinical use of the OQ-45, such that normative data for treatment expectations are available across a large number of settings, treatments and patient categories. The utility of the OQ-45 in identifying patients who are expected to have negative outcomes has been established, as have procedures for informing clinicians (and patients) of treatment expectations. Clinical support tools have been developed that further augment the OQ system and serve to provide clinicians with a range of options to address patients who are not progressing as expected.

Given the large sample sizes of the individual studies in this summary, and a combined overall sample size of over 4,000 cases in our clinical trials, the current findings are compelling, though they are not without limitations. First, the majority of the data on ongoing treatment monitoring and therapist feedback were collected in a university outpatient clinic. Studies in other settings, and with different treatments and patient samples, are needed. For example, as our samples are composed of predominately young adult patients, we have limited data on children and adolescents, and on older adults. Although a recent study of 30-day inpatient treatment in Switzerland (Berking, Orth & Lutz, 2005) using similar methods has replicated the effects of treatment monitoring and feedback, many more studies will be needed before the limitations and generalizability of such interventions are known.

Second, there were no evaluations or controls of how therapists made use of feedback or clinical support tools. While this methodological limitation increases the likelihood that the results reflect what will happen in other clinical settings, clinicians' actions with regard to looking at feedback, sharing it with clients, seeking supervision or consultation, and modifying treatment, remain largely unknown, with the exception of our two studies where we delivered feedback directly to patients (Harmon et al., 2007; Hawkins et al., 2004). This raises the issue of clinician acceptance of feedback, which is another potential limitation of this type of research and clinical management. Generally speaking, clinicians do not see the value of frequent assessments based on standardized scales (Hatfield & Ogles, 2002), likely because they are confident in their ability to accurately observe patient worsening and provide an appropriate response. Despite evidence that suggests psychotherapists are not alert to treatment failure (Hannan et al., 2005; Yalom & Lieberman, 1971), and strong evidence that clinical judgments are usually found to be inferior to actuarial methods across a wide variety of predictive tasks (Garb, 2005), therapist confidence in his/her own clinical judgment stands as a barrier to implementation of monitoring and feedback systems. In addition, clinicians are used to practicing in private and with considerable autonomy. Monitoring patient treatment response makes the effects of practice somewhat public and transparent. Such 'transparency' inevitably raises evaluation anxiety and fears of losing control. Implementation requires the cooperation of therapists and takes time before it is apparent to clinicians that the feedback is helpful.

Finally, our research is limited to a single self-report measure of improvement (OQ-45) and therefore provides only one view of the impact of therapy on patients. The OQ system was designed to be a tool to aid clinical decision making rather than to dictate or proscribe to clinicians. We are well aware of the fact that decisions regarding the continued provision of treatment, the modification of ongoing treatment, obtaining case consultation or supervision, or the application of clinical support tools or other techniques, cannot be made on the basis of a single questionnaire or independent from clinical judgment. Thus we envision the OQ system as analogous to a 'lab test' in medical treatment, which can supplement and inform clinical decision making, rather than as a replacement for the clinician's judgment.

References

Barkham, M., Margison, F., Leach, C., Lucock, M., Mellor-Clark, J. et al. (2001). Service profiling and outcomes benchmarking using the CORE-OM: Toward practice-based evidence in the psychological therapies. *Journal of Consulting and Clinical Psychology, 69,* 184–196.

Berking, M., Orth, U. & Lutz, W. (2006). Wie effektiv sind systematische Rückmeldungen des Therapieverlaufs an den Therapeuten? Eine empirische Studie in einem stationär-verhaltenstherapeutischen Setting. *Zeitschrift für Klinische Psychologie und Psychotherapie, 35,* 21–29.

Brown, G.S., Lambert, M.J., Jones, E.R. & Minami, T. (2005). Identifying highly effective therapists in a managed care environment. *American Journal of Managed Care, 8,* 513–520.

Finch, A.E., Lambert, M.J. & Schaalje, B.G. (2001). Psychotherapy quality control: The statistical generation of expected recovery curves for integration into an early warning system. *Clinical Psychology & Psychotherapy*, 8, 231–242.

Garb, H.N. (2005). Clinical judgment and decision making. *Annual Review of Clinical Psychology*, 55, 13–23.

Hannan, C., Lambert, M.J., Harmon, C., Nielsen, S.L., Smart, D.W. et al. (2005). A lab test and algorithms for identifying clients at risk for treatment failure. *Journal of Clinical Psychology: In Session*, 61, 155–163.

Hansen, N.B., Lambert, M.J. & Forman, E.V. (2002). The psychotherapy dose-response effect and its implications for treatment delivery services. *Clinical Psychology: Science and Practice*, 9, 329–343.

Harmon, S.C., Lambert, M.J., Smart, D.W., Hawkins, E.J., Nielsen, S.L. et al. (2007). Enhancing outcome for potential treatment failures: Therapist/client feedback and clinical support tools. *Psychotherapy Research*, 17, 379–392.

Hatfield, D.R. & Ogles, B.M. (2004). Use of outcome measures by psychologists in clinical practice. *Professional Psychology: Research and Practice*, 35, 485–491.

Hawkins, E.J., Lambert, M.J., Vermeersch, D.A., Slade, K. & Tuttle, K. (2004). The effects of providing patient progress information to therapists and patients. *Psychotherapy Research*, 14, 308–327.

Hendryx, M., Dyck, D. & Srebnik, D. (1999). Risk-adjusted outcome models for public mental health outpatient programs. *Health Services Research*, 34, 171–195.

Jacobson, N.S. & Truax, P. (1991). Clinical significance: A statistical approach to defining meaningful change in psychotherapy research. *Journal of Consulting and Clinical Psychology*, 59, 12–19.

Kordy, H., Hannöver, W. & Richard, M. (2001). Computer-assisted feedback-driven quality management for psychotherapy: The Stuttgart-Heidelberg model. *Journal of Consulting and Clinical Psychology*, 69, 173–183.

Lambert, M.J., Whipple, J.L., Smart, D.W., Vermeersch, D.A., Nielsen, S.L. et al. (2001). The effects of providing therapists with feedback on client progress during psychotherapy: Are outcomes enhanced? *Psychotherapy Research*, 11, 49–68.

Lambert, M.J., Whipple, J.L., Bishop, M.J., Vermeersch, D.A., Gray, G.V. et al. (2002a). Comparison of empirically derived and rationally derived methods for identifying clients at risk for treatment failure. *Clinical Psychology & Psychotherapy*, 9, 149–164.

Lambert, M.J., Whipple, J.L., Vermeersch, D.A., Smart, D.W., Hawkins, E.J. et al. (2002b). Enhancing psychotherapy outcomes via providing feedback on client progress: A replication. *Clinical Psychology & Psychotherapy*, 9, 91–103.

Lambert, M.J., Whipple, J.L., Hawkins, E.J., Vermeersch, D.A., Nielsen, S.L. et al. (2003). Is it time for clinicians to routinely track patient outcome?: A meta-analysis. *Clinical Psychology: Science and Practice, 10,* 288–301.

Lambert, M.J., Morton, J.J., Hatfield, D., Harmon, C., Hamilton, S. et al. (2004a). *Administration and Scoring Manual for the Outcome Questionnaire-45.* SLC, UT: OQMeasures.

Lambert, M.J., Whipple, J.L., Harmon, C., Shimokawa, K., Slade, K. et al. (2004b). *Clinical Support Tools Manual.* Provo, UT: Department of Psychology, Brigham Young University.

Lueger, R.J., Lutz, W. & Howard, K.I. (2000). The predicted and observed course of psychotherapy for anxiety and mood disorders. *The Journal of Nervous & Mental Disease, 188,* 127–143.

Lueger, R.J., Howard, K. I., Martinovich Z., Lutz, W., Anderson, E.E. et al. (2001). Assessing treatment progress of individual clients using expected treatment response models. *Journal of Consulting and Clinical Psychology, 69,* 150–158.

Lutz, W., Lambert, M.J., Harmon, S.C., Tschitsaz, A., Schürch, E. et al. (2006). The probability of treatment success, failure and duration – what can be learned from empirical data to support decision making in clinical practice? *Clinical Psychology & Psychotherapy, 13,* 223–232.

Lutz, W., Leach, C., Barkham, M., Lucock, M., Stiles, W.B. et al. (2005). Predicting rate and shape of change for individual clients receiving psychological therapy: Using growth curve modeling and nearest neighbor technologies. *Journal of Consulting and Clinical Psychology, 73,* 904–913.

Spielmans, G.I., Masters, K.S. & Lambert, M.J. (2006). A comparison of rational versus empirical methods in prediction of negative psychotherapy outcome. *Clinical Psychology & Psychotherapy, 13,* 202–214.

Whipple, J.L., Lambert, M.J., Vermeersch, D.A., Smart, D.W., Nielsen, S.L. et al. (2003). Improving the effects of psychotherapy: The use of early identification of treatment failure and problem solving strategies in routine practice. *Journal of Counseling Psychology, 58,* 59–68.

Yalom, I.D. & Lieberman, M.A. (1971). A study of encounter group casualties. *Archives of General Psychiatry, 25,* 16–30.

7

Treatment Outcome Package (TOP) – Development and use in Naturalistic Settings

David Kraus[1] and Louis G. Castonguay[2]

[1] *Behavioral Health Laboratories, Marlborough, MA, USA,* [2] *Pennsylvania State University, USA*

Introduction

This chapter describes the development of a widely used outcome tool designed specifically for naturalistic, real-world treatment settings. From large networks like Blue Cross and Blue Shield of Massachusetts, to solo-practice clinicians in Canada and other countries, TOP (the Treatment Outcome Package) has emerged as a popular outcome tool for a wide variety of provider groups. By the beginning of 2007, TOP, created and processed by Behavioral Health Labs (BHL), had been used by more than 30,000 clinicians to assess more than 600,000 clients, their treatment needs and their progress towards defined treatment plan goals.

The TOP features a number of characteristics that makes it suitable to both evidence-based practice and clinically relevant research. For example, based on Lambert-style alert methodology (see Chapter 6), it provides individualized client feedback to warn clinicians of potentially poor outcomes. Aggregate report feedback is risk adjusted and benchmarked with ties to empirically based quality improvement suggestions, helping providers to maximize the type of feedback that can accelerate treatment effectiveness. With an anonymous (patient de-identified) benchmarking database exceeding a million clients, the opportunities for research and fine-tuned benchmarking are remarkable. With such a massive and centralized database, BHL is able to provide detailed,

Developing and Delivering Practice-Based Evidence   By Michael Barkham, Gillian E Hardy, and John Mellor-Clark   © 2010 John Wiley & Sons, Ltd

risk-adjusted benchmarking that allows clinicians to discover their strengths and weaknesses compared to their peers who treat similar populations.

To us, this is the ultimate example of evidence-based practice – if your benchmarked results are excellent, you have well-measured evidence assuring you to keep doing what you have been doing – good work. If your results in a particular area are subpar, then you should consider incorporating practice-based changes like empirically validated, evidence-based treatments.

Using quartile analyses, the TOP system will compare your best-treated and worst-treated populations, painting a clear picture of the demographic and clinical characteristics of the clients who could benefit from your practice improvement (e.g. consultation, focused continuing education and reading professional publications). Then, with a library of catalogued evidence-based principles and therapies tied to each TOP outcome domain, and within several minutes of clicking a button to access the benchmarking and quartile analyses, the treatment provider can know what concrete actions to consider taking. Below, we detail the vision, development and application of this system.

Vision and philosophy

In the early 1990s, as the first author was planning to leave his post as a team leader of an inpatient adolescent program to join a group practice outside Boston, Hillary Clinton was talking about national healthcare reform. Although her efforts eventually failed, she gave extraordinary momentum to the concept of accountability in healthcare. The concept was bold yet simple – all healthcare providers should be able to document that, on average, their patients were benefiting from the services provided. No longer would we be paid for delivering services on blind faith.

In an ideal world, the concept of measuring outcomes is hard to argue with. As providers, we probably should not be arguing against the measurement of quality, even if it is difficult and it may never be error free. Resisting measurement looks like we have something to hide. Nevertheless, the concept, while supported whole-heartedly by my brain, sent shivers up my spine. How would this newly minted, solo-practice provider compare to all the experienced therapists on managed care panels? Would I be first on the chopping block if the industry moved forward with its first, half-baked plans to throw a third of us into the ocean if our outcomes were subpar (Geigle & Jones, 1990)?

It was this anxiety that started the snowball rolling, leading to the development of the TOP. The first author's initial, counter-phobic response was to research the field and look for the best outcome system for his group practice to adopt. We were not willing to wait for Hillary or local managed care companies to decide how to measure our quality behind our backs while we sat back idly waiting for their verdicts. We wanted to know where we stood before they did, and afford ourselves the chance of taking action if it looked like action was necessary.

The snowball grew as these trips to the library failed to find a world-class outcome system for real-world providers. From practical issues of cost, to the scientific problems of risk adjustment, basic issues could not be answered to our satisfaction. For example, if insurance companies were really planning to compare our results to others, they should not do this based on raw outcome data. This was particularly obvious for the first author who, at the time, specialized in treating adolescents and young adults with multigenerational issues of abuse and trauma and whose outcomes were more likely to differ from those specializing in treating younger children, or the worried well. However, we saw no system or methodology that took these case-mix variables seriously, and certainly no outcome tool that did either.

Frankly, there were too many concerns to list here. Rather than crying foul and waging war against managed care, we decided to take action and begin the development of an outcome system built by, and for, providers. The five guiding principles that launched the development of TOP still guide our vision today: utility, cost, timing, risk adjustment and benchmarking.

Utility

We believe that the entire philosophy and approach to most outcome movements have been off-target. We certainly believe that the pressure for accountability is here to stay; however, it should neither be the single, nor the most important use of outcome data. As hinted to above, the entire process got off on the wrong foot when the major healthcare players gathered in the late 1980s to discuss the use of health outcomes (Geigle & Jones, 1990). Their meeting had overwhelmingly punitive tones. For example, the consensus, number-one use of outcome data was to profile clinicians on outcomes and eliminate those with 'documented poor quality'. With such approaches, there is little reason to expect clinician buy-in, or evidence-based use of the data; clinicians would be running scared.

We believe the principal focus of outcomes should be to guide and assist the psychotherapist in planning the treatment process. Such a tool should never prescribe a certain intervention, but provide the clinician with information, tailored to the patient's assessment and condition, about the relative success of various treatment options, and outline current advances in standard care by pointing to evidence-based interventions. By properly guiding clinicians, a system of outcomes management can facilitate communication between the patient and clinician while helping to identify budding problems before they become serious. Such a system is much more likely to be embraced by clinicians because it can inform and potentially improve the therapeutic process, rather than just evaluating and judging it.

Cost

To be used in clinical practice, we believe that outcomes management tools need to be free of royalty charges. Data processing services should be offered at cost to encourage use and capitalize on economies of scale. In line with this philosophy, BHL does not charge any royalty fees for the use of TOP. Unless you make other arrangements, however, you do need to use their service bureau to process the data. The advantages of this requirement are highlighted below (see section below on Benchmarking).

Timing

The major reason previous generation outcome projects failed is because of data processing. From Georgia to Washington State there are countless examples of massive amounts of data being dumped into black holes. Needless to say, it is impossible to sustain a project that cannot deliver useful results to its key participants – the patient and the psychotherapist. Whether the data is processed electronically or on paper, the BHL TOP system is designed to return useful results with this urgency in mind. Paper processing is obviously the most challenging:

- After the patient completes a TOP, the form is faxed to BHL's central computer system. There, it never touches paper again. A TIFF file image (the computer graphic file generated by your fax machine) is transferred to three data processing engines that translate the images into data.
- A human verifier looks over every form and makes sure the computers have correctly processed the information. The data is then transferred to the data warehouse where it is scored, compared to general population norms and any historical patient records, and a report is generated.
- These reports are returned via fax or e-mail to the clinician with an average return time (from hitting send on your fax machine) of 14 minutes.
- As an alternative to a fax-based system, BHL also has an electronic/web system where the results are returned within three seconds.

BHL also provides toll-free customer service, a training video and extensive documentation, making startup simple. By offloading the time-consuming process of warehousing and scoring reports, clinicians can stay focused on what they do best – treatment.

Similar to psychological testing, outcome assessment data and their reports need to be fed back to clinicians in a timely manner so that the results can be integrated into treatment planning, evaluation and diagnostic formulations. Only by delivering reports that facilitate the treatment process can a system meet clinicians' needs and win their buy-in.

Risk adjustment

Variables that are beyond the control of the therapeutic process, but nonetheless influence the outcome, are defined as case-mix variables (Goldfield, 1999). Naturalistic research typically lacks the experimental controls used in efficacy research to militate against the need to statistically control for (or measure) these case-mix variables. Without measuring and controlling for such variables, comparing or benchmarking naturalistic datasets can be quite misleading. Hsu (1989) has shown that even with randomization, when the samples are small, the chances of a 'nuisance' case-mix (e.g. AIDS) variable being disproportionately distributed across groups, is not only common, but very likely (in some cases exceeding 90%). Therefore, without extensive case-mix data, results have limited administrative value in real-world settings. These data need to be used to disaggregate and/or statistically adjust outcome data to produce fair and accurate benchmarking. Unless your clients' levels of life stress, or co-morbid medical conditions were measured and adjusted for, we believe your benchmarked outcomes would likely lead to misleading results.

Benchmarking

Outcome data is of little use if we do not have a reference group for comparison. Furthermore, since most payers probably will not blindly trust outcome data presented to them by providers (see Bilbrey & Bilbrey, 1995), we made a strategic decision to take on the difficult work of becoming a neutral, third-party data-processing organization. Like the consumer reports of the behavioural health field, BHL can certify outcome results as free from bias and fraud while offering the largest possible benchmarking reference database.

Whether it is looking for a sample of eating-disorder clients treated in residential treatment settings, or a sample of solo-practice providers specializing in treating sexual dysfunction, BHL is able to offer this level of specificity when creating a reference sample for your results. From here, with sophisticated risk adjustment, it is much easier to know where our relative strengths and weaknesses really lie.

Development

The TOP and its supporting infrastructure are designed to bring to the forefront the positive and beneficial aspects of outcomes management. For a kinder or

Table 7.1   Core Battery Conference criteria for a universal core battery

---

Not bound to specific theories
Appropriate across all diagnostic groups
Must measure subjective distress
Must measure symptomatic states
Must measure social and interpersonal functioning
Must have clear and standardized administration and scoring
Norms to help discriminate between patients and non-patients
Ability to distinguish clients from general population
Internal consistency and test–retest reliability
Construct and external validity
Sensitive to change
Easy to use
Efficiency and feasibility in clinical settings
Ease of use by clinicians and relevance to clinical needs
Ability to track multiple administrations
Reflect categorical and dimensional data
Ability to gather data from multiple sources

Source: Horowitz, L.M. et al. (eds.), *Measuring patient change in mood, anxiety, and personality disorders: Toward a core battery.* Washington, DC: American Psychological Association Press, 1997

friendlier outcomes management system (Kraus, Castonguay & Wolfe, 2006) to be clinically helpful, however, it needs to rest on solid psychometric properties. In this next section we will discuss the empirical basis of the TOP's development, which parallels the recommendations of the 1994 Core Battery Conference that was organized by the Society for Psychotherapy Research and the American Psychological Association (Horowitz, Lambert & Strupp, 1997). These recommendations are listed in Table 7.1.

As a universal core battery, the TOP is not tied to any specific theoretical orientation and measures many categories within symptom, functional and quality-of-life domains. The current version of the TOP is in its fourth incarnation with 48–58 questions, depending upon the age version (child, adolescent and adult).

Construction of the TOP

Initial development of the first version of TOP consisted of the first author generating more than 250 atheoretical items that spanned diagnostic symptoms and functional areas identified in the Diagnostic and Statistical Manual of Mental Disorders-IV (DSM-IV; American Psychiatric Association, 1994). All DSM-IV Axis I diagnostic symptoms were reviewed and those symptoms that the first author thought clients could reliably rate on a self-report measure were formulated into questions. Many assessment tools were also reviewed for item inclusion, but most were based on theoretical constructs inconsistent with DSM-IV symptomatology.

These questions were then presented to other clinicians for edit and review. They made suggestions for modifications and deletions, based on relative importance and clarity of items. Clients were administered initial versions of the questionnaires and asked for feedback as well. Questions were reworded based on feedback, and items that were less important or appeared to measure a similar symptom were eliminated. The tool was then revised and re-introduced for feedback. Such expert clinical and client review in the development process ensured adequate face validity. Subsequent versions of TOP were also used in clinical practice and the data factor analysed with increasingly robust sample sizes. The instrument presented here is the result of four iterations of this process.

The current version of the TOP is a battery of distinct modules that can be administered all together or in combinations as needed. The various modules of the TOP include:

- Chief complaints
- Demographics
- Treatment utilization and provider characteristics
- Co-morbid medical conditions and medical utilization
- Assessment of life stress
- Substance abuse
- Treatment satisfaction
- Functioning
- Quality of life/Subjective distress
- Mental health symptoms.

Psychometric overview

Factor structure

The development of stable and clinically useful subscale structures is a long-term process that is often short-changed in tool development. Nevertheless, it is a critically important step in creating a tool that is rich in reliable, valid and clinically useful information. A 13-year path aimed at creating a robust and parsimonious questionnaire with subscales that meet the criteria of the Core Battery Conference led to the current version of the TOP.

In the latest iteration, the 93 mental health symptom, functional and quality-of-life items from the third TOP version were administered to a large sample of newly admitted psychiatric clients. Participants were instructed to rate each question in relation to 'How much of the time during the last month you have . . .'. All questions were answered on a 6-point Likert frequency scale: 1 (*All*), 2 (*Most*), 3 (*A lot*), 4 (*Some*), 5 (*A little*), 6 (*None*).

The sample consisted of 19,801 adult patients treated in 383 different behavioural health services across the United States who completed all questions of the TOP at intake, as part of standard treatment. The sample was split into five random subsamples as a cross-validation strategy.

Sample 1 was used to develop a baseline factor model. Responses to the 93 items were correlated, and the resulting matrix was submitted to principal-components analysis (PCA) followed by correlated (Direct Oblimin) rotations. The optimal number of factors to be retained was determined by the criterion of eigenvalue greater than one supplemented by the scree test and the criterion of interpretability (Cattell, 1966; Tabachnick & Fidell, 1996). Items that did not load greater than 0.45 on at least one factor, and factors with fewer than three items were trimmed from the model.

Sample 2 was then used to develop a baseline measure of acceptability in a Confirmatory Factor Analysis (CFA) and revise the model using fit diagnostics in AMOS 4.0 (Arbuckle & Wothke, 1999). Goodness of fit was evaluated using the root mean square error of approximation (RMSEA) and its 90% confidence interval (90% CI; cf. MacCallum, Browne & Sugawara, 1996), comparative fit index (CFI), and the Tucker-Lewis index (TLI). Acceptable model fit was defined by the following criteria: RMSEA (<0.08, 90% CI<0.08), CFI (>0.90), and TLI (>0.90). Multiple indices were used because they provide different information about model fit (i.e. absolute fit, fit adjusting for model parsimony, fit relative to a null model); used together these indices provide a more conservative and reliable test of the solution (Jaccard & Wan, 1996). Few outcome tools' substructures have passed this state-of-the-art method of confirming a tools' factor structure.

For the TOP, most of the revised models were nested; in these situations, comparative fit was evaluated by χ^2 differences tests (χ^2 diff) and the interpretability of the solution. The final model that resulted from Sample 2 exploratory procedures was then comparatively evaluated in three independent CFAs (Samples 3–5) using the criteria above with excellent results (exceeding all pre-defined criteria as demonstrated in Table 7.2). Taken together, these analyses provide strong support for the stability and strength of the TOP factors.

Test–retest reliability

In order to assess the test–retest reliability, 53 behavioural health clients recruited by four community mental health centres completed the Treatment Outcome Package one week apart while they were waiting for outpatient

Table 7.2 Confirmatory factor analysis fit statistics

Confirmatory Factor Analysis	Description	N	DF	Tucker-Lewis Index	Comparative Fit Index	Root Mean Square Error of Approximation Indices	
						RMSEA	RMSEA Upper
Sample 2 initial	Derived from EFA model	3960	1218	0.898	0.906	0.045	0.046
Sample 2 final	Modified model	3960	1007	0.945	0.951	0.033	0.034
Sample 3	Confirmatory Analysis 1	3960	1007	0.940	0.946	0.035	0.036
Sample 4	Confirmatory Analysis 2	3960	1007	0.942	0.948	0.034	0.035
Sample 5	Confirmatory Analysis 3	3961	1007	0.940	0.947	0.035	0.036

treatment to begin. The stability of the TOP over time was assessed by computing intraclass correlation coefficients using a one-way random model. Except for the subscale Mania, all reliabilities for subscales (factors presented in Study 1) were excellent (see Table 7.3), ranging from 0.87 to 0.94. The subscale Mania's reliability was acceptable, but considerably lower at 0.76. This is due to the bi-modal distribution of mania items like: 'Feeling on top of the world'. These items do not have a linear relationship to health as feeling on top of the world all of the time might be an indication of mania, while never feeling on top of the world might be a sign of depression.

Discriminant and convergent validity

An important step in the establishment of the validity of a measure is the testing of whether it correlates highly with other variables with which it should theoretically correlate (convergent validity), and whether it does not correlate significantly with variables from which it should differ (discriminant validity). For the purpose of examining convergent and divergent validity, 312 participants completed the TOP and one or more validity questionnaires, outlined as follows: 110 completed the BASIS 32 (51 general population, 23 outpatient and 36 inpatient), 80 completed the SF-36 (43 general population, 3 outpatient and 34 inpatient), and 69 completed the BSI, BDI and MMPI-2 (69 outpatient).

Results provided evidence to the effect that TOP factors are measuring the constructs they were intended to measure. The TOP depression scale, for instance, correlated 0.92 with the Beck Depression Inventory (for more details, see Kraus, Seligman & Jordan, 2005).

Floor and ceiling effects

For an outcome tool to be widely applicable (especially for populations like the seriously and persistently mentally ill) it must accurately measure the full spectrum of the construct, including its extremes. Using a measure that fails to capture extreme level of psychopathology would be comparable to the use of a basal body thermometer (with a built-in ceiling of only 102 degrees) to study air temperature in the desert. On a string of hot summer days, one might conclude that the temperature never changes and stays at 102 degrees.

For a psychiatric patient who scores at the ceiling of the tool but actually has much more severe symptomatology, the patient could make considerable progress in treatment, but still be measured at the ceiling on follow-up. Incorrectly concluding that a client is not making clinically meaningful changes can lead to poor administrative and clinical decisions. The SF-36, for example,

Table 7.3 Subscale intercorrelations

FACTOR	DESCRIPTION	DEPRS	VIOLN	SCONF	LIFEQ	SLEEP	SEXFN	WORKF	PSYCS	PANIC	MANIC	Alpha	Intraclass test–retest
DEPRS	Depression											0.93	0.93
VIOLN	Violence	0.33										0.81	0.88
SCONF	Social Conflict	0.55	0.33									0.72	0.93
LIFEQ	Quality of Life	−0.78	−0.24	−0.45								0.85	0.93
SLEEP	Sleep Functioning	0.64	0.26	0.41	−0.50							0.86	0.94
SEXFN	Sexual Functioning	0.51	0.21	0.38	−0.41	0.36						0.69	0.92
WORKF	Work Functioning	0.55	0.43	0.53	−0.41	0.37	0.34					0.72	0.90
PSYCS	Psychosis	0.66	0.55	0.42	−0.46	0.51	0.42	0.50				0.69	0.87
PANIC	Panic	0.73	0.33	0.43	−0.52	0.59	0.43	0.46	0.67			0.83	0.88
MANIC	Mania	−0.26	0.11	−0.09	0.37	−0.12	−0.09	0.01	0.05	0.04		0.53	0.76
SUICD	Suicidality	0.44	0.44	0.26	−0.33	0.27	0.23	0.36	0.61	0.38	−0.02	0.78	0.90

has been shown to have significant ceiling effects in clinical samples (Nelson et al., 1995), suggesting that the tool has limited applicability to the Medicaid population for which it was being tested. For the TOP to be reliable and valid, it must demonstrate that it can measure the full range of pathology.

This important issue was examined using the TOP administrations for all adult clients from a diverse array of service settings that contracted with Behavioral Health Laboratories between the years of 1996 and 2003 to process and analyse their clinical outcome data (N = 216, 642). The dataset was analysed for frequency counts of clients who scored at either the theoretical maximum or minimum score of each TOP scale (Table 7.4). TOP scores are presented in Z-scores, standardized by using general population means and standard deviations. All scales are oriented so that higher scores indicate more symptoms or poorer functioning.

Analysis of the TOP revealed no substantial ceiling effects on any TOP scales, suggesting that the TOP sufficiently measures into the clinically severe extremes of these constructs. Furthermore, each TOP subscale measures at least a half to more than two standard deviations into the 'healthy' tails of its construct. Therefore, from this very large clinical sample it is reasonable to conclude that each TOP scale measures the full range of clinical severity and, as such, represents a substantial improvement over the widely used naturalistic outcome tools reported previously.

Sensitivity to change

The more accurately an outcome measure is able to measure important (even subtle) changes in clinical status, the more useful it is as an outcome tool. Unfortunately, many state governments and private payers have mandated the use of outcome tools that have inadequate sensitivity to change, costing all involved extensive time and wasted resources, only to have the project abandoned after the data are unable to demonstrate differences in provider outcomes. For example, the functional scales of the Ohio Youth Scales are not showing change in functional status in treatment (Ogles et al., 2000).

To examine its sensitivity to change, 20,098 adult behavioural health clients were administered the TOP at the start of treatment and later after several therapy sessions. For each TOP subscale, within group Cohen's d effect sizes were calculated comparing subscale scores at first TOP administration to subscale scores at the second TOP administration. In addition, a reliable change index was calculated for each TOP factor using procedures outlined in Jacobson, Roberts, Berns and McGlinchey (1999). The reliable change index can be used to determine if the change an individual client makes is beyond the measurement error of the instrument. We used the indices to classify each client as having made reliable improvement (or reliable worsening), or not, on each TOP subscale.

Table 7.4 Floor and ceiling effects

Factor	Theoretical Minimum	Theoretical Maximum	Number of clients at Minimum	Number of clients at Maximum	Total Sample Size (N)	Percentage of clients at Minimum	Percentage of clients at Maximum
DEPRS	−1.67	4.63	7,519	2,406	212,589	3.5	1.1
VIOLN	−0.44	15.44	121,625	978	205,932	59.1	0.5
SCONF	−1.44	2.87	11,606	726	145,695	8.0	0.5
LIFEQ	−2.34	5.05	4,430	6,210	156,738	2.8	4.0
SLEEP	−1.43	3.73	23,106	5,907	206,677	11.2	2.9
SEXFN	−1.15	3.79	48,905	1,264	150,576	32.5	0.8
WORKF	−1.54	5.95	22,081	163	152,511	14.5	0.1
PSYCS	−0.93	13.23	33,900	339	202,306	16.8	0.2
PANIC	−1.13	7.59	30,444	1,153	212,474	14.3	0.5
MANIC	−1.57	4.75	16,779	474	211,802	7.9	0.2
SUICD	−0.51	15.57	58,388	702	211,836	27.6	0.3

In addition, the same indices were used to calculate the number of clients who showed reliable improvement (or reliable worsening) on at least one TOP subscale.

For each TOP subscale, Table 7.5 presents sample size, mean and standard deviation of first and second TOP administrations, within-group Cohen's d effect size, and the percentage of clients who showed reliable improvement or worsening. With an average of only seven treatment sessions, Cohen's d effect sizes ranged from 0.16 (Mania) to 0.53 (Depression). Most TOP measures showed reliable improvement for at least a quarter of participants, and 91% of clients showed reliable improvement on at least one TOP subscale. As one might expect, the functional domains (Social Conflict, Work and Sex) tended to show less change than the symptom domains.

Criterion validity

The criterion validity of the TOP was examined in a study involving 94 members of the general population. Binary logistic regression was applied to each set of the 94 general population participants and a matched sample from the clinical population. These analyses combined all of the TOP measures into a binary stepwise logistic regression to determine the most parsimonious collection of subscales accounting for independent prediction of client vs. general population status. In this type of analysis, independent variables are entered into the equation one at a time based on which variable will add the most to the regression equation. The 10 available TOP scales (Depression, Violence, Quality of Life, Sleep, Sexual Functioning, Work Functioning, Psychosis, Mania, Panic and Suicide) served as the independent variables and client/general population status served as the dependent variable.

To explore the amount of variance accounted for in client/general population status by the six significant predictors in Analysis 1, we employed the Nagelkerke R^2 test (Nagelkerke, 1991). Quality of Life accounted for 28% of the variance in client/general population status, Psychosis accounted for another 6%, Mania accounted for another 8%, Suicidality accounted for another 5%, Work Functioning accounted for another 3%, and Sexual Functioning accounted for another 4%. Thus, together these six variables accounted for 54% of the variance in predicting client/general population status.

Ten separate samples and analyses were performed. The percentage of participants correctly classified as being from a client or general population sample ranged from 80% to 89%, with an average of 84%. Nagelkerke R^2 for the complete models ranged from 0.54 to 0.77 with a mean of 0.65. In addition, the variables that were significant predictors of client/general population status were fairly consistent across the ten analyses. In ten of the analyses, Quality of Life and Mania were significant predictors; in nine of the analyses Sexual

Table 7.5 Reliable improvement and worsening

Variable	N	Initial Mean	Follow-up Mean	Initial SD	Follow-up SD	Cohen's d	Percentage of clients showing reliable improvement	Percentage of clients showing reliable worsening
DEPRS	19,660	1.34	0.48	1.68	1.55	0.53	54	14
VIOLN	18,765	1.25	0.68	2.97	2.37	0.21	31	17
SCONF	8,047	0.28	-0.04	1.08	1.01	0.31	38	18
LIFEQ	10,039	2.19	1.44	1.83	1.81	0.41	52	21
SLEEP	18,869	0.68	0.16	1.46	1.32	0.37	47	20
SEXFN	9,407	-0.12	-0.31	1.12	1.04	0.18	25	15
WORKF	9,600	0.30	-0.10	1.44	1.29	0.29	39	20
PSYCS	18,320	2.02	1.14	2.85	2.42	0.33	44	18
PANIC	19,701	1.36	0.75	1.93	1.73	0.33	41	17
MANIC	19,561	-0.31	-0.47	1.00	0.96	0.16	10	6
SUICD	19,562	2.38	1.14	3.69	2.80	0.38	42	14

Functioning was a significant predictor; in eight of the analyses Psychosis was a significant predictor, and in six of the analyses Work Functioning and Panic were significant predictors. Other significant predictors included Suicidality (three analyses), Violence (three analyses), Depression (two analyses), and Sleep (one analysis). The most important predictor of client/general population status for each of the ten analyses was Quality of Life. This result, in and of itself, is important, as most of the frequently used outcome measures do not assess for the quality of life. By only focusing on level of distress and impairment, these instruments may fail to capture issues of meaning, purpose and/or satisfaction about oneself and his/her life. Such issues of human existence may well be a determinant in leading some people to decide to go into therapy. They are also likely to reflect some of the benefits that both client and therapist expect (implicitly or explicitly) from therapy. Similarly, this finding is consistent with Frank's (1976) demoralization hypothesis, which states that most clients do not enter therapy solely because of psychiatric symptoms. In addition to such psychological problems, clients come to therapy in a state of mind that is characterized by feelings of alienation, isolation, hopelessness, helplessness, impotence and/or a sense of meaninglessness. Such experiences, needless to say, are likely to impact on, and/or reflect, one's view of the quality of his/her life.

The results demonstrate that the TOP has some ability to discriminate between clients and members of the general population with an average correct classification rate of 84%. The consistency across the 10 separate analyses lends credence to these results. It is possible that the analyses could be further improved by adding several other scales to the analysis. The Social Conflict and Substance Abuse subscales of the TOP were not available for this analysis because these scales have been revised since the general population sample was collected.

Current applications

With more than 13 years of experience and a database that is doubling in size every few years, BHL and the TOP have a wealth of developed applications. In this section, we will highlight several of them.

Patient reports that inform

TOP questions have high-face validity to patients and psychotherapists alike. Questions are easy to read (5th grade level) and are related to DSM symptoms that are key to an initial interview (e.g. 'felt little or no interest in most things'). Years of exploratory and confirmatory factor analytic work on the TOP items reduced the number of questions to the three-to-five most powerful questions in a broad array of clinically useful domains. For the adult version, TOP domains include: Depression, Panic, Mania, Psychosis, Sleep, Sex, Work, Quality of Life, Substance Abuse, Suicide and Violence. In contrast with outcome tools that address only one or a few dimensions of functioning, the TOP patient reports provide a wealth of clinically useful assessment data that can be easily integrated into treatment planning. Results are reported as normalized Z-scores that represent their deviation from population norms. In addition to clinical domains (along Axis I) mentioned above, diagnostic considerations are reported for Axis III (medical considerations) and IV (life stress).

BHL is also finalizing a pre-filled, yet modifiable treatment plan (based on TOP responses) that is returned along with the standard TOP report, helping the therapist save time in developing an individualized course of treatment.

With assessment of dimensions like medical utilization, prior treatments, life stress and co-morbid medical conditions, the TOP also helps paint a full picture of the patient. Clinicians can give a new patient an access code to go online and complete the TOP before the appointment. This allows the clinician to get an excellent picture of the patient's perspective of his/her difficulties before actually conducting the initial interview.

Links to the research

As an empirically anchored outcomes management system, BHL has incorporated many features of the current evidence-based movement within the development of the TOP. For example, each of the TOP domains has been linked to a library of evidence-based practices, guidelines and research findings that should help clinicians find the most effective treatments for patients with different TOP profiles. For example, if a patient scores very high on the Depression Scale, this TOP library integrates findings compiled by Castonguay and Beutler (2005) and other sources into an easy-to-read summary of state-of-the-art treatments.

Moreover, building on the seminal research of Michael Lambert – who has single-handedly demonstrated that outcomes management makes us all more effective clinicians – the TOP provides early warnings if treatment appears to be heading in an unhelpful direction. Whether it might be by suggesting strategies to repair alliance ruptures, or the need to incorporate adjunctive interventions to increase client's social support, the evidence-based interventions that BHL will soon be able to suggest to clinicians is likely to help them reduce the number of patients categorized as 'negative responders'.

The rich database accumulated by BHL is also providing opportunities to study new ways of administering items to patients that could lead to further development of the TOP. Recent developments in item response theory and computerized adaptive testing indicate that clinically reliable and meaningful results can be obtained from responses to only a few items. The BHL database of TOP results is being analysed to identify those sets of items that have the optimal specificity and clinical 'bandwidth' to evaluate symptoms and change. The results of analyses is likely to lead to a shorter version of the TOP, which could potentially increase its clinical usefulness.

It should also be mentioned that some of recommendations for the use of the TOP in routine clinical practice have also been influenced by empirical research. Among these recommendations is the review of initial reports with patients in order to facilitate an informed discussion of the priorities and challenges of their treatment. This practice guideline is based not only on clinical experience, but also on the findings of six controlled studies showing that patients are more honest about shame-based issues on questionnaires than they are in face-to-face initial evaluations (Carr & Ghosh, 1983; Erdman, Klein & Greist, 1985; Hile & Adkins, 1997; Lucas, 1977; Searles et al., 1995; Turner et al., 1998). As such, integrating an outcome questionnaire is likely to open beneficial channels of communication between clients and therapists.

Enlightening aggregate data

Every month, BHL sends an aggregate report that summarizes the changes of a psychotherapist's average patient from intake and plots the changes their patients report over the course of treatment. Since more than 91% of patients report clinically and statistically significant change in at least one dimension of functioning, the TOP can provide very rewarding statistics to help psychotherapists guide their work.

In addition, BHL provides psychotherapists with unlimited access to its enormous benchmarking database. Psychotherapists can profile the types of patients with whom they work best and those patients with whom they need to improve their clinical skills. We have tried to use this database to identify the proverbial 'supershrink', the ideal psychotherapist who is well above average on everything. However, the data suggests that there is no such psychotherapist – we all have our strengths and weaknesses. A more realistic goal is for all clinicians to monitor their personal strengths and weaknesses by comparing their clinical outcomes with other professionals using a standardized instrument. Designed by, and for, clinicians TOP and its extensive benchmarking database is designed to facilitate this quest for learning and professional development.

References

American Psychiatric Association (1994). *Diagnostic and statistical manual of mental disorders* (4th edn.). Washington, DC: American Psychiatric Press.

Arbuckle, J. & Wothke, W. (1999). *AMOS 4.0 User's Guide.* Chicago: Smallwaters Corporation, Inc.

Bilbrey, J. & Bilbrey, P. (1995). Judging, trusting, and utilizing outcomes data: A survey of behavioral healthcare payors. *Behavioral Healthcare Tomorrow, 4,* 62–65.

Carr, A.C. & Ghosh, A. (1983). Response of phobic patients to direct computer assessment. *British Journal of Psychiatry, 142,* 60–65.

Castonguay, L.G. & Beutler, L.E. (eds.) (2005). *Principles of therapeutic change that work.* New York, NY: Oxford University Press.

Cattell, R.B. (1966). The scree test for the number of factors. *Multivariate Behavioral Research, 1,* 245–276.

Erdman, H.P., Klein, M. & Greist, J.H. (1985). Direct patient computer interviewing. *Journal of Consulting and Clinical Psychology, 53,* 760–773.

Frank, J.D. (1976). Restoration of morale and behavior change. In A. Burton (ed.), *What makes behavior change possible?* New York: Brunner/Mazel.

Geigle, R. & Jones, S.B. (1990). Outcomes measurement: A report from the front. *Inquiry, 27,* 7–13.

Goldfield, N. (ed.) (1999). *Physician profiling and risk adjustment.* Frederick, MD: Aspen Publishers.

Hile, M.G. & Adkins, R.E. (1997). Do substance abuse and mental health clients prefer automated assessments? *Behavior Research Methods, Instruments & Computers, 29,* 146–150.

Horowitz, L.M., Lambert, M.J. & Strupp, H.H. (eds.) (1997). *Measuring patient change in mood, anxiety, and personality disorders: Toward a core battery.* Washington, DC: American Psychological Association Press.

Hsu, L.M. (1989). Random sampling, randomization, and equivalence of contrasted groups in psychotherapy outcome research. *Journal of Consulting and Clinical Psychology, 57,* 131–137.

Jaccard, J. & Wan, C.K. (1996). *LISREL approaches to interaction effects in multiple regression.* Thousand Oaks, CA: Sage Publications.

Jacobson, N.S., Roberts, L.J., Berns, S.B. & McGlinchey, J.B. (1999). Methods for defining and determining the clinical significance of treatment effects: Description, application, and alternatives. *Journal of Consulting and Clinical Psychology, 67,* 300–307.

Kraus, D.R., Castonguay, L.G. & Wolfe, A. (2006). The Outcomes Assistant: A kinder philosophy to the management of outcomes. *Psychotherapy Bulletin, 41,* 23–31.

Kraus, D.R., Seligman, D. & Jordan, J.R. (2005). Validation of a behavioral health treatment outcome and assessment tool designed for naturalistic settings: The Treatment Outcome Package. *Journal of Clinical Psychology, 61,* 285–314.

Lucas, R.W. (1977). A study of patients' attitudes to computer interrogation. *International Journal of Man-Machine Studies, 9,* 69–86.

MacCallum, R.C., Browne, M.W. & Sugawara, H.M. (1996). Power analysis and determination of sample size for 575 covariance structure modeling. *Psychological Methods, 1,* 130–149.

McHorney, C.A., Ware, J.J. & Raczek, A.E. (1993). The MOS 36-Item Short-Form Health Survey (SF-36): II. Psychometric and clinical tests of validity in measuring physical and mental health constructs. *Medical Care, 31,* 247–263.

Nagelkerke, N.J.D. (1991). A note on the general definition of the coefficient of determination. *Biometrika, 78,* 691–692.

Nelson, D.C., Hartman, E., Ojemann, P.G. & Wilcox, M. (1995). Breaking new ground: Public/private collaboration to measure and manage Medicaid patient outcomes. *Behavioral Healthcare Tomorrow, 4,* 31–39.

Ogles, B.M., Melendez, G., Davis, D.C. & Lunnen, K.M. (2000). *The Ohio Youth Problem, Functioning, and Satisfaction Scales: Technical Manual.* Columbus, OH: Ohio University.

Searles, J.S., Perrine, M.W., Mundt, J.C. & Helzer, J.E. (1995). Self-report of drinking using touch-tone telephone: Extending the limits of reliable daily contact. *Journal of Studies on Alcohol, 56,* 375–382.

Tabachnick, B.G. & Fidell, L.S. (1996). *Using multivariate statistics* (3rd edn.). New York: Harper Collins College Publishers.

Turner, C.F., Ku L., Rogers, S.M., Lindberg, L.D., Pleck, J.H. et al. (1998). Adolescent sexual behavior, drug use, and violence: Increased reporting with computer survey technology. *Science, 280,* 867–873.

8

Clinical Outcomes in Routine Evaluation (CORE) – The CORE Measures and System: Measuring, Monitoring and Managing Quality Evaluation in the Psychological Therapies

Michael Barkham[1], John Mellor-Clark[2], Janice Connell[3], Chris Evans[4], Richard Evans[5] and Frank Margison[6]

[1] Centre for Psychological Services Research, University of Sheffield, UK, [2] CORE IMS, Rugby, UK, [3] University of Sheffield, UK, [4] University of Nottingham, UK, [5] CORE System Trust, Bath, UK, [6] Manchester Mental Health and Social Care Trust, UK

Introduction

The CORE (Clinical Outcomes in Routine Evaluation) measures make up a battery of client-completed outcome measures derived from a 34-item parent measure – the CORE-OM – which taps the domains of subjective well-being, problems, functioning and risk. The measures share the common method fundamental to all outcome measures identified as *patient reported outcome measures* (PROMs) and which are a central plank in healthcare evaluation. The CORE measures lie at the heart of the broader CORE System that comprises practitioner-completed forms capturing information relating to pre-therapy variables, treatment delivery and post-therapy impacts. This CORE System, in its paper form, is supported by optional software support systems using personal

Developing and Delivering Practice-Based Evidence   By Michael Barkham, Gillian E Hardy, and John Mellor-Clark   © 2010 John Wiley & Sons, Ltd

computer (PC) and the Internet (Net) formats (i.e. CORE PC and CORE Net) which offer analysis, reporting, benchmarking, performance development and clinical decision aids. This combination of measurement and monitoring tools has become widely used in the UK for evaluating the outcomes of psychological therapies and also the quality of service delivery (e.g. waiting times).

The origins of work relating to CORE lie in the seminal work of two people: Ernest Codman and Irene Elkin. Ernest Codman was a practising surgeon in Boston at the turn of the twentieth century who believed so strongly in the use of outcomes to assess the quality of surgery that he formed his own hospital, the End-Result Hospital, in Boston in 1914 and called for a compilation and analysis of surgical outcomes (for a succinct account, see Spiegelhalter, 1999). He believed that studying what happened to a patient would provide insight into better processes and practices. Codman kept a pocket-sized card, that he called an end-results card, on which he recorded each patient's case number, preoperative diagnosis, the names of operating team members, procedures and results. He used the cards to study outcomes, the basis for quality improvement.

Irene Elkin is an outstanding psychotherapy researcher who was principal investigator in the now classic National Institute of Mental Health's Treatment of Depression Collaborative Research Project. Earlier, as Irene Waskow, she had contributed a chapter entitled 'Selection of a core battery' to a text on *Psychotherapy change measures* (1975) that arose out of a 1970 American Psychological Association scientific conference of the same name. In essence, she proposed drawing together a core set of outcome measures which could be adopted in all studies of the psychological therapies and thereby bring coherence to the research effort focusing on clinical outcomes. The concept of a core outcome measure, widely adopted in research and practice, combined simple logic with a vision for how to ensure that measurement within the psychological therapies was standardized but flexible.

Codman was forced out of his post and died with his work unacknowledged. Neither did the initiative of the *Psychotherapy change measures* conference yield a core outcome battery. Like so many other innovative ideas, the work of Codman and Elkin was ahead of its time. But for us, the work of Elkin provided the initial impetus for the development of what eventually became the CORE-OM while the work of Codman provided a wider context for the development of the CORE System aimed at providing the tools for the quality assurance of psychological therapy service delivery.

The purpose of this chapter is to set out the development, implementation and yield of the CORE System components with specific reference to routine practice settings. We have framed the content of this chapter under three main headings that are consistent with quality evaluation: measurement, monitoring and management. These components laid the foundations for the first generation of quality evaluation using CORE and provide the basis for development of the second generation of quality evaluation that concludes this chapter.

Measurement

In the first part of this chapter, we set out the development and status of the suite of CORE measures. Our developmental model is one in which CORE measures can be used by themselves but they also lie at the heart of the broader (CORE) System. The CORE measures and associated tools provide a comprehensive assessment and outcomes toolkit. The measures are listed in the UK's *Mental Heath Outcomes Compendium* and recommended on the basis of quality and views of stakeholder groups (NIMHE, 2009). The CORE-OM has been used in randomized controlled trials (RCTs) (e.g. Morrell et al., 2009), practice-based service evaluations (e.g. Gibbard & Hanley, 2008), and large-scale surveys of psychological well-being (Royal College of Nursing, 2002). We first address the CORE measures as tools in their own right and then the additional yield gained from the broader CORE System that enables outcomes and service delivery to be monitored and ultimately performance managed.

Origins of the CORE measures

In 1994, the Mental Health Foundation (MHF) funded a conference on psychotherapy research at Balliol College Oxford (see Aveline & Shapiro, 1995). One specific outcome of this event was a Psychotherapy Research Initiative funded by the MHF which set out to support research in three areas, one being the development of a core outcome battery. The developmental work that ensued was a collaborative effort between practitioners and researchers based in Leeds, London and Manchester. Initially the work was funded by the MHF and subsequently by a series of grants from the Counselling in Primary Care Trust (CPCT), the Artemis Trust, and Department of Health Priorities and Needs Research and Development funding via Leeds Community Mental Health NHS Trust.

The development of the CORE-OM has been fully documented in earlier articles outlining the stakeholder survey, assessment of the prevailing measures, and the development of the CORE-OM itself (see Barkham et al., 1998, 2001, 2006a; Evans et al., 2000, 2002). In effect, our aim was to deliver something close to what has been described as the optimal outcome measure: 'the clinical equivalent of the Swiss Army knife – something small and easily taken into the field, with enough blades and attachments to fit any number of circumstances that may arise' (Kane, 1987, p. 95S). Accordingly, the consensus was that the measure should meet six specific criteria as follows: (1) be as short as is compatible with acceptable psychometric properties; (2) avoid specific difficulties identified in the preliminary work (e.g. bias regarding socio-demographic factors); (3) be simple to read and user-friendly; (4) be computer-scannable and hand-scorable; (5) be supported from a coordinating centre; and (6) be pan-theoretical and applicable across the range of settings routinely delivering psychological therapy (e.g. health, welfare, education, staff support, private practice, etc.). The resulting product was a 34-item outcome measure. To reflect its *core* nature (i.e. central domains) and its purpose (i.e. widespread use across services, clients and sessions), we named it the Clinical Outcomes in Routine Evaluation-Outcome Measure (CORE-OM).

The family of CORE measures and their psychometric properties

In this section, we describe the measures which make up the core outcome battery or, as we conceptualize it, the *CORE family of measures* (see Figure 8.1). We begin logically with the parent measure – the CORE-OM – and then move to the related CORE measures. Thumbnail summaries of the CORE outcome measures and specific population measures are presented in Tables 8.1A and 8.1B respectively. With the exception of versions for young people and learning disabilities, the measures have been drawn from the original 34-item pool.

The CORE-OM

- *Rationale and use:* The CORE-OM was designed to obtain assessment and outcome information at pre- and post-therapy. It is the preferred measure when there is sufficient time because of its coverage of items for assessment, including a group of risk items and the increased sensitivity that results from using a longer measure (Barkham et al., 1998, 2001; Evans et al., 2000, 2002). Figure 8.2 shows the CORE-OM.
- *Description*: The CORE-OM comprises 34 items tapping four domains: Subjective well-being (4 items); Problems (12 items); Functioning (12 items); and Risk (6 items). Each domain comprises both high- and low-intensity items and eight items are positively worded to minimize scoring bias. Subjective well-being was viewed as tapping one core construct while each of the other domains comprises *clusters* of items: Problems comprises Depression, Anxiety, Physical and Trauma, and Functioning comprises General day-to-day functioning, Social relationships and Close relationships. The Risk domain comprises Risk to Self and Risk to Others (Barkham et al., 2005b; Evans et al., 2002). Evidence to date suggests that the internal consistency is good at both the domain and cluster level except for Physical Problems and for Risk to Others. However, there is also evidence of strong interdependence between the domains with the exception of Risk (Evans et al., 2002).
- *Utility*: The measure is most commonly used to derive a single score and all published articles have consistently reported the mean item score for all items and also the mean item score for all the non-risk items. This gives

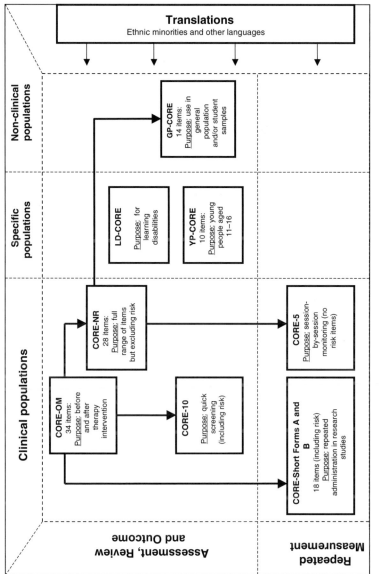

Figure 8.1 Map of the CORE family of measures. *Source:* Barkham, M. et al., A CORE approach to practice-based evidence: A brief history of the origins and applications of the CORE-OM and CORE system, *Counselling & Psychotherapy Research*, 6, 3–15. Taylor & Francis Group, 2006

Table 8.1A   CORE family of measures: Outcome measures

CORE measure	*Thumbnail summary*
CORE-OM: Parent outcome measure	The CORE-OM is a 34-item generic measure of psychological distress that is pan-theoretical (i.e. not associated with a school of therapy), pan-diagnostic (i.e. not focused on a single presenting problem), and draws upon the views of what practitioners considered to be the most important aspects of mental health to measure. The CORE-OM comprises 4 domains: Well-being (4 items); Symptoms (12 items – depression × 4, anxiety × 4, trauma × 2, physical × 2); Functioning (12 items – general × 4, social × 4, close relationships × 4); and Risk (6 items – to self × 4 or to others × 2). It takes between 5–10 minutes to complete.
Short Forms A and B: Session-by-session repeated administration (research)	Two parallel 18-item psychometrically balanced measures for use at alternate therapy sessions and which together make up the CORE-OM. The use of two short forms at alternate sessions rather than the CORE-OM measure at every session reduces memory effects. Due to administrative complexities, repeated administration of the two short forms is usually used only in research studies.
CORE-10: Review or quick initial assessment	A short 10-item version of the CORE-OM to be used as a screening tool and outcome measure when the CORE-OM is considered too long for routine use. Items cover anxiety (2 items), depression (2 items), trauma (1 item), physical problems (1 item), functioning (3 items – general day-to-day functioning, close relationships, social relationships) and risk to self (1 item). The measure has 6 high intensity/severity and 4 low intensity/severity items.
CORE-5: Session-by-session monitoring	The CORE-5 comprises 5 items drawn from the CORE-OM and was designed to provide a brief tool for practitioners to monitor ongoing progress session by session. Items cover anxiety, depression and functioning.

practitioners and researchers the option of including or excluding risk items. In addition, domain and cluster scores for items relating to, for example, depression or anxiety, can be reported separately (Barkham et al., 2005b; Evans et al., 2002). Hence, the structure of the CORE-OM provides a range of options for practitioners in terms of which level of presentation they wish to use for their particular purpose.

- *Scoring the CORE-OM*: The *original* scoring method required practitioners to calculate a mean item score – that is, to sum the total items marked and divide by 34 (providing all items are completed, or the number of items

Table 8.1B   CORE family of measures: Population-specific measures

CORE measure	Thumbnail summary
GP-CORE: General population For use with general or student populations	A short 14-item measure derived from the CORE-OM suitable for use with general populations, including students. In contrast to the CORE-OM, the GP-CORE does not comprise items denoting high-intensity of presenting problems or risk, and over half the items are positively keyed. These aspects increase its acceptability in a non-clinical population.
YP-CORE: Young person's	A 10-item measure derived from the CORE-OM and designed for use in the 11–16 age range. Structure is similar to that of the CORE-OM but with items rephrased to be more easily understood by the target age group.
LD-CORE: Learning disability	LD-CORE is being developed by therapists and adults with LD in Scotland and England. The measure includes simplified items from the CORE-OM selected by therapists and adults with LD, and also includes new items designed to cover the major issues they face that are not in the CORE-OM.
CORE translations	Approved translations now exist for Gujarati, Norwegian, Italian, Slovak, Swedish, Icelandic, Albanian, Dutch, Danish, German, Croatian, Serbian, Bosnian and Greek. Referential and psychometric data for the Slovak, Italian and Norwegian translations are available. People seeking other translations or wishing to help produce them should contact ✉ core-trans@psyctc.org

completed if there are missing items) yielding a mean item total ranging from 0 to 4 (Evans et al., 2002). However, feedback from practitioners identified the 0–4 range for the score difficult to use because of the fractional nature of the resulting score (i.e. 1.83). It tends to be easier to assign meaning to whole numbers rather than to fractions of numbers.

The *revised* scoring method took account of this feedback by adopting a procedure of multiplying the mean score by 10 and calling this a *clinical score* (Leach et al., 2006). This does not alter the psychometric properties of the measure (although the standard deviation also needs to be multiplied by 10). Procedures for scoring the CORE-OM are set out in Table 8.2 and a look-up table of total scores and equivalent clinical scores is presented in Table 8.3 (see also Barkham et al., 2006a). However, the look-up table will only work correctly if there are no missing items. When clients miss out items, the total needs to be divided by the number of items completed to get the mean score, and multiplied by 10 to get the clinical score.

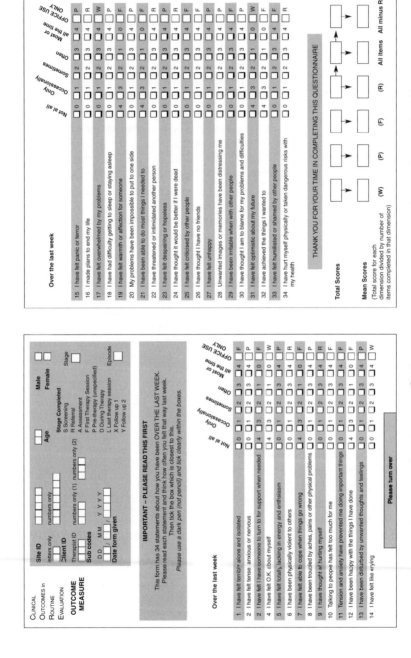

Figure 8.2 The CORE-OM © The CORE System Trust: www.coreims.co.uk/copyright.pdf

Table 8.2   Methods for scoring the CORE-OM

Method A: To obtain the mean item score
   Stage 1: Add the total score
   Stage 2: Divide by 34 (or number of items completed if there are missing responses)
   Stage 3: Result is a mean item score ranging from 0 to 4
   Example 1: A total score of 58 divided 34 = 1.71

Method B: To obtain the clinical score
This is the mean item score multiplied by 10
   Stage 1: Add the total score
   Stage 2: Refer to look-up table to convert to clinical score which will yield a score
     ranging from 0 to 40
   Example 2 (using look-up table): A total score of 58 = 17.1
   Example 3 (not using look-up table): A total score of 58 divided by 34 = 1.71
     multiplied by 10 = 17.1

Method C: Easy estimate method
   Stage 1: Add all client marked items
   Stage 2: Divide by 10
   Stage 3: Multiple by 3
   Example 4: A total score of 58 divided by 10 = 5.8 and multiplied by 3 = 17.4

Table 8.3 shows that the actual clinical score is 17.1. Hence, the estimate of 17.4 is fairly close to the true score when working at a practical level and wanting to have an immediate sense of the score.

Source: Barkham, M. et al., A CORE approach to practice-based evidence: A brief history of the origins and applications of the CORE-OM and CORE system, *Counselling & Psychotherapy Research, 6*, 3–15. Taylor & Francis Group, 2006

    The meaning of CORE scores: We have developed guidelines on the meaning of CORE-OM scores using severity bands set out in Table 8.3 using a cut-off score of 10. The severe level (25 or higher) was originally defined by a score approximately one standard deviation above the mean of a clinical sample (Barkham et al., 2001) and subsequent data sets have confirmed this score as a pragmatic cut-off for severe distress. In an analysis of distributions of CORE-OM scores for accumulated samples, we found 12% of a general population (N > 500) scoring 10 or above (i.e. in the clinical range) and approximately 18% of a clinical sample (N > 10,000) scoring in the severe range (Connell et al., 2007b).

- *Psychometric properties*:
  - ○ *Acceptability*: In a general population sample fewer than 2% of those who completed a follow-up psychiatric interview refused to complete the CORE-OM or were deemed incapable of completing it. The mean omission rate on all items across the respondent group as a whole was

Table 8.3   Look-up table of CORE-OM scores and severity levels

Non-clinical range

Total score	Clinical Score	Simple score	Severity Level
1	0.3		
2	0.6	0	
3	0.9		
4	1.2		
5	1.5	1	
6	1.8		
7	2.1		
8	2.4	2	
9	2.6		Healthy
10	2.9		
11	3.2		
12	3.5	3	
13	3.8		
14	4.1		
15	4.4	4	
16	4.7		
17	5.0		
18	5.3	5	
19	5.6		
20	5.9		
21	6.2		
22	6.5	6	
23	6.8		
24	7.1		
25	7.4	7	
26	7.6		
27	7.9		Low level
28	8.2		
29	8.5	8	
30	8.8		
31	9.1		
32	9.4	9	
33	9.7		

Clinical range — Mild, Moderate, Moderate-to-severe

Total score	Clinical Score	Simple score	Severity Level
	Clinical cut-off level		
34	10.0		
35	10.3	10	
36	10.6		
37	10.9		
38	11.2		
39	11.5	11	
40	11.8		
41	12.1		Mild level
42	12.4	12	
43	12.6		
44	12.9		
45	13.2		
46	13.5	13	
47	13.8		
48	14.1		
49	14.4	14	
50	14.7		
51	15.0		
52	15.3	15	
53	15.6		
54	15.9		
55	16.2	16	
56	16.5		
57	16.8		
58	17.1		Moderate level
59	17.4	17	
60	17.6		
61	17.9		
62	18.2		
63	18.5	18	
64	18.8		
65	19.1		
66	19.4	19	
67	19.7		
68	20.0		
69	20.3	20	
70	20.6		
71	20.9		
72	21.2		
73	21.5	21	
74	21.8		
75	22.1		Moderate-to-severe level
76	22.4	22	
77	22.6		
78	22.9		
79	23.2		
80	23.5	23	
81	23.8		
82	24.1		
83	24.4	24	
84	24.7		

Clinical range — Severe

Total score	Clinical Score	Simple score	Severity Level
85	25.0		
86	25.3		
87	25.6	25	
88	25.9		
89	26.2		
90	26.5		
91	26.8	26	
92	27.1		
93	27.4		
94	27.6	27	
95	27.9		
96	28.2		
97	28.5	28	
98	28.8		
99	29.1		
100	29.4	29	
101	29.7		
102	30.0		
103	30.3	30	
104	30.6		
105	30.9		
106	31.2		
107	31.5	31	
108	31.8		
109	32.1		
110	32.4	32	Severe level
111	32.6		
112	32.9		
113	33.2		
114	33.5	33	
115	33.8		
116	34.1		
117	34.4	34	
118	34.7		
119	35.0		
120	35.3	35	
121	35.6		
122	35.9		
123	36.2		
124	36.5	36	
125	36.8		
126	37.1		
127	37.4	37	
128	37.6		
129	37.9		
130	38.2		
131	38.5	38	
132	38.8		
133	39.1		
134	39.4	39	
135	39.7		
136	40.0	40	

Guidance notes

The original mean item score can be readily calculated by dividing the clinical score by 10.

The 'simple' score uses the first integer only of the clinical score as a rough guide.

The reliable change index is 5 points and the cut-off level is a clinical score of 10 (or .5 and 1 respectively if using the traditional scoring method).

Source: Barkham, M. et al., A CORE approach to practice-based evidence: A brief history of the origins and applications of the CORE-OM and CORE system, *Counselling & Psychotherapy Research*, 6, 3–15. Taylor & Francis Group, 2006

1.4%. When those who did not turn over to complete the second page were disregarded, this reduced to 0.4% (Connell et al., 2007b).

○ *Internal reliability*: In a general population sample the internal consistency coefficient alpha was 0.91 (Connell et al., 2007b) and in a large primary care sample it was 0.93 (Barkham et al., 2005b). For older adults, the alpha was 0.90 in a clinical sample and 0.83 in a non-clinical sample (Barkham et al., 2005a). The reliability of the domains has been reported as follows: Well-being = 0.70, Problems = 0.87, Functioning = 0.85, and Risk = 0.77 (Evans et al., 2002). Within these domains, all item clusters have obtained alpha values greater than 0.70 with the exception of 'close relationships' (0.65). The item clusters of 'physical' and 'risk to others' comprise only two items each and would not be expected to reach 0.70 (see Barkham et al., 2005b).

○ *Test–retest reliability*: In a large clinical population the reliability was 0.88 at 1 month, 0.81 at 2 months, 0.83 at 3 months and 0.80 at 4 months (Barkham et al., 2007).

- *Validity:*
  ○ *Construct validity*: Analyses of construct validity have consistently shown domain scores other than for risk to intercorrelate strongly, tapping into general psychological distress, while scores on the Risk domain are much less correlated with the other scores (Evans et al., 2002; Lyne et al., 2006). Though the various domain scores are highly intercorrelated, they are conceptually different, have construct and face validity, and reflect dimensions of change consistently rated as *core* issues both by therapists of varied modalities and by clients.
  ○ *Convergent validity*: Studies have reported high correlations between the CORE-OM and Beck Depression Inventory-I (BDI-I; Beck et al., 1961) of 0.85 to 0.86 and between the CORE-OM and BDI-II (Beck et al., 1996) of 0.75 to 0.81 (Cahill et al., 2006; Evans et al., 2002; Leach et al., 2006). The correlation between the Hamilton Rating Scale for Depression (HRSD; Hamilton, 1960) and the CORE-OM has been reported as 0.67 compared with 0.56 between the HRSD and the BDI-II (Cahill et al., 2006). The correlation with the Beck Anxiety Inventory (BAI; Beck et al., 1988) has been reported as 0.65. Transformation tables have also been produced to convert between BDI-I and CORE-OM scores (Leach et al., 2006). The CORE-OM and Patient Health Questionnaire-9 (PHQ-9; Kroenke, Spitzer & Williams, 2001) have been evaluated against the SCID diagnosis of depression resulting in the area under the curve for the CORE-OM of 0.92, and a depression cut-off score of 13, compared with 0.94 for the PHQ-9 (Gilbody, Richards & Barkham, 2007). This illustrates that depression, whether interviewer-rated or self-rated, correlates very strongly with the more general self-rating of distress and dysfunction on the CORE-OM as operationalized by the total mean score.

- *Normative baseline severity* (see Table 8.4 for summary): The CORE-OM has been used with clinical and non-clinical populations from which normative data have been derived. The mean clinical score for primary care settings has consistently been in the region of 17–18. Data from secondary (psychology and psychotherapy) services have yielded a mean score very similar to that

Table 8.4 Normative data: Baseline severity

	Total N	Men and Women	Men	Women	Description	Reference
Non-clinical Populations						
Non-distressed	118	2.5 (1.8)	2.9 (2.0)	2.2 (1.4)	Sample from ONS Psychiatric Morbidity Survey	Connell et al. 2007b
General population	535	4.8 (4.3)	4.9 (4.1)	4.8 (4.5)	Sample from ONS Psychiatric Morbidity Survey	Connell et al. 2007b
Older age non-clinical	184	-	5.4 (4.4)	6.3 (3.3)	Via community organizations (e.g. Age Concern centres	Barkham et al. 2005a
Non-clinical	1084	7.6 (5.9)	6.9 (5.3)	8.1 (6.1)	University students and sample of convenience	Evans et al. 2002
Clinical Populations						
Older age clinical	98	-	15.0 (6.0)	15.5 (5.7)	Over 65 yrs attending mental health out-patient or day hospital services	Barkham et al. 2005a
Lowest primary care service	-	15.6	-	-	Sample from Primary care 2	Mullin et al. 2006
Primary care 2	11953	17.5 (6.3)	17.3 (6.2)	17.5 (6.3)	32 sites collecting data using CORE PC. Clients completing pre- and post-measures	Mullin et al. 2006

Primary care 1	5733	18.1 (6.7)	17.5	18.3	33 NHS primary care services, forms scanned using Formic	Evans et al. 2003
Secondary care	1918	18.1 (7.4)	-	-	17 Clinical psychology and psychotherapy services	Barkham et al. 2005b
Student counselling	1109	18.2 (6.0)	17.6 (6.2)	18.4 (5.9)	11 university counselling services	Connell et al. 2007a
Clinical population	890	18.6 (7.5)	18.8 (7.8)	18.5 (7.7)	23 sites recruited via Society for Psychotherapy Research (SPR)	Evans et al. 2002
BME	279	18.8 (6.8)	-	-	Sample from Primary care 1	Evans et al. 2003
Secondary care	2710	19.0 (7.4)	18.5 (7.6)	19.3 (7.3)	39 secondary care services	Barkham et al. 2001
Primary care age 16–24	578	19.3 (6.7)	-	-	From sample Primary care 1	Connell et al. 2007a
Highest primary care service	-	20.3	-	-	Sample from Primary care 2	Mullin et al. 2006
Leeds research clinic – major depression	77	20.7 (5.5)	-	-	Research clinic for clients with major depression	Cahill et al. 2006

from primary care services. The Risk score, however, has been found to be higher for secondary care when compared with primary care services. In the clinical samples, as is often found with mental health measures, there is a tendency for females to score higher than males though this is not a consistent finding in all samples.

- *Evaluating change*: Summaries of pre-post change on CORE-OM scores together with uncontrolled (i.e. pre-post) effect sizes are presented in Table 8.5. In addition to these standard forms of reporting change, two components have been identified as central to determining meaningful change: reliable change, and clinically significant change (for further details, see Evans et al., 1998; Jacobson & Truax, 1991).
  - ○ *Reliable change index*: The reliable change index (RCI) reflects the extent of change in a measure that might be expected by chance alone or measurement error. To date, we have used an RCI of 0.48 for the CORE-OM. Rounding this to 0.50 would yield a clinical score of 5. Hence, to be confident of a client making reliable change, we would be looking for changes of 5 or more in the clinical score (or 0.5 using the mean item scoring method).
  - ○ *Clinical cut-offs*: The originally reported mean item cut-off scores were set at 1.19 for men and 1.29 for women (Evans et al., 2002). Translating these to the new scoring yields values of 11.9 and 12.9 – and rounding up for ease of practical use – yields scores of 12 and 13 respectively. Subsequent work using a larger clinical population and a general population sample yielded a cut-off score of 9.3 for men and 10.2 for women (Connell et al., 2007b). For ease of use these are rounded to 10.
  - ○ The score of 10 is somewhat easier to work with in busy routine settings and saves separate calculations for male and female clients. The lower cut-off score of 10 means that more clients are included in the clinical sample for a service but it also requires, by definition, a lower score than previously for a client to meet clinical improvement although the extent of change (i.e. 5) remains the same.

Shorter versions for specific purposes

We have enhanced the utility of CORE-OM by complementing it with a series of directly derived measures aimed at responding to service needs. These versions are identified by the addition of a suffix (e.g. CORE-SF, CORE-10 and CORE-5) and are briefly summarized below.

CORE Short Forms: CORE-SFs

- *Rationale and use:* The CORE-SFs provide an option to researchers carrying out repeated measurement over time (i.e. session-by-session). Two very

Table 8.5 Normative data: Change from pre- to post-therapy ordered from smallest to largest pre–post therapy effect size for samples comprising more than a single service

Service setting	Sample description	N Service	N Client	Pre-therapy clinical score	Post-therapy clinical score	Difference in pre-post therapy clinical score	Pre-post therapy effect size	Reference
Secondary care	Clients receiving a range of therapies	6	224	18.5 (7.1)	12.3 (8.4)	6.2	0.87	Barkham et al. 2001
Primary and secondary*	Clients receiving CBT/PCT/PDT therapy	33	1309	17.4 (6.5)	8.5 (6.3)	8.9	1.36	Stiles et al. 2006
Primary care	Clients receiving CBT/PCT/PDT therapy	32	5613	17.6 (6.3)	8.8 (6.4)	8.8	1.39	Stiles et al. 2008
Primary care*	Clients with planned endings	33	1868	17.9 (6.5)	8.4 (6.1)	9.5	1.51	Barkham et al. 2006b
Student counselling	Student counselling services	7	323	17.8 (5.6)	9.1 (5.5)	8.7	1.57	Connell et al. 2008

*denotes these samples are drawn from the same overall data set and therefore the clients are not necessarily independent

CBT = cognitive behavioural therapy; PCT = person-centred therapy; PDT = psychodynamic therapy similar short versions were devised: Short Form A (SF-A) and Short Form B (SF-B). We designed the forms to be used alternately, thereby reducing memory effects for clients (Evans et al., 2002). However, using them alternately does add a degree of complexity unless automated within a software package (see later).

- *Description:* Each short form comprises 18 items and covers all four domains as follows: Subjective well-being = 4 items (the same items in SF-A and SF-B); Problems = 6 items, Functioning = 6 items, and Risk = 2 items (Cahill et al., 2006; Evans et al., 2002).
- *Psychometric properties:* The psychometric properties of these two versions as determined by the analysis of the items embedded within the CORE-OM have been reported as: SF-A: all items, M = 13.3 (SD = 9.1), alpha = 0.94; SF-B: all items, M = 13.3 (SD = 9.0), alpha = 0.94 (Evans et al., 2002). Subsequent use of the short forms for monitoring purposes yielded the following average from 703 sessions: SF-A: M = 16.3, SD = 8, n = 377, alpha = 0.93; SF-B: M = 16.6, SD = 7.8, n = 326, alpha = 0.92 (Cahill et al., 2006).

CORE-10

- *Rationale and use:* The CORE-10 (see Figure 8.3) was designed for use as an initial screening measure in busy clinical settings and complements the CORE-OM by providing a short and easy to score measure that can be used for reviewing progress and for the purposes of case management (Barkham et al., 2008a; Connell & Barkham, 2007).
- *Description:* In designing the CORE-10, we were cognizant of the need to sample both high and low intensity items in relation to *depression* and *anxiety* due to their high prevalence. Accordingly, there is a total of four items covering depression and anxiety. In terms of functioning, we selected one item from each of the three clusters – *general, social, and close relationships* – and we selected single items from both *physical* and *trauma* together with a single *risk* item as a key component in screening.
- *Psychometric properties:*
  - *Acceptability and feasibility:* Feedback to date indicates the CORE-10 to be both acceptable in GP and primary care settings. The format of the CORE-10 minimizes missing items due to (a) it being on one side of A4, and (b) exclusion of those items more commonly omitted by clients.
  - *Internal reliability:* The internal consistency of the CORE-10 is high with an alpha of 0.82 (CI 0.79 to 0.85). For women the alpha was 0.82 (CI 0.78 to 0.86) and for men 0.81 (CI 0.76 to 0.86). For details, see Connell and Barkham (2007).
  - *Sensitivity and specificity:* Sensitivity and specificity values have been generated in relation to a range of CORE-10 scores such that the

CLINICAL

OUTCOMES in

ROUTINE

EVALUATION

CORE-10 v.1

Site ID								Stage Completed

S Screeening
R Referral
A Assessment
F First Therapy Session
P Pre-therapy (unspecified)
D During Therapy (review)
L Last therapy session
X Follow up 1
Y Follow up 2

Client ID

letters only   numbers only

Sub codes

Therapist ID   numbers only (1)   numbers only (2)

Episode   Stage

Date form given
D D   M M   Y Y Y Y

Gender
☐ Male   Age
☐ Female

IMPORTANT - PLEASE READ THIS FIRST
This form has 10 statements about how you have been OVER THE LAST WEEK.
Please read each statement and think how often you felt that way last week.
Then tick the box which is closest to this.
Please use a dark pen (not pencil) and tick clearly within the boxes.

Over the last week...

Not at all / Only occasionally / Sometimes / Often / Most or all of the time

1 I have felt tense, anxious or nervous	☐ 0	☐ 1	☐ 2	☐ 3	☐ 4
2 I have felt I have someone to turn to for support when needed	☐ 4	☐ 3	☐ 2	☐ 1	☐ 0
3 I have felt able to cope when things go wrong	☐ 4	☐ 3	☐ 2	☐ 1	☐ 0
4 Talking to people has felt too much for me	☐ 0	☐ 1	☐ 2	☐ 3	☐ 4
5 I have felt panic or terror	☐ 0	☐ 1	☐ 2	☐ 3	☐ 4
6 I made plans to end my life	☐ 0	☐ 1	☐ 2	☐ 3	☐ 4
7 I have had difficulty getting to sleep or staying asleep	☐ 0	☐ 1	☐ 2	☐ 3	☐ 4
8 I have felt despairing or hopeless	☐ 0	☐ 1	☐ 2	☐ 3	☐ 4
9 I have felt unhappy	☐ 0	☐ 1	☐ 2	☐ 3	☐ 4
10 Unwanted images or memories have been distressing me	☐ 0	☐ 1	☐ 2	☐ 3	☐ 4

Total (Clinical Score*)

---

* Procedure: Add together the item scores, then divide by the number of questions completed to get the mean score, then multiply by 10 to get the Clinical Score.
Quick method for the CORE-10 (if all items completed): Add together the item scores to get the Clinical Score.

Thank you for your time in completing this questionnaire

Figure 8.3 The CORE-10 © The CORE System Trust: www.coreims.co.uk/
copyright.pdf

relative trade-off between sensitivity and specificity can be taken into account when considering the adoption of a cut-off for a specific condition, for example, depression (Barkham et al., 2008a).

- *Validity:*
  - *Concurrent validity*: Correlations between the CORE-10 items and other measures are as follows: Symptom Checklist-90-R (SCL-90-R; Derogatis, 1994) = 0.81, Brief Symptom Inventory (BSI; Derogatis & Melisaratos, 1983) = 0.75, BDI-I = 0.77, BDI-II = 0.76, BAI = 0.65, Clinical Interview Schedule-Revised (CIS-R; Lewis et al., 1992) = 0.74, and PHQ-9 = 0.56 (Connell & Barkham, 2007).
  - *Convergent validity*: The CORE-10 items and PHQ-9 have been evaluated against a diagnosis of depression and the area under the curve for the CORE-10 was 0.90 and for the PHQ-9 was 0.94 (Barkham et al., 2008a).
- *Sensitivity to change and norms:* The mean CORE-10 clinical score has been reported as 20.2 (SD = 0.79) with no significant difference between men (M = 19.8, SD = 0.76) and women (M = 20.4, SD = 0.80). The mean score is slightly higher than for the CORE-OM because the smaller number of items (i.e. 10) yield a higher proportion of items that are scored as being present as compared with the CORE-OM where it is more likely that some items will score '0', especially the risk items. In screening for depression, a cut-off score of 13 on the CORE-10 yields sensitivity and specificity values of 0.92 and 0.72 respectively. For general psychological distress, the cut-off score to discriminate between a clinical and non-clinical population has been calculated as 11.0 with the difference between men (10.6) and women (11.1) being less than 1 full point (see Barkham et al., 2008a).

CORE-5: Ongoing monitoring

- *Rationale and use:* The CORE-5 was devised as a session-by-session monitoring tool – a thermometer – and an aid for signalling clinical concern. It can be used repeatedly in the traditional paper and pencil format and also be administered verbally in the session by a practitioner. Its use differs from the CORE-OM and CORE-10 in that it is not a pre-post change measure. Rather, it is a potential signal for action by the practitioner. In this context and with only five items, a maximum score is more likely on the CORE-5 than on the other measures together with a wider spread of scores (Bewick et al., 2009).
- *Description:* It comprises two positive and three negatively-keyed items covering the domains of subjective well-being, problems (anxiety, depression) and functioning (close relationships and general). There is no specific risk item.
- *Psychometrics and norms:* The alpha has been reported as 0.81 and the overall mean score as 19.80 (SD = 9.33) compared with 18.44 (SD = 6.91)

for the sample on the CORE-OM. The CORE-5 items and PHQ-9 have been evaluated against a diagnosis of depression and the area under the curve for the CORE-5 was 0.92 and for the PHQ-9 was 0.94 (Bewick et al., 2009).

Shorter versions for specific populations

We have also derived measures from the CORE-OM designed for specific populations. These versions are identified by the addition of a prefix (e.g. GP-CORE, YP-CORE and LD-CORE) and are briefly summarized below.

General population: GP-CORE

- *Rationale and use:* The GP-CORE is a 14-item measure for use in a general population. It is intended for use in samples that are not explicitly clinical (e.g. students, occupational samples). Crucially, no item contains the word 'problem' and there are no items explicitly tapping risk.
- *Description:* Item selection was driven by acceptability to users and psychometric properties were checked after item selection rather than the other way around. Six negatively keyed low intensity items were selected which, with the eight positively keyed items, made for a total of 14 items that are presented in the same order as they appear in the full version.
- *Psychometric properties and norms:* Internal consistency is high (alpha of 0.83: men = 0.80; women = 0.86) and there is no reported significant difference in scores between men (M = 12.7, SD = 5.6) and women (M = 13.1, SD = 6.2). The means and SDs for males and females in non-clinical and clinical samples are as follows: *Non-clinical* men = 10.2 (SD = 6.3), women = 10.7 (SD = 7.1); *Clinical* men = 19.8 (SD = 6.6), women = 21.6 (SD = 6.6). The resulting clinical cut-off scores are 14.9 for males and 16.3 for females (Sinclair et al., 2005).

Young persons: YP-CORE

- *Rationale and use:* The YP-CORE was devised to succeed an earlier version, named Teen-CORE, and focuses on the adolescent years (age range 11–16), thereby extending the application of CORE into child and adolescent mental health services. It was designed using 10 items in order to minimize demands on young people and to ease scoring in busy settings (Twigg et al., 2009).
- *Description:* The YP-CORE comprises four problem and four functioning items together with single risk and well-being items.
- *Psychometric properties and norms:* The YP-CORE has a Flesch-Kincaid grade level score of 2.1 with reading level scores for individual items ranging from 0.8 ('My problems have felt too much for me') to 5.2 ('I have felt unhappy').

It has high reliability (alpha of 0.85: young men = 0.83; young women = 0.85) and reliability was satisfactory over all age groups and within the age bands. Based on a sample of adolescents completing the YP-CORE at pre- and post-therapy, the mean pre-therapy score for all items has been reported as 18.5 (SD = 7.44) and 19.6 (SD = 7.64) for the non-risk items. The associated post-therapy score for all items was 8.8 (SD = 5.62) or 9.6 (SD = 5.86) for the non-risk items (for details, see Twigg et al., 2009).

Learning disabilities: LD-CORE

- *Rationale and use:* The CORE-OM is being adapted for people with learning disabilities (see Brooks & Davies, 2007; Marshall & Willoughby-Booth, 2007).
- *Description:* The measure includes simplified items from the CORE-OM selected by therapists and adults with LD, and also includes new items designed to cover the major issues faced by people with LD that are not contained in the CORE-OM.

CORE translations

We have also worked with colleagues to produce a range of translations for use in the UK and through international collaborations.

- *Rationale and use:* The CORE System Trust has actively supported translations of the CORE-OM, and hence the shortened versions, into other languages, both for non English speaking UK residents and for use outside the UK.
- *Description:* A translation protocol ensures a consistent methodology is applied to translations involving multiple independent forward translations being produced by native speakers of the target language aiming to have an absolute minimum of one lay person, one mental health professional and one professional translator or interpreter. All forward translations are collected and as many translators as possible come together to discuss the differences between them and finalize a penultimate version. This is then checked with an independent back-translation and with people of different ages and, where possible, from different locations where dialect or culture vary from those of the translators. Final versions are approved by the CORE System Trust. Examples of approved translations include Gujarati, Norwegian, Italian, Slovak, Swedish, Icelandic, Albanian, Greek and Dutch. People seeking other translations or wishing to help produce them should contact ⊠ core-trans@psyctc.org

CORE System

A key part of our philosophy has been to place the information gained from the use of measurement tools in their appropriate context – that is, the world of the client, their presentation, and the service they are receiving. Accordingly, the CORE measures are a component – albeit a central one – of a *system approach* to measurement called the *CORE System*.

- *Rationale and use:* The CORE System comprises three tools: a) the client completed CORE-OM, completed at least pre and post-therapy; b) the pre-therapy practitioner completed Therapy Assessment Form, and c) the post-therapy practitioner completed End of Therapy Form. The content of the system was informed by extensive collaboration with practitioners, managers and service commissioners and some of the work used local Practice Research Networks (PRNs). For full details, see Mellor-Clark et al. (1999), and Mellor-Clark and Barkham (2000, 2006).
- *Description:* To complement the CORE-OM and provide client contextual detail, the double-sided CORE Therapy Assessment Form (see Figure 8.4) captures a core set of information that aids the quality of both client assessment and overall service development. The form collects contextual information that includes client support, previous/concurrent attendance for psychological therapy, medication, as well as a categorization system to record presenting difficulties, their impact on day-to-day functioning, and any associated risk. To aid the development of service quality, the form collects data on critical assessment audit items that profile the accessibility and appropriateness of service provision. These include client demographics, waiting times and the suitability of referral.

  Finally, for client discharge, the CORE End of Therapy Form (see Figure 8.5) captures a core set of treatment descriptors that aid the interpretation of CORE-OM scores and help contextualize therapy outcomes and inform service development. The form collects profile information that includes therapy length, type of intervention, modality and frequency. The form collects data on critical discharge audit items that profile the effectiveness and efficiency of service provision, including problem and risk reviews, therapy benefits, session attendance rates, and whether the therapy ending was planned or unplanned.

Monitoring

Having outlined the components of the CORE System, this section describes their use, starting with the measures used on their own, and then as part of the wider system.

CLINICAL OUTCOMES in ROUTINE EVALUATION

THERAPY ASSESSMENT FORM v.2

Site ID [ ]
Client ID [ ] letters numbers
Sub codes [ ] TH ID number [ ] SC2 numbers [ ] SC3 numbers [ ]
Referrer(s) [ ]

Age [ ]
Male [ ] Female [ ]
Employment [ ]
Ethnic Origin [ ]

Referral date D D / M M / Y Y Y Y
First assessment date attended D D / M M / Y Y Y Y
Last assessment date D D / M M / Y Y Y Y

Total number of assessments [ ]
Previously seen for therapy in this service? Yes [ ] No [ ]
Months since last episode [ ]
Is this a follow-up/review appointment? Yes [ ] No [ ] Episode [ ][ ][ ]

Relationships/support Please tick as many boxes as appropriate

Living alone (not including dependents) [ ]
Living with partner [ ]
Caring for children under 5 years [ ]
Caring for children over 5 years [ ]
Living with parents/guardian [ ]
Living with other relatives/friends [ ]
Full time carer (of disabled/elderly etc) [ ]
Living in shared accommodation (e.g. lodgings) [ ]
Living in temporary accommodation (e.g. hostel) [ ]
Living in institution/hospital [ ]
Other [ ]

Current/previous use of services for psychological problems?
Please tick as many boxes as appropriate

Primary GP or other member of primary care team (eg practice nurse, counsellor)... Community [ ] <12 mins [ ] >12 mins [ ]

Secondary In primary care setting...
In community setting...
In hospital setting or sessional basis...
Day care services (e.g. day hospital)...
Hospital admission <= 10 days...
Hospital admission >= 11 days...

Specialist Psychotherapy/psychological treatments from specialist team (sessional)...
Attendance at day therapeutic programme...
Inpatient treatment...

Other Counsellor in eg voluntary, religious, work, educational setting...

Is the client currently prescribed medication to help with their psychological problem(s)? Yes [ ] No [ ]

If yes, please indicate type of medication:
Anti-psychotics (neuroleptics/major tranquillizers) [ ] Anti-depressants [ ] Anxiolytics/Hypnotics (minor tranquillizers) [ ] Other [ ]

Brief description of reason for referral

Identified Problems/Concerns

	severity					
	<6 months	6–12 months	12 months	Recurring/continuous		
Depression						
Anxiety/Stress						
Psychosis						
Personality Problems						
Cognitive/Learning						
Eating Disorder						
Physical Problems						
Addictions						

	severity			
	<6 months	6–12 months	>12 months	Recurring/contin.
Trauma/abuse				
Bereavement/loss				
Self esteem				
Interpersonal/relationship				
Living/Welfare				
Work/Academic				
Other (specify below)				

Risk

	None	Mild	Mod	Sev
Suicide				
Self Harm				
Harm to others				
Legal/Forensic				

ICD-10 CODES

	F/Z Main Code	Sub-code		F/Z Main Code	Sub-code
1		.	3		.
2	F/Z Main Code	Sub-code .	4	F/Z Main Code	Sub-code .

What has the client done to cope with/avoid their problems? Please tick, and then specify actions
Positive actions [ ] Negative actions [ ]

Assessment outcome (tick one box only)
Assessment/one session only [ ]
Accepted for therapy [ ]
Accepted for trial period of therapy [ ]

*If the client is not entering therapy give brief reason

Figure 8.4 Therapy assessment form (TAF) © The CORE System Trust: www.coreims.co.uk/copyright.pdf

CLINICAL OUTCOMES in ROUTINE EVALUATION

END OF THERAPY FORM v.2

Site ID

Client ID — letters — numbers

Sub Codes — Therapist ID — SCA numbers — SC5 numbers

Date therapy commenced — D D / M M / Y Y Y Y
Date therapy completed — D D / M M / Y Y Y Y

Number of sessions planned
Number of sessions attended
Number of sessions unattended

What type of therapy was undertaken with the client? *Please tick as many boxes as appropriate*

Psychodynamic — Person-centred
Psychoanalytic — Integrative
Cognitive — Systemic
Behavioural — Supportive
Cognitive/Behavioural — Art
Structured/Brief — Other *(specify below)*

What modality of therapy was undertaken with the client? *Please tick as many boxes as appropriate*

Individual — Family
Group — Marital/Couple

What was the frequency of therapy with the client?

More than once weekly — Less than once weekly
Weekly — Not at a fixed frequency

Which of the following best describes the ending of therapy?

Unplanned — Planned
Due to crisis — Planned from outset
Due to loss of contact — Agreed during therapy
Client did not wish to continue — Agreed at end of therapy
Other unplanned ending *(specify below)* — Other planned ending *(specify below)*

Review of Identified Problems/Concerns

	Severity	Therapy Issue		Severity	Therapy Issue
Depression			Trauma/abuse		
Anxiety/Stress			Bereavement/Loss		
Psychosis			Self esteem		
Personality Problems			Interpersonal/relationship		
Cognitive/Learning			Living/Welfare		
Physical Problems			Work/Academic		
Eating Disorder			Other *(specify below)*		
Addictions					

Risk

	None	Mild	Mod	Sev
Suicide				
Self Harm				
Harm to others				
Legal/Forensic				

Contextual Factors

	Poor	Moderate	Good
Motivation			
Working Alliance			
Psychological Mindedness			

Benefits of Therapy

	Improved Yes / No	Not addressed		Improved Yes / No	Not addressed
Personal insight/understanding			Control/planning/decision making		
Expression of feelings/problems			Subjective well-being		
Exploration of feelings/problems			Symptoms		
Coping strategies/techniques			Day to day functioning		
Access to practical help			Personal relationships		
Other benefits					

Tick box and then specify below

Has contact with this service resulted in a change of medication? Yes □ No □ Not applicable □
If yes, is this change likely to be of benefit to the client? Yes □ No □
Details of change: Started □ Discontinued □ Increased □ Decreased □ Modified □

Has the client been given a follow-up appointment? Yes □ No □ Number of months until appointment □

Figure 8.5 End of therapy (EOT) © The CORE System Trust: www.coreims.co.uk/copyright.pdf

Monitoring using CORE measures only

Underpinning the CORE System is the principle that in its paper and pencil form it was free to use and photocopy and thereby available and flexible to be used by practitioners in ways that best suited their needs. Outcomes monitoring can be undertaken by independent practitioners working alone, by groups of practitioners, or by varying sizes of services. The hand-scored forms are shared in discussion between peers or in supervision of therapy.

Using the CORE-OM within a session

The CORE-OM can be used to frame and guide the conversation between client and practitioner. Two common reasons for using CORE measures within a session are to build rapport and to encourage both therapist and client to explore any positive answers to the risk items. This helps to keep a clear focus on risk management. The form can be used as a vehicle for communicating aspects of a client's experience that can then become part of the conversation and integral to the therapeutic process. In addition, CORE forms can be completed before or after a session or, pre- and post-therapy depending on how closely the therapist wants the focus on specific outcomes.

Case identification

Whether using hand-scored forms or data that has been summarized in a database, it is easy to identify specific cases that need closer attention. A strategy of comparing best and worst outcomes can provide practitioners with immediate feedback in the context of their own caseload. In order to make this possible data need to be available at both pre- and post-therapy.

Summaries

A more sophisticated use of forms is to produce summaries, whether the comparisons are internal to a department or using external comparative data (e.g. published data). Overall summaries might include gender balance, age (mean, median, range and numbers of younger and older patients), mean initial scores, mean change scores, numbers and percentages improved, deteriorated, reliably and/or significantly changed. Summaries using CORE intake scores can be used to generate simple plots of the distribution in severity accordingly to the severity bandings (see Figure 8.6A) and also for rates of 'recovery' or 'deterioration' (see Figures 8.6B and 8.6C respectively). Monitoring over quarterly time periods has clear benefits in accommodating seasonal variations in client referral patterns (see Figure 8.6D).

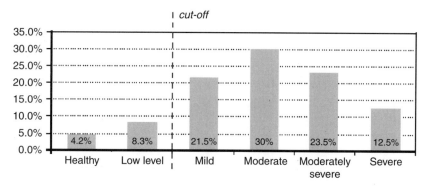

Figure 8.6A Examples of summary plots using CORE-OM data: Intake profile. *Source:* Is initial overall CORE-OM score an indicator of likely outcome?, CORE Partnership Occasional Paper No. 1. Rugby: CORE IMS, 2007

A particularly powerful way of demonstrating clinical change is to plot every client seen on a graph designed to show reliable and clinically significant change. Figure 8.6E shows an example of a Jacobson plot using pre-post CORE-OM measures from a sample of 9,761 clients and yielding a recovery rate (i.e. those clients meeting criteria for reliable and clinically significant improvement) of 61.9%. This can be achieved by hand with smaller numbers using a simple chart showing the CORE-OM score at the beginning of therapy on the horizontal

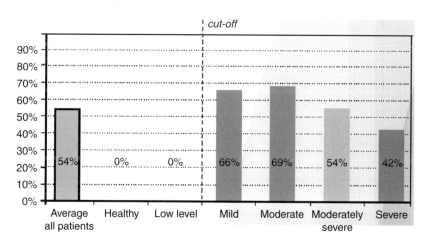

Figure 8.6B Examples of summary plots using CORE-OM data: Recovery rates. *Source:* Is initial overall CORE-OM score an indicator of likely outcome?, CORE Partnership Occasional Paper No. 1. CORE IMS: Rugby, 2007

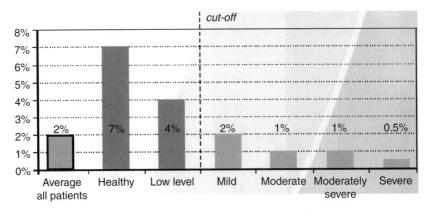

Figure 8.6C   Examples of summary plots using CORE-OM data: Deterioration rates. *Source:* Is initial overall CORE-OM score an indicator of likely outcome?, CORE Partnership Occasional Paper No. 1. CORE IMS: Rugby, 2007

axis and the score at the end of therapy on the vertical axis. The 45° diagonal then represents *no change* and the *tramlines* on either side represent the change that could be just from errors of measurement. The horizontal line represents the cut-off score such that people whose scores fall below the line are deemed members of a non-clinical population.

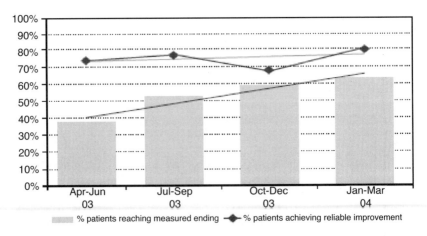

Figure 8.6D   Examples of summary plots using CORE-OM data: Quarterly monitoring of improvement rates and completion rates together. *Source:* Impact of the use of the CORE system on service quality, CORE Partnership Occasional Paper No. 3. Rugby: CORE IMS: Rugby, 2007

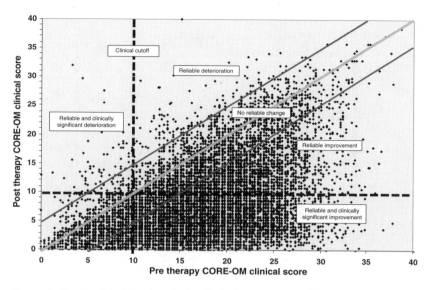

Figure 8.6E Graphical (Jacobson) plot displaying groupings of clients meeting criteria for reliable and clinically significant improvement, reliable change, no change and reliable deterioration

Comparison with referential parameters/benchmarks

Comparison of data across services can provide clues to relative service performance. There are several sources of benchmarks against which a service can be compared. Examples of such benchmarks are provided in the literature (e.g. Evans et al., 2003; Mullin et al., 2006) together with examples of services using a benchmarking approach (e.g. Gilbert et al., 2005). In this specific context, suitable benchmarks include: (a) CORE-OM completion rates for pre-and post-therapy; (b) intake severity; (c) percentage of clients 'improved'; and (d) percentage of clients 'recovered'. The reported figures for these benchmarks are provided here (see Table 8.6) and have been rounded for ease of use in practice (i.e. rounded to nearest whole percentage). The benchmarks will vary slightly as data accumulates, but the data currently available appear to be reasonably robust.

Overall, these three levels – case identification, summaries, and benchmarks – provide different ways of organizing and using data for individual clinical and service needs by enabling comparisons between any single client and other similar clients. In relation to benchmarking activities, these can focus on summary outcomes at the end of treatment (see Lueger & Barkham, Chapter 9), or at each session on an ongoing basis through what has been termed case-tracking (see Leach & Lutz, Chapter 10).

Table 8.6 Key performance indicators for UK NHS primary care psychological therapy and counselling services and their profiles

Indicator	Overall mean (SD)	Best performing service	Poorest performing service	Percentiles		
				25th	50th	75th
Waiting times from referral to 1st assessment (days)	57 (36)	11	182	24	55	84
Pre-therapy CORE-OM completion rates (%)	86 (17)	100	20	77	93	97
Pre- and post-therapy CORE-OM completion rates (%)	39 (23)	99	3	22	38	53
Clients accepted for ongoing therapy following assessment (%)	81 (13)	100	34	74	82	89
Differences in clients' and practitioners' ratings of risk (%)	17 (7)	1	32	12	17	22
Clients initiating termination of therapy by undeclared discontinuation (%)	50 (20)	5	86	38	49	58
Clients meeting criteria for recovery and/or improvement (%)	72 (8)	86	54	67	73	78

Monitoring using the CORE system

Although using the CORE measures alone provides a good starting point from which to monitor the impact of an intervention or effectiveness of a service, there is a wider context within which outcomes occur. We now consider the use of the CORE system in monitoring services and practice. We consulted with system users and explored the potential usefulness of developing software that would support the use of CORE running on a personal computer (PC) – hence, the development of CORE PC – to support in-house analysis and reporting. In essence, this would provide a 'researcher-in-a-box' solution.

Development of CORE PC

CORE PC was designed to promote *quality evaluation* as a dynamic activity that recommended ongoing data quality monitoring, and quarterly data analysis, reporting, and in-house review. In short, CORE PC provides services with a unique resource to take control of their own evaluation on an ongoing basis and promote a research-practitioner model rather than the traditional model of exporting data to external experts for analysis. The four key strengths of having such an on-site support tool include: (a) the ability to provide information to service stakeholders as and when it is required; (b) the ability for service practitioners to analyse their own data and use it as part of the process of personal reflection and development; (c) making it easy to categorize client outcomes according to whether their CORE outcome profile identified them as improved, deteriorated, or the same; and (d) the ability to explore differing subsets of clients for insight into potential problems with service organization and delivery (Mellor-Clark et al., 2006). This approach encompassed three key features: following the client's journey, traffic light signals (i.e. benchmarks) and data-drilling.

Following the client's journey

First, we designed an analysis model within the CORE PC software that focused on *tracking the client journey* through a set of discrete stages in their journey into and through services. Building a step-wise approach to data analysis encouraged services to consider the progressive attrition of clients over their journeys and helped them focus on specific aspects of their CORE data that could enable them to understand and ultimately reduce attrition. To support this process, we developed a set of performance indicators and service descriptors that were refined for publication in a special edition of *Counselling & Psychotherapy Research* (March, 2006) to act as a suitable benchmarking resource. (Table 8.6)

Thermometers and traffic lights

Second, we developed a graphical indicator that took the form of a *thermome-ter* as illustrated in Figures 8.7A and 8.7B which show the representations for planned endings and recovery and/or improvement rates respectively. The thermometer format presents services along a continuum but grouped into quartiles. In its usual coloured representation the band at the top of the ther-mometer is green (represented on the diagram as dark shading) and shows the range of percentages profiled for the top 25% (i.e. quartile) of services – that is, the most desirable practice. For the two examples presented here, the top quartile ranges from 95% to 62% in Figure 8.7A and from 86% to 78% in Figure 8.7B. The middle portion of the graphs (which represent the services in the middle 50% of the distribution) are usually coloured amber and are dis-played here in lighter shading. The actual values for each benchmark are 62% to 42% in Figure 8.7A and 78% to 67% in Figure 8.7B. The bottom quartile represents services falling in the lowest 25% of the spread and this portion of the graph is usually coloured red and is displayed here in moderate shading so as to contrast with the middle portion. The values for each benchmark are 42% to 14% in Figure 8.7A and 67% to 54% in Figure 8.7B. A percentile to the right of the thermometer is usually displayed to indicate the national average profile (in these cases 50% and 72% respectively). However, where the indicator functions such that a low rate is the desired outcome (e.g. waiting times), then the ordering of colours is reversed such that 'green' appears at the bottom.[1]

In use, a service compares their own service profile on a specific indicator to those of the performance thermometer to get an indication of their relative performance. As stated, roughly speaking if a service's profile is in the 'green', it is assumed to be high or desirable, whilst 'red' equates to low or not so desirable.

Data-drilling

The third innovation was developing *data-drilling* in order to enable the practi-tioner to identify the clients who fall into a specific category of data, for example, the identification of client ID numbers for all clients waiting over a specified time for their first contact session, or the identification of those clients scoring below clinical cut-off on the CORE-OM. Having identified the case numbers, practitioners can discuss these individual clients within a meaningful clinical context. For example, a discussion might focus on all those clients who have left the service unilaterally resulting in total loss of contact through client-initiated termination.

---

[1] Alternatively, the order of colours could remain the same but the anchor points would need to be reversed.

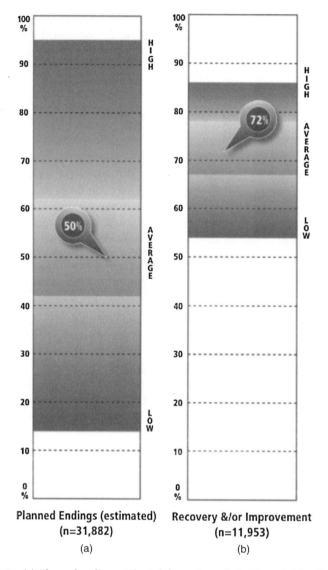

Planned Endings (estimated)
(n=31,882)

(a)

Recovery &/or Improvement
(n=11,953)

(b)

Figure 8.7 (a) Planned endings. Adapted from Connell, J., Client-initiated termination of therapy at NHS primary care counselling services, *Counselling & Psychotherapy Research, 6,* 60–67. Taylor & Francis Group, 2006 © CORE Information Management Systems: www.coreims.co.uk/copyright.pdf (b) Recovery and/or improvement rates. Adapted from: Mullin, T. et al., Recovery and improvement benchmarks in routine primary care mental health settings, *Counselling & Psychotherapy Research, 6,* 68–80. Taylor & Francis Group, 2006 © CORE Information Management Systems: www.coreims.co.uk/copyright.pdf

Collectively, we believe that these procedures help practitioners *quantify* their service profile and *qualitatively* explore individual cases to better understand important local service phenomena, an approach which encourages a healthy methodological pluralism.

Developing multilevel feedback systems for routine management

In this third section we consider ways that CORE data can be used for feedback and outcomes management. We consider the evolving development of a series of national databases for practice-based evidence and then move from a *national* to a *local* focus exploring the empirical and practical use of such benchmarks in service management and clinical performance development.

Collating practice-based evidence national databases (PBE-NDs)

As of 2008, over 400 UK services had purchased licenses to help collate data for a combined total of well over 500,000 therapy service users, thereby offering a unique potential to develop large naturalistic data sets. We define these data sets as practice-based evidence national databases (PBE-NDs; for an earlier conception see Evans et al., 2006) and have built separate PBE-NDs for specific sectors of therapy service delivery to help control for setting effects such as referral quality in medical settings, semester breaks in academic settings, and volunteer availability in voluntary sectors. To date the PBE-NDs have been developed from donated samples comprising NHS primary care psychological therapies, university counselling services, and staff support services/employment assistance programmes. These data sets are, of course, anonymous when they are collated nationally. They are updated regularly and have yielded important research contributions (e.g. Barkham et al., 2008b; Connell, Barkham & Mellor-Clark, 2008; Stiles et al., 2006, 2008a, 2008b).

Resourcing local feedback for service management

Table 8.6 profiles a series of published key performance indicators along with their empirical profiles taken from our NHS primary care psychological therapy and counselling NDs (for details, see special issue of *Counselling and Psychotherapy Research*, 2006, March). These show both the potential utility of such data, as well as the breadth of service delivery quality evident in the sample. To illustrate, we present a worked example.

Service management: illustrative example

The final two indicators in Table 8.6 provide information on undeclared termination (i.e. unplanned) rates and improvement rates. Logically, low rates of unplanned endings signify high rates of planned endings (and vice versa). Hence while the average is 50%, by taking the minimum and maximum values for *unplanned endings* of 5% and 86%, we can extrapolate that the range of planned endings is between 95% and 14%. These extremes frame the benchmark data when presented as quartiles as shown in Figure 8.7A. This figure presents the data showing the boundaries between the upper quartile, labelled 'high' (62% and above), and the lower quartile, labelled 'low' (42% and below). Thus a service with a planned endings rate of, for example, 70% will fall into the top quartile while a service with a rate of 35% will fall into the bottom quartile. In this way services can locate themselves in the context of other similar services. But making comparisons between indicators can also be informative. So, while the spread is considerable for planned endings, this is less true for rates of improvement as shown in Figure 8.7B where the range is only between 54% and 86% with the boundaries for the upper and lower quartiles at 78% (high) and 67% (low) respectively. The average percentage rate for services is 72%.

Because performance varies, services can be located at differing points on a continuum for differing indicators. This can produce positive feedback for some service managers but for others it can deliver challenging information. In the latter situation, there are a number of responses including: (a) seeking evidence that the service is in some way distinct and different from other services that helped generate the benchmarks (McInnes, 2006); (b) exploring whether the below-average service performance profile can be equally attributed to all service practitioners (Mothersole, 2006); and (c) exploring whether there are differential performance profiles that could benefit from in-house continuing professional development (CPD) training (e.g. Grant, 2006) or enhanced supervision (e.g. McNaughton, Boyd & McBride, 2006).

We have found that access to such performance indicators for the purposes of local feedback, together with *bottom-up* and confidential benchmarking, not only helps services engage in exploring the relative profile of their service performance but also helps identify areas where they may potentially benefit from peer-to-peer support from others in the CORE User Network in a higher (ideally top quartile) performance category. Data is also disseminated via a series of *CORE Partnership Occasional Papers* (available at www.coreims.co.uk/index.php?name=EZCMS&page_id=45) that highlight specific challenging areas of service delivery.

Individual feedback: illustrative example

Crucially, however, data capture and use needs to work at the level of the individual practitioner, and a key component is feeding back the performance of each practitioner in relation to their service and national benchmarks. CORE PC provides an appraisal tool yielding a summary profile of an individual practitioner's contribution to overall service quality. This data is, in turn, benchmarked against local and national indicators that managers, supervisors and practitioners can review together in order to support and guide continuing professional development.

An anonymized appraisal feedback template from CORE PC is presented in Figure 8.8 as an example of the potential of feedback from the information captured by the various CORE tools. In the illustrated example the first column in the centre of the table introduces the range of key performance indicators

Therapist	Report Date	Filter By
Demo Therapist	08/05/2009 12:53:03	None

		Service Range				Comments
		Min	Max	Avg	Demo Therapist	
Number of clients attending first session		10	110	46	60	Above average

		National range			Service range			Demo Therapist	Comments
		Min	Max	Avg	Min	Max	Avg		
Use of CORE	OM1	61	91	82	0	100	88	50	May be struggling to use CORE with clients. Explore
	OM1 + 2	15	83	45	0	100	38	15	Very low proportion of outcomes. Explore
KPI's	Clinical and/or Reliable Improvement	52	88	70	0	100	70	100	Excellent figures for feedback
	Deterioration	0	6	3	0	100	3	0	Excellent figures for feedback
	Unplanned Endings	9	35	19	0	100	18	15	Lower than service average
	DNAs	7	34	17	0	98	21	14	Lower than service average
First Sessions	Not Suitabale for Therapy	0	8	1.5	0	100	3	29	Very high levels of selectivity. Explore
	Referred on	0	5	1.5	0	100	3	1	OK
	Single Session	0	7	4	0	100	8	0	No single session work. Explore
	Accepted for Therapy	74	98	87	0	100	68	71	OK
Below Cutoff at Referrals		8	25	20	0	100	22	5	Very high clinical rates. Explore.
Avg Waiting Times		22	90	54	0	565	71	6	Very fast access. Explore

General Appraisal	
Some excellent examples of client management and clinical effectiveness. Seems to be high levels of client selectivity and low levels of completion of the CORE Outcome Measure which we usefully explored.	
Action Plan	
Give Positive Feedback	Great outcomes for those clients with measures and evident effective client selection.
Focus 1	The introduction of the CORE measure at assessment which Demo feels uncomfortable about.
Focus 2	The selection criteria that Demo uses could be used by other team practitioners. Explore further.
Focus 3	Waiting time management is something Demo should share with rest of team.
Focus 4	Some single sessions must be therapeutically beneficial but Demo reports not doing single session work. Explore further.
Focus 5	Explore DNA management in next appraisal/mentoring session.

Figure 8.8   Example of (anonymized) individual appraisal template from CORE PC with sample comments for performance management © CORE Information Management Systems: www.coreims.co.uk/copyright.pdf

including: (a) their use of CORE (as measured by client pre- and post-therapy completion rates); (b) level of reliable and clinically significant change; and (c) unplanned endings.

At an individual practitioner level, the data provides summary information on how the practitioner is constructing and delivering their service. This practitioner provides fast access (average six-day wait) but is selective in terms of clients accepted (i.e. 29% deemed not suitable). Given that only half their clients complete a CORE-OM at intake, it raises the question as to what information is being used to inform this decision. The data shows 100% of clients achieve reliable and clinically significant change but, crucially, this is based on only 15% of their caseload (i.e. the percentage of pre- and post-therapy completed CORE-OMs). The data suggests the practitioner could potentially benefit from peer-to-peer support by identifying methods for capturing an above-average proportion of CORE-OMs both at the onset and end of therapy (see row labelled Use of CORE), with other colleagues who have greater levels of success.

Towards a second generation of quality evaluation

The measurement, monitoring and management framework outlined above presents a review of what we see as *first generation* development and implementation of the CORE measures and system. However, outcome measurement systems need to evolve to be responsive to the developing requirements for transparency and accountability. Accordingly, we have used the lessons learned from the initial decade of work to enhance the quality of the measurement system and move into a *second generation* of quality evaluation (for an overview, see Gray & Mellor-Clark, 2007). There is a potential danger in having a system that is stable for practitioners and managers as it can then become static and consequently impede necessary developments. This can lead to tensions which we have sought to keep in balance by developing both the methodology and supporting software, the key developments of which are outlined in this final section.

CORE Net

The responses to the challenges and observations outlined above guided the development and implementation of CORE Net as a second generation support system launched within a competency and user accreditation framework.[2] It is web-based technology and offers the ability to analyse and report on client and

---

[2] CORE Net is second generation software from CORE Information Management Systems Ltd. who are the authorized change agency and software supplier working in partnership with the CORE System Trust.

service data in real-time. This methodology complements the well-established CORE-OM with the new shorter 10-item and 5-item measures that can generate immediate clinical feedback and flag (alert) reports that require further attention. User recovery and improvement is fostered by the attention to warning flags that require action by the therapist. CORE-Net also includes clinical support tools such as a five-item measure of the client-practitioner alliance. This can be used to elicit information that can help identify problems in the alliance (Cahill et al., submitted). Functional profiles of CORE Net are available online in the form of video presentations at www.coreims-online.co.uk

Using CORE Net

In UK NHS services the use of CORE Net revolves around the patient routinely completing a CORE-10 measure at the first screening session with their General Practitioner (GP: Primary care physician), within a stepped care programme. The initial measure is followed by further CORE measures at each subsequent consultation with either Step 1 or Step 2 practitioners (e.g. GPs, nurse practitioners, mental health workers, etc.), Step 3 practitioners (primary care psychologists, counsellors, etc.) or Step 4 specialist workers. This results in an *open* information system in which the patient's progress can be tracked for recovery and improvement on an ongoing basis and case-managed by the GP or other designated professional.

The patient can complete the tool online on the practitioner's computer screen. However, practitioners could equally administer the form as a paper tool and later enter the data onto CORE Net (as illustrated by Figure 8.9A). Once the measure has been completed, the practitioner has the option to

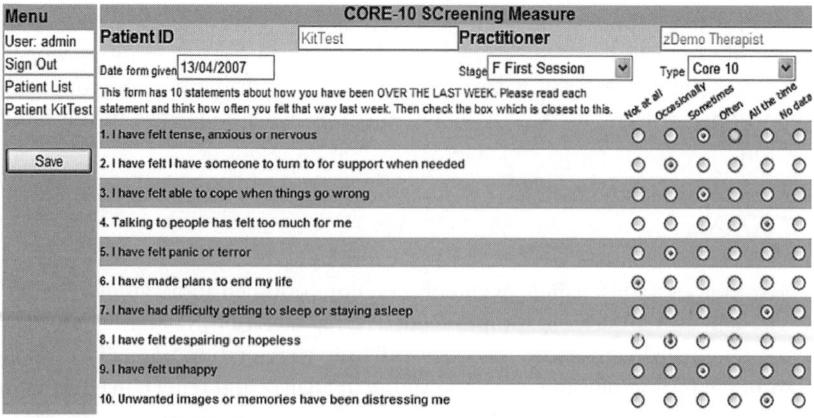

Figure 8.9A   CORE Net data entry screen for CORE system measures (CORE-10 is illustrated) © CORE Information Management Systems: www.coreims.co.uk/copyright.pdf

Answer	Question
2.Sometimes	1. I have felt tense, anxious or nervous
1.Often	2. I have felt I have someone to turn to for support when needed
2.Sometimes	3. I have felt able to cope when things go wrong
3.Often	4. Talking to people has felt too much for me
2.Sometimes	5. I have felt panic or terror
1.Occasionally	6. I made plans to end my life
2.Sometimes	7. I have had difficulty getting to sleep or staying asleep
2.Sometimes	8. I have felt despairing or hopeless
2.Sometimes	9. I have felt unhappy
2.Sometimes	10. Unwanted images or memories have been distressing me

Figure 8.9B   CORE Net item display summaries © CORE Information Management Systems: www.coreims.co.uk/copyright.pdf

review the results privately or to share them with the patient. In practice it is generally found to be more desirable for clients to complete CORE-10 early in a consultation in order to provide progress feedback to practitioner and client. This feedback can take a tabular form of the item responses as illustrated in Figure 8.9B or a graphical form as illustrated in Figures 8.10A and 8.10B by the upper plotted line. Paper copies of the progress graphs can be used to inform and enhance patient feedback.

In Figures 8.10A and 8.10B the shaded bands provide a quick picture of severity of distress, as a reflection of NICE guidance steps. A score above the cut-off score of 10 indicates that the patient is in the clinical population. Subsequent improvement (statistically a five-point score change – or the movement from one severity band to another) and recovery (movement below clinical cut-off) are easily highlighted as and when they occur. In subsequent consultations, when the measure has been completed the measurement tool immediately displays a progress chart which adds the patient's latest score and therefore the trajectory of progress.

Additionally, Figures 8.10A and 8.10B illustrate a lower plotted line that shows the risk score with a grey dotted line showing whether the patient is clinically at risk – if the patient is at significant risk, then fuller risk assessment becomes the first priority (using CORE-OM). The annotations at the bottom of the charts show the date of each consultation and the version of the CORE measure used: F = Full (CORE-OM), A or B = Short Forms, and the CORE-10. The CORE-5 would also be a candidate version. Other data relating to medication, support and referral routes can also be recorded on the graph. As illustrated by Figure 8.9B, higher scoring items on the measure are highlighted in progressively darker shades of grey, and the practitioner can use this as a rapid visual cue to areas that are troubling the client more, and as a focus to expand the consultation content into the more distressing areas, as they wish.

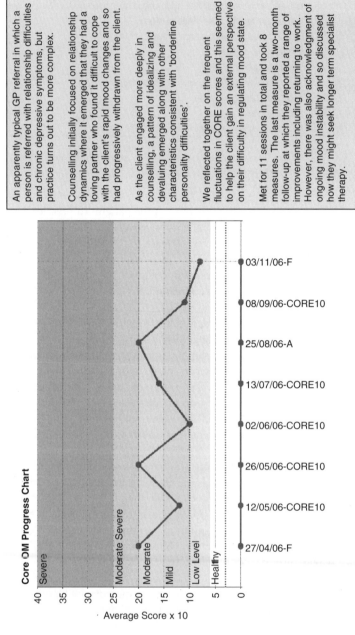

An apparently typical GP referral in which a person is referred with relationship difficulties and chronic depressive symptoms, but practice turns out to be more complex.

Counselling initially focused on relationship dynamics where it emerged that they had a loving partner who found it difficult to cope with the client's rapid mood changes and so had progressively withdrawn from the client.

As the client engaged more deeply in counselling, a pattern of idealizing and devaluing emerged along with other characteristics consistent with 'borderline personality difficulties'.

We reflected together on the frequent fluctuations in CORE scores and this seemed to help the client gain an external perspective on their difficulty in regulating mood state.

Met for 11 sessions in total and took 8 measures. The last measure is a two-month follow-up at which they reported a range of improvements including returning to work. However, there was also acknowledgment of ongoing mood instability and so discussed how they might seek longer term specialist therapy.

Figure 8.10A CORE Net progress tracking chart © CORE Information Management Systems: www.coreims.co.uk/copyright.pdf

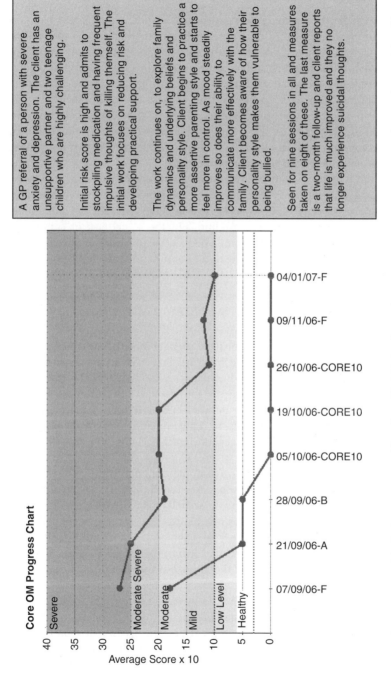

Figure 8.10B CORE Net progress tracking chart © CORE Information Management Systems: www.coreims.co.uk/copyright.pdf

A true patient-centred system

Used optimally, the system reflects patient centred practice at its best. Not only do clients provide responses to the measure items, but practitioners and patients work collaboratively to understand and interpret the patient's progress chart (e.g. Figures 8.10A & 8.10B) and recognize, in real time, where progress is being made or, if not, review alternative strategies. Intriguingly, at the first session the position of their score on the severity bands often provides the client with a sense of validation that things are not right, that they need help, and that their seeking help is legitimate – and then at subsequent consultations their most recent score provides them with tangible evidence that they are making progress and so provides positive reinforcement.

One result of this patient-centred use of the completed measure is that completion of questionnaires is not commonly experienced as a burden by the client since their answers and their scores are seen as being valued by the practitioner and integral to their treatment. Additionally, the actual task of completing measures is also reduced to a minimum because the practitioner can choose the shortest measure that is appropriate to the consultation and the client's state.

Conclusions

The CORE System has always prioritized client completed measures and now has a wide spread of self-report instruments that have been shortened from, or based upon, the CORE-OM. But these are complemented with context setting information from instruments completed by practitioners at initial contact and discharge. These can be used in simple ways, particularly with peer support, and even the simplest set-up with handscoring and comparison of results within a peer group can generate positive change in a department, or an individual's practice.

Realizing the full potential requires computer support. The CORE System has had two main generations of such support so far: the first in the form of a stand-alone PC solution – CORE PC – and the second in the form of a network-based system – CORE Net. The former provides excellent tools for data collection and then for service and practitioner level aggregated data analysis. The latter adds more extensive tools for individual client progress tracking and has been adopted not just by psychological therapists but by general practitioners (i.e. primary care physicians) and other primary care healthcare workers.

Underpinning these developments, however, is our central philosophy that the approach of engaging and sustaining the use of such systems needs to be *bottom-up*. Using data *routinely* to improve practice needs to be *rooted* in daily practice so that it can then filter upwards to contribute not only to improving practice but also to enhancing the scientific evidence for the effectiveness of the psychological therapies.

Acknowledgements

We would like to thank all clients, practitioners, managers and commissioners who have contributed to the development of the CORE measures and system. We also thank Barry McInnes for his helpful comments on an earlier version of this chapter.

References

Aveline, M. & Shapiro, D.A. (eds.) (1995). *Research foundations for psychotherapy practice*. Chichester: John Wiley & Sons, Ltd.

Barkham, M., Mellor-Clark. J., Connell, J. & Cahill J. (2006a). A CORE approach to practice-based evidence: A brief history of the origins and applications of the CORE-OM and CORE System. *Counselling & Psychotherapy Research, 6*, 3–15.

Barkham, M., Culverwell, A., Spindler, K., Twigg, E. & Connell, J. (2005a). The CORE-OM in an older adult population: Psychometric status, acceptability, and feasibility. *Aging and Mental Health, 9*, 235–245.

Barkham, M., Gilbert, N., Connell, J., Marshall, C. & Twigg, E. (2005b). Suitability and utility of the CORE-OM and CORE-A for assessing severity of presenting problems in psychological therapy services based in primary and secondary care settings. *British Journal of Psychiatry, 186*, 239–246.

Barkham, M., Mullin, T., Leach, C., Stiles, W.B. & Lucock, M. (2007). Stability of the CORE-OM and BDI-I: Psychometric properties and implications for routine practice. *Psychology and Psychotherapy: Theory, Research and Practice, 80*, 269–278.

Barkham, M., Bewick, B.M., Mullin, T., Gilbody, S., Connell, J. et al. (2008a). The CORE-10: A short assessment and outcome measure for core common mental health problems in routine primary care practice. Centre for Psychological Services Research, CPSR Memo 2, University of Sheffield.

Barkham, M., Connell, J., Stiles, W.B., Miles, J.N.V., Margison, F. et al. (2006b). Dose-effect relations and responsive regulation of treatment duration: The good enough level. *Journal of Consulting and Clinical Psychology, 74*, 160–167.

Barkham, M., Evans, C., Margison, F., McGrath, G., Mellor-Clark, J. et al. (1998). The rationale for developing and implementing core batteries in service settings and psychotherapy outcome research. *Journal of Mental Health, 7*, 35–47.

Barkham, M., Margison, F., Leach, C., Lucock, M., Mellor-Clark, J. et al. (2001). Service profiling and outcomes benchmarking using the CORE-OM: Towards practice-based evidence in the psychological therapies. *Journal of Consulting and Clinical Psychology, 69*, 184–196.

Barkham, M., Stiles, W.B., Connell, J., Twigg, E., Leach, C. et al. (2008b). Effects of psychological therapies in randomized trials and practice-based studies. *British Journal of Clinical Psychology, 47,* 397–415.

Beck, A.T., Steer, R.A. & Brown, G. (1996). *Manual for Beck Depression Inventory-II.* San Antonio, TX: Psychological Corporation.

Beck, A.T., Epstein, N., Brown, G. & Steer, R.A. (1988). An inventory for measuring clinical anxiety: Psychometric properties. *Journal of Consulting and Clinical Psychology, 56,* 893–897.

Beck, A.T., Ward, C.H., Mendelson, M., Mock, J. & Erbaugh, J. (1961). An inventory for measuring depression. *Archives of General Psychiatry, 4,* 561–571.

Bewick, B.M., Barkham, M., Connell, J. & Twigg, E. (2009). A 5-item measure for the ongoing monitoring of psychological therapy outcomes. Centre for Psychological Services Research, CPSR Memo 3, University of Sheffield.

Brooks, M. & Davies, S. (2007). Pathways to participatory research in developing a tool to measure feelings. *British Journal of Learning Disabilities, 36,* 128–133.

Cahill, J., Barkham, M., Stiles, W.B., Twigg, E., Rees, A. et al. (2006). Convergent validity of the CORE measures with measures of depression for clients in brief cognitive therapy for depression. *Journal of Counseling Psychology, 53,* 253–259.

Cahill, J., Stiles, W.B., Barkham, M., Hardy, G.E., Agnew-Davies, R. et al. (submitted). Two short forms of the Agnew Relationship Measure: The ARM-5 and ARM-12.

Connell, J. & Barkham, M. (2007). CORE-10 user manual (version 1.0). Centre for Psychological Services Research, CPSR Memo 1, University of Sheffield.

Connell, J., Barkham, M. & Mellor-Clark, J. (2007a). Mental health CORE-OM norms of students attending university counselling services benchmarked against an age-matched primary care sample. *British Journal of Guidance and Counselling, 35,* 41–56.

Connell, J., Barkham, M. & Mellor-Clark, J. (2008). The effectiveness of UK student counselling services: An analysis using the CORE System. *British Journal of Guidance and Counselling, 36,* 1–18.

Connell, J., Grant, S. & Mullin, T. (2006). Client initiated termination of therapy at NHS primary care counselling services. *Counselling & Psychotherapy Research, 6,* 60–67.

Connell, J., Barkham, M., Stiles, W.B., Twigg, E., Singleton, N. et al. (2007b). Distribution of CORE-OM scores in a general population, clinical cut off points, and comparison with the CIS-R. *British Journal of Psychiatry, 190,* 69–74.

Derogatis, L.R. (1994). *Administration, scoring and procedures manual* (3rd edn). Minneapolis, MN: NCS Pearson Inc.

Derogatis, L.R. & Melisaratos, N. (1983). The Brief Symptom Inventory: An introductory report. *Psychological Medicine, 13*, 595–605.

Evans, C., Margison, F. & Barkham, M. (1998). The contribution of reliable and clinically significant change methods to evidence-based mental health. *Evidence Based Mental Health, 1*, 70–72.

Evans, C., Connell, J., Barkham, M., Marshall, C. & Mellor-Clark, J. (2003). Practice-based evidence: Benchmarking NHS primary care counselling services at national and local levels. *Clinical Psychology and Psychotherapy, 10*, 374–388.

Evans, C., Connell, J., Barkham, M., Margison, F., Mellor-Clark, J. et al. (2002). Towards a standardised brief outcome measure: Psychometric properties and utility of the CORE-OM. *British Journal of Psychiatry, 180*, 51–60.

Evans, C., Mellor-Clark, J., Margison, F., Barkham, M., McGrath, G. et al. (2000). Clinical Outcomes in Routine Evaluation: The CORE-OM. *Journal of Mental Health, 9*, 247–255.

Evans, R., Mellor-Clark, J., Barkham, M. & Mothersole, G. (2006). Routine outcome measurement and service quality management in NHS primary care psychological therapy services. *European Journal of Psychotherapy and Counselling, 8*, 141–161.

Gibbard, I. & Hanley, T. (2008). A five-year evaluation of the effectiveness of person-centred counselling in routine clinical practice in primary care. *Counselling & Psychotherapy Research, 8*, 215–222.

Gilbert, N., Barkham, M., Richards, A. & Cameron, I. (2005). The effectiveness of a primary care mental health service delivering brief psychological interventions: A benchmarking study using the CORE System. *Primary Care Mental Health, 3*, 241–251.

Gilbody, S., Richards, D.A. & Barkham, M. (2007). Diagnosing depression in primary care using self-completed instruments: a UK validation of the PHQ-9 and CORE-OM. *British Journal of General Practice, 57*, 650–652.

Grant, S. (2006). Making sense of CORE System data: Attrition, effectiveness, concordance and information capture. *European Journal of Psychotherapy and Counselling, 8*, 193–208.

Gray, P. & Mellor-Clark, J. (2007). *CORE: A decade of development*. www.coreims.co.uk/modules.php?op=modloadandname=Newsandfile=articleandsid=24

Hamilton, M. (1960). A rating scale for depression. *Journal of Neurology, Neurosurgery and Psychiatry, 23*, 56–62.

Jacobson, N.S. & Truax, P. (1991). Clinical significance: A statistical approach to defining meaningful change in psychotherapy research. *Journal of Consulting and Clinical Psychology, 59*, 12–19.

Kane, R.L. (1987). Commentary: functional assessment questionnaire for geriatric patients – or the clinical Swiss Army knife. *Journal of Chronic Disorders*, *40* (Suppl.), 95S.

Kroenke, K., Spitzer, R.L. & Williams, J.B. (2001). The PHQ-9: validity of a brief depression severity measure. *Journal of General Internal Medicine*, *16*, 606–613.

Leach, C., Lucock, M., Barkham, M., Stiles, W.B., Noble, R. et al. (2006). Transforming between Beck Depression Inventory and CORE-OM scores in routine clinical practice. *British Journal of Clinical Psychology*, *45*, 153–166.

Lewis, G., Pelosi, A.J., Araya, R. & Dunn, G. (1992). Measuring psychiatric disorder in the community: A standardised assessment for use by lay interviewers. *Psychological Medicine*, *22*, 465–486.

Lyne, J., Barrett, P., Evans, C. & Barkham, M. (2006). Dimensions of variation on the CORE-OM amongst patients attending for psychological therapy. *British Journal of Clinical Psychology*, *45*, 185–203.

McInnes, B. (2006). Management at a crossroads: The service management challenge of implementing routine evaluation and performance management in psychological therapy and counselling services. *European Journal of Psychotherapy and Counselling*, *8*, 163–176.

McNaughton, K-A., Boyd, J. & McBride, J. (2006). Using CORE data in counselling supervision: An initial exploration. *European Journal of Psychotherapy and Counselling*, *8*, 209–225.

Marshall, K. & Willoughby-Booth, S. (2007). Modifying the Clinical Outcomes in Routine Evaluation measure for use with people who have a learning disability. *British Journal of Learning Disabilities*, *35*, 107–112.

Mellor-Clark, J. & Barkham, M. (2000). Quality evaluation: methods, measures and meaning. In C. Feltham & I. Horton (eds.), *Handbook of counselling and psychotherapy* (pp. 255–270). London: Sage Publications.

Mellor-Clark, J. & Barkham, M. (2006). The CORE System: Developing and delivering practice–based evidence through quality evaluation. In C. Feltham & I. Horton (eds.), *Handbook of counselling and psychotherapy* (2nd edn). London: Sage Publications.

Mellor-Clark, J., Barkham, M., Connell, J. & Evans, C. (1999). Practice-based evidence and the need for a standardised evaluation system: Informing the design of the CORE System. *European Journal of Psychotherapy, Counselling and Health*, *2*, 357–374.

Mellor-Clark, J., Curtis Jenkins, A., Evans, R., Mothersole, G. & McInnes, B. (2006). Resourcing a CORE Network to develop a National Research Database to help enhance psychological therapies and counselling service provision. *Counselling & Psychotherapy Research*, *6*, 16–22.

Mothersole, G. (2006). The use of CORE system data to inform and develop practitioner performance assessment and appraisal: An experiential account. *European Journal of Psychotherapy and Counselling, 8*, 177–191.

Morrell, C.J., Slade, P., Warner, R., Paley, G., Dixon, S. et al. (2009). Clinical effectiveness of health visitor training in psychological interventions for postnatal women – a pragmatic cluster-randomised trial in primary care. *British Medical Journal, 338*: a3045.

Mullin, T., Barkham, M., Mothersole, G., Bewick, B.M. & Kinder, A. (2006). Recovery and improvement benchmarks in routine primary care mental health settings. *Counselling & Psychotherapy Research, 6*, 68–80.

National Institute for Mental Health England (NIMHE) (2009). *Mental Health Outcomes Compendium.* London: Department of Health.

Royal College of Nursing. (2002). *Working well? Results from the RCN Working well survey into the wellbeing and working lives of nurses.* London: Author.

Sinclair, A., Barkham, M., Evans, C., Connell, J. & Audin, K. (2005). Rationale and development of a general population well-being measure: Psychometric status of the GP-CORE in a student sample. *British Journal of Guidance and Counselling, 33*, 153–174.

Spiegelhalter, D.J. (1999). Surgical audit: Statistical lessions from Nightingale and Codman. *Journal of the Royal Statistical Society (Series A), 162*, 45–58.

Stiles, W.B., Barkham, M., Mellor-Clark, J. & Connell, J. (2008a). Effectiveness of cognitive-behavioural, person-centred, and psychodynamic therapies in UK primary care routine practice: Replication with a larger sample. *Psychological Medicine, 38*, 677–688.

Stiles, W.B., Barkham, M., Connell, J. & Mellor-Clark, J. (2008b). Responsive regulation of treatment duration in routine practice in United Kingdom primary care settings. *Journal of Consulting and Clinical Psychology, 76*, 298–305.

Stiles, W.B., Barkham, M., Twigg, E., Mellor-Clark, J. & Cooper, M. (2006). Effectiveness of cognitive-behavioural, person-centred, and psychodynamic therapies as practiced in UK National Health Service settings. *Psychological Medicine, 36*, 555–566.

Twigg, E., Barkham, M., Bewick, B.M., Mulhern, B., Connell, J. et al. (2009). The Young Person's CORE: Development of a brief outcome measure for young people. *Counselling & Psychotherapy Research, 9*, 160–168.

Waskow, I.E. (1975). Selection of a core battery. In I.E. Waskow & M.B. Parloff (eds.), *Psychotherapy change measures* (DHEW Pub. No (ADM) 74-120) (pp. 245–269). Washington, DC: US Government Printing Office.

Section IV

Monitoring Strategies for Individual Practitioners and Services

9

Using Benchmarks and Benchmarking to Improve Quality of Practice and Services

Robert J. Lueger[1] and Michael Barkham[2]

[1]Creighton University, Omaha, NE, USA, [2]Centre for Psychological Services Research, University of Sheffield, UK

Introduction

Overview

Benchmarking involves seeking quality improvement by examining the processes of more successful interventions that are superior in outcomes and efficiency. The application of benchmarking can occur in an organization that is collectively focused on quality improvement or in an organization that is seeking improvement within a more limited domain of operations. Organizations with a collective focus on quality improvement typically epitomize a Total Quality Management (TQM) or Continuous Quality Improvement (CQI) organizational environment. The practice of benchmarking without a collective organizational focus on quality improvement can produce valuable information, but is probably less likely to be acted on at a corporate level.

In this chapter, we first provide an overview of benchmarking, and then provide examples and an overview of applications of benchmarking to mental health services. We then explore the use of benchmarking in the separate research traditions of treatment-based and patient-focused studies. We identify specific procedures and also issues and caveats in relation to benchmarking, and conclude with suggested directions for future research and practice.

Developing and Delivering Practice-Based Evidence   By Michael Barkham, Gillian E Hardy, and John Mellor-Clark   © 2010 John Wiley & Sons, Ltd

Origins of benchmarking

In the late 1970s, competitive pricing and quality in the area of copy and reproduction equipment became a major challenge to the Xerox Corporation's primary facility located in Rochester, New York. Much of this challenge came from companies producing similar equipment in Japan. Japanese companies, in turn, had benefited in quality and efficiency in industrial productivity by imitating the best practices of highly performing companies. This concept of imitating quality processes, *dantotsu,* or *the best of the best*, provided a competitive advantage both within Japanese markets and internationally.

Robert C. Camp, an engineer with advanced degrees in logistics and operations research and prior work experience with Mobil and DuPont, was then the Manager of Planning in the Logistics and Distribution division at Xerox. He introduced benchmarking at Xerox in 1979 with the goal of analysing unit production costs in manufacturing operations and meeting the lower Japanese costs as targets. The subsequent success of Xerox's efforts raised the salience of benchmarking as a means of improving quality and efficiency in industrial production, and Robert Camp became the acknowledged expert in benchmarking with a decade of applications and publication of an article in the *Harvard Business Review* (Tucker, Zivan & Camp, 1987) and the first of several books, *The Search for Industry Best Practices that Lead to Superior Performance* (Camp, 1989). Camp defined benchmarking as 'the continuous process of measuring products, services, and practices against the competition or leading-edge companies'. Benchmarking, then, means *to find and implement the best practices*.

Types of benchmarking

Camp (1989) has identified four types of benchmarking for quality improvement. These four types – internal, competitive, functional and generic – theoretically can produce progressively increasing levels of performance, but also require increasingly greater effort, resources, and organizational experience and maturity to be effectively implemented.

Internal benchmarking

Internal benchmarking involves the collection and comparison of outcomes data within a unit of service delivery. For example, within a clinic there may be multiple therapists and multiple modalities of treatment. The identification of the most effective therapist among a group of therapists can invite examination of the processes used by that most successful therapist. Within a healthcare delivery system, one might compare the outcomes of clinics to identify the one with the highest quality parameters, and then examine the processes of that clinic to mimic or adapt its processes to the other clinics. Internal benchmarking is a logical starting point for benchmarking, but has several limitations. Service delivery personnel may be reluctant to share outcomes data publicly in a comparative format. A strong sense of collegiality and professional respect seems important for this public sharing to be positively motivating. As we shall see, initial efforts to introduce benchmarking to counselling and psychotherapy have been adversely affected by this limitation. Secondly, internal benchmarking is limited to the best practices of the highest performing individual or unit in that system, and it may be that better exemplars of service delivery are available in other clinics or health delivery systems.

Competitive benchmarking

Competitive benchmarking involves comparisons with units or individuals outside the system but in a similar delivery industry. For example, outcomes in a government-sponsored service might be compared against outcomes in a private service delivery system. Or the outcomes of two or more private healthcare systems might be compared against one's own outcomes. The advantages of using competitive data are that disparate processes and potentially higher levels of quality might be available in those sources to improve one's own services. Competitive benchmarking depends on the availability of published outcomes, and sometimes requires masking the identity of the data source through a third party. Internal and competitive benchmarking both involve within-industry comparisons. That is, the outcomes of therapists or counsellors are being compared to those of others providing those same services. A limitation shared by these two types of benchmarking is that individuals, whether as clinicians or as managers, may exhibit defensiveness in allowing the comparison of performance data.

Functional benchmarking

In non-competitive or functional benchmarking, similar functions of service delivery are identified in the services of a different industry and comparisons with those outcomes are made. For example, both counsellors in mental health services and physical therapists in rehabilitation services typically identify a set of goals for an episode of treatment involving multiple sessions. Continuation in treatment through the prescribed course has been shown to be influenced by the degree to which the goals of treatment are salient and addressed (Wierzbicki & Pekarik, 1986). Although counsellors and physical therapists usually offer non-competing services, similarities of functions might provide a basis of comparison. The difficulty of functional benchmarking is finding similarity in the processes across differing industries, and the advantage is the lack of defensiveness among those being compared.

Generic process benchmarking

Generic process benchmarking involves the identification of distinct processes in an episode of service delivery and examines each specific process across all industries that might include that process. For example, early in counselling or psychotherapy it is important for the patient or client to become hopeful about the potential success of the treatment (Frank, 1973; Howard et al., 1993). This process can be found in many other domains of healthcare delivery, including surgery, dentistry, primary care medicine and weight-loss programmes. Even beyond healthcare, hopefulness in a positive outcome as a process can be found in remedial education, legal disentanglement and product design. Generic process benchmarking would examine a process such as instilling hope across these contexts to identify the activities most likely to elicit hopefulness in the potential outcomes. Generic process benchmarking has the potential to redefine the prescriptions for the delivery of a service, and for counselling or psychotherapy services, that could mean abandoning theoretically-informed actions in favour of assembling atheoretical, generic processes of known effectiveness.

Performance parameters indicating quality

Differences in quality can be marked with a single outcome variable or with a set of variables. The latter are often called a scorecard of outcomes. In studies of psychotherapy and counselling interventions, an omnibus measure of behavioural health status or pathology can provide an easy-to-interpret marker of quality provided the therapists/counsellors accept that measure as meaningful to their therapeutic interventions. A number of single-index outcome measures have received widespread use in behavioural healthcare systems. Among these measures are the BASIS-32 (Eisen, Dill & Grob, 1994), Clinical Outcomes in Routine Evaluation-Outcome Measure (CORE-OM; Barkham et al., 2001; Evans et al., 2002), COMPASS/Integra (Howard et al., 1993), Outcome Questionnaire-45 (OQ-45; Lambert et al. 1996), Treatment Evaluation and Management (TEAM; Grissom, Lyons & Lutz, 2003), Treatment Outcome Package (TOP; Kraus, Seligman & Jordan, 2004), and the Outcome Rating Scale (ORS; Miller et al., 2003). These measures have the advantages of being relatively short, possessing good reliability and concurrent validity, being atheoretical, and having normative data from both patient and non-patient samples. Because these measures include both symptoms and elements of functioning, they tend to have face validity with both patients and therapists. An important advantage of all of these measures is that they were designed to be used as outcome measures in contrast to commonly used measures of constructs grounded in theories (e.g. the Beck Depression Inventory (BDI); Beck, Steer & Garbin, 1988) or diagnosis (e.g. Personal Health Questionnaire-9 (PHQ-9); Kroenke, Spitzer & Williams, 2001).

The report card approach to outcomes assessment attempts to include outcomes that are important to multiple stakeholders. Some commonly used indicators relevant to counselling or psychotherapy might include: (1) waiting time for the service; (2) specification of a treatment plan with mutually-agreed goals; (3) completion of the prescribed course; (4) satisfaction with the service; and (5) post-treatment quality of life. Hermann (Hermann et al., 2004) had a panel of 12 stakeholders rate 116 measures for their feasibility (clear specifications, acceptable assessment burden, adequate case-mix adjustment) and meaningfulness (clinically important, assesses gap between actual and optimal care, associated with improved performance and outcome) as report card indicators. A set of 28 measures were rated at least moderately high on both dimensions. However, only 16 of these measures were supported by the results of outcomes research, and only 12 addressed treatment issues. Over 90% of these report card indicators were based on administrative or patient chart data. The import of this study is that further measure development is needed, consensus is elusive, and validity for report card measures is limited. A difficulty of the report card approach is achieving consensus among stakeholders on a set of measures that transcend the presenting problems, treatments and service delivery settings in various behavioural healthcare systems.

The context of benchmarking within quality improvement efforts

Although the initial point of benchmarking application at Xerox was within a prescribed area of the company's operations, the success that followed its implementation in that sector led to a corporation-wide mandate to use benchmarking processes as a means of quality improvement. There is an important point here, namely, administrative endorsement of a quality enhancement process is important for realizing the value that benchmarking provides, and a systems-wide commitment to quality improvement supports the intended changes from the older set of practices. Indeed, the use of benchmarking at the Xerox Corporation must be understood within the context of the company's adoption of *Total Quality Management* (TQM) principles, which also had a pre-existing utilization among Japanese industrial producers.

TQM efforts are system-wide, data-informed, customer-oriented, team-based and senior-management led. TQM is concerned with quality during the production of an output rather than with a post-production audit of outcomes. There is a dynamic quality in which feedback on the development of an output can be altered based on information regarding the efficiency of the processes. Thus the delivery of an output can be adjusted with feedback evidence before the output is completed. In recognition of this evolving and continuous approach to quality improvement, the name *Continuous Quality Improvement* (CQI) is popularly used to describe a system-wide commitment to quality, efficiency and feedback-based adjustments. CQI or TQM can be distinguished from *quality assurance* in that the latter.emphasizes changes implemented with evidence of after-the-fact reflection, whereas the former attempts to understand and improve the underlying work processes within a system before the actual production of the outcome.

Later in this chapter we will explore in greater detail two studies (Merrill, Tolbert & Wade, 2003; Wade, Treat & Stuart, 1998) that were conducted in a mental health clinic environment that had adopted a quality improvement initiative under the following mandate: 'The Center will operate only those mental health treatments, services, and programs for which there exists evidence in the professional literature of their efficacy' (Morrison, 2004, p. 485). When issued in the late 1980s, this expectation from the clinic's board of directors, challenged the clinical professionals to begin using techniques different from those that many had been trained to deliver. The clinicians' first concern was an ethical dilemma: If I adopt these new ways of treating patients, am I meeting my responsibilities to the clients? Once those concerns had been met, the challenge was to integrate a culture change in treatment orientation into all aspects of treatment delivery so that measurement of outcomes was part of treatment delivery, outcomes were compared to those of peers in the clinic, and feedback was provided to clinicians to effect improvements in their skills. This example of benchmarking clearly reflects the corporate endorsement to effect a corporate environment of standard-setting.

Hermann et al. (2004) draw some further distinctions between quality assurance (QA) and CQI as they apply to healthcare as follows: (1) QA focuses on individual cases whereas CQI aggregates all service episodes; (2) QA traditionally has used peer review to audit completed cases whereas CQI has used measures of outcome; (3) QA historically has been invoked in response to a problem, whereas CQI attempts to shape a culture of routine performance assessment as a part of service delivery; and (4) CQI attempts to integrate evidence of clinical improvement with cost and personnel efficiencies.

Hermann et al. (2004) have summarized the principles of CQI as they apply to quality improvement in healthcare settings. These principles include the following:

- Healthcare is a series of processes in a system leading to outcomes;
- Quality problems can be seen as the result of defects in processes;

- Quality improvement efforts should draw on the knowledge and efforts of individuals involved in these processes, working in teams;
- Quality improvement work is grounded in measurement, statistical analysis and scientific method;
- The focus of improvement efforts should be on the needs of the customer (i.e. patients, but also the referrers, payers and other components of the healthcare system);
- Improvement should concentrate on the highest priority problems (i.e. those having the greatest impact on patient outcomes, costs and other critical areas).

The use of feedback to adjust the delivery of counselling and psychotherapy is an emerging example of the practice of CQI in the mental health services system. When paired with attention to processes known to effect positive outcomes, this feedback can inform adjustments to processes in favour of a potentially better treatment outcome. For CQI to be effectively applied to ongoing mental health services delivery, it is essential to establish linkages between processes and outcomes, preferably in the stochastic model that characterizes psychotherapy and counselling delivery.

CQI and benchmarking as interventions in health services

Clinical outcomes research as an example of CQI

The appropriation of quality improvement principles such as CQI and benchmarking to mental healthcare began in the 1990s (Camp & Tweet, 1994). Several large-scale collaborative efforts such as the National Outcomes Management Project (NOMP; Dewan et al., 2000) were initiated with patients in psychiatric care. As an example, the NOMP began with 16 sites in 9 states. Data were collected at three-month intervals on the BASIS-32 (Eisen et al., 1994), the SF-36 (Ware & Sherbourne, 1992), and a brief survey assessing need for care and reasons for seeking behavioural health treatment. A centralized data collection unit based at the Department of Psychiatry at the University of Cincinnati provided analysis of data collected at the sites. In turn, collaborating sites regularly received a large report summarizing data across all participating sites in order to compare performances and to seek out the processes and practices of the best-performing sites. Although generally described as an exercise in benchmarking, the NOMP programme, in fact, initially functioned more as a quality assurance or post-treatment audit of outcomes.

Clinical informatics

Ken Howard was among the first psychotherapy researchers to advocate the use of clinical information – *clinical informatics* – to inform the efficient delivery of mental health services. Howard et al. (1996) drew distinctions between efficacy, effectiveness and efficiency research. Efficacy research examines whether a particular treatment is sufficient to produce desirable outcomes, whereas effectiveness research focuses on the outcomes of treatment delivered in typical treatment settings. Efficiency research involves the aggregation of outcomes data of individual cases that has been gathered periodically and regularly during treatment. Data from a clinic, and when combined with the data from other clinics within a system, provides the possibility of greater sampling representativeness. Within the clinic, the multiple cases of each therapist provide a level of analysis, as do the modalities of treatment such as individual counselling, couples therapy, group therapy, or medication management.

The aggregation of large data sets provides normative data that can be used to assess the efficiency with which a treatment is progressing. Standards of outcome in the form of expected treatment responses can be developed that take into account the clinical characteristics that influence the patient's response to treatment. An expected course of response to treatment, adjusted for clinical characteristics, can be used to monitor an individual patient's response to therapy against the trajectory of change predicted by the modelled clinical variables.

Howard's work in quality improvement was stimulated by the development of a self-report measure of mental health status (Howard et al., 1992, 1995) that was based on principles of the dose-effect (Howard et al., 1986) and the phase models (Howard et al., 1993) of outcome development. The 68-item Integra Outpatient Tracking Assessment (later called the COMPASS) provides an omnibus measure of mental health status (the Mental Health Index), that in turn is comprised of three domains: subjective well-being, symptoms, and life functioning. Additional self-report data are collected from patients about presenting problems, and during therapy, about the therapeutic relationship. Therapists also provide ratings of severity, patient well-being, and treatment progress. The Integra/COMPASS measure was administered to clients of managed care networks operated by Integra, Inc. (later, COMPASS, Inc.) primarily in the east coast states of the United States.

Within several years of its implementation, an initial database of over 16,000 users provided normative standards against which to compare patients. Follow-up administrations of the measure allowed managed care supervisors to track the progress of patients while they were in treatment, and to have conversations with therapists about the progress of the patient in therapy. Initial administrations involved faxing scoring sheets to a central office for scoring, but later efforts used electronic response measures that provided immediate scoring and printed reports of completed forms. The work schedules of several managed care case supervisors were dedicated to reviewing tracking reports, discussing problematic cases in conferences, and dialoguing with therapists. These efforts clearly exhibited many of the features of quality improvement efforts, if not all the features of a CQI system (for descriptions of the instruments and review processes, see Sperry et al., 1996).

Feedback systems

Michael Lambert (e.g. Lambert, Hansen & Finch, 2001) has further advanced the concepts of efficacy research and has developed a systematic research programme examining the clinical utility of providing feedback on patient response to treatment. Lambert developed a self-report outcome assessment instrument, the Outcome Questionnaire-45 (OQ-45; Lambert et al., 1996), for tracking patients on a weekly basis while in counselling or psychotherapy. Brigham Young University's Comprehensive Clinic, Aetna Insurance, Human Affairs International and PacifiCare Behavioral Health, among other healthcare providers, adopted the OQ-45 for use as a quality improvement tool in their behavioural care operations. In the more than 10 years of use, over 100,000 patients have provided evidence of their mental health status on the instrument. Lambert (2007) has shown that providing clinicians with feedback while the treatment is in progress that a patient is not on track for improvement results in improved outcomes for those patients. Lambert and his colleagues have experimented also with the provision of clinical support tools to suggest alternative strategies to managing a failing case. The objective of these interventions is to prevent a treatment failure when knowledge of patient response to treatment can be assessed.

Through the Institute for the Study of Therapeutic Change, a consortium of private practice psychotherapists and counsellors has developed an outcomes assessment system, the Partners for Change Outcome Management System (PCOMS). The OQ-45 is one component of this feedback system. Miller et al. (2004) describe the use of this system in using feedback to make adjustments to ongoing therapies. Positive effects of this feedback include improved retention and outcomes for clients most at risk for failure.

Quality evaluation and national databases (NDs)

In the UK the CORE System Trust has aggregated clinical outcomes data on large samples of clients serviced in the clinics of multiple systems of service delivery. The resultant data sets provide excellent representativeness of potential patient clinical characteristics and enable more specific normative standards of treatment response to be developed. These have been used to monitor change over time (Barkham et al., 2001), benchmarking a range of service variables against normative data (Evans et al., 2003), and the development of a range of service benchmarks via an infrastructure (Mellor-Clark et al., 2006).

Benchmarks have been developed for amongst others, completion rates for measures (Bewick et al., 2006), initial contact (Cahill et al., 2006), unilateral termination (Connell, Grant & Mullin, 2006), recovery and improvement rates (Mullin et al., 2006), and waiting times (Trusler et al., 2006). To date the NDs that have been developed from donor samples include NHS primary care psychological therapies, university counselling services, and staff support services/employment assistance programmes. These data sets are updated at regular intervals and provide the basis for academic collaborations with colleagues to ensure that the yield of the data feeds into the national and international scientific community.

Later, we will explore the implications of each of these approaches to efficacy research for their application of benchmarking. Although these three approaches, COMPASS, OQ-45 and CORE, as well as other systems, use different outcomes assessment instruments, all three monitor mental health status at an omnibus level, all make multiple assessments within the course of a single treatment and all generate sufficient data to formulate norms or standards of response given clinical characteristics of the patient or client. Finally, all provide the opportunity for management of quality improvement at the systems level, use patient-focused (provided) data on status, and emphasize continuous adjustments of treatments. These features, as we have seen, are the essential ingredients of TQM and CQI approaches within which benchmarking seems to produce the most positive impact.

Empirical studies

Although logical in its design and rational in its principles, it remains an empirical question whether the implementation of a quality improvement system such as CQI is associated with more positive outcomes and greater cost efficiency in healthcare. Beginning in the 1990s, a number of reports on the use of CQI and benchmarking have appeared in the mental health literature. Many of these reports are conceptual pieces extolling the value of using CQI principles in mental health treatment. Others are in essence case studies involving partial or system-wide implementation of CQI. For example, Keller (1997) examined the impact of implementing a CQI process to reduce waiting times for patients at a health maintenance clinic offering outpatient psychotherapy. Over a two-year period, waiting times were reduced from an average of 22 days to 6 days while the CQI process was being implemented.

Very few studies have examined the empirical impact of implementing CQI across service delivery sites, or in the context of other potential causes of any positive changes that might be observed. A study by Solberg et al. (2001) involving many clinics is one of the few exceptions. Solberg assessed the impact of using a continuous quality improvement intervention in primary care clinics to improve outcomes of treatments for depression, but found no effect for the intervention. Shortell et al. (1995) conducted one of the early studies assessing the impact of CQI in a healthcare setting using multiple service delivery sites. Their study involved data from 61 hospitals in the United States examining the impact of hospital culture, use of CQI, implementation approach, and hospital size (number of beds) on objective measures of patient outcomes and clinical efficiency. Hospital culture was assessed for the degree of group, developmental, hierarchical and rational features. Implementation was assessed with a scale comprised of dimensions of leadership, information and analysis, human resources management, quality management and strategic quality planning that showed strong criterion validity with activities such as greater use of quality improvement tools, and higher levels of involvement with quality improvement teams. Patient outcomes included treatment success, reduced errors and inappropriate treatment, increased patient satisfaction, and improved continuity of care. Clinical efficiency examined charges and length of stay grouped by specific problems.

Thirty-seven of the hospitals met all five criteria for a CQI process – emphasis on systems and processes rather than individuals, data-driven problem-solving approaches, use of cross-organizational teams, empowerment of workers, and a customer focus. Hospital culture and implementation approach both influenced patient outcomes and clinical efficiency. Hospitals with group/developmental cultures emphasizing teamwork, support and development of workers' potential, and willingness to undertake some degree of risk were more likely to implement quality improvement processes. Also, hospitals emphasizing decentralized control, empowerment of workers, and just-in-time training of physicians reported greater implementation of quality improvement practices. Culture and implementation were related to patient but not efficiency outcomes. Whether or not the hospital met CQI criteria did not influence patient outcomes (proportion of successes) but did influence efficiency (lower length of stay and charges). Thus, a major implication of this study is that healthcare organizations that have a group/developmental culture are more likely to implement quality improvement practices.

A few studies have examined the cost efficiency of mental health interventions, and have linked those interventions to actual or potential quality improvement activities. For example, Ackerberg, Machado and Riordan (2006) used an econometric approach together with case-mix adjustment to examine the performance of alcohol-abuse treatment providers in the State of Maine. Their data showed that alcohol-abuse treatment agencies differed substantially in their ability to improve the health of participants, completion thresholds, initial status of participants, and retention rates in treatment. Using a sophisticated model of (1) time in treatment and health improvement, (2) a correction for dropout hazard, (3) probability of completing treatment, and (4) different treating clinics, Ackerberg et al. modelled the economic cost of providing

alcohol treatment in programmes of varying lengths of time. Their econometric model suggested that the most efficient and effective treatments, if copied,
would reduce costs and improve treatment outcomes.

Although it is not the purpose of this chapter to thoroughly review the empirical literature on either continuous quality improvement or benchmarking, it
is important to note that continuous quality improvement and benchmarking,
when studied empirically, have not always yielded the predicted positive results.
Whether this is a function of limited effect size, insufficient power of the study,
an interaction of these two issues, or failure to implement a CQI intervention
as designed is not well established.

Paradigms of outcomes research for mental health services

Empirical studies of mental health interventions have represented two
paradigms that differ in their focus on four key components: on treatments
(treatment-focused research) or patients (patient-focused research), in methodology (confirmatory versus exploratory studies), in prescribed processes of
the treatment package (theoretically-informed, controlled interventions versus
treatments as actually delivered), and in group versus individual patient predictions (Donnenberg, Lyons & Howard, 1999; Howard et al., 1996; Lambert
et al., 2001; Lueger, 2002).

Donnenberg et al. (1999) have presented a dichotomy of these various approaches as illustrated in Table 9.1. This dichotomy organizes features on a
continuum characterized on one end of the continuum as mental health services research, and on the other end of the continuum as clinical trials research.
Others have labelled this continuum as a Federal Drug Administration regulatory paradigm versus a public health paradigm of research (Pilkonis & Krause,

Table 9.1   Features of research models for assessing outcomes of psychotherapy

Public Health Model	*Drug Regulatory Model*
Effectiveness	Efficacy
Exploratory	Confirmatory
Inductive reasoning	Deductive reasoning
Patient-focused	Treatment-focused
External validity	Internal validity
Large heterogeneous samples	Homogeneous diagnostic samples
Natural course of treatment	Protocol-determined treatment
Statistical control of clinical risk factors	Methodological control of risk factors

Adapted from Donnenberg, G.R. et al., Clinical trials versus mental health services research:
contributions and connections, *Journal of Clinical Psychology, 55,* 1135–1146. John Wiley &
Sons, 1999

Table 9.2 Four approaches to generalizing psychotherapy research

	Participants Focus of the Research	
	Treatment	*Patient*
Population	Technology Transfer Studies	Naturalistic Studies
Case	Single Case Design Studies	Clinical Decision Support Studies

Adapted from Lueger, R.J., Practice-informed research and research-informed psychotherapy, *Journal of Clinical Psychology, 58,* 1265–1276. John Wiley & Sons, 2002

1999). This dichotomy is useful for examining the application of benchmarking in quality improvement efforts. As we shall see, benchmarks can be constructed from actual therapy as delivered, drawn from large samples collected in many service delivery settings, or can be designed from prototype clinical trials of well-defined interventions.

Lueger (2002) has extended this dichotomy to emphasize a focus on groups or populations of patients or, alternatively, individual patients. As illustrated in Table 9.2, this quadratic approach recognizes that clinical trials of treatments are examined for generalizability to differing clinical settings and populations through the technology transfer study. The technology transfer study maintains strict controls for the delivery of the treatment, but may relax controls on other parameters such as co-morbidity of diagnoses, demographic characteristics of patients, or the presence of other active treatments such as medication management. Although trained in the delivery of the empirically supported treatment, the therapists may not be identified as experts in that particular treatment. As we shall see, the results of a technology transfer study are usually compared with the results of a clinical trial study that is more selective of the patient-participants. Because the focus is on the efficacy of the treatment, standards of therapist proficiency or flexibility of using alternative techniques generally are restricted in a clinical utility study. Services research studies typically focus on the validity of a class of interventions (e.g. psychotherapy, broadly defined) as expressed in outcomes, on access to care, on characteristics of service users, or on combinations of treatment components (intensity) in order to make statements applicable and generalizable to groups or populations of service users. Services research is more likely to include heterogeneous interventions that often lack the specificity of definition of those of clinical utility studies. Thus, it may be unclear which processes characterize the clinical delivery sites with the most effective outcomes.

The distinction between case and population focus evokes the differing scientific approaches of Aristotle and Galileo (Eells, 2007). In the Aristotelian approach, the essence of an event is recognized in the commonality of a large sample of an entity, with specific instances differing in degree from the commonality. Thus measures of central tendency identify a group centroid (mean or median) that captures the most prototypical qualities of that essence. Predictions generated by measures of central tendency, as evidenced in multiple regression techniques, can only be properly assessed by application to groups of individuals. One problem of multiple regression modelling is the fragility of covariance structures among the variables of a data set. The application of maximization techniques to establish similar groups in small data sets often leads to shrinkage in application to subsequent data sets. In addition, in a multivariate model of prediction, the potential contribution of lower order variables can be suppressed by more dominant relationships, thus masking mediating and moderating relationships among variables. Moreover, there still are no tests of error variance when group results are applied to the individual case. By contrast, in the Galilean approach, essence is embodied in each case as a concrete event. The features of an event such as similarity of treatment processes applied, similarity of a case to a prototypical case, similarity in qualities and style of the therapist, are referenced to the case at hand and understood in terms of geometric distances from the centroid case. Measures of Euclidean distance are more favoured than are multiple regression measures.

Case-focused research can address either (or both) efficacy and efficiency. In single case design treatment studies, prototypical cases are recognized as belonging to a class of disorder or problem presentation that is sufficiently well described as to have a high generalizability factor. Well-defined interventions are documented with individual cases. Aggregations of those cases make a more compelling argument for the generalizability of findings. In patient-focused research at the case level, the question of interest is how well a treatment is progressing for the particular patient being seen in treatment at this time (the efficiency question). As Pilkonis and Krause have stated, 'clinicians want to know (or ought to know) whether to take on a next patient and what to do if they do so . . . clinicians want to know what results can reasonably be expected from doing what they can do, which of these alternatives should be performed, and whether alternatives exist to providing therapy themselves' (Pilkonis & Krause, 1999, p. 204).

In making such decisions, clinicians rely on their own experience as the best source of evidence (high similarity of therapist), on the results of similar therapists in similar settings with patients like this one receiving similar treatment. Thus other instances of treatment differing in therapist qualities, patient characteristics, treatment processes and feature of setting are seen as geometric distances from the concrete case confronting the therapist. Benchmarking, when derived from this research, would cluster therapist, patient, treatment and setting variables to identify standards of outcome that would apply to the case at hand. Success in outcome is defined as a good-enough approximation of these combined similarities with minimum distances of variance.

Effectiveness paradigm

Treatment-focused benchmarking studies

Several technology transfer studies that focus on generalizing empirically supported treatments to service delivery settings serve as examples of the process of benchmarking treatment results. Wade has reported on two clinical utility studies that examined the transportability of empirically supported treatments to a community service delivery setting (Merrill et al., 2003; Wade et al., 1998).

Benchmarking treatments for panic disorder

Wade et al. (1998) used therapists who had received training in an empirically supported treatment designed and tested by Barlow et al. (1989) to treat 110 patients who met criteria for a diagnosis of panic disorder. Some of these participants were recruited by advertisements that a treatment for panic was available, the clinical staff members of the community clinic were specifically trained to deliver this treatment, treatment integrity was carefully monitored, and treatment length was prescribed. On the other hand, the participants were more heterogeneous with respect to presenting problems and demographic characteristics than were participants in the clinical trial establishing the efficacy of the treatment. The Barlow study results and the results of a clinical trial by Telch et al. (1993) served as the benchmark data for comparisons on eight variables: (a) panic-free status; (b) frequency of panic attacks; (c) daily self-monitoring of anxiety; (d) daily self-monitoring of depression; (e) agoraphobia symptoms; (f) symptomatic depression; (g) percentage of clients taking anxiolytic medications; and (h) percentage of clients taking depression medications.

Of the 110 clients who began treatment, 81 (74%) completed at least 8 of the first 11 sessions and were known as *completers.* By contrast, only one of the participants in the Barlow study dropped out of treatment. This, of course, elicits the much-discussed issue of which sample to compare with the benchmark data – the completers or the entire sample. Using the completer sample, the authors observed, 'CMHC [community mental health center] treatment completers improved on virtually every measure, and the magnitude of these improvements was comparable to those of the improvements reported in the controlled efficacy studies' (Wade et al., 1998, p. 236). Although pre- and post-test differences on outcome variables were reported for the community-based study, no statistical tests of difference or equivalence were reported to support the assertion of comparability.

Benchmarking treatments of depression

Merrill et al. (2003) compared a cognitive therapy treatment of depression with two benchmark clinical trial studies involving cognitive therapy for depression

(Elkin et al., 1989; Hollon et al., 1992). Inclusion in the study sample required a primary diagnosis of depression; no substance dependence, antisocial personality, bipolar disorder or psychosis; and completion of study measures. Of the 322 clients seeking treatment for depression, 192 met the above criteria. Unlike the clinical trials, length of therapy was open-ended. The cognitive therapy protocol prescribes a treatment lasting 12 to 20 sessions, and the definition of a treatment completer in the clinical trials is more than 11 sessions. The authors reported that only 32% of the clients met this completion threshold, and that treatments lasted an average of 7.8 sessions. Data in the clinic sample were organized to reflect the 164 clients who attended at least one session, and a subsample of patients who more closely matched the symptom severity parameters of the benchmark studies and who attended a minimum of four sessions of cognitive therapy. The authors tested the differences between this subsample against the results of the Elkin et al. (1989) study and observed that the differences were small, with effect sizes (Cohen's d) of 0.16 for a self-report measure of depression and 0.21 for a clinician rating of functioning. The authors concluded, 'Most CBH [Center for Behavioral Health] clients attended substantially fewer sessions than clients in the RCTs [randomized clinical trials], yet still showed similar levels of improvement' (Merrill et al., 2003, p. 408).

Minami and Wampold (Minami et al., 2006, 2007, 2008) have advanced the practice of benchmarking for mental health services involving treatment of depression. Using meta-analytic aggregates of pre- and post-treatment effect sizes, they established clinical trial benchmarks and tested for treatment efficacy against these benchmarks. They also identified natural history benchmarks using the aggregated pre-post scores of wait-list controls from clinical trial studies. The effect size outcomes of a managed care treated group of patients were compared with these benchmarks. The comparisons indicated that managed care treatments were comparable to those of clinical trials outcomes.

Weersing and Weisz (2002) attempted to identify a research-based standard of care by combining the results of 13 randomized clinical trials involving the cognitive behavioural treatment of depression in youths. The clinical trials ranged in session length from 6 to 25 with a median of 12 sessions. Unfortunately, the number of clients participating in the 13 studies contributing to the benchmark standards was not provided in the Weersing and Weisz (2002) manuscript. In addition to the use of multiple studies to establish the benchmark, a notable feature of their benchmark data was the identification of a trajectory of change over a 12-month period following treatment. Using this benchmark, they compared the treatment response of 67 depressed youths treated in a community clinic setting. Treatment lengths ranged from 1 to 90 sessions with a median of 11 sessions. Therapists reported practices more congruent with a mix of psychodynamic, cognitive and behavioural techniques. The clinic group began therapy with levels of depression similar to those of the benchmark standards, but did not respond as positively as assessed at the end of treatment. However, by 12 months post-treatment, the clinic group's depression scores had reduced to the level of the benchmark standard. Nevertheless, the authors concluded: 'The results are not encouraging with regard to the effects of community treatment ... CMHC [community mental health centre] youth took twice as long as [benchmark] youth to achieve a similar level of symptom relief' (Weersing & Weisz, 2002, p. 307).

Westbrook and Kirk (2004) studied the effectiveness of cognitive behaviour therapy (CBT) in a service delivery system and used the outcomes of clinical trials as the benchmark to assess those outcomes. The sample size of the naturalistically treated patients with depression was large (N = 1,276), but the results indicated that the results in a naturalistic setting did not reach the levels reported for the clinical trials.

Benchmarking with other treatments of other disorders

Hunsley and Lee (2007) have reported on efficacy benchmarks for psychological treatments in order to establish comparisons with the results from effectiveness studies. The authors determined the efficacy benchmark for improved or recovered clients at post-therapy, represented in terms of clinically significant change, for five clinical presentations in adults as follows: depression – 51%, panic disorder – 63%, generalized anxiety disorder – 52% (Westen & Morrison, 2001), and obsessive-compulsive disorder – 64% (Eddy, Dutra & Westen, 2004). Clearly, the results of efficacy studies show that a majority of treated patients improve or recover, but that those rates, even in highly controlled studies, have considerable room for improvement.

Scheeres et al. (2008) used the outcomes of four clinical trials of CBT for chronic fatigue syndrome as a benchmark to assess the quality of treatment outcomes of 112 patients treated in a mental health centre. Although treatment effect sizes were 'in a range of those found in the benchmark studies' (p. 163), approximately one-third of the patients left treatment shortly after or before the treatment began.

Issues

Several observations can be made before considering other examples of benchmarking empirically supported treatments. First, in comparing the results of a clinic-based outcomes study with that of a benchmark standard, researchers might do well to consider conducting analyses of equivalence (see Rogers, Vessey & Howard, 1993) as well as tests for the significance of differences. Secondly, in benchmarking studies with a focus on treatments, there is the problem of differences in treatment lengths. In the studies described above, the clinic samples all had significantly fewer sessions of psychotherapy than did the participants in the benchmark clinical trials. Thirdly, the selection of a clinical trial data set as the benchmark does not ensure that it contains the best outcomes among possible treatment interventions. That is, within any clinical trial, some therapists using a treatment might be more successful with some patients than the average of those therapists and patients with that treatment. Finally, as Weersing and Weisz (2002) demonstrated in their study, it is necessary to conduct risk or case-mix adjustments to identify moderators of treatment response.

Benchmarking for practice-based studies

We now turn to issues relating to establishing benchmarks for the psychological therapies as delivered in routine practice. Unlike treatment-focused studies reported above that emphasize transporting evidence-based treatments into clinical settings and testing generalizability, practice-based studies focus on routine treatment as it exists without any imposition or constraint akin to trials methodology (for more details, see Barkham et al., Chapter 2).

Patient-focused benchmarking studies

In the past 15 years, several research programmes have developed with the goal of aggregating outcomes data collected from treatments involving psychotherapy or counselling services. These efforts typically involve a brief measurement instrument that provides an omnibus measure of mental health status, are guided by the efforts of a team of researchers, are informed by the principles of patient-focused research, and that involve extensions into large service delivery systems. The aggregated data sets constitute naturalistic studies of psychotherapy effectiveness, but these patient-focused efforts involve at least pre- to post-therapy changes in addition to a profile of patients/clients at intake. Moreover, these efforts involve statistical definitions of change as statistically reliable improvement or deterioration, and clinically significant change.

The programmes of practice-based research can be identified by the measurement instrument as well as by the recognized research-practitioner guiding the programme of research. We include among these efforts the following: programmes by Ken Howard using the Integra Outpatient Tracking System (Howard et al., 1992), which later was called the COMPASS (Howard et al., 1993); the COMPASS-PC (primary care version; Grissom & Howard, 2000) and later evolved into the TEAM (Grissom et al., 2003); the Outcome Questionnaire-45 (OQ-45; Lambert et al., 1996) and the youth-normed equivalent, the YLSQ (Burlingame, Jasper & Peterson, 2001); the BASIS-32 (Eisen et al., 1994; Dewan et al. 2000); the CORE System (Barkham et al., 2006; Mellor-Clark & Barkham, 2006); the TOP (Treatment Outcome Package; Kraus et al., 2004); and the body of work entitled Client Directed, Outcome Informed (CDOI) clinical work (Duncan, Miller & Sparks, 2004). We have included the CDOI clinical work in this list because, although not used for research benchmarking, it is an exemplar of practice-based outcomes implementation in which the two central tools, four-item outcome and session rating scales, are used to inform and enhance naturally occurring clinical work. In the sense that the aim of benchmarking is to improve the quality of service provided to clients, the CDOI approach embraces this philosophy within the work of the individual practitioner.

Internal benchmarking

Work with the CORE-OM is illustrative of efforts to bring these large data sets to benchmarking. Barkham et al. (2001) reported early data from the CORE-OM from 2,710 psychotherapy and counselling recipients in 39 National Health Service secondary care clinics in the United Kingdom. He further focused on 1,455 service recipients in a single clinic. Three issues were explored: (1) whether the percentage of patients achieving outcomes maintains from year to year; (2) how levels of severity at intake compare in their change; and (3) whether clinically significant outcomes are influenced by the amount of therapy received. An important point of using benchmarking data is that a service should be examined over time rather than at a single point in time.

In a more recent series of articles in the journal, *Counselling & Psychotherapy Research*, a team of researchers with the CORE-OM System used data collected from over 30,000 service recipients in the NHS system to address issues of wait times for services, the rate of completion of outcome measures, service safety and risk assessment, and therapy allocation to those who need it most (Mellor-Clark, 2006). Figures 9.1A and Figure 9.1B present outcome graphs for mild/moderately severe and severe initial levels of presenting problems respectively. Each graph is divided into quartiles showing the percentage of clients for mild/moderate (N of practitioners = 372) and severe (N of practitioners = 166). Hence, a practitioner achieving a recovery rate of 72% or more for their clients presenting with mild, moderate, or moderate-to-severe problems, would place that practitioner in the top quartile. But for practitioners seeing clients presenting with severe problems, a recovery rate of 58% or more would place the practitioner in the top quartile. This division between severity bands introduces a simple adjustment for case-mix, a procedure that is outlined in detail later.

Multi-level modelling and therapist effects

With large data sets, there are possibilities for analysing nested variables in a hierarchical order (Baer & Lueger, 2003). For example, comparisons can be made between multiple therapists in the same clinic, multiple clinics within

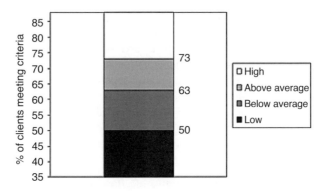

Figure 9.1A   Case-mix adjusted recovery benchmarks for mild and moderate severity problems in UK primary care psychological therapies. *Source*: Mullin, T. et al., Recovery and improvement benchmarks in routine primary care mental health settings. *Counselling & Psychotherapy Research, 6*, 68–80. Taylor & Francis Group, 2006

the same service, service delivery systems, and at an international level by aggregating systems of care within each country. To date, efforts to benchmark outcomes at an international level have focused on identifying common quality measures (Hermann et al., 2006) or on policy discussions (Ferlie & Shortell, 2001). A few empirical studies have focused on profiling the outcomes of therapists with case-mix adjustment. For example, Lutz et al. (2002) used a

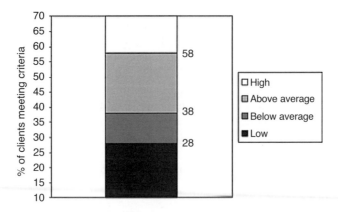

Figure 9.1B   Case-mix adjusted recovery benchmarks for severe presenting problems in UK primary care psychological therapies. *Source*: Mullin, T. et al., Recovery and improvement benchmarks in routine primary care mental health settings. *Counselling & Psychotherapy Research, 6*, 68–80. Taylor & Francis Group, 2006

growth curve analysis of patient trajectories of change to determine whether patients did better or worse than expected, given their clinical characteristics. The caseloads of each of eight therapists were examined to determine whether the patients did better or worse than expected with case-mix adjustment for severity of presenting symptoms and functioning. The analysis of outcome by cases adjusted for severity revealed that a few therapists did well with cases of mild severity, whereas a few therapists had better outcomes with cases of greater severity.

Brown et al. (2005) examined the variability of the outcomes of 281 therapists who provided psychotherapy or counselling to a total of 10,812 patients. The sample of therapists was selected on the basis of a minimum of 15 cases of outcomes data. The outcome measure was the LSQ (Burlingame et al., 2001), and case-mix was controlled using a multiple regression model with residual change scores as the dependent variable and intake score, age group, sex, diagnostic group (eight groupings) and session number of the first assessment as case-mix variables. Based on case-mix adjusted outcomes, a subset of 71 highly effective therapists was identified. Highly effective therapists averaged more than three times the average change per case compared to the other therapists. Secondary analyses of outcomes with patients who score above the clinical cut-off (i.e. have significant symptomatic problems) indicated that these highly effective therapists still had outcomes at least 2.7 times better than the rest of the therapists had with patients of similar severity.

These examples at the therapist level of analysis illustrate potential usefulness of benchmarking outcomes to those of the most effective therapists when the severity of the patient's problems is taken into consideration. A caveat for interpreting these findings is that the therapist variable is crossed with clinic, and possibly service delivery system, variables. That is, the caseloads were not nested within clinics, within systems, and so forth.

Finding the critical processes in cases with desirable outcomes

Although much research has been conducted on the processes leading to positive outcomes of psychotherapy, this research has not revealed many predictive variables that replicate across studies (Castonguay & Beutler, 2005; Orlinsky, Grawe & Parks, 1994). Thus the task of finding processes that characterize more favourable outcomes when the caseloads of highly successful therapists or high performing clinics are benchmarked is challenging. One variable with staying power as a predictor of positive outcomes is the alliance between therapist and patient. Other candidates might include an increased sense of hope (Frank, 1973; Howard et al., 1993) early in treatment, agreement on therapeutic goals (Wierzbicki & Pekarik, 1993), the presence of social support for being in therapy from a significant other, and mutual agreement on termination (Connell et al., 2006).

Clinical trials as benchmarks for routine practice

As with effectiveness studies, a logical – albeit not necessarily a natural – source of benchmarks is the trials literature. The issue being addressed by this approach is to locate the outcomes under routine practice conditions against a standard deemed to represent the effectiveness of such an intervention under optimal conditions. Because our focus is more naturally on practice-based approaches, we have outlined below the procedures for implementing such a strategy.

Benchmarking methodology

Minami et al. (2006) have detailed the necessary stages in devising benchmarks as follows: (1) constructing pre-post benchmarks from clinical trials; (2) estimating the effectiveness of routine practice as denoted by the pre-post effect size (ES); and (3) benchmarking the routine practice ES against the benchmark for the trials data. In terms of the first stage, their recommendation is to carry out a meta-analysis of clinical trials in which data is reported as intent-to-treat as this best mimics routine practice. In addition, benchmarks should be measure-specific in that outcome measurement can vary in terms of reactivity and specificity. Measures completed by practitioners or assessors are known to be more reactive than self-report measures completed by clients, while measures higher in specificity (i.e. focused on specific symptoms) will yield larger effects. Also, it is recommended that only a single ES per study should be aggregated for one benchmark. Formulae for calculating the ES in clinical trials are provided by Minami et al. (2008) which, when aggregated, yield a single value for the benchmark which is fixed. The formulae for the routine practice ES – the second stage – is broadly similar to that for the individual clinical trial (see Minami et al., 2008 for details). Both procedures use the pre-treatment standard deviation as the denominator in calculating the ES.

In terms of the third stage of actually benchmarking routine outcomes against efficacy benchmarks, Cohen's rule of $d = 0.2$ is applied as the margin around the clinical benchmark. As an additional comparator, Minami et al. (2007) also established a benchmark for the natural history of improvement for, in this instance, depression by drawing on a meta-analytic review by Posternak and Miller (2001). In effect, this is the baseline for no treatment such that any intervention should be expected to exceed. In this way, treatments delivered in routine settings can be judged to be (a) not effective, (b) more effective than no treatment but not as effective as an appropriate comparator treatment delivered under optimal conditions, or (c) equivalent to treatment as an appropriate comparator treatment delivered under optimal conditions. There is also, logically, a further category, namely that the routine treatment is more effective than the efficacy benchmark. It might be assumed that it would be unlikely for this final category to occur. However, a service might select an efficacy benchmark that

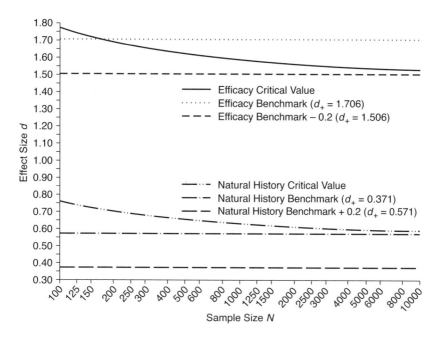

Figure 9.2 Routine against efficacy for low reactive-high specificity measure (BDI). *Source*: Minami, T. et al., Benchmarks for psychotherapy efficacy in adult major depression. *Journal of Consulting and Clinical Psychology, 75*, 232–243. American Psychological Association, 2007

is, at one level, plausible and enables it to show that the service is effective, although under closer scrutiny it might be shown that it is neither the logical nor appropriate comparator. In other words, it has been selected because it is the lowest threshold and, as such, it is possible for the routinely delivered treatment to equal the benchmark.

These methods yielded distinct efficacy and natural history benchmarks for a range of measures of depression (i.e. BDI, Hamilton Rating Scales for Depression, and generic measures). Figures 9.2 and 9.3 present the benchmarks based on the BDI (Beck et al., 1988) and the low-specificity and low-reactive measures respectively.

As an illustration, if the BDI is used as the outcome measure (Figure 9.2), a practice-based sample (N = 500) would need to yield a pre-post ES (Cohen's *d*) of 0.65 to equal the natural history benchmark and an ES of 1.62 to equal the efficacy benchmark. However, with a low reactive-low specificity measure, the respective values are considerably lower. Perhaps what is most striking here is the influence of the specific measure itself in relation to a specific clinical presentation – in this instance, depression. Hence, the implication is that there would need to be benchmarks for specific measures for specific

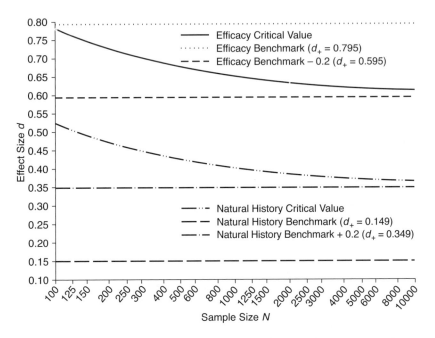

Figure 9.3   Routine against efficacy for low reactive-low specificity measures. *Source*: Minami, T. et al., Benchmarks for psychotherapy efficacy in adult major depression. *Journal of Consulting and Clinical Psychology, 75,* 232–243. American Psychological Association, 2007

clinical presentations. This implies considerable work on developing these aids but it might also indicate the need for developing such work with a generic *patient reported outcome measure* – known in the UK as PROMs – such as the EQ-5D (The EuroQol Group, 1990), which could facilitate comparisons and heath utilities across healthcare settings as well as internationally.

Cautionary note regarding effect sizes and other metrics

Notwithstanding the appeal and utility of the procedures described above, there are certain properties of ESs – both technical and conceptual – that any user needs to take into account. In the descriptions above, it was noted that the denominator used in calculations is the pre-treatment SD. In trials, pre-treatment SDs have a relatively tight band because inclusion criteria invariably specify a minimum intake score on the primary outcome measure. In addition, they may also indirectly exclude clients presenting with very high scores as this is likely to signal other complex issues on which bases they might be excluded. Either way, the effect of this greater exclusion results in reduced variance which yields a smaller denominator and thereby a more favourable ES. By contrast, routine services will have a clinically responsive procedure and are likely to use any pre-measure as only one part of the intake assessment and may not exclude higher scoring clients (although this might signal another part of the service as more appropriate to their needs). But, the result is likely to be larger variance and, as a result, a comparatively smaller ES. The impact of a slightly greater SD combined with slightly reduced change can result in an appreciable reduction in the overall ES. Indeed, Barkham et al. (2008) considered ESs for the treatment of depression from RCTs compared with unselected clients from practice-based studies and found that the advantage in ES, despite broadly similar pre-post change, was mainly accounted for by the restricted standard deviation within trials. And pooling the pre- and post-treatment SDs made relatively little difference.

In addition, there are clinical and conceptual issues worthy of brief mention. Clinically, an ES is a neutral term – that is, it carries no intrinsic clinical meaning. And conceptually, it is worth remembering that Cohen assigned the labels *small*, *medium* and *large* somewhat tentatively making it clear that the terms are relative to each other but that the definitions are arbitrary, a theme taken up in a critique of the methods of measurement underpinning evidence-based treatments (for details, see Kazdin, 2006). Hence, there is a questionable logic concerning assigning a specific attribute to, for example, an ES of 0.50, as has been the case in the UK where $d = 0.5$ has been taken as the criterion for proven effectiveness by the National Institute for Health and Clinical Excellence (NICE).

Risk or case-mix adjustment

Risk adjustment, or case-mix adjustment, is a process of statistically correcting outcomes using variables known to correlate with treatment outcomes. This process allows the comparison of treatment outcomes across patients, between therapists, among clinics, or systems of service delivery where severity, distress, chronicity, previous exposure to therapy, medical conditions, co-morbidity, and demographic variables differ among the comparison cases or groups. Risk adjustment is critical to meaningful comparisons using benchmarking data and two approaches have dominated: stratification and multivariate statistical controls.

Stratification

Stratification typically focuses on one or two critical variables such as distress, severity, or co-morbidity. For example, Lambert et al. (2001) have used stratification of initial level of patient distress and functioning to identify expected patterns of response to psychotherapy in the early sessions. Patients with higher levels of symptomatic distress and poorer functioning are not expected to respond as rapidly as patients with milder levels of distress. The National Center for Quality Assurance's Health Plan Employer Data and Information Set (HEDIS), which is a frequently referenced source of benchmarking data in the United States, uses the stratification approach by identifying phases of treatment for specific disorders (e.g. acute phase medication treatment of acute depression; Kerr et al., 2000). One problem with the use of stratification is that only a few variables can be used to correct the observed outcomes, and there is the possibility that an unknown mediating or moderating variable is having an impact on the outcomes under scrutiny.

Multivariate statistical controls

The multivariate approach to case-mix adjustment allows the inclusion of more variables that might directly or indirectly contribute to outcomes. Some techniques such as random regression models can allow examination of nested factors such as patients, therapists, clinics and service delivery systems. Kramer et al. (2001) used a multivariate statistical correction in comparing case-mix adjusted outcomes of treatments for depression. Howard et al. (1996) used hierarchical linear modelling (also known as random regression modelling) to identify first-order (the outcome index itself) and second-order (risk adjustment variables) to identify patterns of change adjusted for seven clinical characteristics (subjective well-being, symptomatic distress, life functioning, severity, chronicity, motivation and previous treatment). To better understand the clinical variables that might contribute to the unpromising comparisons between clinic-treated and efficacy study outcomes, the authors of the benchmark study of child/adolescent depression (Weersing & Weisz, 2002) used hierarchical linear modelling to identify second-order characteristics affecting treatment response. Two variables, ethnic status and dosage, predicted the treatment outcomes of clinic youth. Racial minority youth, and those who received fewer than eight sessions of psychotherapy had poorer outcomes. Lutz et al. (2005) have used clustering algorithms to identify, from a large database, patients with clinical characteristics similar to a target patient in order to adjust for treatment comparisons.

Multivariate case-mix adjustment is a helpful tool, but is not a panacea for understanding the contribution of clinical variables to benchmarking results. This tool requires large data sets to conduct nesting studies, and to counter the risk of unstable covariance matrices. Moreover, some multivariate approaches using covariance analysis tend to suppress latent variables, and thus might unwittingly diminish true variability in the outcome index because of shared covariance characteristics. Finally, the use of multivariate corrections typically requires the expertise and services of highly trained statistical researchers.

Practical issues for implementing benchmarking practices

A number of issues are important to the successful implementation of benchmarking practices. Among these issues are: (1) how well therapists accept measurement as a part of treatment; (2) agreement among stakeholders on the value of outcome indices; (3) a culture shift of focusing on outcomes of the therapy process rather than on therapist training, experience and process-inputs during therapy; (4) therapists overcoming a fear of practicing unethically; and (5) commitment to a culture of improvement based on feedback of outcomes data. Each of these topics is worthy of extensive, separate consideration, but suffice it to say that the cultural social shift to accountability of services will support, or even push, therapists and clinics to address these issues.

One issue that repeats in the examination of benchmarking efforts is the need for confidentiality. Comparisons of outcomes among therapists in the same clinic can be confirming to a few and embarrassing for a few others. The anticipatory fear of exposure will be a barrier for effective implementation of benchmarking. Similarly, clinics are likely to be reluctant to share data if their identities can be established. As a result, researchers will have to employ data-blind procedures and may need to include data managers with a reputation for honesty and confidentiality to serve as gatekeepers of the data.

Future directions for research

One of the difficulties of benchmarking data from clinical trials is that the clinic groups often reflect treatment lengths that differ (i.e. involve fewer sessions) than do the benchmarked clinical trials. Also, more clinic patients leave therapy before a dose threshold is reached than in clinical trials. The resulting samples can be very difficult to compare and interpret. One potential solution is to provide the data from clinical trials disaggregated to the case level. Then, cases with the best outcomes can be examined for potential contributions to their positive outcomes and held as a standard for treatment. It might be possible to use a simple severity stratification (mild, moderate, severe) mixed with dosage (less than dosage, met or exceeds dosage) to examine cases as standards of care.

With the development of large data sets, it has now become possible to examine nested variables of risk-adjusted patients, therapists, clinics, systems and nationalities to examine the quality outcomes of psychotherapy and counselling. Of course these ambitious efforts at benchmarking will require collaboration at an international level of researchers willing to share their data sets. The foundations for this work have already been established and research manuscripts are emerging that indicate the feasibility of addressing questions of quality at an international level.

To date, most efforts at benchmarking psychological therapy outcomes have used the internal type of benchmarking, or possibly the competitive type if one allows that other clinics are potential competitors for the same services. There has been little use of functional benchmarking or generic process benchmarking. The use of single outcome indices of quality might hamper such comparisons, and probably we need to know more about the processes that characterize successful outcomes before turning to these two types of benchmarking.

References

Ackerberg, D.A., Machado, M.P. & Riordan, M.H. (2006). Benchmarking for productivity improvement: A health-care application. *International Economic Review*, *47*, 161–201.

Baer, S.M. & Lueger, R.J. (June, 2003). *Benchmarking psychotherapy outcomes.* Paper presented at the annual meeting of the Society for Psychotherapy Research, Santa Barbara, CA.

Barkham, M., Mellor-Clark, J., Connell, J. & Cahill, J. (2006). A core approach to practice-based evidence: A brief history of the origins and applications of the CORE-OM and CORE system. *Counselling & Psychotherapy Research*, *6*, 3–15.

Barkham, M., Margison, F., Leach, C., Lucock, M., Mellor-Clark, J. et al. (2001). Service profiling and outcomes benchmarking using the CORE-OM: toward practice-based evidence in the psychological therapies. *Journal of Consulting and Clinical Psychology*, *69*, 184–196.

Barkham, M., Stiles, W.B., Connell, J., Twigg, E., Leach, C. et al. (2008). Effects of psychological therapies in randomized trials and practice-based studies. *British Journal of Clinical Psychology*, *47*, 397–415.

Barlow, D.H., Craske, M.G., Cerny, J.A. & Klosko, J.S. (1989). Behavioral treatment of panic disorder. *Behavior Therapy*, *20*, 261–282.

Beck, A.T., Steer, R.A. & Garbin, G.M. (1988). Psychometric properties of the Beck Depression Inventory: Twenty-five years of evaluation. *Clinical Psychology Review*, *8*, 77–100.

Bewick, B.M., Trusler, K., Mullin, T., Grant, S. & Mothersole, G. (2006). Routine outcome measurement completion rates of the CORE-OM in primary care psychological therapies and counselling. *Counselling & Psychotherapy Research*, *6*, 33–40.

Brown, G.S., Lambert, M.J., Jones, E.R. & Minami, T. (2005). Identifying highly effective psychotherapists in a managed care environment. *American Journal of Managed Care*, *11*, 513–520.

Burlingame, G.M., Jasper, B.W. & Peterson, G. (2001). *Administration and Scoring Manual for the YLSQ.* Salt Lake City, UT: American Professional Credentialing Services.

Cahill, J., Potter, S., & Mullin, T. (2006). First contact session outcomes in primary care psychological therapy and counselling services. *Counselling and Psychotherapy Research, 6,* 41–49

Camp, R.C. (1989). *Benchmarking: The search for industry best practice.* New York: ASQC Press.

Camp, R.C. & Tweet, A.G. (1994). Benchmarking applied to health care. *Journal on Quality Improvement, 20,* 229–238.

Castonguay, L.G. & Beutler, L.E. (eds.) (2005). *Principles of therapeutic change that work.* New York: Oxford University Press.

Connell, J., Grant, S. & Mullin, T. (2006). Client initiated termination of therapy at NHS primary care counselling services. *Counselling & Psychotherapy Research, 6,* 60–67.

Dewan, N.A., Daniels, A., Zieman, G. & Kramer, T.L. (2000). The national outcomes management project: A benchmarking collaborative study. *The Journal of Behavioral Health Services and Research, 27,* 431–436.

Donnenberg, G.R., Lyons, J.S. & Howard, K.I. (1999). Clinical trials versus mental health services research: contributions and connections. *Journal of Clinical Psychology, 55,* 1135–1146.

Duncan, B.L., Miller, S.D. & Sparks, J.A. (2004). *The heroic client: A revolutionary way to improve effectiveness through client-directed, outcome-informed therapy.* San Francisco, CA: Jossey-Bass.

Eddy, K.T., Dutra, L. & Westen, D. (2004). *A multidimensional meta-analysis of psychotherapy and pharmacotherapy for obsessive-compulsive disorder.* Unpublished manuscript, Emory University, Atlanta, GA.

Eells, T.D. (2007). Generating and generalizing knowledge about psychotherapy from pragmatic case studies. *Pragmatic Case Studies in Psychotherapy, 3,* 1.

Eisen, S.V., Dill, D.L. & Grob, M.C. (1994). Reliability and validity of a brief patient-report instrument for psychiatric outcome evaluation. *Hospital and Community Psychiatry, 45,* 242–247.

Elkin, I., Shea, M.T., Watkins, J.T., Imber, S.T., Sotsky, S.M. et al. (1989). National Institute of Mental Health Treatment of Depression Collaborative Research Program: General effectiveness of treatments. *Archives of General Psychiatry, 46,* 971–982.

Evans, C., Connell, J., Barkham, M., Margison, F., Mellor-Clark, J. et al. (2002). Towards a standardised brief outcome measure: Psychometric properties and utility of the CORE-OM. *British Journal of Psychiatry, 180,* 51–60.

Evans, C., Connell, J., Barkham, M., Marshall, C. & Mellor-Clark, J. (2003). Practice-based evidence: Benchmarking NHS primary care counselling services at national and local levels. *Clinical Psychology & Psychotherapy*, *10*, 374–388.

Ferlie, E.B. & Shortell, S.M. (2001). Improving the quality of health care in the United Kingdom and the United States: A framework for change. *The Millbank Quarterly*, *79*, 281–315.

Frank, J.D. (1973). *Persuasion and healing: A comparative study of psychotherapy*. Baltimore: Johns Hopkins University Press.

Grissom, G.R. & Howard, K.I. (2000). COMPASS-PC. In M. Maruish (ed.), *Handbook of psychological assessment in primary care settings*. Hillsdale, NJ: Erlbaum Associates.

Grissom, G.R., Lyons, J. & Lutz, W. (2003). Standing on the shoulders of a giant: Development of an outcome management system based on the dose model and phase theory of psychotherapy. *Journal of Psychotherapy Research*, *12*, 397–412.

Hermann, R.C., Mattke, S., Somekh, D., Silfverhielm, H., Goldner, E. et al. (2006). Quality indicators for international benchmarking of mental health care. *International Journal for Quality in Health Care*, *18*, (Supplement 1), 31–38.

Hermann, R.C., Palmer, R.H., Leff, S., Shwartz, M., Provost, S. et al. (2004). Achieving consensus across diverse stakeholders on quality measures for mental healthcare. *Medical Care*, *42*, 1246–1253.

Hollon, S.D., DeRubeis, R.J., Evans, M.D., Wiemer, M.J., Garvey, M.J. et al. (1992). Cognitive therapy and pharmacotherapy for depression: Singly and in combination. *Archives of General Psychiatry*, *49*, 774–781.

Howard, K.I., Brill, P.L., Lueger, R.J. & O'Mahoney, M. (1992). *Integra outpatient tracking assessment*. Radnor, PA: Integra, Inc.

Howard, K.I., Brill, P.L., Lueger, R.J. & O'Mahoney, M. (1995). *The COMPASS outpatient tracking system*. King of Prussia, PA: COMPASS, Inc.

Howard, K.I., Kopta, S.M., Krause, M.S. & Orlinsky, D.E. (1986). The dose-effect relationship in psychotherapy. *American Psychologist*, *41*, 159–164.

Howard, K.I., Lueger, R.J., Maling, M. & Martinovich, Z. (1993). The phase model of psychotherapy outcome: Causal mediation of change. *Journal of Consulting and Clinical Psychology*, *61*, 678–685.

Howard, K.I., Moras, K., Brill, P.L., Martinovich, Z. & Lutz, W. (1996). The evaluation of psychotherapy: Efficacy, effectiveness, and patient progress. *American Psychologist*, *51*, 1059–1064.

Hunsley, J. & Lee, C.M. (2007). Research-informed benchmarks for psychological treatments: Efficacy studies, effectiveness studies, and beyond. *Professional Psychology*, *38*, 21–33.

Kazdin, A. (2006). Arbitrary metrics: Implications for identifying evidence-based treatments. *American Psychologist*, *61*, 42–49.

Keller, G.A. (1997). Management for quality: Continuous quality improvement to increase access to outpatient mental health services. *Psychiatric Services*, *48*, 821–825.

Kerr, E., McGlynn, E., Van Vorst, K. & Wickstrom, S. (2000). Measuring antidepressant prescribing practice in a health care system using administrative data: Implications for quality measurement and improvement. *Joint Commission Journal on Quality Improvement*, *26*, 203–216.

Kramer, T.L., Evans, R.B., Landes, R., Mancino, M., Booth, B.M. et al. (2001). Comparing outcomes of routine care for depression: The dilemma of case-mix adjustment. *The Journal of Behavioral Health Research*, *28*, 287–300.

Kraus, D.R., Seligman, D.A. & Jordan, J.R. (2004). Validation of a behavioral health treatment outcome and assessment tool designed for naturalistic settings: The Treatment Outcome Package. *Journal of Clinical Psychology*, *61*, 285–314.

Kroenke, K., Spitzer, R.L. & Williams, J.B.W. (2001). The PHQ-9: Validity of a brief depression severity measure. *Journal of General Internal Medicine*, *16*, 606–613.

Lambert, M.J. (2007). Presidential address: What we have learned from a decade of research aimed at improving psychotherapy outcome in routine care. *Psychotherapy Research*, *17*, 1–14.

Lambert, M.J., Hansen, N.B. & Finch, A.E. (2001). Patient-focused research: using patient outcome data to enhance treatment effects. *Journal of Consulting and Clinical Psychology*, *69*, 159–172.

Lambert, M.J., Hansen, N.B., Umphress, V., Lunnen, K., Okiishi, J. et al. (1996). *Administration and scoring manual for the Outcome Questionnaire (OQ-45.2)*. Wilmington, DE: American Professional Credentialing Services.

Lueger, R.J. (2002). Practice-informed research and research-informed psychotherapy. *Journal of Clinical Psychology*, *58*, 1265–1276.

Lutz, W., Martinovich, Z., Howard, K.I. & Leon, S. (2002). Outcomes management, expected treatment response, and severity-adjusted provider profiling in outpatient psychotherapy. *Journal of Clinical Psychology*, *58*, 1291–1304.

Lutz, W., Leach, C., Barkham, M., Lucock, M., Stiles, W.B. et al. (2005). Predicting rate and shape of change for individual clients receiving psychological therapy: Using growth curve modeling and nearest neighbor technologies. *Journal of Consulting and Clinical Psychology*, *73*, 904–913.

Mellor-Clark, J. (2006). Developing CORE performance indicators for benchmarking in NHS primary care psychological therapy and counselling services: An editorial introduction. *Counselling & Psychotherapy Research*, *6*, 1–2.

Mellor-Clark, J. & Barkham, M. (2006). The CORE System: Developing and delivering practice-based evidence through quality evaluation. In C. Feltham & I. Horton (eds.), *Handbook of counselling and psychotherapy* (2nd edn., pp. 207–224). London: Sage Publications.

Mellor-Clark, J., Curtis Jenkins, A., Evans, R., Mothersole, G. & McInnes, B. (2006). Resourcing a CORE Network to develop a National Research Database to help enhance psychological therapies and counselling service provision. *Counselling & Psychotherapy Research*, 6, 16–22.

Merrill, K.A., Tolbert, V.E. & Wade, W.A. (2003). Effectiveness of cognitive therapy for depression in a community mental health center: A benchmarking study. *Journal of Consulting and Clinical Psychology*, 71, 404–409.

Miller, S.D., Duncan, B., Sorrell, R. & Brown, G.S. (2004). The Partners for Change Outcome Management System. *Journal of Clinical Psychology*, 61, 199–208.

Miller, S.D., Duncan, B.L., Brown, J., Sparks, J.A. & Claud, D.A. (2003). The Outcome Rating Scale: A preliminary study of the reliability, validity, and feasibility of a brief visual analog measure. *Journal of Brief Therapy*, 2, 91–100.

Minami, T., Serlin, R.C., Wampold, B.E., Kircher, J.C. & Brown, G.S.(Jeb) (2006). Using clinical trials to benchmark effects produced in clinical practice. *Quality & Quantity*, 42, 513–525.

Minami, T., Wampold, B.E., Serlin, R.C., Kircher, J.C. & Brown, G.S.(Jeb) (2007). Benchmarks for psychotherapy efficacy in adult major depression. *Journal of Consulting and Clinical Psychology*, 75, 232–243.

Minami, T., Wampold, B.E., Serlin, R.C., Hamilton, E.G., Brown, G.S.(Jeb) et al. (2008). Benchmarking the effectiveness of psychotherapy treatment for adult depression in a managed care environment: A preliminary study. *Journal of Consulting and Clinical Psychology*, 76, 116–124.

Morrison, D. (2004). Real-world use of evidence-based treatments in community behavioral health care. *Psychiatric Services*, 5, 485–487.

Mullin, T., Barkham, M., Mothersole, G., Bewick, B.M. & Kinder, A. (2006). Recovery and improvement benchmarks in routine primary care mental health settings. *Counselling & Psychotherapy Research*, 6, 68–80.

Orlinsky, D.E., Grawe, K. & Parks, B.K. (1994). Process and outcome in psychotherapy –Noch einmal. In S.L. Garfield & A.E. Bergin (eds.), *Handbook of psychotherapy & behavior change* (4th edn., pp. 270–376). New York: John Wiley & Sons, Inc.

Pilkonis, P.A. & Krause, M.S. (1999). Summary: paradigms for psychotherapy outcome research. *Journal of Clinical Psychology*, 55, 201–205.

Posternak, M.A. & Miller, I. (2001). Untreated short-term course of major depression: A meta-analysis of outcomes from studies using wait-list control groups. *Journal of Affective Disorders, 66,* 139–146.

Rogers, J., Vessey, J. & Howard, K.I. (1993). Using statistical tests to establish equivalence between two experimental groups. *Psychological Bulletin, 113,* 553–565.

Scheeres, K., Wensing, M., Knoop, H. & Bleijenberg, G. (2008). Implementing cognitive behavioral therapy for chronic fatigue syndrome in a mental health center: A benchmarking evaluation. *Journal of Consulting and Clinical Psychology, 76,* 163–171.

Shortell, S.M., O'Brien, J.L., Carman, J.M., Foster, R.W., Hughes, E.F.X. et al. (1995). Assessing the impact of continuous quality improvement/total quality management: Concept versus implementation. *HSR: Health Services Research, 30,* 378–401.

Solberg, L.I., Fischer, L.R., Wei, F., Rush, W.A., Conboy, K.S. et al. (2001). A CQI intervention to change the care of depression: A controlled study. *Evaluation Studies, 4,* 239–249.

Sperry, L., Brill, P., Howard, K.I. & Grissom, G. (1996). *Treatment outcomes in psychotherapy and psychiatric interventions.* New York: Brunner/Mazel.

Telch, M.J., Lucas, J.A., Schmidt, N.B., Hanna, H.H., Jaimez, T.L. et al. (1993). Group cognitive-behavioral treatment of panic disorder. *Behavior Therapy and Research, 31,* 279–287.

The EuroQol Group (1990). EuroQol – a new facility for the measurement of health-related quality of life. *Health Policy, 16,* 199–208.

Trusler, K., Doherty, C., Mullin, T., Grant, S. & McBride, J. (2006). Waiting times for primary care psychological therapy and counselling services. *Counselling & Psychotherapy Research. 6,* 23–32.

Tucker, F.G., Zivan, S.M. & Camp, R.C. (1987). How to measure yourself against the best. *Harvard Business Review, 65,* 8–10.

Wade, W.A., Treat, T.A. & Stuart, G.L. (1998). Transporting an empirically supported treatment for panic disorder to a service clinic setting: A benchmarking strategy. *Journal of Consulting and Clinical Psychology, 66,* 231–239.

Ware, J.E. & Sherbourne, C.D. (1992). The MOS 36-item short form health survey (SF-36): Conceptual framework and item selection. *Medical Care, 30,* 473–483.

Weersing, V.R. & Weisz, J.R. (2002). Community clinic treatment of depressed youth: Benchmarking usual care against CBT clinical trials. *Journal of Consulting and Clinical Psychology, 70,* 299–310.

Westbrook, D. & Kirk, J. (2004). The clinical effectiveness of cognitive behaviour therapy: Outcome for a large sample of adults treated in routine practice. *Behaviour Research and Therapy, 45,* 1243–1261.

Westen, D. & Morrison, K. (2001). A multidimensional meta-analysis of treatments for depression, panic, and generalized anxiety disorder: An empirical examination of the status of empirically supported therapies. *Journal of Consulting and Clinical Psychology, 69*, 875–899.

Wierzbicki, M. & Pekarik, G. (1993). A meta-analysis of psychotherapy dropout. *Professional Psychology: Research and Practice, 24*, 190–195.

10

Constructing and Disseminating Outcome Data at the Service Level: Case Tracking and Benchmarking

Chris Leach[1] and Wolfgang Lutz[2]

[1] *South West Yorkshire Partnership NHS Foundation Trust & University of Huddersfield, UK* [2] *University of Trier, Germany*

Introduction

This chapter offers suggestions for presenting and disseminating data collected as part of routine service delivery. Our examples come mainly from a data set collected over the past 10 years in an adult psychological therapies service in the National Health Service (NHS) of the United Kingdom. We start with simple methods of data exploration and presentation that can be used without access to statistical packages before moving on to techniques that require widely available spreadsheet or statistical packages and then consider more complex techniques requiring specialist software. We also suggest simple ways of presenting service-level data for audit and feedback to clinicians. Throughout we look at the key principles underlying making sense of data; these should be helpful for users at any level of statistical sophistication.

The simplest methods can be used with a single case without reference to how other clients with similar problems or therapies or levels of distress have done. Once a database of such similar clients is available, it can be used to provide a reference distribution that will allow more sophisticated case tracking, showing how a client's progress compares to that of others already treated. This also allows services to provide feedback and alerts to clinicians and clients as therapy progresses. We look at a number of approaches based on growth modelling, which predict a client's progress by estimating the average progress of a reference group of already-treated clients. The methods differ principally in how this

Developing and Delivering Practice-Based Evidence   By Michael Barkham, Gillian E Hardy, and John Mellor-Clark   © 2010 John Wiley & Sons, Ltd

reference group is identified and how the shape of progress is estimated. The Expected Treatment Response (ETR) approach (Lutz, Martinovich & Howard, 1999) and the nearest neighbour (NN) approach (Lutz et al., 2005) both model change as a log-linear function of session number, but differ in how the reference group is selected. The ETR approach uses a broad heterogeneous group of clients who enter therapy with a similar intake score on the outcome measure to the target client, while the NN approach homes-in on a small reference group of clients who resemble the target client on a broader range of variables at intake, including the specific outcome measure of interest. The more recent Growth Mixture Models (GMMs; Stulz et al., 2005) allow choice of reference groups with qualitatively different average growth curves. These techniques will become increasingly important as services are required to demonstrate their effectiveness and to make use of evidence to improve services (cf. Lambert, 2007).

Example data sets

The data set we use throughout this chapter is one collected in a United Kingdom NHS setting (Lucock et al., 2003). The service is a multiprofessional adult psychological therapies service receiving about 1,200 referrals a year. About 80% of referrals are from general practitioners. Most clients are seen in one of three main clinical bases or in general practice settings. The service comprises clinical psychologists, a specialist psychotherapy team, counsellors, nurse therapists, cognitive behavioural therapists and an art therapist. A range of therapies is provided, including cognitive behaviour therapy (CBT), eye movement desensitization and reprocessing (EMDR), psychodynamic and psychoanalytical psychotherapies, person-centred approaches and integrative psychotherapy including cognitive analytical therapy. Between 1997 and 2004, all clients referred were posted four measures (CORE-OM, BDI-I, BAI and IIP-32) on up to five occasions: (a) at referral, (b) before clinical assessment, (c) before therapy, (d) at discharge, and (e) six months after discharge. The second and third occasion measures were sent only if the time after the previous measures were sent was greater than six weeks. Over 5,500 clients completed at least one outcome measure on one of the five occasions. In addition, a subset of 357 clients gave informed consent to participate in a research study (e.g. Lutz et al., 2005; Stiles et al., 2003), which involved completing a short form (CORE-SF) of the CORE-OM before each therapy session, and returned one or more pre-session CORE-SF forms.

The large database recording before and after therapy measures has been used to evaluate, audit and benchmark the service (see, for example, Barkham et al., 2001; Lucock et al., 2003; Lucock, Leach & Iveson, 2005), as well as providing large amounts of data for checking psychometric properties of the outcome measures (e.g. Barkham et al., 2005; Leach et al., 2005, 2006). The smaller session-by-session database has been used to track client progress (e.g. Lutz et al., 2005), test specific hypotheses (e.g. Davies et al., 2006; Stiles et al., 2003), and provide case studies (e.g. Greenwood et al., 2007). We give examples of these uses later, focusing mainly on the CORE-OM outcome measure for the purposes of illustration.

Statistical packages

Constructing and making use of a database can be done in a number of ways, using in-house information or contributing to national or international databases. Our example database started life using the statistical package SPSS in-house, but later was able to use the local NHS database of client information to record client ongoing clinical information (such as referral and discharge dates, as well as data from questionnaires completed by the client), which could be downloaded and merged with the SPSS database. As we write, the database is on hold, anticipating the introduction of another new NHS IT system that promises greater flexibility and availability across a much larger patch. Setting such a system up and modifying it as local and national NHS IT systems are introduced takes a great deal of time and computer expertise. Staying with just the local SPSS system would have been much more straightforward technically but more inefficient in administrative time. If local statistical and computing expertise is lacking, then using simpler packages such as Excel still allows straightforward case exploration. Alternatively, using some of the available software for reporting outcome measures may be an alternative worth considering, with the cost of the package and support often being far less than the local staff salaries and expertise required to do everything in-house. For example, for users of the CORE System, there is PC-based software and the CORE Net System (see Chapter 8) that will allow local users to contribute to national databases.

Some of the analyses we offer below can be done using simpler, widely available packages, such as Excel or SPSS, while the later ones require more specialist software, with some procedures being possible in SPSS but much more straightforward in other statistical packages such as Systat, SAS, SPlus or Mplus.

When tracking both individual client and service-level progress, it is helpful to detect both *patterns* in the data and *exceptions* to the patterns, drawing on the standard exploratory data analysis strategy suggested by Tukey (1977) amongst others. The patterns may emerge from careful consideration of the data or may be suggested by external hypotheses, as illustrated in our first example. Both patterns and exceptions are important and both can carry helpful clinical insights into the process of change in therapy.

Single case presentation

Tracking individual client progress can be done very straightforwardly using simple programs. Figure 10.1A shows data collected from a 34-year-old man who had been involved in a road traffic accident in which he was knocked off his motorbike and sustained a broken leg. He was receiving treatment using EMDR (Shapiro, 2001) for post-traumatic stress (PTS) symptoms, including severe flashbacks to the accident and the hospital procedures, and nightmares related to the accident. At assessment, he scored 22.9 on the CORE-OM, well above the clinical cut-off of 10 and close to the severe cut-off of 25. From the 8th to the 11th sessions, he was scoring below the clinical cut-off, and reported few further stress symptoms. EMDR was used in sessions 2, 3 and 4 to re-expose him to the images, feelings, thoughts and bodily sensations, with a further EMDR procedure being required at session 9 to help reprocess images triggered by an experience at work that reminded him of the physical damage to his leg in a very visual way.

The client's progress fits well with the dose-response model of change (Howard et al., 1986), which suggests a positive relationship between the logarithm ($\log_{10}$) of the number of sessions (dose) and the probability of client improvement (response). In this model, greater improvement is hypothesized to occur early in therapy and then slowly decelerating over time, and Howard et al. report data supporting the theory. The predicted course, obtained by doing a simple linear regression of the log of the session number on the CORE-OM clinical scores to produce a so-called log-linear regression line, is shown as a

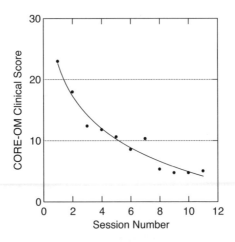

Figure 10.1A   CORE-OM scores for each session for Client 1: Graph produced using SYSTAT 10.0 with best-fitting log-linear regression line

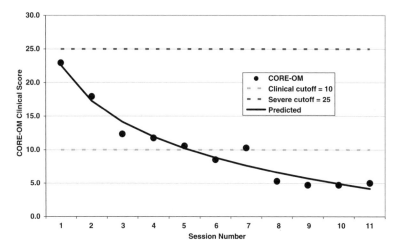

Figure 10.1B   CORE-OM scores for each session for Client 1: Graph produced using Excel with best-fitting log-linear regression line and clinical cut-offs added

continuous line in the figure. The observed data fit quite well, with session 7 being a noticeable outlier, in which the client scored higher than predicted. He reported severe physical pain, picked up by item 8 of the CORE-OM ('I have been troubled by aches, pains or other physical problems) in all sessions up to and including session 7, with the pain reducing substantially at all later sessions, and he noted that the pain was mainly responsible for a higher score overall in that session, at a time when he was feeling emotionally stronger. Figure 10.1A was produced using the statistical package SYSTAT, while Figure 10.1B shows that the same information can be produced using a spreadsheet such as Excel. In the Excel version, we also include the two clinical cut-off lines.

Once a database of clients completing the same outcome measures is available, this can provide a reference distribution against which to compare the client's progress. From our database of 357 clients completing CORE-OMs at each session, such a reference distribution is easily incorporated into these graphs. In Figure 10.1C, the client's scores at each session have been transformed into percentile ranks by comparing his scores against the session 1 scores for the whole sample. Details of how to do this are given in Leach et al. (in preparation). This simple transformation allows you to say that the client's scores at session 1 are at the 69th percentile, so he is scoring higher than 69% of clients; by session 8, he is scoring as low as the bottom 5% of clients.

The fit of data such as these to the predicted log-linear trend is one of the reasons log-linear models are typically used in more complex analyses of data from groups of clients such as those illustrated later.

Figure 10.2A (with the CORE-OM clinical scores transformed into percentile ranks) shows an example of a client whose progress followed a different path.

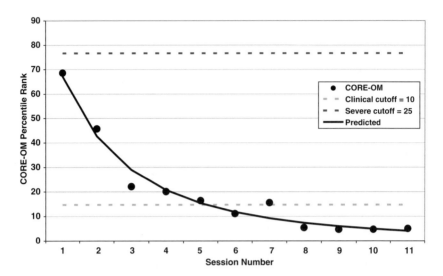

Figure 10.1C   CORE-OM scores for each session for Client 1: CORE-OM clinical scores transformed into percentile rank with best-fitting log-linear regression line and clinical cut-offs added (using SWYT sessional database as reference distribution)

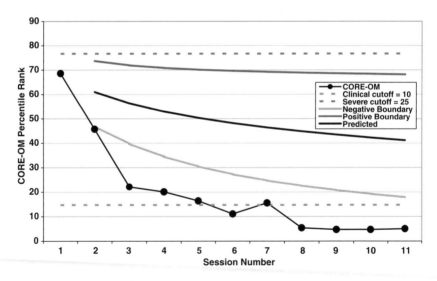

Figure 10.1D   CORE-OM scores for each session for Client 1: Expected Treatment Response model – CORE percentile ranks with predicted CORE-OM and positive and negative boundaries

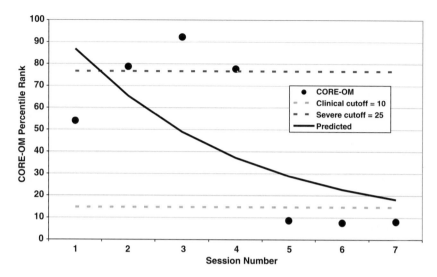

Figure 10.2A CORE-OM scores for each session for Client 2: CORE-OM percentile rank scores with best-fitting log-linear regression line and clinical cut-offs (using SWYT sessional database as reference distribution)

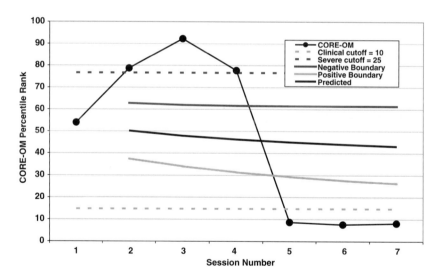

Figure 10.2B CORE-OM scores for each session for Client 2: Expected Treatment Response model – CORE percentile ranks with predicted CORE-OM and positive and negative boundaries

Client 2 was again receiving EMDR for post-traumatic stress symptoms, this time following a sexual assault a year earlier. She was a 17-year-old woman, who coped by blocking feelings more extremely than Client 1, showing some evidence of dissociation. At assessment, she scored 19.7 (56th percentile) on the CORE-OM. Once EMDR was set up (in session 2) and used (in sessions 3 and 4), her scores increased dramatically to 26 (80th percentile), 31 (93rd percentile) and 25 (79th percentile), going above the severe cut-off of 25 at the beginning of each of these sessions, before reducing well below the lower cut-off of 10 for the final three sessions, with CORE-OM scores of 7 (9th percentile) at each of these sessions. Prior to session 5, she managed to internalize that the assault was not her fault and was able to progress without further treatment. Sessions 6 and 7 were follow-up sessions a month apart to check that she was symptom-free. Such a pattern of symptoms getting worse, once therapy exposes a client to buried feelings, before they get better is very common, particularly with PTS symptoms. It is not well captured by the simple log-linear curve shown in Figure 10.2A and would be better modelled by a more complex curve (quadratic or cubic). However, the simple curve shows a pattern against which progress can be monitored. We return to this sort of monitoring with these two examples later.

Simple presentations of service data

Tracking data from a whole service can be done straightforwardly, as shown in Figure 10.3A. Figure 10.3A shows a simple bar chart of average (mean) scores on the CORE-OM for clients at the five occasions on which before-after information was collected. This shows that the mean scores were stable for the three pre-therapy measures, but dropped below the clinical cut-off at discharge and at six-month follow-up. Such a graph is very uninformative, however, at it does not show any of the variation typical of such data. A simple set of box plots, as in Figure 10.3B (which can be plotted using SPSS or any of the other statistical packages) gives much more information about typical patterns and exceptions in the data. In a box plot, the average (median) score is shown by the bar inside each box, with the boxes enclosing the middle 50% of the data, and the whiskers extending to the top and bottom 25% of the data, excluding outlying observations. The outliers are shown as diamonds. In this figure also, occasion labels have been added, making it easier to understand the graph. The box plots make clear the same overall pattern shown in Figure 10.3A, but against a background of wide variation both before and after therapy.

Figure 10.3C adds more information. The clinical and severe cut-offs (10 and 25) are plotted as reference lines, making it immediately obvious that the three pre-therapy occasions have well over 75% (the proportions in the box and

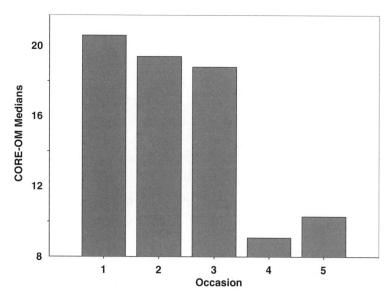

Figure 10.3A CORE-OM scores at five occasions for 5,563 clients from SWYT database: Bar chart of median scores

the top whisker) above the clinical threshold, while at discharge over 50% have scores below the threshold. Figure 10.3C is a notched box plot, with notches in each box showing 90% confidence intervals for the median. For data that are independent, this means that if any two of the boxes have notches that do not overlap, there is evidence of a statistically significant difference between them (using a 5% significance level). Thus, the two post-therapy medians are reliably lower than the three pre-therapy ones, which do not differ reliably from each other. Notched box plots can be produced in the more specialist packages such as SYSTAT or SPlus, but not in current versions of SPSS. This significance test only strictly applies to data that are independent. The data here have overlapping clients, with some clients producing data on more than one occasion, but this display still provides a helpful guide to patterns in the data.

Figure 10.3C also shows the numbers of clients completing questionnaires at each data point and makes obvious a pattern that typically occurs for any services collecting such data. The figures reduce from over 4,500 at referral to about 500 at six-month follow-up. Some of the differences in data points at the five occasions are a result of the clinical choices made in collecting the data. For example, clients were not sent questionnaires before assessment if the time between assessment and the referral questionnaires being completed was less than six weeks; similarly, clients were not sent pre-therapy questionnaires if the time between assessment and therapy was less than six weeks. Also, some clients

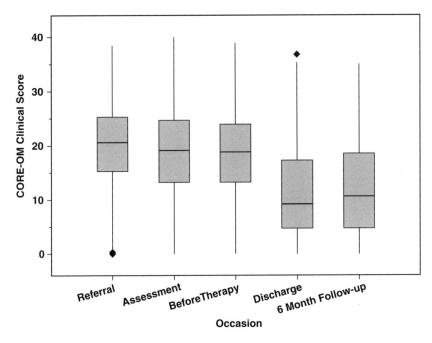

Figure 10.3B   CORE-OM scores at five occasions for 5,563 clients from SWYT database: Box plots for each occasion. Adapted from Leach, C. et al., Evaluating psychological therapies services: A review of outcome measures and their utility, *Mental Health and Learning Disabilities Research and Practice, 1,* 53–66. South West Yorkshire NHS Mental Health Trust and the University of Huddersfield, 2004

may still be waiting for therapy or may not have been discharged, so have not had the opportunity to contribute to data at later occasions. In addition, some clinicians may have decided that it would not be helpful for particular clients to complete later measures. This database allows for the clinicians to note such information. However, the most obvious reason for the attrition is that clients are much less likely to complete measures after discharge, when they may wish to have no further contact with the service, than before therapy, when they are asking for help. There is evidence that clients who do not complete discharge or follow-up questionnaires are those who score higher on the questionnaires before therapy (see, for example, Stiles et al., 2003). Such problems are typical of attempts to collect service-level information following treatment. They make it difficult to draw accurate conclusions about how well a service is doing, and may give a misleadingly positive picture. In generating statistical models of such data, extreme caution is necessary, as missing data in many standard statistical approaches are either ignored (by making use of only clients with complete data) or handled by assuming the data are missing at random. Attempts to

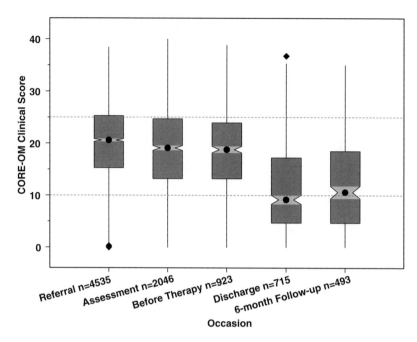

Figure 10.3C   CORE-OM scores at five occasions for 5,563 clients from SWYT database: Notched box plots for each occasion, with clinical cut-offs and sample sizes. Adapted from Leach, C. et al., Evaluating psychological therapies services: A review of outcome measures and their utility, *Mental Health and Learning Disabilities Research and Practice, 1*, 53–66. South West Yorkshire NHS Mental Health Trust and the University of Huddersfield, 2004

model non-randomness in missing data (so-called informative drop-out) are possible, by explicitly modelling the process by which they are missing, but can be complex and depend on a clear understanding of why the data are missing (see, for example, Diggle & Kenward, 1994; Diggle et al., 1994). Such problems of attrition are also apparent in research clinics, where more time is available to chase missing questionnaires than is possible in routine service settings. For example, the data analysed by Howard, Orlinsky & Lueger (1995) show similar attrition.

The box plots shown so far do not allow tracking of individual client progress. For this, different strategies are required. Figure 10.3D shows a scatter plot comparing before and after therapy data for 478 clients who completed one of the before therapy measures and a measure at discharge. Again, from the numbers involved, the small proportion of clients with both before and after data available is apparent. What is plotted is the average of any CORE-OM scores collected before therapy against the discharge data for each client. It is helpful to have the main diagonal drawn in, with the plot showing those clients below

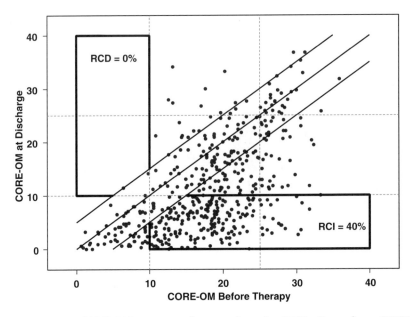

Figure 10.3D CORE-OM scores at five occasions for 5,563 clients from SWYT database: Jacobson plot of pre-therapy scores compared with discharge scores for 478 clients. *Source*: Leach, C. et al., Evaluating psychological therapies services: A review of outcome measures and their utility, *Mental Health and Learning Disabilities Research and Practice, 1*, 53–66. South West Yorkshire NHS Mental Health Trust and the University of Huddersfield, 2004

the diagonal as improving and those above as deteriorating. The tramlines on either side of the diagonal reflect the reliability of the CORE-OM and occur at 5 points above and below the diagonal. Clients whose before and after CORE-OMs differ by 5 or more points are deemed to have improved reliably. In addition, this plot (known as a Jacobson plot) shows boxes for clients who are above the clinical cut-off for the CORE-OM before therapy and below it afterwards (showing reliable and clinical improvement (RCI)) and those who score below the cut-off before therapy but above it afterwards (showing reliable and clinical deterioration (RCD)). When tracking client progress, those who deteriorate following therapy, either by showing reliable deterioration (i.e. those above the upper tramline) or by showing reliable and clinical deterioration (those in the upper box), are the ones who should be drawn to the therapists' attention.

In the service from which these data were drawn, feedback has been given to therapists on a regular basis using both box plots and Jacobson plots to show both overall trends and the individual progress of clients. Where session-by-session data are available, even more detailed progress reports are possible as shown in our more complex examples below (see also Lambert, 2007).

Estimating client change using growth modelling procedures

Over the past decade, there has been a growing interest in modelling change in psychotherapy research. Whereas in experimental research the focus is on comparing the pre-intervention baseline assessment with the post-intervention or follow-up assessment, applied practice–based research is also concerned with describing patterns of change. We view this latter approach as top-down. Psychotherapies are seen as a class of treatments defined by overlapping techniques, mechanisms and proposed outcomes. Outcomes and change are measured by summing items related to many disorders and are not assessed in relation to specific diagnoses. Instead of identifying particular treatments for particular diagnoses by clinical trials (a bottom-up approach), the top-down approach used by this so-called client-focused research is a practical first step for large scale outcome monitoring in clinical practice. In routine clinical practice reliable diagnoses and tailoring of outcomes assessment to specific diagnoses are often not feasible or are difficult to achieve (Barkham et al., 2001; Lambert, Hansen & Finch, 2001; Lutz, 2002).

There are two main reasons for the special interest in patterns of change in practice-based research. First, from a practice-based and outcomes management perspective, focusing on early indicators of later change helps to specify what kind of feedback should be given to the practitioner during the course of therapy. Second, in applied research, oriented towards managing progress in routine care, the relevant time period is less clear. It often varies between persons since the intervention might not be time-limited and/or is adjusted depending on the unique characteristics of the particular client. Several studies have shown that patterns of improvement for individuals can vary significantly from the general trend (see also our Client 2 above). Clearly, every client does not have the same outcome or course of treatment, which also means that the same mean outcome or mean course of recovery cannot be expected for every client (Krause, Howard & Lutz, 1998; Martinovich & Helgerson, 2008).

In the last decade several new statistical methods under the broad category of growth curve analysis have been developed, which bring new possibilities for analysis of individual change (e.g. Little et al., 1996; Raudenbush & Bryk, 2002; Singer & Willett, 2003). These methods, which have a number of different names in the literature (e.g. mixed models, hierarchical linear models, random regression models, multilevel models), assume an underlying path or trajectory of change over time, and are able to deal with the hierarchical structure of psychotherapy data (i.e. repeated assessments are nested within each client, clients are nested within therapists). Growth curve models have a number of advantages over traditional techniques for estimating treatment response over the course of treatment (e.g. repeated measures ANOVA or

ANCOVA). Traditional regression analyses are limited by assumptions of (1) linearity, (2) normality, (3) homoscedasticity, and (4) independence of errors. The first two of these assumptions are maintained in growth curve analyses, but the second two are modified, applying only within each person's data across time.

These methods allow the number and timing of outcome assessment to vary from person to person, which makes them very useful for practice-based research (as well as experimental studies). Traditional analytic techniques (e.g. repeated measures ANOVA) require a fixed assessment schedule for each client as well as the deletion of missing scores or a strategy for estimating missing values (often called imputation). As a result, either information is lost (when clients with missing scores are deleted) or, when imputation is used, the error variance is artificially reduced. In growth curve models, it is possible to estimate random effects (e.g. individual differences in rates of change) and to produce inferential tests of the reliability of these individual differences. Clients with missing scores are included in the analysis, but, because they have less reliable change patterns over the course of treatment, they are automatically given less weight when estimating parameters for the group.

Growth models typically describe change in psychotherapy as a log-linear function of session number, which is well illustrated by Client 1's data (Figure 10.1A and 10.1B). More complex non-linear applications (as would be required to model adequately Client 2's data) are also possible within the framework of growth curve modelling, but would go beyond the scope of this chapter (see, for example, Singer & Willett, 2003). As a first step (also called a *Level 1* model), two parameters are used, the intercept and the slope, to describe the course of recovery for each client. This means the simple linear trajectory describes each person's change over time with an intercept coefficient, indicating the starting score on the change measure, and a slope coefficient multiplied by time (e.g. the session number), indicating rate of change.

The second step uses the differences between individuals (variance in the client-specific intercepts and slopes) as dependent variables for a level 2 model. This *Level 2* model assesses the relationship between potential predictors and intercepts (i.e. initial) and slopes (i.e. rates of change). Other measures obtained at intake can also be used as predictors to provide information about the impact of relevant initial characteristics on differences between individuals in patient courses (slopes). We give an example of this below with Client 3.

Simple case tracking

Figures 10.1D and 10.2B show how a simple version of this approach can be used for case tracking, providing a method for alerting clinicians when client progress does not follow the straightforward log-linear approach of the dose-response model. These graphs have been produced using a simplified version of the methods described by Lutz et al. (1999). First, from session 2 onwards, a predicted value of CORE-OM is plotted. This makes use of data from 181 clients from the SWYT sessional database who completed therapy in 30 or fewer sessions to predict average progress. Then (following Lutz et al.), two threshold boundaries (labelled negative and positive) are constructed at the 25th percentile above and below the predicted value. Any data values falling outside these threshold boundaries are deemed evidence of reliable deterioration or improvement and might be reported to the clinician to alert them to the fact that the client is not progressing as might be expected. Client 1's data in Figure 10.1D fall below the positive boundary by session 3 and stay well below it, so the clinician might be made aware that the client is doing better than expected. Client 2's (Figure 10.2D) dramatic increase in CORE-OMs in sessions 2, 3 and 4 is above the negative boundary, so the clinicians might be alerted here. By session 5, her rapid improvement is clearly captured by her scores falling below the positive boundary. Details of how to calculate the boundaries are given in Leach et al. (in preparation), together with methods to further refine the predictions by using subsets of the data based on severity bands determined by the first session scores.

These two examples use only the session-by-session CORE-OM data to predict the likely trajectory for a client and the positive and negative boundaries. The original Lutz et al. (1999) paper shows how to extend this approach to incorporate other intake information, in their case using seven pre-treatment measures, including subjective well-being, current life functioning, clinician's global assessment of functioning, past use of therapy, duration of problem and client's expectations of therapy.

Further work using this model found that predictions for change in later sessions were enhanced by incorporating information about the change clients experienced during early sessions (Lutz et al., 2002). An evaluation of the clinical usefulness of this method, and the reliability of the initial predictions based on patient characteristics, was presented by Howard et al. (1996) and Lueger et al. (2001). Additional research has supported the application of this model to different diagnostic groups and various symptom patterns (Lutz et al., 2001) as well as further outcome instruments (Lutz & Barkham, 2007). In a recent study this concept was extended to a three-level model in order to determine the influence of therapist differences on patient change (Lutz et al., 2007). Lambert et al. (2002) compared a 'rational method' of predicting patient treatment failure (as the basis of a feedback concept) with a statistical growth curve technique as described above and showed essential equivalence between both feedback approaches, though the statistical approach was marginally more accurate. Finch, Lambert and Schaalje (2001) modelled recovery curves separately for initial level of disturbance in small score bands.

Extending growth modelling concepts by using nearest neighbour approaches

In the versions of this methodology described above, the validity of the use of growth curve prediction weights for any particular client depends on the extent to which the study sample (reference group) is representative of the population of which that client was a member. For this reason, most predictors work only for specific subsets of clients (Krause et al., 1998). To address this problem, an extended growth curve methodology was recently introduced, which employs nearest neighbour (NN) techniques (Lutz et al., 2005, 2006a, 2006b). Hypothesizing that particular predictors may work best for restricted subsets of clients, the NN approach identifies those previously treated clients in the reference group who most closely match the target client (hence 'nearest neighbours') on intake variables. It then uses this homogeneous subgroup to generate predictions of treatment progress for the target client. This strategy has been used to estimate the probabilities of alpine avalanches occurring (e.g. Brabec & Meister, 2001).

In developing NN prediction models for avalanches (Brabec & Meister, 2001), researchers used a large database of days with many kinds of potentially relevant parameters (e.g. temperature, barometric pressure, depth of snow, recent rainfall). To make a prediction for a given day, they chose the most similar days and used the relative frequency of avalanches among those nearest neighbours as the prediction. In adapting the NN approach to predicting clients' progress in psychotherapy, our aim was to make predictions based on the course of similar already-treated clients, that is, we aimed to select samples of clients similar to an incoming client and predict that the incoming client's course will resemble theirs. This approach mirrors the way clinicians often talk about how they use their clinical experience.

Although the traditional growth curve model and the NN growth curve approach may use the same variables, they differ in the way they model change. The traditional approach is essentially an advanced regression (level 1) model which uses the intake variables for the full sample to predict individual change (see, for example, Raudenbush, 2001). Individual slopes form the input for the regression model and weights show the influence of the intake variables on the prediction of individual change. In the NN approach, the intake variables are used only to find the nearest neighbours. Individual change is then predicted using an unconditional growth model using the average growth (slope) for the nearest neighbours as the prediction.

The NN approach can be illustrated with data from client 3 from the UK NHS database described above (see Lutz et al., 2005, for further details of this example). Client 3 was a 37-year-old woman referred for anxiety and post-traumatic stress following a car accident. At intake, she scored 17.4 on the CORE-OM, 16

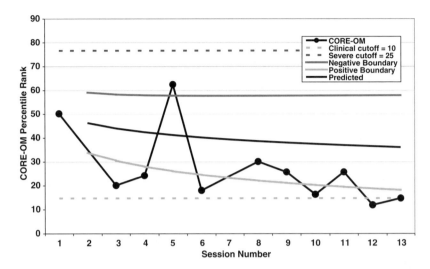

Figure 10.4A   CORE-OM scores for each session for Client 3: CORE percentile ranks with predicted CORE-OM and positive and negative boundaries

on the BDI-I (indicating moderate depression), 20 on the BAI (indicating moderate anxiety) and 1.16 on the IIP-32. She was seen by a counsellor, was offered 14 sessions of counselling therapy and attended 12, completing the CORE-SF before 11 sessions. Figure 10.4A shows her CORE-SF scores dropping from 18.9 (51st percentile) at the first session to 10.0 (15th percentile) by session 13. The CORE-SF improvement shown in the final sessions was confirmed by discharge scores of 3.8 on the CORE-OM, 2 on the BDI-I, 4 on the BAI and 0.31 on the IIP, all well below clinical cut-offs. For comparison, Figure 10.4A also shows her predicted trajectory and positive and negative boundaries from the ETR approach described above. She clearly does better than the predicted values based on all clients with a similar initial score on the CORE-SF, although the high score at session 5 (above the negative boundary) would have led to the clinician being alerted.

The NN approach with this client finds her nearest neighbours, based on the 10 clients in the database who are closest to her in the key intake variables (age, gender, CORE-OM, BDI, BAI and IIP-32). The dotted line in Figure 10.4B shows the predicted trajectory using this approach, which in this case does not improve on the prediction using more heterogeneous clients shown in Figure 10.4A. Figure 10.4C shows that the prediction in the NN approach can be improved for this client by adding CORE-SF scores for the first three sessions to the search for nearest neighbours.

Lutz et al. (2005) give a further example of a client whose prediction based on the intake information only is as good as that incorporating information

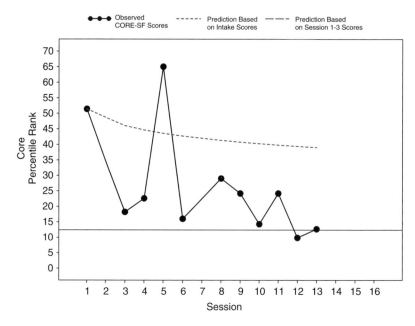

Figure 10.4B CORE-OM scores for each session for Client 3: Nearest neighbour model – prediction based on intake scores. *Source*: Lutz, W. et al., Predicting rate and shape of change for individual clients receiving psychological therapy: Using growth curve modeling and nearest neighbor technologies, *Journal of Consulting and Clinical Psychology, 73*, 904–913. American Psychological Association, 2005

from the first three sessions. They also show that, for the clients in this database, the NN approach tends to outperform the ETR approach in predicting rate of change. They also investigated the effect of varying the number of neighbours between 10 and 50, finding 10 adequate for this dataset. They further looked at the ability of the models to predict variability during the course of treatment, finding a less clear advantage of the NN over the ETR approach in this respect.

In another study (Lutz et al., 2006b), the predictive validity and clinical utility of the NN approach was tested in generating optimal expected treatment response profiles for two treatment modalities (a CBT protocol and an integrative cognitive behavioural and interpersonal therapy (IPT) protocol). The 30 clients most similar to those from each of the groups (CBT and IPT) were selected as homogeneous sub-samples, which were used to generate expected trajectories for each case under each treatment modality. The NN method created meaningful and different predictions between the treatment modalities for about 27% of the patients. Validation analyses compared the prediction to actual outcomes within the conducted treatment modality. Results supported the validity of the method.

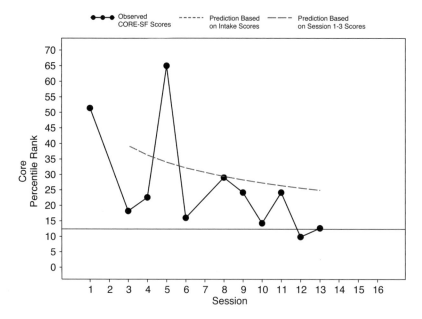

Figure 10.4C CORE-OM scores for each session for Client 3: Nearest neighbour model – prediction based on session 1–3 scores. *Source*: Lutz, W. et al., Predicting rate and shape of change for individual clients receiving psychological therapy: Using growth curve modeling and nearest neighbor technologies, *Journal of Consulting and Clinical Psychology, 73,* 904–913. American Psychological Association, 2005

Finally the NN method was used to predict the probability of treatment success, failure and duration in order to identify optimal decision rules to evaluate progress during the course of treatment (Lutz et al., 2006a). The empirically derived decision system was found to be superior to a rational clinically based one in almost all measures of prediction accuracy and indicated its potential to identify patients at risk of treatment failure.

This method has to be further tested and evaluated, but, if it proves valuable, it might be used further in clinical settings either to evaluate the progress of an individual client by comparing actual progress with expected progress in that treatment modality or to determine what treatment modality (e.g. psychotherapy, a combination of medication and psychotherapy) is most likely to result in positive change. Whereas, in most clinical cases, progress is evaluated by comparing current scores to pre-treatment scores, this method allows comparison of predicted and actual progress of clients. For example, if expected progress is minimal, subsequent actual minimal progress might be considered successful. In contrast, expected progress might be substantial, such that actual moderate progress might be considered insufficient. Furthermore, if used in a team of service providers, the approach could be used to identify therapists with experience of similar clients (defined by the NN) who might provide supervision for a specific client.

Using Growth Mixture Models to detect patterns of early change and variability

The models discussed in the previous sections take account of individual differences in change, but are built on the assumption of one specific shape of change for all clients in the data set. Now this assumption makes sense in order to estimate a general trend over time, but it has been noted that client change may follow highly variable temporal courses and that this variation may be clinically important (e.g. our Client 2 and Barkham, Stiles & Shapiro, 1993; Barkham et al., 2006; Krause et al., 1998).

While the growth modelling procedures described above assume that all individuals are drawn from the same population with common population parameters, i.e. with a common average growth curve, and capture individual heterogeneity in development over time by individual variation in continuous latent growth factors (e.g. Lutz et al., 1999), recently introduced Growth Mixture Models (GMMs) relax this single population assumption and allow for parameter differences across unobserved populations by implementing a categorical latent variable (e.g. Muthén, 2004; Stulz et al., 2007). This categorical variable captures individual variation around qualitatively different average growth curves that are shared within homogenous latent classes (Colder et al., 2002). Moreover, and in contrast to cluster analytic approaches (e.g. Stiles et al., 2004), GMMs also take into account the often not perfectly reliable assignment of individuals to latent classes by estimating each individual's probability of membership in each of the latent classes.

To estimate the parameters used in GMMs, the statistical package Mplus, which provides maximum likelihood estimations based on the accelerated expectation maximization procedure, is often used (Muthén et al., 2002). This software also allows estimation of models with missing values in continuous outcome variables under the assumption that data are missing at random, i.e. that unmeasured covariates related to missingness are not related to variables critical to this study (Colder et al., 2002; Diggle & Kenward, 1994).

In using such an advanced growth curve model, researchers are able to identify clusters of clients with a similar change pattern and those clusters can have different patterns of change and do not have to be the same for the whole population.

Figure 10.5 shows an example application of such a model in a sample of 192 clients who received between 7 and 203 sessions, drawn from our UK database

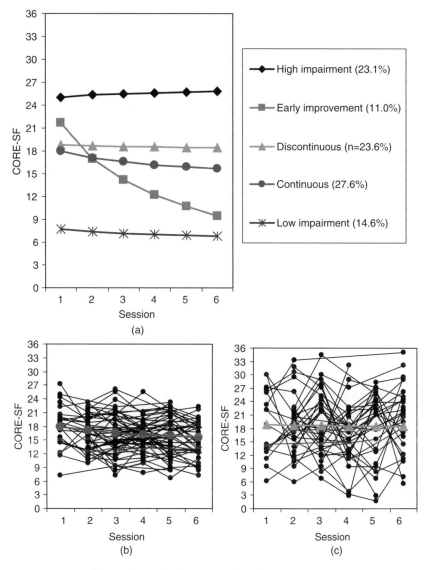

Figure 10.5 Different shapes of early change identified using Growth Mixture Models (GMMs). *Source*: Stulz, N. et al., Shapes of early change in psychotherapy under routine outpatient conditions, *Journal of Consulting and Clinical Psychology, 75*, 864–874. American Psychological Association, 2007

described above (Stulz et al., 2005, 2007). In this example shapes or client clusters of early change (up to session 6) have been identified to predict later outcome and treatment duration. Figure 10.5A shows five different shapes of early change identified with the GMM, including:

1 An *early improvement* cluster of clients (11%), who start with high CORE-SF scores and show a quick reduction in symptoms;
2 A *high impairment* cluster (23.1%) with little or no change; and
3 A *low impairment* cluster of clients (14.6%), with little or no change.

The two remaining clusters show two moderately impaired groups with similar average growth curves, but very different individual treatment courses as can be seen in Figures 10.5B and 10.5C, where the observed client courses around the mean latent growth curve for two example groups are plotted. While the clients in the 'continuous' (27.6%) and in the 'discontinuous' (23.6%) groups have quite similar mean latent growth curves, the plots of the actual individual treatment courses reveal that clients in the 'discontinuous' group (Figure 10.5C) show much more session-by-session variation than clients in the 'continuous' group (Figure 10.5B) in the early phase of treatment.

Discussion and recommendations

The methods discussed in this chapter are at different stages of development. At the simplest level, collecting outcome data before and after therapy within a service (as in Figure 10.3) and feeding back to therapists and referrers is now being recommended as good practice (Department of Health, 2004). Hurdles to implementing such monitoring are administrative cost and the need to bring clinicians and administrative staff on board, as well as having sufficient expertise to produce graphs like those we illustrate. Going further than this and collecting data on a session-by-session basis makes it possible to feed back results to therapists and clients during the course of therapy, which in our experience is beneficial to clients. As illustrated in Figure 10.1A, such monitoring is possible even without access to a reference group of similar clients.

Once a reference distribution is available, simply plotting the data on a percentile rank scale, as in Figures 10.1B, 10.2A and Figure 10.4A, allows comparison of the current client's level of distress with that of other clients. Failing a local reference group, using the distribution used in this chapter will allow a comparison if the client groups are not too dissimilar. All that is required for the percentile rank transformation is the mean and standard deviation of the CORE-OM scores for the reference distribution. The reference group used here (of all clients referred to a UK secondary care adult psychological therapies service who completed a CORE-OM at the beginning of therapy) has a mean of 18.44 and an SD of 8.52. Leach et al. (in preparation) give details of the calculations required to do the transformation.

Moving on to simple case tracking, again a reference group is required. The examples here (Figures 10.1D and 10.2B) use the same database of session-by-session CORE-OM scores, restricting the data used to those from clients with short- or medium-term therapy (fewer than 30 sessions). Leach et al. (in preparation) show how to produce these graphs, which allow clinicians to be alerted when clients go outside the boundary values for the reference group. Leach et al. also show how to do the calculations when a tighter prediction is required, for example, by comparing the current client to others in the same severity band of CORE-OM scores at session 1. All the methods so far can straightforwardly be implemented now. They can also be used when data is missing, either by design (for example when a clinician chooses to monitor client progress only irregularly during therapy) or by accident (for example when a client does not complete a questionnaire for some of the sessions).

The later, more complex methods, including the NN and GMM models, are still in development and need optimizing before routine use. They show how to narrow the focus even further, by comparing the current client with an even more tightly specified reference group. They differ in how they do this. For the future, such methods will be helpful in capturing the complexity of individual client change and variability of change amongst clients. These further developments can easily be added to the simple case-tracking methods and tested further under routine conditions.

The beauty of these methods is that they interweave research and practice in a real-time manner, with the main aim of improving practice as it happens. In our view, this goes beyond the frequently used horse-race research design of comparing manualized treatments in an artificial research clinic setting, where it takes much longer for research findings to influence practice.

Acknowledgement

We would like to thank Niklaus Stulz for helping to prepare Figure 10.5.

References

Barkham, M., Stiles, W.B. & Shapiro, D.A. (1993). The shape of change in psychotherapy: Longitudinal assessment of personal problems. *Journal of Consulting and Clinical Psychology, 61*, 667–677.

Barkham, M., Connell, J., Stiles, W.B., Miles, J.N.V., Margison, F. *et al.* (2006). Dose-effect relations and responsive regulation of treatment duration: The good enough level. *Journal of Consulting and Clinical Psychology, 74,* 160–167.

Barkham, M., Margison, F., Leach, C., Lucock, M., Mellor-Clark, J. *et al.* (2001). Service profiling and outcomes benchmarking using CORE-OM: Toward practice-based evidence in psychological therapies. *Journal of Consulting and Clinical Psychology, 69,* 184–196.

Barkham, M., Rees, A., Leach, C., Shapiro, D.A., Hardy, G. *et al.* (2005). Rewiring efficacy studies of depression: An empirical test in transforming BDI to CORE-OM scores. *Mental Health and Learning Disabilities Research and Practice, 2,* 11–18.

Brabec, B. & Meister, R. (2001). A nearest-neighbor model for regional avalanche forecasting. *Annals of Glaciology, 32,* 130–134.

Colder, C.R., Campbell, R.T., Ruel, E., Richardson, J.L. & Flay, B.R. (2002). A finite mixture model of growth trajectories of adolescent alcohol use: Predictors and consequences. *Journal of Consulting and Clinical Psychology, 70,* 976–985.

Davies, L., Leach, C., Lucock, M., Stiles, W.B., Iveson, S. *et al.* (2006). Therapists' recall of early sudden gains in routine clinical practice. *Psychology and Psychotherapy: Theory, Research and Practice, 79,* 107–114.

Department of Health (2004). *Organising and delivering psychological therapies.* London: HMSO.

Diggle, P.J. & Kenward, M.G. (1994). Informative dropout in longitudinal data analysis (with discussion). *Applied Statistics, 43,* 49–93.

Diggle, P.J., Liang, K.Y. & Zeger, S.L. (1994). *Analysis of longitudinal data,* Oxford: Oxford University Press.

Finch, A.E., Lambert, M.J. & Schaalje, B.G. (2001). Psychotherapy quality control: The statistical generation of expected recovery curves for integration into an early warning system. *Clinical Psychology and Psychotherapy, 8,* 231–242.

Gibbons, R.D., Hedeker, D., Elkin, I., Waterneaux, C., Kraemer, H. *et al.* (1993). Some conceptual and statistical issues in analysis of longitudinal psychiatric data. *Archives of General Psychiatry, 50,* 739–750.

Greenwood, H., Leach, C., Lucock, M. & Noble, R. (2007). The process of long-term art therapy: A case study combining art work and clinical outcome. *Psychotherapy Research, 17,* 588–599.

Howard, K.I., Orlinsky, D. & Lueger, R.J. (1995). The design of clinically relevant outcome research: Some considerations and an example. In M. Aveline & D.A. Shapiro (eds.), *Research foundations for psychotherapy practice.* Chichester: John Wiley & Sons, Ltd.

Howard, K.I., Kopta, S.M., Krause, M.S. & Orlinsky, D.E. (1986). The dose-response relationship in psychotherapy. *American Psychologist, 41,* 159–164.

Howard, K.I., Moras, K., Brill, P., Martinovich, Z. & Lutz, W. (1996). The evaluation of psychotherapy. *American Psychologist*, *51*, 1059–1064.

Krause, M.S., Howard, K.I. & Lutz, W. (1998). Exploring individual change. *Journal of Consulting and Clinical Psychology*, *66*, 838–845.

Lambert, M. (2007). Presidential address: What we have learned from a decade of research aimed at improving psychotherapy outcome in routine care. *Psychotherapy Research*, *17*, 1–14.

Lambert, M.J., Hansen, N.B. & Finch, A.E. (2001). Patient-focused research: Using patient outcome data to enhance treatment effects. *Journal of Consulting and Clinical Psychology*, *69*, 159–172.

Lambert, M.J., Whipple, J.L., Bishop, M.J., Vermeersch, D.A., Gray, G.V. *et al.* (2002). Comparison of empirically derived and rationally derived methods for identifying patients at risk for treatment failure. *Clinical Psychology and Psychotherapy*, *9*, 149–164.

Leach, C., Lucock, M., Iveson, S. & Noble, R. (2004). Evaluating psychological therapies services: a review of outcome measures and their utility. *Mental Health and Learning Disabilities Research and Practice*, *1*, 53–66.

Leach, C., Lutz, W., Barkham, M. & Lucock, M. (in preparation). Case tracking with CORE-OM: A manual for clinicians and researchers.

Leach, C., Lucock, M., Barkham, M., Noble, R. & Iveson, S. (2006). Transforming between Beck Depression Inventory and CORE-OM scores in routine clinical practice. *British Journal of Clinical Psychology*, *45*, 153–166.

Leach, C., Lucock, M., Barkham, M., Noble, R., Clarke, L. *et al.* (2005). Assessing risk and emotional disturbance using the CORE-OM and HoNOS outcome measures. *Psychiatric Bulletin*, *29*, 419–422.

Little, R.C., Milliken, G.A., Stroup, W.W. & Wolfinger, R.D. (1996). *SAS System for mixed models*. Cary, NC: SAS Institute Inc.

Lucock, M.P., Leach, C. & Iveson, S. (2005). Using evidence to improve psychological therapy services. *Mental Health and Learning Disabilities Research and Practice*, *2*, 51–60.

Lucock, M., Leach, C., Iveson, S., Lynch, K., Horsefield, C. *et al.* (2003). A systematic approach to practice-based evidence in a psychological therapies service. *Clinical Psychology and Psychotherapy*, *10*, 389–399.

Lueger, R.J., Howard, K.I., Martinovich, Z., Lutz, W., Anderson, E. *et al.* (2001). Assessing treatment progress with individualized models of predicted response. *Journal of Consulting and Clinical Psychology*, *69*, 150–158.

Lutz, W. (2002). Patient-focused psychotherapy research and individual treatment progress as scientific groundwork for an empirically based clinical practice. *Psychotherapy Research*, *12*, 251–272.

Lutz, W. & Barkham, M. (2007). The expected treatment response model using the CORE: Procedures manual. (Research Report.) Berne/Leeds: University of Leeds, University of Berne, Department of Psychology.

Lutz, W., Martinovich, Z. & Howard, K.I. (1999). Patient Profiling: An application of random coefficient regression models to depicting the response of a patient to outpatient psychotherapy. *Journal of Consulting and Clinical Psychology, 67*, 571–577.

Lutz, W., Rafaeli-Mor, E., Howard, K.I. & Martinovich, Z. (2002). Adaptive modeling of progress in outpatient psychotherapy. *Psychotherapy Research, 12*, 427–443.

Lutz, W., Leon, S.C., Martinovich, Z., Lyons, J.S. & Stiles, W.B. (2007). Therapist effects in outpatient psychotherapy: A three-level growth curve approach. *Journal of Counseling Psychology, 54*, 32–39.

Lutz, W., Leach, C., Barkham, M., Lucock., Stiles, W.B. *et al.* (2005). Predicting change for individual psychotherapy clients based on their nearest neighbors. *Journal of Consulting and Clinical Psychology, 73*, 904–913.

Lutz, W., Lambert, M.J., Harmon, C.J., Tschitsaz, A., Schürch, E. *et al.* (2006a). The probability of treatment success, failure and duration – what can be learned from empirical data to support decision making in clinical practice? *Clinical Psychology and Psychotherapy, 13*, 223–232.

Lutz, W., Saunders, S.M., Leon, S.C., Martinovich, Z., Kosfelder, J. *et al.* (2006b). Empirical and clinical useful decision making in psychotherapy: Differential predictions with treatment response models. *Psychological Assessment, 18*, 133–141.

Martinovich, Z. & Helgerson, J. (2008). Applications of trajectory analysis in research and outcomes management. In J. Lyons & D. Aron-Weiner (eds.), *Strategies in behavioral healthcare: Total clinical outcomes management.* New York City, NY: Civic Research Institute, Inc.

Muthén, B.O. (2004). Latent variable analysis: growth mixture modeling and related techniques for longitudinal data. In D. Kaplan (ed.), *Handbook of quantitative methodology for social sciences* (pp. 345–368). Newbury Park, CA: Sage Publications.

Muthén, B.O., Brown, C.H., Maysn, K., Jo, B., Khoo, S-T. *et al.* (2002). General growth mixture modeling for randomized preventive interventions. *Biostatistics, 3*, 459–475.

Raudenbush, S.W. (2001). Comparing personal trajectories and drawing causal inferences from longitudinal data. *Annual Review of Psychology, 52*, 501–525.

Raudenbush, S.W. & Bryk, A.S. (2002). *Hierarchical linear models: Applications and data analysis methods* (2nd edn.). Newbury Park, CA: Sage Publications.

Shapiro, F. (2001). *Eye movement desensitization and reprocessing: Basic principles, processes, and procedures.* New York: Guilford Press.

Singer, J.D. & Willett, J.B. (2003). *Applied longitudinal data analysis: Modeling change and event occurrence.* New York: Oxford University Press.

Stiles, W.B., Glick, M.J., Osatuke, K., Hardy, G.E., Shapiro, D.A. *et al.* (2004). Patterns of alliance development and the rupture-repair hypothesis: Are productive relationships U-shaped or V-shaped? *Journal of Counseling Psychology, 51,* 81–92.

Stiles, W.B., Leach, C., Barkham, M., Lucock, M., Iveson, S. *et al.* (2003). Early sudden gains in psychotherapy under routine clinic conditions: Practice-based evidence. *Journal of Consulting and Clinical Psychology, 71,* 14–21.

Stulz, N., Lutz, W., Leach, C., Lucock, M. & Barkham, M. (2005). *Patterns of early change in outpatient psychotherapy and their relation to treatment outcome and duration.* Poster presented to the Swiss Psychological Society, Geneva.

Stulz, N., Lutz, W., Leach, C., Lucock, M. & Barkham, M. (2007). Shapes of early change in psychotherapy under routine outpatient conditions. *Journal of Consulting and Clinical Psychology, 75,* 864–874.

Tukey, J.W. (1977). *Exploratory data analysis.* New York: Addison Wesley.

Section V

Managing Improvement via Organizations and Practice Networks

11

Organizational and Conceptual Framework for Practice-Based Research on the Effectiveness of Psychotherapy and Psychotherapy Training

Robert Elliott[1] and Alberto Zucconi[2]

[1] University of Strathclyde, UK, [2] University of Siena, Italy

Introduction

The oft-lamented gap between psychotherapy research and practice has led to the near disenfranchisement of many forms of therapy, including person-centred/experiential, psychodynamic and systems approaches, all of which are currently under-represented on lists of empirically-supported or evidence-based treatments (e.g. Chambless et al., 1996; Roth & Fonagy, 2004). The key to maintaining and increasing the recognition of these and other therapies in the current political-historical moment is for us to study them using a variety of methods, quantitative and qualitative, single case and randomized clinical trials, treatment development and practice-based. The moment is ripe for this for several reasons: accrediting bodies, insurance companies and governments are increasingly calling for accountability in therapy practice and training. Exciting developments in research methods are also opening up new possibilities. This situation has inspired researchers and educators in several countries to develop demonstration programmes featuring practice-based research and Practice Research Networks (PRNs; e.g. Barkham & Mellor-Clark, 2000; Borkovec et al., 2001; Stinckens et al., 2009).

In this chapter, we describe some organizational structures and conceptual frameworks for encouraging collaborative practice-based research. In

Developing and Delivering Practice-Based Evidence   By Michael Barkham, Gillian E Hardy, and John Mellor-Clark   © 2010 John Wiley & Sons, Ltd

particular, we present a practice-based research framework and protocols for studying treatments and training experiences in psychotherapy training centres and institutes. We conclude with a discussion of recent methodological developments that promise to enhance this research and a list of suggestions for getting involved in therapy research collaborations.

Research-practice gap in an era of evidence-based mental health

The gap between research and the practice of psychotherapy has been discussed for more than 30 years, with empirical documentation going back at least to Morrow-Bradley and Elliott's (1986) survey demonstrating that practising therapists make very little use of research in their work with clients. Over the past 20 years numerous attempts to link or unify research and practice in psychotherapy have been made. In most of these solutions researchers and policy-makers have tried to dictate to therapists. In the United States the best known of these efforts has been the empirically supported treatments (EST) movement (Chambless et al., 1996). Controversy continues to rage over this approach, even 15 years after its inception; for a summary of the main points on each side see Elliott (1998). Evidence-based mental health is the term for the larger, international movement towards basing therapy practice on scientific evidence (Roth & Fonagy, 2004; Rowland & Goss, 2000). Other examples of this approach can be found in recent books attempting to integrate scientific evidence on therapy outcome (Kazdin & Weisz, 2003; Nathan & Gorman, 2002); the *empirically supported relationships* task force (Norcross, 2002); and more recently, the *empirically supported principles* task force (Beutler & Castonguay, 2005).

What all these efforts have in common, however, is that they are based on a top-down, therapist-as-research-consumer model, in which committees of scientists sift through 25 to 50 years of accumulated research evidence in order to come up with recommendations for how to do therapy. The task forces and editorial teams involved in these various efforts most typically do not include either practising therapists or clients/mental health service users. From the point of view of front-line practising therapists, therefore, such projects are typically seen as simply not relevant to the complexities of clinical practice, in which implicit, tacit knowledge operates to a great extent (Thornton, 2006).

Although it is too early to fully judge the impact of these approaches on therapy practice, it seems that one of their major effects so far has been a negative one: discouraging practice and training in therapies not favoured by CBT-oriented academician-researchers, whilst not particularly improving the uptake of research-based therapy approaches on the part of practising therapists.

Practice-based therapy research

In this chapter, we argue that successful integration of therapy research and practice will be more likely if a more integrative, bottom-up strategy is used. A promising development along this line is the Practice Research Network (PRN) approach, promoted in the USA by Borkovec, Castonguay and colleagues (e.g. Borkovec et al., 2001), and in the UK by Barkham and Mellor-Clark (2000). Interestingly, the third generation of the Pennsylvania PRN project (Castonguay et al., 2004) is now being carried out at a training site (the psychology training clinic at Pennsylvania State University). This ongoing demonstration project offers a prototype for the subject of this chapter – practice-based therapy research in training sites. The rationale for this approach to practice-based therapy research is as follows: first, in spite of 60-plus years of systematic psychotherapy research, we know relatively little about contemporary applications of most types of psychotherapy, including many of those for which systematic postgraduate training is offered. Second, being able to use and carry out therapy process and outcome research is an essential aspect of therapist competence. Third, the best way to learn therapy research methods is for students to begin doing research during their basic or specialist therapy training. Fourth, being part of interesting, clinically relevant therapy research from the beginning of one's training as a therapist is the best way to develop positive attitudes about research and the integration of research and practice.

The principles of this approach to therapy research and research-practice integration are spelled out in Table 11.1, and include relying on inexpensive, user-friendly measurement instruments; involving therapists in the selection of research questions; starting by assessing with a small number of key elements of therapy and expanding on these as needed; using both quantitative and qualitative research methods; and collaborating with other training centres to foster larger-scale research. Together, these principles provide a set of practical guidelines for the sort of research we are talking about.

International Project on the Effectiveness of Psychotherapy and Psychotherapy Training (IPEPPT)

In order to reduce the research-practice gap and to foster practice-based research in psychotherapy training centres, the International Project on the Effectiveness of Psychotherapy and Psychotherapy Training was formally initiated in June 2004 by the Italian Coordinamento Nazionale Scuole di Psicoterapia (CNSP), and by the 21 psychotherapy associations belonging to the Italian Federation of Psychotherapy Associations (FIAP). To date, a scientific steering committee has been formed along with working groups for person-centred/

Table 11.1   Principles of practice-based therapy research

---

1. Practical: Employ inexpensive and easy-to-use instruments that can enhance therapy rather than interfere with it.
2. Stakeholder-based: Actively involve therapists (and clients where possible) in the selection of research questions and methods.
3. Focused: Instead of trying to be comprehensive, start by measuring key elements of therapy process and outcome (e.g. therapeutic alliance, client problem severity).
4. Incremental: Once the key elements are in place, consider adding measures of other important concepts (e.g. interpersonal problems).
5. Methodologically pluralist: Encourage the use of a variety of research methods (qualitative and quantitative; group and single case).
6. Collaborative: Create research networks of training sites using similar, pan-theoretical instruments, in order to make planning more efficient and to create opportunities for data sharing.

---

experiential psychotherapies and Dutch-language research protocols. The general goal of this project is to improve psychotherapy and psychotherapy training in a broad range of theoretical approaches, by encouraging systematic research in therapy training institutes and university-based training clinics. The person-centred/experiential and Dutch-language working groups maintain a demonstration website and currently include members from Australia, Austria, Belgium, Canada, Greece, Portugal, Slovakia, the UK and the USA (www.communityzero.com/pcepirp).

The first component of this project involves facilitating practice-based research on the effectiveness of psychotherapy in universities and training institutes in Europe, North America and elsewhere. In these settings, randomized clinical trials are generally impractical and tend not to be useful for understanding or improving therapy. Such research requires the development of a conceptual framework for assessing therapy process and outcome that can be used across a range of theoretical orientations, modalities and client populations. We have proposed the use of a 'star' design for this component: a common protocol shared by all orientations (the main body of the star), to serve as a common metric or base, plus specialized protocols for different therapy approaches (the star rays; Elliott & Zucconi, 2006). The purpose of such a research framework is to inspire, focus and facilitate practice-based therapy research in training sites. At the same time, it is important to develop clearing houses of measures of therapy process, outcome and change processes, suitable for assessing a wide range of therapeutic approaches, and to provide education and dissemination of knowledge about useful easy-to-use practice-based therapy research measures and designs to training institutions. Later stages may include the creation of comprehensive shared databases, creating opportunities for collaborative research via data pooling.

The second component of the project involves promotion of research evaluating the effectiveness of therapy training in university- and institute-based training programmes. Relatively little is known about the effectiveness of therapy training, in part because of technical and logistical difficulties. These difficulties include, among other things, the absence of agreed-upon measures of therapist functioning and the need to measure therapist change longitudinally over several years of training. Nevertheless, it is important to begin systematic evaluation of therapy training outcomes. These evaluation activities should be able to provide both formative and summative functions. That is, they should enable us to improve training by providing feedback about effective and ineffective training processes; and they should also enable us to demonstrate the effectiveness of training programmes to accrediting and funding agencies. A multi-orientation star design is also planned for this component, with a common core of key training outcomes, amplified by specialized evaluation protocols for particular therapy approaches or orientations.

Research framework with examples of specific concepts and treatment components

The star design is appealing because it provides a way to balance the common and divergent interests of researchers. This design relies on the development of common protocols, which requires agreement among researchers and therapists representing different theoretical orientations. However, competing interests favouring particular instruments have long frustrated attempts to obtain consensus *core battery* (e.g. Strupp, Horowitz & Lambert, 1997). Here, we propose to avoid such controversies by taking a different approach: the development of a more generic research framework that focuses on concepts rather than specific instruments and that seeks to balance comparability and flexibility. This flexible framework allows both specific treatment and training outcome protocols for particular stakeholder groups (e.g. theoretical orientations) and also choice among comparable measurement instruments.

The general framework for selecting instruments for evaluating psychotherapy and psychotherapy training follows three dimensions that organize twelve therapy measurement domains (see Table 11.2). The first dimension is research focus on psychotherapy vs. psychotherapy training. The second dimension consists of three research topics corresponding to the traditional distinction between outcome, process, and background characteristics. Crossing these two dimensions produces six research domains:

I-A.   *Therapy outcome*: How clients change over the course of therapy
I-B.   *Therapy process*: What happens within therapy sessions

Table 11.2   Therapy and therapy training measurement domains with examples of key concepts

Research Theme	1. General (pan-theoretical)	2. Treatment Specific (e.g *person-centered/experiential therapy*)
	I. Psychotherapy	
A. Therapy Outcome	General clinical distress	*Self-concept*
B. Therapy Process	Therapeutic alliance	*Client in-session depth of experiential processing*
C. Client/Therapist Characteristics	Demographics	*Client independence vs. dependence*
	II. Psychotherapy Training	
A. Training Outcome	Productive vs. unproductive practice pattern	*Therapist facilitative conditions*
B. Training Process	Training programme components	*Experiential component of training*
C. Trainee/Trainer Characteristics	Demographics	*Personal endorsement of person-centred values*

I-C. *Client/therapist characteristics*: Important features of clients and therapists that may affect therapy outcome or process

II-A. *Training outcome*: How therapists change over the course of training

II-B. *Training process*: What happens during the training programme

II-C. *Trainee/trainer characteristics*: Important features of trainees and trainers that may affect training outcome or process.

The third dimension is the generality of the concepts studied, and corresponds to the star model; it consists of two levels:

- Generic/pan-theoretical concepts agreed to as important by a broad range of therapists and researchers;
- Specific concepts held to be important within a particular theoretical orientation (e.g. person-centred/experiential), client treatment population (e.g. people living with schizophrenia), or national or language group (e.g. Belgium/Flemish-speaking).

The proposed framework is a nested set of priority lists, intended to allow necessary flexibility while at the same time encouraging consistency within and across treatment approaches. This is accomplished by first prioritizing measurement domains, then prioritizing concepts within measurement domains. Once the relevant concepts are identified, then instruments available in a given language or for a particular client population can be examined. In this way, the draft protocol makes recommendations as to what is probably most important to measure, thus encouraging standardization so that data from different sites can be combined or compared, while still allowing flexibility for individual centres.

It is important to note that the priorities given here are meant as examples only; they express our personal opinions and should be seen as tentative. Different research teams, particularly working from different orientations or suborientations and modalities and with different client groups, will have different views on what the priorities should be and will need to develop lists of treatment-specific instruments within each domain.

Table 11.3 summarizes the current state of the generic or pan-theoretical components of the research framework, including recommended concepts for each of the six generic research domains. This list focuses on general concepts rather than specific instruments, and offers short definitions or examples for each concept. The list reflects input from various groups, but is still provisional. It currently includes 26 pan-theoretical concepts. Obviously, no single study could measure all of these; instead, the list is more like a restaurant menu with multiple courses to choose from, although ideally a sizeable consortium of research and training sites might together manage to collectively measure all the concepts. Thus, the framework itself is programmatic and also points to the need for collaboration.

Examples of general therapy concepts

A complete explication of all 26 pan-theoretical concepts, with examples of corresponding quantitative or qualitative instruments, is beyond the scope of this chapter. Instead, we will offer examples of one key concept within the General Therapy Outcome and General Therapy Process research domains.

Severity of client problems

Arguably, the most important general therapy outcome variable is severity of client symptom or problem distress. The four most important English-language client symptom severity instruments currently used to assess adult clients are the CORE-OM (Evans et al., 2002), the SCL-90-R (Derogatis, Rickels & Rock, 1976), the Outcome Questionnaire (Lambert et al., 1996), and the Treatment Outcome Package (TOP; Kraus, Seligman & Jordan, 2005). All of these instruments have extensive, strong reliability and validity data and consist of less than 100 items, which means that they take no more than 15 minutes to complete. All have short forms appropriate for more frequent administration (weekly or biweekly). The CORE-OM and the TOP are free; the SCL-90-R (Derogatis et al., 1976) and Outcome Questionnaire (Lambert et al., 1996) require either per-form or licensing fees. All of these instruments can be administered and scored by hand,

Table 11.3 Generic research domains and recommended key concepts

Domain I-A-1: General Therapy Outcome:

*1. Quantitative improvement in general severity of problems/symptoms (pre- to post- differences in symptom frequency or distress on standard instruments)

+2. Retrospective qualitative view of change (post-therapy report of changes experienced by client)

3. Progress on individualized problems/goals (improvement on problems or goals selected by client)

4. Life functioning improvement (e.g. improvement in interpersonal, relationship or work problems)

5. Quality of life (e.g. improvement in subjective well-being or life satisfaction improvement)

6. Cost effectiveness (e.g. decrease in healthcare utilization or burden of illness)

Domain I-B-2: General Therapy Process:

*1. Therapeutic alliance (e.g. client or therapist ratings)

+2. Client perception of helpful factors or events in therapy (post-session or post-therapy qualitative reports)

+3. Records of what happened in the session (recordings or therapist process notes)

4. Client perception of session value (ratings of qualities or effects of session)

Domain I-C-3: General Client/Therapist Pre-therapy Characteristics:

*1. Client/therapist demographics (e.g. gender, age, education level, ethnicity, household income)

*2. Therapist professional background (e.g. experience, discipline, theoretical orientation)

*3. Client presenting difficulties/problem description/diagnosis (e.g. self-report inventory psychopathology measures)

4. Client psychiatric medications (e.g. medications, including dose, condition treated, when last changed

5. Client social support (e.g. number and quality of friends, supportive others; religious or other community involvement)

6. Client personality style (e.g. five factor model)

Domain II-A-1: General Training Outcome:

1. Therapist facilitative interpersonal skills (e.g. pre-post improvement on performance measures of general therapeutic relational skills)

2. Professional functioning (e.g. post-training level of continuing work involvement or professional growth vs. burnout or stagnation)

3. Students' qualitative perceptions of process and effects of their practice over the course of training

4. Improvements in client retention rates, outcome (early to late training)

Table 11.3 (*Continued*)

Domain II-B-1: Training Process:

1. Training programme components (presence and amount; e.g. lecture, experiential, practice, self-development, research)
2. Training alliance/atmosphere (trainee relationships with trainers, fellow trainees; programme morale)
3. Trainee perceived helpful and problematic aspects of training

Domain II-C-1: Trainee/Trainer Characteristics:

1. Trainee/trainer demographics (e.g. gender, age, ethnicity, household income)
2. Trainee level of previous therapeutic experience
3. Trainee initial values/theoretical orientation

---

*Recommended concept for minimum protocol
+Additional recommended concepts for systematic case study protocol

but have optional fee-based online administration and scoring services. (For more information, see Elliott & Zucconi, 2006.)

Therapeutic alliance

Over the past 50 years, researchers have developed hundreds of different therapy process instruments measuring a wide range of concepts or variables; however, most of these are impractical for routine use in practice and training settings, because they are specific to a particular type of therapy, involve fairly long instruments (e.g. Therapy Session Report; Orlinsky & Howard, 1986), or require trained raters. Thus, the most obvious choices for the kind of general therapy process to measure come down to: (a) quantitative measures of the therapeutic alliance; (b) qualitative reports of client-perceived helpful events or factors in therapy; (c) records of what happened in the session; and (d) quantitative assessments of the value of therapy sessions.

While each of these concepts has its advocates, the most logical and generally studied kind of general therapy process is the therapeutic alliance (Horvath & Greenberg, 1994). Several different alliance measures have been developed over the past 25 years; those used most frequently today include the Working Alliance Inventory (WAI; Horvath & Greenberg, 1989); the California Psychotherapy Alliance Scale (CALPAS; Gaston & Marmar, 1994); the Penn Helping Alliance Questionnaire-II (Haq-II; Luborsky et al., 1996); and the Agnew Relationship Measure (ARM; Agnew-Davies et al., 1998). These instruments are summarized in Table 11.4. All have very good reliability and validity, exist in multiple versions and, as unpublished tests available from their developers, are essentially free. The most widely used is the 12-item version of the Working Alliance Inventory, as revised first from the original 36-item version by Tracey and Kokotovic (1989)

Table 11.4 Common English language therapeutic alliance instruments

Instrument (items)	Reference	Scale Basis, Points & Time Frame	Subscales	Informant	Non-English Translations
Working Alliance Inventory (WAI) (36 items; 12-item short form)	Horvath & Greenberg, 1989; Hatcher & Gillaspy, 2006[a]	Frequency 7 points (revised short form: 5 points)	Bond Task agreement Goal agreement	Client Therapist Observer	Dutch Danish French
California Psychotherapy Alliance Scale (CALPAS; 24 items)	Gaston & Marmar, 1994	Agreement-Disagreement 6 points	Patient Working Capacity Patient Commitment Therapist Understanding and Involvement Working Strategy Consensus	Client Therapist	French Portuguese Italian
Penn Helping Alliance Questionnaire-II (Haq-II; 19 items)	Luborsky et al. 1996	Agreement 7 points	–	Client Therapist	German French Norwegian Dutch (earlier version)
Agnew Relationship Measure (ARM; 28 items)	Agnew-Davies et al. 1998	Agreement 7 points	Bond Partnership Confidence Openness Initiative	Client Therapist	–

[a] Revised 12-item short form

and most recently using more powerful psychometric methods by Hatcher and Gillaspy (2006).

Example of treatment-specific research domains

Table 11.5 provides examples of 18 concepts specific to person-centred or experiential therapies, organized into six research domains parallel to the generic research domains. Thus, it contains lists of outcome, process, client-therapist background and training outcome concepts relevant to studying person-centred and experiential psychotherapies. For example, trainers at a person-centred postgraduate training course might want to administer measures of client positive mental health (outcome), client perceptions of the therapist facilitative conditions of warmth, empathy and genuineness, and client preference for a directive vs. non-directive therapist approach. They might also track their trainees' ability to communicate the facilitative conditions over the course of their training, the nature and extent of experiential components in their training, and trainees' initial endorsement of person-centred values.

Research protocols

This research framework can be used to describe various levels of practice-based research design: *Minimum protocols* are appropriate for use in busy agencies or private practice settings with one's own clients, where only a small number of things can be measured. *Systematic case study protocols* are slightly more elaborate, appropriate for carrying out a careful study of a single therapy case for a case-presentation course requirement or for publication using the Pragmatic Case Study (Fishman, 1999) or Hermeneutic Single Case Efficacy Design (Elliott, 2002). By contrast, *maximal protocols*, in which all domains are assessed by at least one instrument, are appropriate only for well-resourced research centres or research consortia, and include at least one instrument for each key concept in each of the eight measurement domains. Finally, *training protocols* are required for systematic evaluation of psychotherapy training programmes. Two of these designs are most relevant to the purpose of this chapter: minimum and systematic case study protocols.

Recommended minimum protocol

What, in practical, concrete terms, is the least that one could do by way of monitoring one's – or one's students' work – with clients? Such a minimum

Table 11.5 Example of treatment-specific research domains and recommended key concepts: person-centred/experiential psychotherapy (PCEP)

Domain I-A-2: PCEP-Specific Therapy Outcome:

1. Positive mental health (e.g. improved optimism, resilience)
2. Self-concept (e.g. improvement in quantitative self-evaluation or qualitative self-description)
3. Experiential processing (e.g. decreased alexithymia, increased experiencing)
4. Coping strategies (e.g. decreased external/avoidant or increased internal/ emotion-based strategies)

Domain I-B-2: PCEP Specific Therapy Process:

1. Therapist facilitative relationship conditions (rated by client, therapist or observer raters)
2. Theory-specific client post-session reactions (e.g. feeling understood; resolution of therapeutic tasks)
3. Orientation-specific therapist adherence (e.g. observer or therapist ratings of key therapist attitudes, principles, responses or tasks)

Domain I-C-2: PCEP-Specific Client/Therapist Background:

1. Client preference/dispreference for a directive vs. non-directive therapist approach
2. Client personal resources for making use of offered treatment (e.g. pre-therapy level of experiential processing; client qualitative interview report of personal resources, limitations for using the therapy)

Domain II-A-2: PCEP-Specific Training Outcome:

1. Person-centred facilitative conditions (e.g. improvements in client or observer ratings)
2. Specific person-centred/experiential therapist skills (improvement in student or supervisor ratings, e.g. of reflection of feelings; therapeutic tasks)
3. Therapist emotional intelligence (e.g. access to experience, self-soothing)
4. Maturity (e.g. social awareness)
5. Authenticity (e.g. ability to be appropriately transparent with significant others, internal coherence, positive relationship with self)

Domain II-B-3: PCEP-Specific Training Processes:

1. Experiential components of training (e.g. amount, depth, richness)
2. Self-determination processes (e.g. student-led components, self-assessment)

Domain II-C-3: PCEP-Specific Trainee/Trainer Characteristics:

1. Personal endorsement of person-centred values (e.g. authenticity, experiencing, self-determination, pluralism, wholeness, growth)
2. Trainer suborientation within person-centred approach (e.g. classical person-centred, process-experiential)

design could be useful for busy practice or training settings. It seems to us that the smallest meaningful practice-based research design consists of three components (marked with an asterisk in Table 11.3):

Client problem severity

A general measure of client problem severity (general therapy outcome), as discussed in the previous section, is a good starting point and is likely to be most widely accepted. Such measures should be given at the first session of therapy, providing a description of the client's initial clinical state and providing a baseline against which to gauge progress in therapy. In addition, the instrument should be repeated at frequent intervals, preferably every week or two, in order to reduce data loss from clients dropping out of therapy, a perennial problem in practice-based research.

Therapeutic alliance

Second, it would be a good idea to use a general therapy process measure, specifically, a measure of therapeutic alliance. Such a measure (e.g. Working Alliance Inventory-12-Revised; Hatcher & Gillaspy, 2006) could be given at alternate sessions, as with the problem severity instrument, or less frequently (e.g. session 3, 5, 10, etc.).

Client and therapist background information

The third component of the minimum design is basic descriptive information about the client and therapist. Such information is important for characterizing the therapies studied and provides an interpretive context for the results obtained. No generally accepted demographic questionnaires exist, but such forms typically provide the following information:

- Gender (client, therapist)
- Age (client, therapist)
- Educational background (client, therapist)
- Ethnicity (client, therapist)
- Occupation (client)/discipline (therapist)
- Experience level (therapist)/previous therapy (client)
- Theoretical orientation (therapist)
- Presenting problems (client).

Most training clinics collect this information from clients during the intake process, so only forms for the desired therapist information need be added to routine procedures.

The case for the minimum protocol

This minimal recommended research protocol has multiple strengths as a starting place for practice-based research, even on less-studied treatments such as
psychodynamic, experiential and systemic therapies. To begin with, it provides
a basic audit of therapy outcome, process and relevant descriptive background
information, which can be used for administrative monitoring purposes. In
addition, this information provides a starting point for evaluating the generalizability of the results.

More importantly, in spite of frequent objections (e.g. Bohart, O'Hara &
Leitner, 1998), there is now evidence that these instruments are appropriate
for the study of non-CBT treatments. Certainly there should be little to object
to about including a measure of the therapeutic alliance, which has roots in
both psychodynamic (e.g. Bordin, 1994) and experiential-systemic (Horvath &
Greenberg, 1989) traditions. Furthermore, even though a pathology-oriented
measure of client symptom severity would not be a first choice for most researchers and therapists working within the psychodynamic, experiential or
systemic traditions, it is now clear that these instruments are sensitive to change
in non-behavioural treatments (e.g. Elliott, 2001).

Systematic case study protocol

A potentially useful research protocol would be one that could be used to
provide data for a systematic case study. Case presentations are a common requirement in psychotherapy training clinics and institutes, where they are often
used to assess students' abilities to develop case formulations, carry out effective
therapeutic interventions, and integrate research into their work as therapists.
Such case presentations can now benefit from the recent development of a
new generation of systematic case study designs. Thus, Fishman (1999), Elliott
(2002) and Schneider (1999) have all put forward expanded single case designs
that take a more interpretive approach to examining client change and its
causes. In general, these designs aim to (1) demonstrate that change occurred,
(2) examine the evidence for concluding that therapy was responsible for
the change, (3) look for alternative explanations for the change, and (4)
assess which processes in therapy might have been responsible for change.
These methods emphasize the use of a rich case record of comprehensive
information on therapy outcome and process (e.g. using multiple perspectives,
sources and types of data), as well as systematic and critical reflection by the
researcher.

Thus, with a moderate degree of extra effort, traditional therapy case presentations can be converted into systematic case study research, potentially for
publication in clinically-oriented or case-research journals, such as *Pragmatic*

Case Studies in Psychotherapy (available at pcsp.libraries.rutgers.edu/). For example, in order to carry out a Hermeneutic Single Case Efficacy Design (HSCED; Elliott, 2002), the therapist must develop a case record of information about a client's therapy. This includes background information, as well as data on therapy process and outcome, using multiple sources or measures. This is a generic research procedure, intended for use across a wide variety of types of therapy and client populations. The following data are typically used with adult outpatients (marked with an asterisk or plus-sign in Table 11.3):

(a) *General client/therapist background* information, as noted earlier, is essential for providing interpretive context for the case, as well as a basis for generalizing the conclusions of the case study.

(b) *General quantitative outcome measures*, for example, client symptom distress (e.g. Symptom Checklist-90-R; Derogatis et al., 1976), client life functioning (e.g. Inventory of Interpersonal Problems; Horowitz et al., 1988), and individualized change measure (e.g. Simplified Personal Questionnaire; Elliott, Mack & Shapiro, 1999). Many of these measures can be given at the beginning and end of therapy, but it is also a good idea to give one of them every session or every other session.

(c) *Qualitative Interview about client change and important therapy processes.* It is also useful to employ a semi-structured interview (e.g. the Change Interview; Elliott, Slatick & Urman, 2001) to complement the quantitative measures. Such an interview can be used to help understand the quantitative data, and can easily provide both general outcome and process information, such as client descriptions of changes experienced over the course of therapy, their attributions for these changes, and helpful and hindering aspects of their therapy. Such interviews typically take 30–60 minutes (depending on the level of detail desired, can be given at the end of therapy (or, better, every 10 sessions), and are best carried out by a third party (although in some cases it may be appropriate for the therapist to do them).

(d) *General therapy process: qualitative post-session assessment of helpful aspects of therapy.* Another very helpful research tool is a weekly open-ended questionnaire that asks clients what they found helpful in that particular session (e.g. Helpful Aspects of Therapy [HAT] Form; Llewelyn, 1988). Such questionnaires can be used to pinpoint significant therapeutic processes that may be associated with change on the weekly outcome measure or to corroborate change processes referred to in later qualitative interviews.

(e) *Records of therapy sessions.* Finally, detailed therapist process notes and audio or video recordings of therapy sessions are very useful for pinpointing, corroborating, or clarifying issues or contradictions elsewhere in the data.

To this general template, we would recommend the addition of a measure of therapeutic alliance, as described under the minimal protocol. For children or psychotic adults some or all of the client self-reports can be replaced by therapist or observer-based instruments.

Expanded research protocols

Applying the minimum or systematic case study protocols in a wide variety of training sites would be an excellent start, but would clearly be limited from the point of view of studying a wider range of general concepts, not to mention more theoretically relevant types of therapy outcome and process. Thus, it would be useful for particular training sites to add one or several more general or orientation-specific instruments. These could be chosen from lists of general concepts in Table 11.3 and from a treatment-specific list, such as the one given in Table 11.5. For example, qualitative assessment of client views of change over the course of therapy might be added, or a measure of life functioning (e.g. improvement on interpersonal problems). Alternatively, adding a separate training outcome component would provide another dimension to the research, perhaps by doing qualitative interviews with former or advanced trainees or quantitatively assessing their professional functioning using one or both of the new professional functioning scales developed by Orlinsky and Rønnestad (2005). Thus, adding one or two measures of some of these other concepts might add considerable interest and breadth to the minimum protocol.

Consortia arrangements

Expanded protocols could be also implemented in a consortium arrangement involving several training programmes or clinics (possibly within a language community), with different sites drawing different sets of concepts and measures from the larger framework. Such consortia could be run by a working group responsible for selecting concepts and instruments, setting up and coordinating data collection, and eventually overseeing data pooling and analysis.

Promising methodological developments to facilitate collaborative research

Beyond the arguments made at the beginning of this paper for the timeliness and appropriateness of practice-based research, recent advances in research methods can support and enhance this kind of work. These include systematic case study research (discussed in the previous section); systematic qualitative research methods; early outcome signal methods; new, powerful psychometric methods; and web-based resources. Some of these have already been alluded to but will be elaborated in the final section of this paper.

Systematic qualitative methods

One of the most exciting developments in psychotherapy research over the past 20 years has been the emergence of systematic, rigorous approaches to qualitative data collection and analysis (Elliott, 1999; Elliott & Timulak, 2005; McLeod, 2001). These methods include (but are not limited to) grounded theory (Strauss & Corbin, 1998), empirical phenomenology (Wertz, 2005); hermeneutic-interpretive research (Packer & Addison, 1989), interpretative phenomenological analysis (Smith, Jarman & Osborn, 1999), Consensual Qualitative Research (Hill, Thompson & Williams, 1997), and discourse analysis (Potter & Wetherell, 1987). These research methods have brought a breath of fresh air to psychotherapy research. Many traditionally minded therapy researchers have now learned that systematic qualitative methods offer a useful complement for enriching, enlivening and illuminating quantitative results.

New, powerful psychometric methods

Earlier, we touched on the problem of competing research instruments as an obstacle for research collaboration. By way of illustration, consider the widely used measures of client problem severity and therapeutic alliance cited earlier. Having so many measures of the same thing has been both a strength and a limitation for the field, in that it provides different options suited to different views of therapy and different measurement preferences. Such diversity, however, also makes it difficult to compare results of studies using different instruments, and also leads to conflicts over whose instrument to recommend for general use. Fortunately, another recent development in psychometric methods can provide a solution to this problem, in the form of Rasch analysis, developed as an alternative to traditional approaches by Danish mathematician Georg Rasch (1980). This measurement model, a form of Item Response Theory (IRT), provides a framework and a set of useful tools for assessing the reliability, validity and utility of psychological measures. Although it is too technical to be described in proper detail here, the underlying theory of Rasch analysis is that useful measurement consists of a unidimensional construct arranged in a hierarchical pattern (e.g. more than/less than) along an equal-interval continuum constructed using log transformations of odds ratios and probabilistic equations (Bond & Fox, 2007). Then, equating studies can be done, tying different instruments to the same metric (Wright, 1993). What this means for an international project with researchers using different instruments in different languages is that this form of analysis can be used to equate the instruments (Bond & Fox, 2007), thus allowing both diversity and comparability. (For an example of how Rasch analysis can be applied to a common outcome instrument – the SCL-90-R – see Elliott et al., 2006.)

Early signal methods

In a series of papers, Lambert and colleagues (e.g. Lambert et al., 2002a, 2002b; Hawkins et al., 2004) have shown (a) that clients who show a poor response early in therapy (e.g. get worse) generally have poorer eventual outcomes, and (b) that providing therapists or clients with feedback about the lack of progress (*signal alarms*) leads to better outcomes in those at-risk clients. In these studies, Lambert and colleagues used the Outcome Questionnaire-45, described earlier. However, Lambert's decision rules for identifying clients as *non-clinical* (white), *progressing well* (green), *showing possible problems* (yellow), or *off-track* (red) can be inferred from the client's beginning level of symptom severity and the amount of positive or negative change shown since pre-treatment; the resulting decision rules can then be applied to other instruments such as the CORE or the SCL-90-R (Breighner & Elliott, 2005).

Web-based resources

In addition to the mix of quantitative and qualitative methodological developments we have listed, the Internet makes various resources available for collaborative practice-based research. For example, there are now many different web-based data collection and test-scoring resources (e.g. Best & Krueger, 2004), which can be used to facilitate collaborative research across geographically separated training sites. However, even prior to this, virtual communities can assist working groups of person-centred and experiential therapy trainers and researchers in planning collaborative research via exchange of ideas, working papers, research instruments and so on. To this end, we have created a demonstration version of such a community at www.communityzero.com/pcepirp, intended to facilitate treatment-specific research on person-centred and experiential psychotherapies, including both English and Dutch-language instruments. This site consists of sections devoted to Assessment Tools (i.e. instruments), Research Protocol, Research Network (links to related sites), Upcoming Events (e.g. conferences and workshops), Discussions (of questions about research methods), Members (list of names and e-mail addresses), and Notice Board (announcements). In order to protect members from spam, this is a closed website, open by invitation only (which requires going to the address given and applying for membership). More recently, we have begun using Google groups as a less expensive, more flexible way of creating virtual communities. An independent informational site has also been set up at www.ipeppt.net.

Conclusion: Carrying practice-based research forward

In this article we have outlined a conceptual framework and research protocols suitable for practice-based research, especially in therapy training courses and centres. We conclude with a list of ways that readers can become involved in this sort of research:

1. They can begin implementing the minimum protocol design with their own clients and in their own training setting.
2. Trainers can convert traditional case presentation training requirements into systematic case study exercises (Stinckens et al., 2009), with an eye toward helping students publish these in one of the new case study journals.
3. Those located in non-English-speaking countries can help with translations of key research instruments.
4. Interested readers can form or join an online discussion group or virtual community, such as www.communityzero.com/pcepirp
5. Finally, trainers and practitioners can take part in more formal collaborations with similarly inclined training centres to generate data to support psychometric research aimed at improving existing instruments and at equating different instruments for the same constructs.

We note that the larger project is by no means restricted to under-studied therapeutic approaches. The methods described are equally applicable to cognitive and behavioural therapies, and also to therapists working with different client populations (e.g. people living with schizophrenia, children), and national or language groups (e.g. Dutch-speakers or Italian therapists).

From our point of view, the research-practice gap is based on a false dichotomy with roots in positivistic and technological models of psychotherapy. These models emphasize therapeutic technique over relationship and observation over lived experience. The result is a fundamental alienation between practice and research. The practice-based research described here does away with this false dichotomy, by integrating research and practice into a single activity. It is our view that our clients can most benefit from a research-practice integration in which psychologists and other mental health professionals bring all their sensitivities and abilities to the task of helping their clients.

Acknowledgements

Earlier versions of this chapter were presented at meetings of the Congress of the Istituto dell'Approccio Centrato sulla Persona, Rome, Italy and the Society for Psychotherapy Research, in Lausanne, Switzerland, in Montreal, Canada and in Toledo, Ohio. We are grateful to Germain Lietaer, David Orlinsky, Louis Castonguay and others for helpful suggestions and encouragement.

References

Agnew-Davies, R., Stiles W.B., Hardy, G.E., Barkham, M. & Shapiro, D.A. (1998). Alliance structure assessed by the Agnew Relationship Measure (ARM). *British Journal of Clinical Psychology*, *37*, 155–172.

Barkham, M. & Mellor-Clark, J. (2000). Rigour and relevance: the role of practice-based evidence in the psychological therapies. In N. Rowland & S. Goss, *Evidence-based counselling and psychological therapies: Research and applications* (pp. 127–144). London: Routledge.

Best, S.J. & Krueger, B.S. (2004). *Internet data collection*. Thousand Oaks, CA: Sage Publications.

Beutler, L. & Castonguay, L. (eds.) (2005). *What works in psychology, and why*. Oxford, UK: Oxford University Press.

Bohart, A.C., O'Hara, M. & Leitner, L.M. (1998). Empirically violated treatments: Disenfranchisement of humanistic and other psychotherapies. *Psychotherapy Research*, *8*, 141–157.

Bond, T.G. & Fox, C.M. (2007). *Applying the Rasch Model: Fundamental measurement in the human sciences* (2nd edn.). New Jersey: Erlbaum.

Bordin, E.S. (1994). Theory and research on the therapeutic working alliance: New directions. In A.O. Horvath & L.S. Greenberg (eds.), *The working alliance: Theory, research and practice*. New York: John Wiley & Sons, Inc.

Borkovec, T.D., Echemendia, R.J., Ragusea, S.A. & Ruiz, M. (2001). The Pennsylvania Practice Research Network and future possibilities for clinically meaningful and scientifically rigorous psychotherapy effectiveness research. *Clinical Psychology: Research & Practice*, *8*, 155–167.

Breighner, E. & Elliott, R. (June, 2005). *Using the Personal Questionnaire to identify early treatment problems: Adapting signal alarm methods*. Paper presented at the conference of the Society for Psychotherapy Research, Montreal, Canada.

Castonguay, L., Pincus, A., Arnett, P., Roper, G., Rabia, B. et al. (November, 2004). *Psychology training clinic as a research practice network: Integrating research and clinical practice in graduate school.* Paper presented at the conference of the Society for Psychotherapy Research, Springdale, Utah.

Chambless, D.L., Sanderson, W.C., Shoham, V., Johnson, S.B., Pope, K.S. et al. (1996). An update on empirically validated therapies. *The Clinical Psychologist*, *49*, 5–18.

Derogatis, L.R., Rickels, K. & Rock, A. (1976). The SCL-90-R and the MMPI: A step in the validation of a new self-report scale. *British Journal of Psychiatry*, *128*, 280–289.

Elliott, R. (1998). Editor's introduction: A guide to the empirically supported treatments controversy. *Psychotherapy Research, 8*, 115–125.

Elliott, R. (1999). Editor's introduction to special issue on qualitative psychotherapy research: Definitions, themes and discoveries. *Psychotherapy Research, 9*, 251–257.

Elliott, R. (2001). Research on the effectiveness of humanistic therapies: A meta-analysis. In D. Cain & J. Seeman (eds.), *Humanistic psychotherapies: Handbook of research and practice* (pp. 57–81). Washington, DC: American Psychological Association.

Elliott, R. (2002). Hermeneutic single case efficacy design. *Psychotherapy Research, 12*, 1–20.

Elliott, R. & Timulak, L. (2005). Descriptive and interpretive approaches to qualitative research. In J. Miles & P. Gilbert (eds.), *A handbook of research methods in clinical and health psychology* (pp. 147–159). Oxford, UK: Oxford University Press.

Elliott, R. & Zucconi, A. (2006). Doing research on the effectiveness of psychotherapy and psychotherapy training: A person-centered/experiential perspective. *Person-Centered and Experiential Psychotherapies, 5*, 82–100.

Elliott, R., Mack, C. & Shapiro, D.A. (1999). *Simplified Personal Questionnaire procedure.* Network for Research on Experiential Psychotherapies website: http://experiential-researchers.org/instruments/elliott/pqprocedure.html

Elliott, R., Slatick, E. & Urman, M. (2001). Qualitative Change Process Research on Psychotherapy: Alternative Strategies. In J. Frommer & D.L. Rennie (eds.), *Qualitative psychotherapy research: Methods and methodology* (pp. 69–111). Lengerich, Germany: Pabst Science Publishers.

Elliott, R., Fox, C.M., Beltyukova, S.A., Stone, G.E., Gunderson, J. et al. (2006). Deconstructing therapy outcome measurement with Rasch analysis: The SCL-90-R. *Psychological Assessment, 18*, 359–372.

Evans, C., Connell, J., Barkham, M., Margison, F., Mellor-Clark, J. et al. (2002). Towards a standardised brief outcome measure: Psychometric properties and utility of the CORE-OM. *British Journal of Psychiatry, 180*, 51–60.

Fishman, D.B. (1999). *The case for pragmatic psychology.* New York: New York University Press.

Gaston, L. & Marmar, C.R. (1994). California psychotherapy alliance scale. In A.O. Horvath & L.S. Greenberg (eds.), *The working alliance: Theory, research, and practice* (pp. 85–108). New York: John Wiley & Sons, Inc.

Hatcher, R.L. & Gillaspy, J.A. (2006). Development and validation of a revised short version of the Working Alliance Inventory. *Psychotherapy Research, 16*, 12–25.

Hawkins, E.J., Lambert, M.J., Vermeersch, D.A., Slade, K. & Tuttle, K. (2004). The therapeutic effects of providing client progress information to patients and therapists. *Psychotherapy Research, 10*, 308–327.

Hill, C.E., Thompson, B.J. & Williams, E.N. (1997). A guide to conducting consensual qualitative research. *The Counseling Psychologist, 25*, 517–572.

Horowitz, L.M., Rosenberg, S.E., Baer, B.A., Ureño, G. & Villaseñor, V.S. (1988). Inventory of interpersonal problems: psychometric properties and clinical applications. *Journal of Consulting and Clinical Psychology, 56*, 885–892.

Horvath, A.O. & Greenberg, L.S. (1989). Development and validation of the working alliance inventory. *Journal of Counseling Psychology, 36*, 223–233.

Horvath, A.O. & Greenberg, L.S. (eds.) (1994). *The working alliance: Theory, research, and practice.* New York: John Wiley & Sons, Inc.

Kazdin, A.E. & Weisz, J.R. (2003). *Evidence-based psychotherapies for children and adolescents.* New York: Guilford Press.

Kraus, D.R., Seligman, D.A. & Jordan, J.R. (2005). Validation of a behavioral health treatment outcome and assessment tool designed for naturalistic settings: The treatment outcome package. *Journal of Clinical Psychology, 61*, 285–314.

Lambert, M.J., Burlingame, G.M., Umphress, V., Hansen, N., Yanchar, S.C. et al. (1996). The reliability and validity of a new psychotherapy outcome questionnaire. *Clinical Psychology and Psychotherapy, 3*, 249–258.

Lambert, M.J., Whipple, J.L., Bishop, M.J., Vermeersch, D.A., Gray, G.V. & Finch, A.E. (2002a). Comparison of empirically derived and rationally derived methods for identifying clients at risk for treatment failure. *Clinical Psychology & Psychotherapy, 9*, 149–164.

Lambert, M.J., Whipple, J.L., Vermeersch, D.A., Smart, D.W., Hawkins, E.J. et al. (2002b). Enhancing psychotherapy outcomes via providing feedback on client progress: a replication. *Clinical Psychology & Psychotherapy, 9, 91–103*.

Llewelyn, S. (1988). Psychological therapy as viewed by clients and therapists. *British Journal of Clinical Psychology, 27*, 223–238.

Luborsky, L., Barber, J.P., Siqueland, L., Johnson, S., Najavits, L.M. et al. (1996). The revised helping alliance questionnaire (HAQ-11): Psychometric properties. *Journal of Psychotherapy Practice and Research, 5*, 260–271.

McLeod, J. (2001). *Qualitative research in counselling and psychotherapy.* London: Sage Publications.

Morrow-Bradley, C. & Elliott, R. (1986). The utilization of psychotherapy research by practicing psychotherapists. *American Psychologist, 41,* 188–197.

Nathan, P.E. & Gorman, J.M. (eds.) (2002). *A guide to treatments that work.* New York: Oxford University Press.

Norcross, J. (ed.) (2002). *Psychotherapy relationships that work.* New York: Oxford University Press.

Orlinsky, D.E. & Howard, K.I. (1986). The psychological interior of psychotherapy: Explorations with the Therapy Session Reports. In L. Greenberg & W. Pinsof (eds.), *The psychotherapeutic process: A research handbook* (pp. 477–501). New York: Guilford Press.

Orlinsky, D.E. & Rønnestad, M.H. (2005). *How psychotherapists develop: A study of therapeutic work and professional growth.* Washington, DC: American Psychological Association.

Packer, M.J. & Addison, R.B. (1989). *Entering the circle: Hermeneutic investigation in psychology.* Albany, NY: SUNY Press.

Potter, J. & Wetherell, M. (1987). *Discourse and social psychology.* Newbury Park: Sage Publications.

Rasch, G. (1980). *Probabilistic models for some intelligence and attainment tests* (expanded edn.). Chicago: University of Chicago.

Roth, A. & Fonagy, P. (2004). *What works for whom?: A critical review of psychotherapy research* (2nd edn.). New York: Guilford Press.

Rowland, N. & Goss, S. (2000). *Evidence-based counselling and psychological therapies: Research and applications* (pp. 127–144). London: Routledge.

Schneider, K.J. (1999). Multiple-case depth research. *Journal of Clinical Psychology, 55,* 1531–1540.

Smith, J.A., Jarman, M. & Osborn, M. (1999). Doing interpretative phenomenological analysis. In M. Murray & K. Chamberlain (eds.), *Qualitative health psychology* (pp. 218–240). London: Sage Publications.

Stinckens, N., Elliott, R. & Leijssen, M. (2009). Bridging the gap between therapy research and practice in a person-centered/experiential therapy training program: The Leuven systematic case-study research protocol. *Person-Centred and Experiential Psychotherapies, 8,* 143–162.

Strauss, A. & Corbin, J. (1998). *Basics of qualitative research: Techniques and procedures for developing grounded theory* (2nd edn.). Thousand Oaks, CA: Sage Publications.

Strupp, H.H., Horowitz, L.M. & Lambert, M.J. (eds.) (1997). *Measuring patient changes in mood, anxiety, and personality disorders: Toward a core battery.* Washington, DC: American Psychological Association.

Thornton, T. (2006). Tacit knowledge as the unifying factor in evidence-based medicine and clinical judgement. *Philosophy, ethics, and humanities in medicine, 1* (2). Published online 2006, March 17. doi: 10.1186/1747-5341-1-2.

Tracey, T.J. & Kokotovic, A.M. (1989). Factor structure of the Working Alliance Inventory. *Psychological Assessment, 1,* 207–210.

Wertz, F.J. (2005). Phenomenological research methods for counseling psychology. *Journal of Counseling Psychology, 52,* 167–177.

Wright, B.D. (1993). Equitable test equating. *Rasch Measurement Transactions, 7,* 298–299.

12

Practice Research Networks and Psychological Services Research in the UK and USA

Glenys Parry[1], Louis G. Castonguay[2], Tom D. Borkovec[2] and Abraham W. Wolf[3]

[1] University of Sheffield, UK, [2] Penn State University, USA, [3] Case Western Reserve University, Ohio, USA

The gap between research and practice: why does it matter?

That there is a gap, possibly a gulf, between research and practice in psychological therapies has long been acknowledged. Most therapists base their practice on the theoretical orientation in which they trained and their own clinical experience rather than on research findings. Much experimental clinical research in psychology is designed to answer questions of little direct interest to clinicians, using methods which militate against clinical realism. For example, in research on the relative efficacy of interventions, to gain experimental control researchers have defended against threats to internal validity at the expense of external validity. Much of this type of research is on manualized treatment packages with patients who present with single conditions (or who are treated as if they do), whereas most practitioners work more eclectically with people who have complex problems, or they intervene at the level of organizational systems, for example through training and organizational development.

One way of applying research to practice, of attempting to bridge the gap, has been to incorporate empirical findings into clinical practice guidelines to attempt to implement such findings and to change professional practice. Unfortunately, the evidence suggests that although it is possible to improve treatment outcomes where a systematic and sustained attempt is made to implement

Developing and Delivering Practice-Based Evidence By Michael Barkham, Gillian E Hardy, and John Mellor-Clark © 2010 John Wiley & Sons, Ltd

them, guidelines alone are a very weak influence on clinician behaviour and in practice make little difference to health outcomes (Parry, Cape & Pilling, 2003). A related strategy has been to use evidence from controlled trials to create lists of 'empirically supported treatments' (in the UK often called 'evidence-based therapies'). This has attracted a chorus of complaint from both practitioners and scientists, who argue that this dichotomous designation is reductionist, unscientific, biased, or has undesirable consequences (Westen, Novotny & Thompson-Brunner, 2004). Perhaps because of its simplicity, the method has had more impact on policy and training courses than a more nuanced approach, although its impact on service outcomes and quality remains untested. These issues have led to a growing interest in 'translational research', including research on how to translate findings into better decision making, improved healthcare outcomes and higher quality services.

Challenges to external validity are problematic for health services researchers as much as for clinicians. For example, the relatively small sample sizes in most trials are unable to address many significant issues, such as health economic questions of cost-effectiveness, the impact of moderator variables, or rare outcomes. From the health services researcher's point of view, there are frequently circumstances in which an experimental approach, even the most pragmatic within a clinical setting, is inappropriate, impossible or inadequate (Black, 1996). For example, experimental trials are inappropriate to study adverse outcomes; impossible where practitioners refuse to cooperate or different service delivery systems are being compared; or inadequate because of limits to generalizability of the findings. There are strong arguments for the complementary role of observational research.

However, observational research using surveys or routinely collected outcomes can continue to serve the researcher's agenda rather than the practitioner's and to exert a form of 'empirical imperialism' (Castonguay & Borkovec, 2005) that gives research questions priority over clinical ones. There is a parallel here with the call to involve service users in research, both as a way of improving research quality but also as a democratic right, captured in the slogan 'nothing about us without us'. Practitioners could take the same stance, calling for a research paradigm that is genuinely co-constructed, allowing researchers and practitioners to collaborate and to focus joint attention on areas of mutual concern. One mechanism that is used successfully in other areas of healthcare (Wolf, 2005, 2007) with the potential for applicability to both research and practice in psychological services is the Practice Research Network (PRN).

Practice Research Networks: the paradigm

Practice-based research can be carried forward in individual departments or even by individual therapists using single case methodologies. For example, there is a long history in the UK of using routinely gathered data on therapy delivery and patient outcomes within a locality, both for clinical audit and quality improvement purposes (Parry, 1998) and research (e.g. Saxon et al., 2007).

Practice-based research networks go beyond individual practitioners or services and have been alternately defined as a 'group of practising clinicians that co-operates to collect data and conduct research studies' (Zarin et al., 1997), and '. . . large numbers of practicing clinicians and clinical scientists brought together in collaborative research on clinically meaningful questions in the naturalistic setting for the sake of external validity and employing rigorous scientific methodology for the sake of internal validity' (Borkovec, 2002).

Research networks can focus on developing research capacity and infrastructure as a form of social and intellectual capital (Fenton et al., 2001) or on capturing snapshots of current practice in terms of descriptions of patient demographics, presenting problems, treatment setting and characteristics, therapy duration and intensity, and contact with other mental health professionals (Pincus et al., 1999). In their mature form, members agree to pool data relating to clinical outcomes, using the same measure or set of measures. In this way, they collaborate in building high-quality clinical databases on large, clinically representative samples. As some have argued (e.g. Borkovec et al., 2001), they can even provide the opportunity to conduct experimental research using component control, parametric, and especially additive designs that allow increasingly specific conclusions about causal elements in therapies and the acquisition of basic knowledge about the nature of the psychological problem and the nature of the mechanisms of change within those therapies.

This has the potential to bridge the gap between efficacy research and practice improvement methods, because so much efficacy research (and much process research) has a poor track record of improving practice and services. Where members of a PRN contribute data to a shared-access dataset, it holds the potential to meet both clinical audit and research purposes. Clinical audit is a process where data are used to give feedback on key features of a service to show where improvements are needed and later to check if they have occurred. It is typically a locally responsive enterprise, and findings often have limited generality. By monitoring outcomes regularly through the PRN, members are able to compare their own clinic case-mix, service standards and outcomes with other clinics and services, showing where improvement is needed. Research on the other hand has generation of new knowledge with general applicability as its key purpose, and here there are major advantages to large data sets of naturalistic evidence, to complement experimental evidence in understanding how best to organize and deliver services effectively and cost-effectively.

In studying outcomes the distinction is often made between efficacy and effectiveness research, but we would argue that this is not a dichotomy. It can be seen as a dimension, from research that above all defends against threats to internal validity to research that above all defends against threats to external validity. At the 'most internally valid' end of this spectrum are laboratory-based analogue studies, then, in order of decreasing internal validity and increasing external validity: university-based explanatory randomized controlled trials (RCTs) including dismantling studies, pragmatic randomized trials in routine clinic settings, interrupted time series and multiple baseline single-case experiments, case-control series, protocol-driven case series in clinical practice settings and, at the 'most externally valid' end of the spectrum, purely observational, non-intrusive studies of routine outcomes. All these methods hold value for different purposes and are best seen as complementary to each other, rather than competing. Large N, practice-based evidence is needed to tackle questions about outcomes and influences on outcomes that are not easily addressed experimentally, such as:

- Clinical utility
- Client acceptability
- Rare outcomes (e.g. adverse outcomes)
- Cost-effectiveness
- Modelling the impact of service configurations and organizational factors
- Gaining statistical power to examine interactions at service level (e.g. case-mix, therapist experience, treatment length).

Second, although they are challenging, internally valid outcome investigations, like additive designs, are possible in the naturalistic setting and within the context of a PRN. Such studies virtually eliminate the efficacy/effectiveness distinction.

Examples of Practice Research Networks

PRNs in the US and UK were established first on health topics other than psychological therapies. UK examples include the International Paediatric Nursing Research Network (IPNRN), Qualitative European Drug Research Network, Ophthalmic Research Network, the National Cancer Research Network, and most recently the Mental Health Research Network. In the US, a pioneer PRN was the Ambulatory Sentinel Practice Network, a network of primary healthcare practices across the United States and Canada (Green et al., 1984).

Although these are all termed 'research networks,' some are more practice-based than others, and even fewer are practice-led. For example, the Mental Health Research Network in the UK is a well-funded 'top-down' infrastructure with a primary function of supporting National Institute of Health Research (NIHR) projects, for example, to improve recruitment into clinical trials and other research. In that sense it is a managed system for clinicians to support researchers' projects rather than a practice-based network.

In the US, Congress enacted legislation in 1999 to encourage the Agency for Healthcare Research and Quality (AHRQ) to develop initiatives that expand understanding of translating research to practice and to address issues of disparities in healthcare quality, outcomes, cost and access. A call for applications for funding PRNs in primary care followed. Since 2002, AHRQ provided support to 36 PRNs comprised of over 10,000 primary care clinicians with practices in 50 states, serving almost 10 million primary care patients.

American Psychiatric Association

In 1993, the American Psychiatric Association formed a network of psychiatrists in clinical practice to study their practice patterns and patient characteristics. It was funded by the American Psychiatric Association, the federal Center for Mental Health Services, and private sources. Membership in the network included both a randomly selected group of practitioners in order to increase generalizability but also a 'volunteer' group for more intensive long-term studies. Data were collected through mailed paper-and-pencil questionnaires. Since 1993 there have been about 20 publications from this project. For example, Pincus et al. (1999) reported a snapshot of psychiatric practice from 417 psychiatrists who generated data on 5,004 patients and detailed information on 1,245. They showed that most patients had a severe mental disorder, many have concurrent Axis I disorders, 24% have a personality disorder and half have a physical health problem. The data suggested that American psychiatrists have shifted to a pharmacological treatment approach with 90% of patients on medication, although 55.4% of outpatients were also receiving psychotherapy. Polypharmacy was common, with 31.2% receiving three or more medications. A further study (Mintz et al., 2004) examined the relationship between utilization management techniques and psychiatrists' modification of treatment plans. In a sample of 1,800 patients treated by 600 psychiatrists, the authors found that PRN psychiatrists in independent practice with non-salaried income were more likely to modify treatment decisions for patients under utilization management. When compared to evidence-based treatment recommendations, these changes seemed likely to result in less than optimal care.

American Psychological Association

The American Psychological Association also has a PRN. Since 2001, PracticeNet has undertaken five studies using an Internet-based method. Developed by the Practice Directorate with grant support from the Center for Substance Abuse Treatment, PracticeNet uses real-time behaviour sampling to capture specific moments of practitioner activity. Participants include licensed psychologists as well as psychology graduate students, interns and post-docs. These volunteer samples participated in surveys on reactions to 9/11, on the effects of war and terrorism, clinical practice patterns and two substance abuse surveys. Sample sizes varied between 200 and 300. One interesting finding from the practice patterns survey was that 24% of patients with private insurance do not use that benefit, presumably because of privacy concerns. Results are available at www.apapracticenet.net.

The Pennsylvania PRN

To illustrate a PRN in psychological therapies, we should like to review the experience of our research team with the Pennsylvania PRN. Such experience is relevant because of the knowledge and skill obtained in working collaboratively with groups of practitioners in conducting clinically meaningful research.

One of the authors (TB), in conjunction with a private practitioner and a director of a psychology department mental health clinic, successfully established a PRN in the state of Pennsylvania in the late 1990s. The first phase of this endeavour involved (a) the creation of a core assessment battery, standardization of assessment procedures, centralized data management and clinician feedback methods, and recruitment of private practitioner participants, and (b) pilot testing of this infrastructure.

Partial or complete data were obtained from 57 clinicians and 220 clients. As expected, analyses revealed significant client improvements on all measures: symptoms, role functioning, interpersonal functioning, and global client and therapist ratings. Group comparisons of client and therapist characteristics and correlational analyses revealed such significant effects as female clients showing greater improvement than male clients in family relationships, male therapists being associated with greater positive change in client intimacy, greater therapist caseload being related to lessened client outcome, and more positive change being correlated with both the number of sessions received and the client's initial expectancy for improvement (Borkovec et al., 2001). Subsequent research within this phase I of the Pennsylvania PRN found that certain variables of the Inventory of Interpersonal Problems predicted treatment length and outcome (Ruiz et al., 2004).

These studies indicated that a PRN infrastructure could be successfully established even within the context of group and individual private practices throughout a state. Built on lessons learned from these first investigations, a second phase of the Pennsylvania Psychological Association (PPA) PRN was launched within a smaller group of full-time clinicians and full-time researchers in Central Pennsylvania. Before the beginning of the study, therapists and researchers met regularly for approximately one year to design the research method and developed a detailed script of the study procedures. For the next 18 months, therapists then invited all their new clients (adults, adolescents and children) to participate in the study (unless therapists judged such participation to be clinically counter-indicated). Working with very limited resources, the first goal of the Phase II project was to identify what client and therapist find especially helpful or hindering at each session (Castonguay et al., 2007). While the findings identified interesting convergence between client and therapist perception of therapeutic events (e.g. both found particularly helpful events aimed at increasing self-awareness and problem clarification), the most important contribution of this study might be that it demonstrates the level of engagement that therapists can show when conducting a study that they themselves designed in collaboration with researchers. Within the context of their own private practice (and thus with paying clients), 13 therapists recruited close to 150 clients. Furthermore, their efforts led to the description and coding of more than 1,500 therapeutic events. The same PRN has now completed, after more than three years of regular meetings, the design of a third study. This study is planned to be an experimental investigation aimed at testing the causal role of providing feedback to practitioners session-by-session regarding the techniques that the client found particularly helpful (or non-helpful).

One of the authors (LC) has also chaired the committee responsible for the transformation of the Psychological Clinic in the Department of Psychology at Penn State as a PRN. Arguably, one of the factors contributing to the weak connection between research and practice is the difficulty of conducting clinically relevant research during graduate school. Because of the tenuous link between their research requirements (Masters and Dissertation) and clinical training, many graduate students fail to see how research can inform their practice and how, in turn, their clinical practice can be a main source for the generation and implementation of research ideas. To address this issue, an infrastructure was created that allows students (and faculty) to build scientifically rigorous and clinically relevant research.

The training efforts of this PRN obviously parallel the PRN initiatives that have been developed with the collaboration of PPA. These efforts have also taken place in the context of creating a network of psychology training clinics sharing the same outcome battery, with the goal of providing opportunities for large-scale studies across multiple sites (see Borkovec, 2002). In addition, the development of the Penn State Training PRN infrastructure has been facilitated by the large number of clients that are being seen at the clinic, which is the second largest clinic associated with the department of clinical psychology in the United States.

The infrastructure of the Penn State training PRN involves three major components, the first of which is a core outcome battery. The Treatment Outcome Package (TOP; Kraus, Seligman & Jordan, 2005) was chosen for this purpose not only because of its numerous pragmatic advantages and psychometric properties (see Chapter 7), but also because it allows the conduct of analyses comparing samples that cut across different PRN initiatives (Angtuaco, Castonguay & Kraus, 2005). With the option of being complemented by any measures assessing the variables of interest to students' specific projects, the

TOP is assigned to all clinic clients before structured assessment, before session 1, and at session 7, session 15 and every 15 sessions thereafter.

The second component of this training infrastructure is a standardized diagnostic assessment procedure. During the first few years of the PRN training, all clients were assessed at pre-treatment with SCID I and SCID II, and all assessment sessions were video-taped and reviewed by an independent assessor, which in turn was followed by a consensus meeting (within a month of the original assessment) between two assessors on all diagnoses. An assessment of inter-rater agreement, however, revealed a disappointing level of reliability for many diagnoses. As a consequence, a systematic training in structured assessment was conducted, which involved the participation (for almost one full year) of all students and faculty members of the adult track of the clinical programme. While the estimates of reliability on the new instruments selected (i.e. ADIS for Axis I and the IPDE for Axis II diagnoses) are yet to be conducted, our experience clearly suggests that diagnostic reliability in natural settings should not be taken for granted and is likely to deserve intense and systematic attention.

The third major component is a selection committee, which includes representatives from the faculty, clinical staff, students and practitioners from the community. The goal of this committee is to evaluate, based on clearly delineated guidelines and specific criteria (e.g. clinical relevance of the project, minimization of burden on clinical staff), the students' proposals for studies within the clinic. Since the creation of this infrastructure (the establishment of which took four years), the committee has evaluated more than 10 projects (most of them from students), approving all but one of them.

The UK CORE Users' Network

The development of the Clinical Outcomes in Routine Evaluation (CORE) System in the UK has had a major impact (see Chapter 8). This global measure of psychological distress was first developed as a free-to-use paper-based system, then a decade of subsequent development has brought a family of versions for use in different contexts (e.g. short forms for screening or case tracking, forms for young people) (Gray & Mellor-Clark, 2007). The paper-based measure has been supplemented by a data collection infrastructure provided by a specialist firm, which develops software, gives training to services in the use of the suite of measures, organizes a CORE System users' network and benchmarking club, provides feedback to users on how their service outcomes compare with national profiles, and collects CORE outcome data across psychological therapy services in the UK to populate a national research database. This combination of a shared outcome measure, an infrastructure for feedback and a national data set has proved very popular.

The CORE System users' network certainly fulfils two of the functions of a PRN, in that members gain feedback from the participation of others in order to implement service improvements and the resultant data set has been used to address research questions of national or international interest (Barkham et al., 2001). Examples of quality improvement methods include a feedback system where the participating service is given feedback on various indicators of its performance in terms of national benchmarks for the whole data set. On a stacked column chart, the poorest performing quartile is marked in red, the second in amber, the third quartile in yellow and the best performing quartile in green. These 'traffic lights' give a user-friendly method for an individual or a group practice to benchmark both process indicators and clinical outcomes to those of the network as a whole.

The scientific yield from the UK CORE National Research Dataset is starting to be realized. For example, Stiles et al. (2006, 2008a) used evidence from the CORE data set in two large-scale practice-based studies on people presenting with common mental health problems in routine practice, showing that although cognitive behaviour therapy gave slightly better outcomes than person-centred therapy or psychodynamic therapy, the difference had little clinical significance. The data set suffers the shortcomings of PRN data discussed further below: uncontrolled bias in client selection from volunteer samples and relatively poor data quality compared with a well-conducted trial. Although these shortcomings were noted by the authors, some psychological researchers believe that because of them, this paradigm is of little value (Clark et al., 2008). However, many of the specific criticisms can be rebutted (Stiles et al., 2008b), and the main argument in its favour is that these descriptive results are more representative of outcomes in routine practice than trials data, and can complement the information obtained from trials.

UK Art Therapists' PRN

A contrasting approach to a PRN is provided in the UK by the Art Therapy Practice Research Network (Huet, Springham & Evans, 2008). This is a single-profession PRN which epitomizes the 'bottom-up' approach. Art therapists struggle to feel comfortable within what many see as a rigid, doctrinaire paradigm of evidence-based practice, a discourse which favours experimental evidence over theory and description (Wood, 1999). The ATPRN aims to bridge the gap between researchers and practitioners through fostering a collaboration of practising art therapists who are engaged in practice-led research and evaluation. The PRN exists through providing the structures for collaboration and mutual support between practitioners to help them evaluate services and produce publishable research evidence. It is explicitly a means of clinicians being involved in research without undertaking specialist training in that discipline. A broad range of practitioner-led projects are undertaken, rather than a pooling of data for a national data set.

UK ACAT PRN feasibility study

Another practitioner-led initiative was taken by the Association for Cognitive Analytic Therapy (ACAT) which commissioned a study to assess the feasibility of setting up a PRN amongst cognitive analytic therapists in the UK (Parry et al., 2006). The aims were: to establish whether secure web-based technology could be used to engage members in a PRN, to explore methods to obtain PRN membership that was representative of the total population of CAT practitioners and to make recommendations about sustainability. An online survey of members gave a 70% response rate, and was informative about the working practice of members. The CORE Net System was used (Gray & Mellor-Clark, 2007) and found to be a feasible method to engage practitioners, in that it was rewarding for participating individuals, giving quick feedback and case-tracking methods. The cost and security of the system were not limiting factors. There were two main barriers to representative participation. First, a large majority of CAT therapists were employed in the UK National Health Service (NHS) and there were potential conflicts between an individual's willingness to participate and the data-sharing policy of his or her employer. Where NHS employers have their own outcomes data collection and analysis systems, they may be unwilling for employees to share data (albeit anonymized and secure) with anyone outside the NHS. Even if this were not the case, therapists may be unwilling to enter data twice, into two entirely separate systems. Second, the membership survey showed that although most respondents did use outcome measures, a large minority did not, so that any PRN would be unlikely to capture the interest and participation of a representative group. Neither of these barriers was insurmountable, but required careful attention prior to setting up the PRN.

Strengths and weaknesses of PRNs for research purposes

There are clearly many advantages to the researcher of PRN-based data (Audin et al., 2001). The network is more able than small-scale trials to capture data on representative patients who are receiving representative treatments, although this is not automatically the case, and care needs to be taken in setting up the PRN to ensure that this is indeed so (Norquist, 2001). It becomes possible to assess the utility of an intervention provided by clinicians with a broad range of training and expertise rather than the more tightly controlled range of therapists typically available in a trial. It is also possible to obtain clinically detailed, patient-level data with the flexibility to collect and analyse data from a variety of perspectives (e.g. clinician, patient, system). With the potential for certain types of experimental design to be employed, the PRN advantage is that very large Ns are possible, meaning that even very small effect sizes can be detected as statistically significant and thus facilitating the identification of causal treatment elements. The more causes of change that can be identified, the more we will be able to include those causes into our developing therapies (see Borkovec & Castonguay, 1998).

The weaknesses and disadvantages of the paradigm are evident (Zarin et al., 1997). In cases of PRN research that do not employ experimental design, there is obviously a limited ability to control for biases or to infer causality. For all types of design, where the psychological therapist treating the patient collects the outcome data, particularly using patient self-report measures, there is likely to be bias compared with independent assessment. Data collection is not often performed in standardized ways, and most clinicians lack specialized research training. For example, even where clinicians agree to use the same outcome measure, there can be a great deal of variability in when and how it is administered (e.g. in the waiting room prior to the session, in the therapy room with or without the therapist present, after the therapy session or in the patient's home and returned by post). Practitioners rarely make data collection their highest priority in a busy clinic, given competing demands and inadequate support from research assistants or administrators, so missing data are universal. Everyone finds that intake data are much easier to collect than repeated measures, end-of-treatment or follow-up data, and high attrition rates (e.g. between 30–60%) are a major bane of PRN data sets. With this level of attrition and resultant bias, the validity of any conclusions drawn about the sample is questionable. Other sources of bias can occur when the PRN is an 'enthusiasts' club', hence unrepresentative of normal practice. Uncontrolled case selection can also introduce bias as the basis for choosing which cases to include in the database. There is a tension between clinicians' and researchers' aims, and balancing the needs of both can be very difficult.

Possibly for all these reasons, the research yield of PRNs has been as yet modest and, we would argue, disappointing. Although it could be argued that the weaknesses of the paradigm are not remediable, we would argue that the PRN approach is in its infancy and has not been adequately resourced or supported to realize its full potential.

The 'top-down' approach, where researchers lead and organize the network to provide research data, is one common response to these problems but is unlikely to retain the active participation and support of practitioners unless they feel some ownership of the enterprise and share its aims. At its most extreme, this approach more closely resembles a practitioner survey than a mutually beneficial network.

There are a number of ways in which, as research infrastructure, PRNs can be improved. First, in setting up a PRN, it is important to give adequate time and resources to data collection and management in a way that is sustainable. It may be easier to obtain infrastructure funding for the role of the PRN in service audit and quality improvement than as a research tool. Research funding tends to be allocated on the basis of specific projects rather than for infrastructure support. Research funding will also be lacking unless PRNs pay detailed attention to data quality and project design. In this respect, it is too easy for a PRN to yield opportunity samples that are of less value than systematic ones. It is therefore valuable to establish the sampling frame carefully. For example, it is important to estimate how representative PRN members are of the population of practitioners from which they are drawn. Volunteer samples can be supplemented with a probability sample of practitioners for specific projects.

One way to improve data quality (i.e. to reduce rates of attrition and missing data) is for the PRN to focus its efforts in collecting very high quality data on a specific sample of patients over a time-limited case series. Here, members agree to gather repeated measures in a prospective sample of all new patients referred over a specific period, rather than obtaining ongoing, sporadic and incomplete data only on a group of patients selected by the therapist.

PRNs are undoubtedly valuable in yielding very large data sets of routinely collected outcome measures, but there is usually a high rate of attrition. It is thus worth analysing results from services with a high data quality separately, to test whether results differ significantly from those with poorer quality data. In addition to this use of PRN data, there is a role for a PRN to address specific research questions. The PRN needs a method to generate and prioritize members' questions and to develop the protocol. Here the large data set is valuable in providing a rich context within which the smaller scale and more specific projects can be embedded.

The longer term success of a PRN is likely to depend on its value to individual practitioners as a source of information about their own clients' progress, possibly benchmarked against other similar clients seen in the PRN. This requires a lot of effort in creating a practitioner-friendly infrastructure, at every level from involvement in PRN strategy and management to end-user satisfaction, by receiving fast and accurate feedback about their own data and the broader work of the PRN. Practitioners may also be under local management pressure to participate within their own organizations' data collection and analysis systems, and discouraged from sharing data in a democratic PRN. Any way to strengthen local management and support for PRN participation is therefore extremely valuable; important issues to clarify in this regard are ethical review, data security, data ownership and intellectual property in relation to PRN products.

Issues for the future

It is hard to see PRNs in their mature form prospering without adequate funding, and this raises the question of who funds PRNs for research purposes?

At present there is no clear answer to this question and to obtain one will require consistent, patient work on developing the paradigm and 'selling' its potential to those responsible for resource allocation in healthcare and health research.

Addressing employers' and funders' concerns is also likely to grow in importance, given potential clashes with local data management systems and outcome monitoring schemes. The details of this specific concern differ between the UK, with its more centralized system of public ownership of most mental health services, and the US, with more regional and topical diversity in private health insurance companies, some of which are very large. However, the steady move in the UK towards greater use of private finance and provision within the NHS may bring the two systems closer over the next decade.

In conclusion, the greatest challenge to PRN enthusiasts in the next few years is demonstrating the value of paradigm in yielding valid evidence, useful not only locally but in international research journals. A key to this is in managing the tension between routine use for clinical audit and the levels of data quality needed for research yield. As the paradigm develops to rise to this challenge, it will be possible to answer the key question – can PRN evidence find an accepted place in research effort?

References

Angtuaco, L.A., Castonguay, L.G. & Kraus, D.R. (June, 2005). *The TOP: A core battery for the assessment of psychotherapy outcome.* Paper presented at the Annual Meeting of the Society for Psychotherapy Research, Montreal, Canada.

Audin, K., Mellor-Clark. J., Barkham, M., Margison, F., McGrath, G. *et al.* (2001) Practice research networks for effective psychological therapies. *Journal of Mental Health, 10,* 241–251.

Barkham, M., Margison, F., Leach, C., Lucock, M., Mellor-Clark, J. *et al.* (2001). Service profiling and outcomes benchmarking using the CORE-OM: Towards practice-based evidence in the psychological therapies. *Journal of Consulting and Clinical Psychology, 69,* 184–196.

Black, N. (1996). Why we need observational studies to evaluate the effectiveness of health care. *British Medical Journal, 312,* 1215–1218.

Borkovec, T.D. (2002). Training clinic research and the possibility of a national training clinics practice research network. *The Behavior Therapist, 25,* 98–103.

Borkovec, T.D. & Castonguay, L.G. (1998). What is the scientific meaning of 'empirically supported therapy?' *Journal of Consulting and Clinical Psychology, 66,* 136–142.

Borkovec, T.D., Echemendia, R.J., Ragusea, S.A. & Ruiz, M. (2001). The Pennsylvania Practice Research Network and future possibilities for clinically meaningful and scientifically rigorous psychotherapy effectiveness research. *Clinical Psychology Science and Practice, 8*, 155–167.

Castonguay, L.G. & Borkovec, T.D. (August, 2005). *Practice Research Networks: An antidote for empirical imperialism.* Paper presented at the Annual Meeting of the American Psychological Association, Washington, DC.

Castonguay, L.G., Boswell, J.F., Zack, S., Montellese, J., Baker, S. et al. (June, 2007). *Helpful and hindering events in psychotherapy: A practice research network study.* Paper presented at the Annual Meeting of the Society for Psychotherapy Research, Madison, Wisconsin.

Clark, D.M., Fairburn C.G. & Wessely S. (2008). Psychological treatment outcomes in routine NHS services: a commentary on Stiles et al. (2007) *Psychological Medicine, 38*, 629–634.

Fenton, E., Harvey, J., Griffiths F., Wild, A. & Sturt, J. (2001). Reflections from organizational science on the development of primary health care research networks. *Family Practice, 18*, 540–544.

Gray, P. & Mellor-Clark, J. (2007). *CORE: A decade of development.* Rugby, UK: CORE Information Management Systems.

Green, L.A, Wood M., Becker, L., Farley, E.S. Jr, Freeman W.L. *et al.* (1984). The Ambulatory Sentinel Practice Network: purpose, methods, and policies. *Journal of Family Practice, 18*, 275–280.

Huet, V., Springham, N. & Evans, C. (2008). Art Therapy Practice Research Network, at http://www.baat.org/atprn.html

Kraus, D.R., Seligman, D. & Jordan, J.R. (2005). Validation of a behavioral health treatment outcome and assessment tool designed for naturalistic settings: The Treatment Outcome Package. *Journal of Clinical Psychology, 61*, 285–314.

Mintz, D.C., Marcus, S.C., Druss, B.G., West, J.C. & Brickman, A.L. (2004). Association of Utilization Management and Treatment plan modifications among practicing US psychiatrists. *American Journal of Psychiatry, 161*, 1103–1109.

Norquist, G.N. (2001). Practice Research Networks: promises and pitfalls. *Clinical Psychology Science and Practice, 8*, 173–175.

Parry, G. (1998). Psychotherapy services, health care policy and clinical audit. In R. Davenhill & M. Patrick (eds.), *Reconstructing clinical audit.* London: Routledge.

Parry, G., Cape, J. & Pilling, S. (2003). Clinical practice guidelines in clinical psychology and psychotherapy. *Clinical Psychology and Psychotherapy, 10*, 337–351.

Parry, G., Dunn, M., Potter, S., Saxon, D. & Sloper, J. (2006). *An ACAT Practice Research Network: Report on a feasibility study*. Association for Cognitive Analytic Therapy, at www.acat.me.uk

Pincus, H.A., Zarin D.A., Tenielian, T.L., Johnson, J.L., West, J.C. *et al.* (1999). Psychiatric patients and treatments in 1997: Findings from the American Psychiatric Practice Research Network. *Archives of General Psychiatry, 56,* 441–449.

Saxon, D., Fitzgerald, G., Houghton, S., Lemme, F., Saul, C. et al. (2007). Psychotherapy provision, socioeconomic deprivation, and the inverse care law. *Psychotherapy Research, 17,* 515–521.

Stiles, W.B., Barkham, M., Mellor-Clark, J. & Connell, J. (2008a). Effectiveness of cognitive-behavioural, person-centred, and psychodynamic therapies in UK primary-care routine practice: replication in a larger sample. *Psychological Medicine, 38,* 677–688.

Stiles, W.B., Barkham, M., Mellor-Clark, J. & Connell, J. (2008b). Routine psychological treatment and the Dodo verdict: Rejoinder to Clark et al. (2007). *Psychological Medicine, 38,* 905–910.

Stiles, W.B., Barkham, M., Twigg, E., Mellor-Clark, J. & Cooper, M. (2006). Effectiveness of cognitive-behavioural, person-centred and psychodynamic therapies as practised in UK National Health Service settings. *Psychological Medicine, 36,* 555–566.

Westen, D., Novotny, C.M. & Thompson-Brunner, H. (2004). The empirical status of empirically supported psychotherapies: assumptions, findings and reporting in controlled clinical trials. *Psychological Bulletin, 130,* 631–663.

Wolf, A.W. (2005). Practice Research Networks in Psychotherapy. *Psychotherapy Bulletin, 40,* 39–42.

Wolf, A.W. (2007). On implementing the scientist-practitioner model in a hospital setting. *Journal of Contemporary Psychotherapy. 37,* 229–234.

Wood, C. (1999). Gathering evidence: expansion of art therapy research strategy. *Inscape, 4,* 51–61.

Zarin, D.A., Pincus, H.A., West, J.C. & McIntyre, J.S. (1997). Practice-based research in psychiatry. *American Journal of Psychiatry, 154,* 1199–1208.

Section VI

Developing and Delivering Practice-Based Evidence

13

Improving Practice and Enhancing Evidence

Michael Barkham[1], Gillian E. Hardy[2] and John Mellor-Clark[3]

[1] Centre for Psychological Services Research, University of Sheffield, UK,
[2] Clinical Psychology Unit, University of Sheffield, UK, [3] CORE IMS,
Rugby, UK.

Introduction

Practice-based evidence is a growing and developing paradigm for building on our existing knowledge base of the psychological therapies. As such, it should be set within the broader context of efforts at bridging the gap between research and practice in the field of the psychological therapies (e.g. see Goodheart, Kazdin & Sternberg, 2006). Powerful arguments for broadening the acceptability of methods by which we collect and evaluate evidence have been presented both in the US (APA, 2006) and in the UK (Rawlins, 2008). The American Psychological Association article entitled *Evidence-based practice in psychology* (2006) was directed specifically to a psychology audience and set out a clear and broad research agenda that included investigating models of treatment based on practitioners yielding the best outcomes. The key oration by Sir Michael Rawlins, Chair of the National Institute for Health and Clinical Excellence, entitled *De Testimonio: On the evidence for decisions about the use of therapeutic interventions* (2008) – also published in *The Lancet* (2008) – was directed to a medical audience and argued for valuing all research methods providing they were fit for purpose. More specifically, he made a clear call for abandoning the traditional hierarchy of evidence in which randomized controlled trials (RCTs) dominate. The issues surrounding this debate have been covered elsewhere and so we will not repeat them here (see Barkham et al., Chapter 2). However, the fact that key professional and strategic authorities in both the US and UK

Developing and Delivering Practice-Based Evidence   By Michael Barkham, Gillian E Hardy, and John Mellor-Clark   © 2010 John Wiley & Sons, Ltd

recognize the need to incorporate both a focus on the practitioner as well as the treatment, and also to encompass a broader base for establishing a relevant evidence base, suggests a critical shift in the future direction of research and the types of evidence that might be valued.

Evidence-based practice has been able to deliver a very clear and defined knowledge base by the adoption of rigorous methods drawn from medicine (see Bower & Gilbody, Chapter 1). By contrast, practice-based evidence encompasses a wide range of approaches that are both its strength and its vulnerability. Unlike trials, which have the hallmark of randomization, the equivalent hallmark of practice-based studies is its mirroring of routine practice: this is indeed the essence of practice-based evidence. One of the main drivers behind this approach is the recognition of the limitations of randomized trials for building a robust and relevant knowledge base and their privileged place in what has traditionally been presented as the hierarchy of evidence. A strong argument has been mounted for practice-based methods to be viewed as complementary to trials methodology, not least on the basis that trials lack key attributes when used in the psychological therapies as compared with genuine double-blind drugs trials, the context for which they were designed (see Barkham & Mellor-Clark, 2003; Barkham et al., Chapter 2). Trials are undoubtedly extremely valuable but they do not answer all the questions we need to know in order to develop a comprehensive knowledge base of the psychological therapies.

In his oration, Rawlins (2008) drew on the concept of *teleoanalysis* – derived from the Greek *teleos* meaning complete or thorough – as a driving rationale for taking a broader view of evidence. The term, which appeared earlier in an article by Wald and Morris (2003), denotes combining studies that utilize differing classes of research that would not otherwise be summarized within a single format (as is the case in meta-analysis). The aspiration of *completeness* captures the intrinsic constraints in adopting any single model of evidence, no matter what form it takes. Hence, our aspiration is to contribute to that completeness by extending the evidence base for the psychological therapies. Against this backdrop, we aim to bring together key themes and implications of practice-based evidence, which have appeared in earlier chapters, and consider how, as a paradigm, it can contribute to and extend our knowledge base of the psychological therapies. We provide examples of practice-based work, locate the approaches presented in the preceding chapters within this broader context, and finally set out some of the opportunities afforded by this developing paradigm.

The world of practice-based evidence

Although the term *practice-based evidence* is in general use, it is unclear where the term first appeared in print. It is certainly likely to have been in use within communities of practitioners before appearing in publications but was sufficiently robust as a concept by the turn of the millennium to appear in documents within a number of professions. For example, accounts of the basic components of an approach to practice-based evidence by individual practitioners, as well as calls for it adoption, appeared within the UK in the field of chiropractics at the close of the 1990s (e.g. Cook, 1999; Osborne, 1999). At the same time, a programme of work focusing on the yield from the adoption of the CORE measures and system also used the term within the field of the psychological therapies (e.g. Barkham & Mellor-Clark, 2000; Margison et al., 2000; Mellor-Clark et al., 1999). Similarly, Krakau (2000) also used the term in commenting on the dual publication in the *New England Journal of Medicine* of articles by Concato, Shah and Horwitz (2000) and by Benson and Hartz (2000) that suggested no difference in estimates of treatment effects between RCTs and non-randomized trials (i.e. observational studies). That these disparate and independent publications made explicit reference to the term at the same time suggests that the recognition of a need for a complementary paradigm to that of evidence-based practice was gaining ground both within professional bodies as well as in research.

These developments were not, however, without a wider context and influence. Within the psychological therapies there was a burgeoning literature utilizing large data sets from health insurance companies in the US and continental Europe emanating from the pioneering work of people such as Ken Howard and Michael Lambert. And there was the related but, in our view conceptually different, literature referred to as *effectiveness* research that was gaining ground in the realization of the need to show that findings from trials could generalize to practice (e.g. Merrill, Tolbert & Wade, 2003; Wade, Treat & Stuart, 1998). However, practice-based evidence differs in fundamental ways from effectiveness research. The latter, as part of its hallmark, incorporates the implementation of trials apparatus into practice settings (e.g. diagnosis, treatment adherence). By contrast, practice-based evidence starts from a position of capturing the reality of everyday routine practice and finding ways of evaluating and improving it by adopting a *bottom-up* approach – that is, starting with the work of practitioners and building the evidence base upwards to the level of policy rather than vice versa.

Notwithstanding the merits of the evidence-based movement, when viewed beyond the confines of medicine however, there appears to have been relatively little – if any – attention paid to adapting the principles and procedures to specific professions or disciplines other than medicine. The assumption appears to have been that evidence-based practice is a universal process that can be transferred from profession to profession without adjustment. But this rigidity has been problematic, not least because we live and work in a multidisciplinary and multicultural environment.

Multidisciplinary and multicultural

In terms of a multidisciplinary environment, practice-based evidence has been considered as having an important role. For example, within the discipline of qualitative inquiry Staller (2006) has presented a well-argued case for adopting *practice-based evidence* with a central role for practitioners and an emphasis on the pluralistic use of evidence. Accordingly, she argues that evidence needs to be viewed as 'situated, contextual, case specific, and requires an interpretive, process-oriented approach to evaluation' (p. 512). And in sociology, Fox (2003) has promoted practice-based evidence as having the objective to 're-privilege the role of the practitioner in generating useful knowledge without rejecting the skills and perspectives of the academic researcher' (p. 82). He identified three underlying propositions for generating practice-based evidence that we briefly summarize here.

First, like Staller, he argues that the pursuit of knowledge should be recognized as a local and contingent process. That is, research activity derives from specific local issues making it context-dependent with these conditions that, by definition, do not necessarily hold for other localities. Underlying this issue is that of generalizability. It has often been argued that a specific vulnerability of research activity is that findings may not generalize to practice settings. However, it is more complex than this because 'practice settings' differ amongst themselves, reflecting differing service configurations, resources, contextual factors, etc. In effect, this is about acknowledging individual differences at multiple levels within and between services and the specific features that may apply to one setting and not another. Second, research activity should be constitutive of difference, by which is meant acknowledging the limitations of seeking universal rules or seeking to impose one form of research over another as a function of a hierarchy of evidence – a notion akin to that mentioned earlier (see Rawlins, 2008). In our context, this proposition most closely relates to that of methodological pluralism that ensures using the multiplicity of research methodologies available in order to be able to capture the richness of experience. And third, theory-building should be seen as an adjunct to practical activity. In other words, there needs to be a direct relevance of any theoretical model-building to practice settings. Put another way, theories need to have practical applications – they need to improve practice.

Because of the flexibility or responsiveness of practice-based evidence, it has been adopted as a paradigm in services and settings in which implementing trials are problematic. For example, working within the field of cultural and ethnic minority groups, Isaacs et al. (2005) defined practice-based evidence as 'a range of treatment approaches and supports that are derived from, and supportive of, the positive cultural attributes of the local society and traditions'. In the context of interventions for children with serious emotional and behavioural problems, Walker and Bruns (2006) have invoked the paradigm of practice-based evidence and report on the wraparound process – a long-term approach to planning and coordinating the provision of both formal and informal services in the community – and describe its being shaped into a consensus by stakeholders. And Lyons and McCulloch (2006) have reported on the application of a practice-based paradigm in a state-wide evaluation of residential care for children. Meanwhile Dupree et al. (2007) reported on a study with the aim of distilling and disseminating the aggregated wisdom from practitioners relating to treating infidelity in couples therapy into a practice-based evidence model. And at a social level, McDonald and Viehbeck (2007) developed the notion of *communities of practice* that emphasize the aim for a community between researchers and practitioners. These examples show the diversity of situations and settings in which a practice-based approach is seen to provide an overarching framework. Indeed, the paradigm has also been invoked in the field of clinical oncology in relation to the impact of positron emission tomography (Larson, 2007).

Practice improvement

In relation to the purpose of practice-based evidence, there is a clear movement in the area of physical health for adopting the paradigm in pursuit of delivering best practice. For example, in the US, Horn and colleagues have espoused a methodology they term *practice-based evidence for clinical practice improvement* (Horn et al., 2005; Horn & Gassaway, 2007). Their work is drawn from the fields of stroke and rehabilitation and yet fits perfectly with the aspirations we have striven to present in the preceding chapters. What is perhaps most striking about this approach is its direct linkage between the principles of practice-based evidence and quality improvements in clinical practice. Horn and colleagues have argued that it is impossible for a randomized clinical trial to test all possible interactions among interventions encountered in routine practice. By contrast, the large and natural variation encountered in current practice within and between services provides the opportunity for evaluating the relative effectiveness of differing treatment combinations. The purpose of this methodology is to identify medications and interventions that are associated with better outcomes for specific types of patients in real-world practice.

Practice-based evidence for the psychological therapies

In the context of the above, we need to consider how the approaches presented in the preceding chapters can develop and deliver a form of practice-based evidence that will yield better practice and enhance our knowledge base of the psychological therapies. The range of approaches set out in earlier chapters derive from methods that can be used by practitioners to address questions of practical relevance to their service delivery. They are, in effect, a practitioner's toolkit. Which approach – or tool – they use depends on the question(s) to be addressed. Different tools are required for differing tasks and no single approach is fit for all purposes.

Hallmarks of practice-based evidence

An account of the activity of practice-based evidence in the psychological therapies has been presented (e.g. Margison, 2001) and a recent review set out seven building blocks (i.e. components) for establishing practice-based evidence (see Barkham & Margison, 2007). The first three blocks comprise: (1) the adoption of practice-based evidence as a complementary approach to evidence-based practice together with (2) support from some form of infrastructure and (3) the collaboration with a broader network of practitioners. Together they reflect the aspiration of adopting a practice-based approach together with the simple support systems required for any form of systematic evidence collection. The next two components comprise (4) the adoption of a common approach to measurement and outcomes together with (5) the application and use of such tools in generating new information. These components provide the engine for practice-based evidence – the collection and results of applying measurement systems in practice. The final two components convey the yield from such efforts via the dual strands of (6) reflective (i.e. improving) practice and (7) synthesizing the information gained from practice-based research with that of evidence-based practice – that is, together they promote the aims of improving practice and enhancing evidence. Each of these components can be seen to facilitate five defined hallmarks of practice-based evidence that encapsulate the endeavour: the practitioner, methodological pluralism and equipoise, theory building, meaningful measurement, and finally ownership and partnership. These hallmarks serve to build a science of routine practice.

The practitioner

Crucially, practice-based evidence starts with the practitioner – and in this sense it is the logical underpinning for delivering an evidence base on the *effective practitioner*. Regardless of theoretical orientation, practitioners work to effect change with their clients. What is required to support this approach is a method, or methods, for collecting and presenting such evidence. A key reason for placing the practitioner centre stage is that, regardless of the organization or context within which they work, people are always an organization's greatest asset and resource. By implication also, they are invariably the most financially costly component. Accordingly, focusing on practitioners and providing them with tools for evaluating their effectiveness makes good sense in terms of human resources and cost, as well as ensuring that treatments as delivered are cost-effective. Krause, Lutz and Saunders (2007) have argued for the logical difficulty in separating between forms of treatment as opposed to separating between practitioners and note the greater confidence that can be achieved in separating between practitioners than between forms of treatment. Accordingly, having such a focus transcends any particular treatment approach. That is, regardless of treatment orientation, practitioners and services will strive to deliver effective and quality services. This is a common language across modalities and settings and is one that practice-based evidence is well suited to address.

Methodological pluralism and equipoise

Practice-based research is *pluralistic* with regards to research methods. In this volume, we have, very explicitly, placed qualitative approaches as the starting point set within the context of the individual practitioner (see Pistrang & Barker, Chapter 3; Stiles, Chapter 4). From the previous chapters we can see the arguments for diverse methods and approaches to research and the frequent statement that no single research method or evidence-base is preferred. Moreover, the argument goes that, used properly, different evidence sources are complementary – they improve our understanding of complex phenomena and they both challenge and develop theory. But this is more than a simple combination of qualitative and quantitative or process and outcomes approaches. Indeed, all these approaches have been successfully combined within existing trials methodology (e.g. see Barkham, Hardy & Shapiro, in press). As Kazdin states: '. . . investing narrowly . . . in a single methodological tradition such as quantitative psychology, invariably bears a cost' (2008, p. 154).

A key feature of practice-based evidence is that it draws on the routine practice of a huge swathe of practitioners of differing theoretical orientations, experience and specialisms. There are undoubtedly large numbers of experienced practitioners who exit the profession each year and whilst some of this experience remains with colleagues, there is no strategy of constructing an evidence base that utilizes that knowledge. Indeed, Kazdin (2008) argues that we are letting knowledge 'drip away' through not capturing the accumulated data that could be collected in routine settings. Capturing this knowledge requires the collection of routine data.

However, within the paradigm of practice-based evidence routine data and its collection need to be owned by practitioners and by the delivery system. Not only this, but they then need to access it and use it in order for the information it yields to become part of their working memory. The use of data and particularly its presentation should enable practitioners to build mental maps of their caseload and provide them with perspectives on their work that otherwise would have been inaccessible. This, then, is about a cultural shift whereby practitioners strive towards being evidence-based and viewing every client as contributing to the evidence regardless of outcome. However, this call should not be confused with the requirement that data is demanded of all clients. Within a practice-based paradigm, a client who resists or refuses to give data is yielding important information providing we place an equal emphasis on data that is missing – that is, missing data has value. Other clients become a rich source of evidence about the process change that would be inaccessible via a group design. This is beautifully portrayed in a single case study of the process and outcomes across therapy that used repeated administration of the CORE-SF measure in conjunction with representations and categories of the client's own art work as indicators of change (Greenwood et al., 2007). Hence the importance of adopting the single case approach and ensuring that this tradition is incorporated into practice-based evidence using both quantitative and qualitative approaches (see McMillan & Morley, Chapter 5; Pistrang & Barker, Chapter 3).

Measurement and meaning

Another facet of ensuring quality is the development of robust measurement systems. Crucially, the adoption of a common methodology enables the accumulation of data from routine settings over time (e.g. Gibbard & Hanley, 2008). However, we need to ensure the principle of meaningful measurement – that is, we need to know that the items being summed into an overall effect size or any other form of outcome indicator really do translate into meaningful change in the world of individual clients. In the same way that trials can provide general principles for interventions, so nomothetic measures provide the ability to locate and place an individual within the population of clients presenting for help. But single or primary indicators of change, as adopted in trials on the basis of pre-defined criteria for determining the impact of the intervention, are relatively poor at capturing the complexity and variation of change and fuel a unidimensional approach to evaluating change. There are good reasons for such measurement approaches to be complemented with patient-generated indices (e.g. idiographic measures) derived from clients' felt experiences so that we have increased confidence that change reported in those items translates directly into specific and meaningful change in that individual client's world.

Increasingly, benchmarking and case tracking – in effect, benchmarking in real time – have come to prominence (see Lueger & Barkham, Chapter 9; Leach & Lutz, Chapter 10). In many ways, case tracking can be seen as containing elements of a supervisory process in which practitioners are required to assimilate information about the process of therapy via a different perspective. It also acts as a safety device – an external voice – which flags up when progress, or lack of it, should be noted and acted upon. However, we should also ensure we use repeated measurement in the best ways possible. As stated earlier, part of the rationale for repeated measures is to seek patterns in how clients are responding to psychological interventions. In addition, it can be used to signal off-track cases (see Lambert et al., Chapter 6). However, we should be careful of adopting repeated measurement only to secure a single final measurement administration (should the client decide to unilaterally terminate treatment). Repeated measurement in practice-based evidence must have an ongoing purpose and yield – that is, in relation to clinical aspects of treatment (e.g. clinical monitoring, identification of work to target, flags for supervision) or building a more in-formed evidence base via utilizing the shapes of change as richer summary descriptives of change than as summarized by simple change scores.

It is undoubtedly true that all concerned with the evaluation of the psycho-logical therapies aspire to more comprehensive data. But we should also be mindful of how, for example, the notion of complete data is a fallacy. Some people will always refuse to complete a measure and others might do so by giv-ing less than honest responses. Hence, there will always be a tipping point where securing more data comes at a cost of unreliable data, thereby undermining the very purpose it set out to achieve. This can also occur on single items within measures where requiring all items to be completed can yield rogue responses on those items that a client would rather omit. In clinical settings, a missing item becomes a vehicle for discussion – that is, missed items provide informa-tion, they tell the practitioner something. It is known as the value of missing data. The availability of large data sets that contain missing items provides an opportunity for researchers to investigate this phenomenon. Hence, the issue is not one of *complete* data but rather one of *meaningful* data.

Ownership and partnership

Finally, in the same way that data needs to be owned by practitioners, it equally needs to be owned by clients and users, and shared (anonymously) within prac-tice networks or other forms of collaboration (see Parry et al., Chapter 12). A key aim is to bring data into the open and make it a shared point of reference between all stakeholders, most notably between client and practitioner. Cru-cially, therefore, data must have meaning and relevance to the clinical activity between client and practitioner. At the heart of this endeavour is the aim of improving the user's experience of psychological therapies and the evidence base upon which decisions are based. But this is reliant on their providing data that is relevant rather than rigid. In effect, we need to fit measurement to the person and not the other way around – hence the need for us to give serious consideration to patient-generated indices. The question is: What do we need to know about this client, at this point in time, that has most meaning for them and their treatment? By approaching the task in this way, we will hopefully place practice-based evidence at the heart of clinical activity and set the task for research to meet that challenge (see Elliott & Zucconi, Chapter 11).

Improving practice

The twin aspiration of improving practice and enhancing evidence is a well-acknowledged aim. Kazdin (2008), amongst others, has promoted this dual agenda as a means of helping to bridge the scientist-practitioner gap. While his suggested strategy comprises shifts in emphases on the part of both research and practice, our focus here is on the latter as a means of providing the best possible evidence base to complement trials and more traditional approaches. At the heart of Kazdin's call regarding practice is the activity of measurement. However, it is probably too simple to view such systems as being only focused on quantitative data or as focusing only on outcomes related to nomothetic (i.e. standardized) measures. A primary concern is to ensure measurement systems capture data that matters and that will inform clinical decision making and/or help build an understanding of change. A key principle of practice improvement has been to work as a change agency using data derived from individual practitioners and services with the purpose of identifying current vulnerabilities within a service and then addressing them.

Capturing the world of the psychological therapies

Ultimately, the aspiration shared with evidence-based practice is that of informing and enhancing practice, and measurement systems, however they are defined or constituted, lie at the heart. In the US, in addition to the systems presented earlier in this text (see Lambert et al., Chapter 6; Kraus & Castonguay, Chapter 7), examples of such work include the client-directed outcome-informed (CDOI) practice as espoused by Barry Duncan, Scott Miller and colleagues (Duncan, Miller & Sparks, 2004, 2007), and also work by Jeb Brown and colleagues (Brown et al., 2005). In the UK, the CAMHS Outcomes Research Consortium (CORC) led by Miranda Wolpert and colleagues (e.g. Wolpert, 2008) and the CORE User Network led by CORE IMS (e.g. Gray & Mellor-Clark, 2007) have pioneered learning collaborations that support services' aspirations to enhance practice. Both the latter initiatives share a common philosophy of utilizing practice networks to support sharing and learning from routine data in service of developing improved psychological therapy services. We present brief profiles of CDOI, CORE and CORC as exemplars of pioneers in the operational growth of practice-based evidence.

Client-Directed Outcome-Informed (CDOI) approach

The CDOI approach is fully described in Duncan, Miller and Sparks' *The Heroic Client: A revolutionary way to improve effectiveness through client-directed, outcome-informed therapy* (2004). This approach espoused by Duncan and colleagues contains no fixed techniques and no causal theory regarding the concerns that bring people to psychological therapy. Their view is that any interaction with a client can be client-directed and outcome-informed when the client's voice is privileged as the source of knowledge and solution and helpers purposefully form strong partnerships with clients with three key objectives. Firstly, to enhance the factors across theories that account for successful outcome. Second, to use the client's ideas and preferences (i.e. their theory of change) to guide choice of technique and model. And third, adopting reliable and valid outcome measures, as well as the therapeutic alliance, to inform practitioners' ongoing therapeutic work. A full profile of the evolving methodology espoused by Miller and colleagues, the software platform that supports it, and the full range of their support can be located at www.talkingcure.com

Clinical Outcomes in Routine Evaluation (CORE) approach

The CORE approach comprises a methodology built initially around an integrated outcome and monitoring system that embeds outcomes within contextual data that profiles key processes and variables considered crucial to influencing how services might vary. The rationale has been to provide a system for *quality evaluation* that encourages practitioners to reflect on profiles of success (i.e. recovered and/or improved clients) or the lack of success (i.e. non-engagement with therapy, non-completion, or clinical deterioration). The philosophy has always been to capture data and develop feedback systems that can generate information for practitioners and managers about how to develop and deliver better quality services to clients. This work has been summarized elsewhere (see Barkham et al., Chapter 8) and an accessible summary of the approach is presented in *CORE: A decade of development* (Gray & Mellor-Clark, 2007).

The original CORE methodology combined CORE-OM with context data tools for assessment and discharge profiling and utilized a traditional pre- and post-therapy methodology. However, informed by the pioneering feedback development studies of Michael Lambert, Jeb Brown and Scott Miller, the CORE methodology has evolved to offer increasing flexibility using a family of tracking and feedback measures (e.g. CORE-10, CORE-5), and further process measures (e.g. alliance) to offer an online platform for routine session-by-session data capture and feedback. The benefits gained from using such a flexible methodology include the following: providing practitioners with clinical tracking tools to reflect (visually) on individual clients' progress; the provision of flags and alerts to draw attention to particularly vulnerable clients; the ability for practitioners to manage and own a personal database to help manage case-mix, supervision and continuing personal development; the provision of feedback for clients and the ability for them to interpret and locate their own outcomes; the provision of personal benchmarks to locate clinical performance and service quality; and information for service managers to assess and develop service performance. A full profile of the evolving methodology, software and support services can be located at www.coreims.co.uk

CAMHS Outcomes Research Consortium (CORC) approach

CORC comprises over 70 services across the UK – more than half of all CAMHS (child and adolescent mental health services). Its main aim is to develop and disseminate a feasible model of routine outcome evaluation that can be used across a range of child and adolescent mental health services. As such, it aims to build a learning environment in which services subscribe and then collaborate in using outcome information to inform and develop good practice both in local services and in policy development. Crucially, it is services that drive the questions they want answering from the data and the hub provides the facility to analyse, benchmark and feedback the data in a visually attractive report.

CORC member services adopt a common approach, namely to collate and centrally analyse data, promote use of data to inform service providers, commissioners, users and others, and finally to facilitate sharing ideas between members. This is achieved by services using a common set of pre-therapy measures for child and parent that include the Strengths and Difficulties Questionnaire (SDQ; Goodman, 1997) in addition to other measures that tap parent and child feedback on the service, overall functioning, and the practitioner-completed Health of the Nation Outcome Scales for Children and Adolescents (HoNOSCA; Gowers et al., 1999). A full profile of the evolving methodology, software and support services can be located at www.corc.uk.net

Improving the client's journey within psychological therapy services

Systems such as those presented above and elsewhere (e.g. Kraus & Castonguay, Chapter 7; Lambert et al., Chapter 6) capture information that then needs to be used in service of delivering better quality care. Three key features that help shape how to use the data – but not the only ones – include the following: (1) tracking the client's journey, (2) using multiple indicators for comparative purposes, and (3) zeroing in (i.e. drilling down in the data) in order to problem solve (Mellor-Clark et al., 2006).

Tracking the client's journey

The notion of tracking the client's journey is premised on viewing it as comprising many differing stages, each of which can be potential exit points for clients or can introduce new challenges or barriers to their remaining in therapy. A model of therapy based only on a two-stage process of assessment and treatment will underestimate the complexity of decisions made within the service system and within the client's world that help determine whether they remain or exit therapy. Of particular importance will be components of engagement during referral, waiting and initial assessment (for a detailed account, see Barkham et al., Chapter 8). Hence, the notion of tracking presented here comprises more than case tracking of outcomes (see Leach & Lutz, Chapter 10): it is, quite simply, about tracking the client's experience throughout.

Multiple indicators and feedback

In order to ensure that each stage of the journey is working best for each client, there need to be ways of making appropriate comparisons with best practice at each of the key stages and then making that information readily available to services in user-friendly formats. Hence, systems need to convert data into relevant information that is usable by services. These can include high impact formats for presenting the data, for example, including traffic light colours to signal the location of one service in terms of any variable as compared with other services.

Data drilling and problem solving

A third feature focuses on using the information to help address particular subsamples of clients, in particular those who might be deemed not to be benefiting as expected from the service. The purpose is to attend to those clients who, for example, are reporting poorer ongoing outcomes (i.e. are off-track), poorer relationship with their practitioner, or are for any other reason at risk of unilaterally exiting therapy. In the public area there is an understandable focus of attention on rates of recovery or improvement. However, we should be mindful of the fact that on the basis of practice-based studies there are likely to be in the region of one-quarter to one-third of clients completing treatment who report no reliable improvement (Barkham et al., 2008). And there will be a much smaller portion of clients who report reliable deterioration and a very small – but crucial – number who may experience adverse effects. And there will be many clients who fail to engage with the service after the initial contact. The major challenge for psychological services research is to understand more about how to facilitate client engagement with psychological therapy services regardless of the specific psychological intervention and to adapt such interventions so as to be maximally responsive to clients' requirements.

The patterns and processes of individual change

The issue of addressing the significant portion of clients who do not engage in or benefit from psychological therapies places attention not only on the service but also on each individual client. As stated by Kazdin (2008): 'scientific study of the individual would bring research much closer to the context of clinical practice' (p. 154). Indeed, the role of case-based time-series analysis has been forcefully made (see Borchardt et al., 2008). The crucial component is the ability to capture change over time, and by implication, the absence of change. The use of repeated measurement has a rich history in psychotherapy research and has been used in earlier work we have carried out investigating differing aspects of therapy: for example, the shape of change using client-generated (i.e. idiographic) items as indicators of outcome (e.g. Barkham, Stiles & Shapiro, 1993), and the therapeutic alliance as a key process variable within a single case study (e.g. Agnew et al., 1994). These diverse examples, albeit carried out within the context of a psychotherapy process-outcome trial, have in common a framework of measurement that sought to establish patterns or shapes beyond that of a single straight line and beyond solely symptom change.

And here lies a central case for embedding process work within practice: 'The key function of process research is to develop a greater understanding of what happens in therapy, which should in turn result in increased effectiveness' (Llewelyn & Hardy, 2001, p. 16). For example, Goodridge and Hardy (2009) report on a series of individual case studies carried out in a clinic that aspired to undertake practice-based research. The purpose was the application of a framework of measures aimed at building an understanding of sudden gains and using thematic analyses of case material to evaluate the level of assimilation associated with the sudden gain. Hence, process work was used to inform our understanding of a particular class of change. Importantly, process work can inform practitioners about the *how* of an intervention rather than only the *what*. In this context, process work becomes a proxy for supervision and there would be considerable merit in investing funding in process research in order for it to support improvements in practice.

Enhancing evidence

Although such systems as those presented above – and others – can serve to enhance practice via common methods (e.g. feedback), they do not necessarily build into a cumulative evidence base. That is, service improvement can be an end in itself. However, the additional step of collating the data from IT systems underpinning the collection of routine practice and using it to build a practice-based evidence for the psychological therapies is one that would strengthen the knowledge base for multiple stakeholders including users, practitioners, service managers, commissioners of services and policy makers.

Developing a body of knowledge

Hence, beyond improving practice, the central thesis being proposed here is that this activity also yields enhanced evidence contributing to the knowledge base for psychological interventions. Such a process can begin with single practitioners by providing them with a way of framing their efforts for generating research and evidence from routine practice across many clinical services and settings (e.g. Bergstrom, 2008; Christie & Wilson, 2005; Gardiner et al., 2003;

Gibbard & Hanley, 2008; Greasley & Small, 2005). Although the opportunity for practitioners to publish individual accounts of research is not new, the existence of an overarching paradigm within which to place such work is a welcome addition. Moreover, it is easy to see how the adoption of common measurement systems enables individual reports to accumulate and provide a more systematic evidence base that, because of a common methodology, would be amenable to a simple form of analysis at a meta-analytic level. Hence, every individual practitioner can contribute to a developing evidence base founded on routine practice. This also applies to professional training courses in which, all too often, the effort and energy afforded by practitioners-in-training yields fragmented research rather than adding to a developing research programme. It also provides a realistic opportunity for developing a viable model of the scientist-practitioner that is within the reach of all professionals. The availability of tools and procedures within practice-based evidence enables practitioners to assess and measure current practice, which includes the use of process data and observations, to make comparisons (i.e. benchmarking in some form) against a defined standard or model, identify areas for improvement, and then implement change to achieve the desired improvement.

Although trials can deliver population-based information, we also need complementary evidence that focuses back into routine settings and on exceptions at the level of the individual case. But lest there is concern that such a strategy is unidirectional and does not also build a more firm knowledge base, consider the position espoused by Kazdin (2008): 'It *is* possible . . . to draw causal inferences from studying the individual, to bring to bear information from the case, to help make rival hypotheses implausible, to test and generate hypotheses, and to provide outstanding and astounding findings that will add to the knowledge base . . .' (p. 155).

Equipoise in privileging data sources

There is undoubtedly a growing interest from academics and policy makers as to the potential value of large routinely collected data sets. In the UK the Improving Access to Psychological Therapies (IAPT) programme has yielded large databases (e.g. Richards & Suckling, 2009) in addition to the practice-based evidence databases built using CORE System data (e.g. Barkham et al., 2006; Mellor-Clark et al., 1999; Stiles et al., 2003, 2006, 2008). Data from such studies, as well as from trials data, can help answer the question: Is this psychological approach generally helpful? By considering the collective span of evidence from trials, effectiveness studies and practice-based evidence, questions can be addressed about whether an intervention is likely to yield a positive result under optimal conditions, when transported to practice settings, and when delivered routinely within service settings over longer periods of time. A knowledge base that does not comprise data from these differing situations cannot be viewed as *complete* (see Rawlins, 2008).

Policy makers may well privilege trials data because they consider them to yield better quality evidence. But users may privilege data from routine settings because this is closer to the source from which they will receive services and may view it as being more representative of the user group and characteristics with which they identify. Evidence from differing sources will not always tell the same story and it is our collective task to weave these differing perspectives into a more complete and thorough evidence-base without undue privileging of specific sources of data.

But equally as important as enabling services to evaluate their practice is the opportunity of contributing and broadening the evidence-base for the psychological therapies. In terms of the process of building an evidence base, Gibbard and Hanley (2008) used their data collected over five successive years to counter questions raised concerning the credibility of practice-based evidence (Clark, Fairburn & Wessely, 2008). This exemplifies the ability of practitioners to use their practice data to address substantive issues in the literature as they arise. Hence, the existence of such data provides the potential for a self-correcting process concerning findings arising from evidence-based practice and practice-based evidence. Of course, relevant data does and will not always be accessible to make a response but it does provide the very real possibility for practitioners, via the use of their practice data, to be equal contributors to building and holding in balance the evidence base that has, for so long, privileged researchers.

Practitioner and supervisor effects

All the studies cited above address the broad class of question concerning the effectiveness of psychological therapies. Beyond this, one crucial component that has received relatively sparse attention in traditional research studies is that of the practitioner. Although arguments for taking account of therapist effects have long existed in the psychological literature (e.g. Martindale, 1975), it is only now being fully acknowledged as a major component in trial designs and analyses (for detailed arguments, see Walwyn & Roberts, in press). Notwithstanding such recent advances, traditional treatment-focused research – that is, the body of evidence upon which much of the current evidence rests – aims largely to make therapist contributions uniform in that the central interest has been the treatment itself. In addition to this, powering a study by the number of practitioners would require a huge study. Leaving aside whether or not prior failure to analyse therapist effects in trials may have resulted in an over-estimate of treatment effects – and all the implications that entails – there is an urgent need to address practitioner effectiveness, a move wholly consistent with practice-based focused research. There is a growing body of studies focusing on practitioner effects (e.g. Lutz et al., 2007; Okiishi et al., 2003; Wampold & Brown, 2005). However, building this literature requires more work and there are opportunities here for a clearer interface between trials and practice-based methodologies.

Crucially, however, it is not about creating another dichotomy – namely, treatment versus therapist – but rather to design better research studies in which the key role of the practitioner is evaluated and also analysed using appropriate statistical procedures that recognize that clients are nested within practitioners. And inasmuch as practitioner effects should be investigated, so too should supervisor effects. It is quite likely that the expertise of a supervisor and differential or targeting of support for practitioners where a client is not showing the expected gains may be a crucial factor in determining a successful outcome. Such a process is potentially problematic if hidden within a trial but it is also hugely important in terms of capturing the skills necessary for supporting practitioners in routine practice. Indeed, building a practice-based evidence for supervision would be of considerable value in serving this agenda and one being taken forward in the UK via the establishment of a new practice research network – Supervision Practitioner Research Network (SuPReNet; for further details, see ✉ suprenet@bacp.co.uk).

Natural theory building

In terms of the process of outcomes, as practitioners we want to understand how change comes about – that is, we need theories to help guide and explain change when it occurs and when it does not occur. Unfortunately, psychological theories do not provide complete descriptions of exact specifications for moment-to-moment interventions. Practitioners use them but have to interpret what is happening and adapt what they do to a combination of emerging circumstances, the client they are with, and the relationship between them. Most practitioners – consciously or not – modify or extend the theories because they are responsive to emerging client requirements. That is, practitioners are privately engaging in theory building. The capacity and inherent variation in practitioners' abilities to build micro-theories is a starting point for looking at what it is practitioners do in their everyday practice. And from this can be built a theory of the effective practitioner, and from there, what is common across cases with good outcomes and also what are the processes associated with poorer outcomes. The proposition for building a theory of the effective practitioner is supported by the consideration that the practitioner may provide at least as convenient a unit of analysis for study as any treatment. Indeed, Krause et al. (2007) have argued for the logical difficulty in separating between forms of treatment as opposed to separating practitioners. They argue that greater confidence can be achieved in separating between practitioners than between forms of treatment. Theory development requires new ideas, exceptions to the rule, practical problems that must be overcome and other challenges to the status quo. Practice-based evidence provides a rich ground for developing new models. It also provides a contrast to tightly controlled studies by showing where treatments may be limited or weak.

Responsiveness and relevance

Individual practitioners as well as services are continually seeking ways to improve the treatments they offer and to be more responsive to client needs and preferences. Indeed, this position determines one of the central needs for developing practice-based evidence. This is because a large part of the activity of therapy is *responsive* – that is, it is determined by the emerging context within which they are working (see Stiles, 2009). To the extent that trials attempt to hold constant all factors other than the contrasting treatments or specific variable of interest, they have difficulty in dealing with the fact that treatment, practitioner and client variables all affect each other – what has been termed *causal entanglements*. These entanglements undermine the apparent neatness of trials logic and argue for building evidence using complementary methodologies.

A focus on practice-based evidence that incorporates qualitative, single case studies and process evidence is more than a simple combination of qualitative and quantitative or process and outcomes approaches. Indeed, all these approaches have been successfully combined within existing trials methodology (e.g. see Barkham et al., in press). Rather, their collective effort is a necessity in order both to capture the richness of the psychological therapies but also to provide a richer source of evidence as to the processes and mechanisms of change (see Elliott & Zucconi, Chapter 11). The point is that although, for example, a trial might establish a causal relationship between a specific therapy and gains made, this is not sufficient to assign the change to some mechanism within the treatment. Our understanding of such processes would be enhanced by the adoption of alternative methodologies. For example, Kazdin (2006) singled out three approaches that he felt were required to ensure a balance with trials methodology: qualitative research methods, single case experimental designs, and the case study. Indeed, failure to encompass such approaches will ultimately yield a more restricted science.

Towards a more complete and thorough evidence base

The future of practice-based evidence lies in addressing questions that are based in routine practice and focus on the complexities of service delivery that cannot be simplified into comparisons carried out in randomized trials. Interestingly, Horn and colleagues argue that studying delivery in routine care in which treatments naturally compete with each other might yield newer and better treatments quicker than via the route of randomized trials. By definition, the procedures in trials need to be defined and delivered as prescribed. The issue becomes the time taken to refine treatments in such a paradigm.

Historically, evidence-based practice derived from evidence-based medicine and, as such, has focused on treatments. This has been one of its strengths, assuming that the one key variable that differs between two conditions within a trial is the treatment. And treatments are, of course, crucial. But treatments are, invariably, delivered by practitioners and practitioners are undoubtedly the most valuable resource we have in any service delivery system that is attempting to meet the needs of people in distress. Consider for a moment the evidence concerning common factors versus active treatment effects. There is an accumulation of evidence showing common factors to have a huge effect – a function of practitioners delivering credible treatments, instilling hope, listening and responding appropriately to service users (see Wampold, 2001). Active treatments improve these effects, but the relative addition is smaller than might be supposed. Of course, anything that improves the effectiveness of interventions is worthy but the relevant point here is that we may be placing treatment techniques unduly in the foreground at the expense of common factors that carry the substantive proportion of outcome variance. In particular, we have paid scant attention to the effects of practitioners – that is, therapist effects. This is not a debate about whether the effects of treatments are attributable to treatments or therapists, or even as to which accounts for a greater portion of outcome variance – but it is an argument that healthcare delivery is a result of a system which comprises treatments delivered by practitioners within the context of an organization. If we are to improve the quality, relevance and applicability of the evidence we capture, then we need to embed evaluations within routine service delivery in which all these major components are monitored.

In this chapter, and through the various preceding chapters, we have attempted to provide an overview of the current status and potential for practice-based evidence with specific reference to the psychological therapies. In one sense, practice-based evidence is a young paradigm, born – in some part – by way of frustration with the dominance of trials methodology. However, as stated by Rawlins (2008): 'The notion that evidence can be reliably placed in hierarchies is illusory. Hierarchies place RCTs on an undeserved pedestal for, although the technique has advantages it also has significant disadvantages' (p. 2). The implication is that differing research paradigms should be equally valued, albeit that they are premised on differing assumptions. To date, RCTs have generated a cumulative evidence base via meta-analytic studies. However, these are constrained by the need for studies to be of a similar class – and invariably requiring identical measurement tools. One of the ironic problems with meta-analytic studies is their reduction to a very thin stratum of evidence. In healthcare systems this level of specificity and precision rarely occurs given the prevalence of co-morbidity and wider social issues. Rather than focusing on this meta level of a single class of data, we need to move towards more thorough and complete analyses, a *teleoanalytic* approach, wherein evidence from differing classes of studies can be considered together.

In conclusion, if one thing can be achieved as a result of this book, we would wish it to be a better basis for recognizing that the complementary paradigm of practice-based evidence is as important as that of trials methodology. Indeed, we require both approaches so we can develop and deliver a more thorough and complete knowledge base for the psychological therapies in order to help optimize the potential for alleviating client distress and discomfort.

Acknowledgements

We are grateful to many people who have, over the years, overtly and sometimes inadvertently, offered ideas about the principles and practices of practice-based evidence. In particular, we would like to thank William B. Stiles for his long-standing collaboration with us and from where many of the ideas presented here have emerged. We would also like to acknowledge ideas that arose from an expert seminar on outcomes monitoring held at the Anna Freud Centre, London, March 2009, in particular contributions by Jeb Brown, Tim Croudace, Peter Fonagy, Michael Lambert and Miranda Wolpert.

References

Agnew, R.M., Harper, H., Shapiro, D.A. & Barkham, M. (1994). Resolving a challenge to the therapeutic relationship: A single case study. *British Journal of Medical Psychology, 67,* 155–170.

American Psychological Association (APA) (2006). Evidence-based practice in psychology: APA Presidential task force on evidence-based practice. *American Psychologist, 61,* 271–285.

Barkham, M. & Margison, F. (2007). Practice-based evidence as a complement to evidence-based practice: From dichotomy to chiasmus. In C. Freeman & M. Power (eds.), *Handbook of evidence-based psychotherapies: A guide for research and practice* (pp. 443–476). Chichester: John Wiley & Sons, Ltd.

Barkham, M. & Mellor-Clark, J. (2000). Rigour and relevance: Practice-based evidence in the psychological therapies. In N. Rowland & S. Goss (eds.),

Evidence-based counselling and psychological therapies: Research and applications (pp.127–144). London: Routledge.

Barkham M. & Mellor-Clark J. (2003). Bridging evidence-based practice and practice-based evidence: Developing a rigorous and relevant knowledge for the psychological therapies. *Clinical Psychology & Psychotherapy, 10,* 319–327.

Barkham, M., Hardy, G.E. & Shapiro, D.A. (in press). The Sheffield-Leeds Psychotherapy Research Program. In J.C. Norcross, G.R. VandenBos & D.K. Freedheim (eds.), *A history of psychotherapy* (2nd edn.). Washington, DC: American Psychological Association.

Barkham, M., Stiles, W.B. & Shapiro, D.A. (1993). The shape of change: Longitudinal assessment of personal problems. *Journal of Consulting and Clinical Psychology, 61,* 667–677.

Barkham, M., Connell, J., Stiles, W.B., Miles, J.N.V., Margison, F. et al. (2006). Dose-effect relations and responsive regulation of treatment duration: The good enough level. *Journal of Consulting and Clinical Psychology, 74,* 160–167.

Barkham, M., Stiles, W.B., Connell, J., Twigg, E., Leach, C. et al. (2008). Effects of psychological therapies in randomized trials and practice-based studies. *British Journal of Clinical Psychology, 47,* 397–415.

Benson, K. & Hartz, A.J. (2000). A comparison of observational studies and randomized, controlled trials. *New England Journal of Medicine, 342,* 1878–1886.

Bergstrom, N. (2008). The gap between discovery and practice implementation in evidence-based practice: Is practice-based evidence a solution? *International Journal of Evidence-Based Healthcare, 6,* 135–136.

Borchardt, J.J., Nash, M.R., Murphy, M.D., Moore, M., Shaw, D. et al. (2008). Clinical practice as natural laboratory for psychotherapy research. *American Psychologist, 63,* 77–95.

Brown, G.S., Jones, E.R., Lambert, M.J., Jones, E.R. & Minami, T. (2005). Identifying highly effective psychotherapists in a managed care environment. *American Journal of Managed Care, 11,* 513–520.

Christie, D. & Wilson, C. (2005). CBT in paediatric and adolescent health settings: A review of practice-based evidence. *Pediatric Rehabilitation, 8,* 241–247.

Clark, D.M., Fairburn, C.G. & Wessely, S. (2008). Psychological treatment outcomes in routine NHS services: a commentary on Stiles et al. (2007). *Psychological Medicine, 38,* 629–634.

Concato, J., Shah, N. & Horwitz, R.I. (2000). Randomized controlled trials, observational studies, and the hierarchy of research designs. *New England Journal of Medicine, 342,* 1887–1892.

Cook, J. (1999). There's more to life than practice: practice-based research. *The British Journal of Chiropractic, 3,* 28.

Duncan, B., Miller, S. & Sparks, J. (2004). *The heroic client: A revolutionary way to improve effectiveness through client-directed, outcome-informed therapy.* New York: Jossey-Bass.

Duncan, B., Miller, S. & Sparks, J. (2007). *Heroic clients, heroic agencies: Partner for change – A manual for client-directed, outcome-informed clinical services.* E-book: ISTC Press.

Dupree, W.J., White, M.B., Olsen, C.S. & Lafleur, C.T. (2007). Infidelity treatment patterns: A practice-based evidence approach. *The American Journal of Family Therapy, 35,* 327–341.

Fox, N.J. (2003). Evidence-based practice: Towards collaborative and transgressive research. *Sociology, 37,* 81–102.

Gardiner, C., McLeod, J., Hill, I. & Wigglesworth, A. (2003). A feasibility study of the systematic evaluation of client outcomes in a voluntary sector counseling agency. *Counselling and Psychotherapy Research, 3,* 285–290.

Gibbard, I. & Hanley, T. (2008). A five-year evaluation of the effectiveness of person-centred counselling in routine clinical practice in primary care. *Counselling and Psychotherapy Research, 8,* 215–222.

Goodheart, C., Kazdin, A.E. & Sternberg, R.J. (2006). *Evidence-based psychotherapy: Where practice and research meet.* Washington, DC: American Psychological Association.

Goodman, R. (1997). The Strengths and Difficulties Questionnaire: A research note. *Journal of Child Psychology and Psychiatry, 38,* 581–586.

Goodridge, D. & Hardy, G.E. (2009). Patterns of change in psychotherapy: An investigation of sudden gains in cognitive therapy using the assimilation model. *Psychotherapy Research, 19,* 114–123.

Gowers, S.G., Harrington, R.C., Whitton, A., Lelliott, P., Wing, J. et al. (1999). A brief scale for measuring the outcomes of emotional and behavioural disorders in children: HoNOSCA. *British Journal of Psychiatry, 174,* 413–416.

Gray, P. & Mellor-Clark, J. (2007). *CORE: A decade of development.* Rugby, UK: CORE Information Management Systems.

Greasley, P. & Small, N. (2005). Evaluating a primary care counselling service: Outcomes and issues. *Primary Health Care Research and Development, 6,* 125–136.

Greenwood, H., Leach, C., Lucock, M. & Noble, R. (2007). The process of long-term art therapy: a case study combining artwork and clinical outcome. *Psychotherapy Research, 17,* 588–599.

Horn, S.D. & Gassaway, J. (2007). Practice-based evidence study design for comparative effectiveness research. *Medical Care, 45,* S50–S57.

Horn, S.D., DeJong, G., Ryser, D.K., Veazie, P.J. & Teraoka, J. (2005). Another look at observational studies in rehabilitation research: Going beyond the

Holy Grail of the randomized controlled trial. *Archives of Physical and Medical Rehabilitation, 86,* Supplement 2, S8–S15.

Isaacs, M.R., Huang, L.N., Hernandez, M. & Echo-Hawk, H. (2005). *The road to evidence: The intersection of evidence-based practices and cultural competence in children's mental health.* Washington, DC: National Alliance of Multi-Ethnic Behavioral Health Associations.

Kazdin, A.E. (2006). Assessment and evaluation in clinical practice. In C. Goodheart, A.E. Kazdin & R.J. Sternberg (eds.), *Evidence-based psychotherapy: Where practice and research meet.* Washington, DC: American Psychological Association.

Kazdin, A.E. (2008). Evidence-based treatment and practice: New opportunities to bridge clinical research and practice, enhance the knowledge base, and improve patient care. *American Psychologist, 63,* 146–159.

Krakau, I. (2000). The importance of practice-based evidence. *Scandinavian Journal of Primary Health Care, 18,* 130–131.

Krause, M.S., Lutz, W. & Saunders, S.M. (2007). Empirically certified treatments or therapists: The issue of separability. *Psychotherapy: Theory, Research, Practice, Training, 44,* 347–353.

Larson, S.M. (2008). Practice-based evidence of the beneficial impact of positron emission tomography in clinical oncology. *Journal of Clinical Oncology, 26,* 2083–2084.

Llewelyn, S. & Hardy, G.E. (2001). Process research in understanding and applying psychological therapies. *British Journal of Clinical Psychology, 40,* 1–21.

Lutz, W., Leon, S.C., Martinovich, Z., Lyons, J.S. & Stiles, W.B. (2007). Therapist effects in outpatient psychotherapy: A three-level growth curve approach. *Journal of Counseling Psychology, 54,* 32–39.

Lyons, J.S. & McCulloch, J.R. (2006). Monitoring and managing outcomes in residential treatment: Practice-based evidence in search of evidence-based practice. *Journal of the American Academy of Child and Adolescent Psychiatry, 45,* 247–251.

Margison, F. (2001). Practice-based evidence in psychotherapy. In C. Mace, S. Moorey & B. Roberts (eds.), *Evidence in the psychological therapies: A critical guide for practitioners* (pp. 174–198). London: Brunner-Routledge.

Margison, F., Barkham, M., Evans, C., McGrath, G., Mellor-Clark, J. et al. (2000). Measurement and psychotherapy: Evidence-based practice and practice-based evidence. *British Journal of Psychiatry, 177,* 123–130.

Martindale, C. (1975). The therapist-as-fixed-effect fallacy in psychotherapy research. *Journal of Consulting and Clinical Psychology, 46,* 1526–1530.

McDonald, P.W. & Viehbeck, S. (2007). From evidence-based practice making to practice-based evidence making: Creating communities of (research) and practice. *Health Promotion Practice*, *8*, 140–144.

Mellor-Clark, J., Barkham, M., Connell, J. & Evans, C. (1999). Practice-based evidence and standardised evaluation: Informing the design of the CORE System. *European Journal of Psychotherapy, Counselling and Health*, *3*, 357–374.

Mellor-Clark, J., Curtis Jenkins, A., Evans, R., Mothersole, G. & McInnes, B. (2006). Resourcing a CORE Network to develop a National Research Database to help enhance psychological therapies and counselling service provision. *Counselling and Psychotherapy Research*, *6*, 16–22.

Merrill, K.A., Tolbert, V.E. & Wade, W.A. (2003). Effectiveness of cognitive therapy for depression in a community mental health center: A benchmarking study. *Journal of Consulting and Clinical Psychology*, *71*, 404–409.

Okiishi, J., Lambert, M.J., Nielsen, S.L. & Ogles, B.M. (2003). Waiting for supershrink: An empirical analysis of therapist effects. *Clinical Psychology & Psychotherapy*, *10*, 361–373.

Osborne, N. (1999). Evidence-based practice and practice based evidence. *The British Journal of Chiropractic*, *3*, 30.

Rawlins, M.D. (2008). *De Testimonio: On the evidence for decisions about the use of therapeutic interventions.* The Harveian Oration of 2008. Royal College of Physicians. Reprinted in *The Lancet* (2008), *372*, 2152–2161.

Richards, D.A. & Suckling, R. (2009). Improving access to psychological therapies (IAPT): Phase IV prospective cohort study. *British Journal of Clinical Psychology*, *48*, 377–396.

Staller, K.M. (2006). Railroads, runaways, & researchers: Returning evidence rhetoric to its practice base. *Qualitative Inquiry*, *12*, 503–522.

Stiles, W.B. (2009). Responsiveness as an obstacle for psychotherapy outcome research: It's worse than you think. *Clinical Psychology: Science and Practice*, *16*, 86–91.

Stiles, W.B., Barkham, M., Mellor-Clark, J. & Connell, J. (2008). Effectiveness of cognitive-behavioural, person-centred, and psychodynamic therapies in UK primary care routine practice: Replication with a larger sample. *Psychological Medicine*, *38*, 677–688.

Stiles, W.B., Barkham, M., Twigg, E., Mellor-Clark, J. & Cooper, M. (2006). Effectiveness of cognitive-behavioural, person-centred, and psychodynamic therapies as practiced in UK National Health Service settings. *Psychological Medicine*, *36*, 555–566.

Stiles, W.B., Leach, C., Barkham, M., Lucock, M., Iveson, S. et al. (2003). Early sudden gains in psychotherapy under routine clinic conditions: Practice-based evidence. *Journal of Consulting and Clinical Psychology*, *71*, 14–21.

Wade, W.A., Treat, T.A. & Stuart, G.L. (1998). Transporting an empirically supported treatment for panic disorder to a service clinic setting: A benchmarking strategy. *Journal of Consulting and Clinical Psychology, 66,* 231–239.

Wald, N.J. & Morris, J.K. (2003). Teleoanalysis: combining data from different types of study. *British Medical Journal, 327,* 616–618.

Walker, J.S. & Bruns, E.J. (2006). Building on practice-based evidence: Using expert perspectives to define the wraparound process. *Psychiatric Services, 57,* 1579–1585.

Walwyn, R. & Roberts, C. (in press). Therapist variation in randomised trials of psychotherapy: Implications for precision, internal and external validity. *Statistical Methods in Medical Research.*

Wampold, B.E. (2001). *The great psychotherapy debate: Models, methods, and findings.* Mahwah, NJ: Erlbaum.

Wampold, B.E. & Brown, G. (2005). Estimating therapist variability in outcomes attributable to therapists: A naturalistic study of outcomes in managed care. *Journal of Consulting and Clinical Psychology, 73,* 914–923.

Wolpert, M. (July, 2008). Making evidence-based practice a reality; what does it mean and can it be done? *Evidence-based practice & practice-based evidence in child & adolescent mental health services (CAMHS) – can they be usefully combined?* CAMHS National Conference, Leicester.

Index

AB design 117, 118, 134
  expansion 129–131
ABC design with counterbalancing
  119–121, 120
abduction 94
accountability 17, 156, 157, 287
adherence effects 28, 29
Agency for Healthcare Research and
  Quality (AHRQ) 315
Agnew Relationship Measure 295,
  296
alcohol abuse 233, 234
Alcoholics Anonymous (AA) 76
alcoholism 74, 76
allegiance effects 29, 33, 38
allocation
  concealment 8, 9
  randomization 7, 29, 31
alternating treatment design (ATD)
  124, 125, 129, 134
Ambulatory Sentinel Practice
  Network 314
American Psychiatric Association 315
American Psychological Association
  160, 176, 315, 316, 329

ANOVA 269, 270
anxiety 35, 73
  and CORE 178, 180, 185, 190, 192,
    213
  social 132
  see also generalized anxiety
    disorder
Aristotelian approach 235, 236
Art Therapist's PRN 319
Artemis Trust 177
assimilation model 98, 100–105
  Assimilation of Problematic
    Experiences Sequence (APES)
    101, 103–105
  enactment of core problems
    in microcosm 102, 103,
    105
  problematic positions 101–105
  voice metaphor 100–102, 105
  zone of proximal development
    101, 103–105
Association for Cognitive Analytic
  Therapy (ACAT), PRN
  feasibility study 320
attrition 265–267, 321, 322

Developing and Delivering Practice-Based Evidence   By Michael Barkham, Gillian E Hardy,
and John Mellor-Clark   © 2010 John Wiley & Sons, Ltd

audio/video recordings of therapy
sessions 71, 96, 100, 301
audit 49, 313, 323
autonomy, of clinical judgment 3, 4,
16, 17
avalanche prediction models 272

bar charts 264, 265
BASIS-32 226, 227, 229, 240
Beck Anxiety Inventory (BAI) 185,
273
Beck Depression Inventory (BDI) 67,
164
and benchmarking 245, 246
Beck Depression Inventory-I (BDI-I)
185, 273
Beck Depression Inventory-II
(BDI-II) 185
Behavioral Health Laboratories
(BHL) 155, 156, 158, 166,
170–172
benchmarking database 155, 156,
159, 170–172
behavioural therapies 26, 27, 305
application to non-behavioural
interventions 127
see also cognitive behavioural
therapy
beliefs 5
benchmarking 43, 223–250, 257–279,
318, 319, 322, 336, 339, 340
and case-mix adjustment 241–243,
247, 248
clinical trials as benchmarks for
routine practice 244–246
competitive 225, 250
and confidentiality 249
context within quality
improvement efforts 227–229
and Continuous Quality
Improvement 223, 228–236

and CORE 201, 202, 205, 207, 208,
226, 227, 241
definition 224
and effect sizes 246, 247
effectiveness paradigm 237–240
functional (non-competitive) 225,
226, 250
generic process 226, 250
identifying critical processes 243
internal 224, 225, 241, 242, 250
multi-level modelling 241–243
origins of 224
patient-focused 240–243
performance parameters
indicating quality 226, 227
practical issues for implementation
249, 250
for practice-based studies 240–248
and single case design studies
235–236, 250
and therapist effects 241–243
and the Treatment Outcome
Package 155, 156, 159,
170–172
treatment-focused 237–240
types 224–226
best practice 333
bias 34
and missing data 150
and Practice Research Networks
321
publication 9
and randomization 26, 29
selection 7, 8
and systematic reviews 8, 9
and the therapist 35
and traditional reviews 8
binary logistic regression 168
bottom-up approaches 207, 214, 215,
289, 319, 331
see also practice-based evidence

box plots 264–268
  notched 265, 267
breast cancer 73
Bridging science and service (NAMHC
  report) 23, 24
brief single case quantitative methods
  132
Brief Symptom Inventory (BSI) 192
brief therapy 100, 105
  psychodynamic 78
British Medical Journal 29, 73

California Psychotherapy Alliance
  Scale (CALPAS) 295, 296
CAMHS Outcomes Research
  Consortium (CORC) 338,
  339, 340
cancer 73, 314
case identification 198, 201
case studies 48, 95, 98, 346
  and conclusions 100
  see also single case methodology;
    theory-building case study
    research
case tracking 43, 201, 257–279, 320,
  336
  simple 262, 263, 270, 271, 279
case-mix (risk) adjustment 241–243,
  247, 248
  multivariate statistical controls
  248
  stratification 247, 248
  see also risk adjustment
causal entanglements 346
causal relationships 6, 14, 29, 31, 68,
  127, 128, 346
ceiling effects 164–166, 167
Center for Mental Health Services
  315
Center for Substance Abuse
  Treatment 315

Central Register of Controlled Trials
  11
central tendency 235, 236
change 335–337
  discussion 130, 131
  dose-respondent model of 260,
  261, 271
  Growth Mixture Models of 276–8,
  277
  growth modelling 269–271
  Kotter's stage model of 49
  measurement principles 336, 337
  nearest neighbour approach to
    272–276, 273–275
  patterns of 269, 270, 276, 341, 242
  processes of 341, 342
  psychological principles of 16
  and single case quantitative
    methods 128, 130, 131
  and systematic case study
    protocols 300, 301
  and the Treatment Outcome
    Package 166–168, 169
  see also progress; Reliable Change
    Index; treatment outcome
    measures
change agency support 48, 49
changing criterion design 121–124,
  123
child and adolescent mental health
  services (CAMHS), CAMHS
  Outcomes Research
  Consortium (CORC) 338,
  339, 340
children, with emotional and
  behavioural problems 119,
  119, 127, 332
chronic fatigue syndrome 239
client-directed outcome-informed
  (CDOI) approach 241, 338,
  339

client-focused research 269
clients
    characteristics 25, 292, 294, 298,
        299, 301
    diverse populations 36
    entry to trial restriction 6
    high risk 341
    journey through psychological
        services 202, 340, 341
    selection 40, 49
    see also patient reported outcome
        measures; patient-centred
        systems
clinical audit 313, 323
clinical expertise 4, 22, 23, 24, 25
clinical guidelines 10, 11
    consensus-based 10
    evidence-based 10
    local interpretation 10, 11
clinical informatics 230, 231
Clinical Interview Schedule-Revised
        (CIS-R) 192
clinical judgment 3, 4, 16, 30
    autonomy 3, 4, 16, 17
    downplaying of the role of 16, 17
Clinical Outcomes in Routine
        Evaluation (CORE) 175–215,
        304, 339
    benchmarks 201, 202, 205, 207,
        208
    as bottom-up system 207, 214, 215
    collating practice-based evidence
        national databases 205
    first generation 209
    management 176, 205–209
    measurement 176–195, 209
        family of measures 178–188,
            179, 180, 181
        origins 177, 178
        resourcing local feedback for
            service management 205–209

monitoring 176, 195–205, 209
    case identification 198, 201
    comparison-making 201
    CORE measure only 198–201
    CORE System 202–205
    summaries 198–201
    and seasonality 199, 200
    second generation 209–214,
        210–213
    translations 179, 181, 194
    see also CORE...
Clinical Outcomes in Routine
        Evaluation-Outcome Measure
        (CORE-OM) 175, 177–188,
        195, 258, 260–264, 265–268,
        267, 268, 271, 272, 273–275,
        278, 279, 293–295, 339
    acceptability 183–184
    and benchmarking 201, 226, 227,
        241
    and change evaluation 188, 189,
        198–200, 199–201
    clinical cut-offs 188
    clinical scores 181, 183
    construct validity 185
    convergent validity 185
    and CORE NET 210
    description 178, 180
    example 182
    Functioning 178, 185
    internal consistency 178
    internal reliability 184–185
    look-up table 181, 184
    management 209
    mean item scores 180–181, 183,
        188
    monitoring 198–201
    normative baseline severity
        185–188, 186, 187
    Problems 178, 185
    psychometric properties 183–185

rationale 178
reliable change index 188
Risk 178–180, 185, 188, 198, 211
score meaning 183
scoring 180–184, 192
self-report measures 214
severity levels 183, 184, 185–188,
    186, 187, 199
shorter versions for specific
    populations 179, 181, 193,
    194
shorter versions for specific
    purposes 179, 180, 188–193
Subjective well-being 178, 185
summary plots 199–200, 199–200
test–retest reliability 185
use 178
utility 178–180
validity 185
clinical supervision 48, 49
    generic aims 48, 49
    supervisor effects 344–345
clinical utility 24–26, 157, 158,
    178–180, 274
clinically relevant interventions,
    selection 36
cluster analytic approaches 276
clustering 34
co-morbidities 14
Cochrane Collaboration 11
Cochrane Database of Systematic
    Reviews 11
Cochrane Library, The 11
cognitions 74
cognitive analytic therapy 73, 117,
    117, 258
cognitive behavioural therapy (CBT)
    26, 27, 48, 258, 274, 288, 319
    benchmarking 238, 239
    changing criterion design 123, 124,
    123

domination 12, 15
multiple-baseline design 121, 122
    and the researcher allegiance effect
        33
    and therapist effects 35
cognitive therapy 74, 237, 238, 305
cognitive-diffusion strategies 124,
    125
Cohen's d 166, 168, 169, 244
collaborative research 302–305
combined model
    evidence-based
        practice/practice-based
        evidence 50, 52
    see also complementary model
common factors (therapeutic
        alliance) 15, 16, 28, 347
    see also therapeutic alliance
communities of practice 333
comparative fit index (CFI) 162, 163
comparison 7, 8, 68
comparison groups 7
COMPASS (previously Integra
        Outpatient Tracking
        Assessment) 226, 227, 230,
        232, 240
COMPASS-PC (primary care) 240
complementary model
    evidence-based
        practice/practice-based
        evidence 50–52, 330, 334, 348
    see also combined model
complexity of treatment 127, 128, 133
comprehensive cohort trial/study 52
comprehensive process analysis 77
computer-assisted analysis 78
confidence interval (CI) 162
confidentiality 249
Confirmatory Factor Analysis (CFA)
    162, 163
conflicts of interest 84

Consensual Qualitative Research
303
consensus 97
CONSORT guidelines 34
consortium arrangements 302
constructionism 69, 71
content analysis 72, 73, 81
context, and therapeutic action 128
Continuous Quality Improvement
(CQI) 223, 228–236
clinical informatics 230, 231
clinical outcomes research 229
empirical studies 232–234
feedback systems 229, 231
national databases 231, 232
paradigms of outcomes research
234–236, 234, 235
quality evaluation 231, 232
control 6, 8
control groups 7
'controlling caretaker' position
102–105
conversation analysis 76, 77, 82, 84
core battery 291
Core Battery Conference criteria 160,
160, 161
core categories 74, 81
CORE End-of-Therapy Form 195,
197
CORE IMS 338
CORE National Practice-based
Evidence Datasets 41, 47, 49
CORE National Research Dataset 319
CORE Net 176, 209–214, 210–213,
259, 320
patient-centred nature 214
progress-tracking charts 211, 212,
213, 214
severity rating 211, 214
using 210–213
core outcome measures 176

Core Partnership Occasional Papers
207
CORE PC 176, 202, 214
data drilling 204, 205
development 202
following the client's journey
202
management 208, 209, 208
thermometers/traffic lights 203,
204
CORE System 175–177, 195, 196,
197, 214, 231, 232, 240, 259,
318, 319, 331, 343
description 195
monitoring 198, 202–205
rationale 195
self-report measures 214
use 195
see also Clinical Outcomes in
Routine Evaluation
CORE System Group 231
CORE System Trust 194
CORE Therapy Assessment Form
195, 196
CORE User Network 207, 318, 319,
338
CORE-5 179, 180, 192, 193
CORE-10 179
acceptability 190
concurrent validity 192
convergent validity 192
and CORE Net 210, 211
description 180, 190–192
example 191
internal reliability 190
norms 192
scoring 192
sensitivity and specificity 190–192
validity 192
CORE-SF 179, 180, 188–190, 258,
273, 278, 336

correlated (Direct Oblimin) rotations
162
correlational studies 30, 32
cost-effectiveness 11, 29
and Continuous Quality
Improvement 232, 233, 234
and the Outcome Questionnaire
System 143, 149
versus clinical effectiveness 14, 15
counselling 273
benchmarking 225–227, 229–232,
240–241, 243, 249
non-directive 35
qualitative research 74, 85
theory-building case study
research 91, 92, 96, 97, 100
Counselling in Primary Care Trust
(CPCT) 177
counsellors, benchmarking 225, 226
counterbalancing 119–121, 120
criterion of eigenvalue greater than
one 162
criterion of interpretability 162
cultural minority groups 332
culture, healthcare 17

dantotsu 224
data
analysis 44
cherry picking 46
complete 337, 344
equipoise in privileging sources
343, 344
meaningful 337
missing 45–47, 150, 265–267, 270,
276, 279, 321, 322, 335, 337
non-independence of 34
normative 142, 151, 230, 231, 232
and practice-based studies 42–49
quality 45–47, 322
sharing 320, 337

and the Treatment Outcome
Package 158, 159
data blind procedures 249
data collection
and methodological pluralism 335
and the Outcome Questionnaire
System 150
and Practice Research Networks
321, 322, 323
qualitative 70, 71
data drilling 204, 205, 341
data points 265, 266
data sets 40–42
aggregation 230, 240, 249
CORE 41, 47, 49, 319
large 41, 47, 49, 230, 240, 249, 318,
319, 331, 337, 343, 344
national 41, 47, 49, 318, 319
naturalistic 205
and Practice Research Networks
318, 319, 322
and routine service delivery
257–279
see also databases
databases 11, 41
benchmarking 257–279
bibliographical 9
case tracking 257–279
large 205–207, 230, 231, 232, 259,
318, 319, 343
national 205–207, 230, 231, 232,
259, 318, 319
and statistical packages 257, 259
decision-making 3, 4, 22, 36, 37, 52
assisting 16, 17
as teleoanalysis 30, 50, 53
demoralization hypothesis 170
Department of Health Priorities and
Needs Research and
Development 177
dependency 104

depersonalization 117, 118
depression 35, 73
    benchmarking treatment 237–239,
        245–248
    and CORE 178, 180, 185, 190, 192,
        212, 213
    meta-analysis 27
    NICE guidelines 11
    and psychodynamic-interpersonal
        therapy 100–105
    and randomized controlled trials
        26, 247
    and the Treatment Outcome
        Package 164, 168, 170, 171
    amongst young people 238, 239,
        248
deterioration
    measurement 198, 200, 201
    monitoring 268, 268
    see also treatment failure
developmental models 50
diagnostic reliability, in natural
        settings 318
Diagnostic and Statistical Manual of
    Mental Disorders-IV
    (DSM-IV) 160, 161
Dialogical Sequence Analysis (DSA)
    101, 102, 105
difference, inclusion of 332
disadvantaged populations 67
discourse analysis 76, 77, 78, 82, 84,
    303
Dissociative Identity Disorder 117,
    117
distress 247, 248, 278, 318
    see also Clinical Outcomes in
        Routine Evaluation
Dodo verdict 27
dose-respondent model of change
    260, 261, 271

double-blind trials 29, 330
drug trials 29

early outcome signal methods 303,
    304
econometric approach 233, 234
effect size 246, 247, 320, 321
effectiveness 11
    evidence of no 12, 13
    no evidence of 12, 13
    and the Treatment Outcome
        Package 155
    versus cost-effectiveness 14, 15
effectiveness research 23–25, 27, 28,
        32, 33, 37, 47, 48, 51, 52, 112,
        113, 130, 133, 331
    benchmarking 230, 234, 237–240,
        243, 244, 258
    and case tracking 258
    dichotomy with efficacy research
        312–314
    lack of robustness 41
    organizational and conceptual
        framework for practice-based
        research 287–305
    Outcome Questionnaire System
        149
efficacy research 23–26, 29, 50, 51, 52,
        111, 112, 133
    benchmarking 230, 231, 232, 236,
        239, 244–246
    data 45
    dichotomy with effectiveness
        research 312–314
    generalizability 41
    practice gap 312, 313
    and single case research 236
efficiency research
    benchmarking 230, 233,
        234

Outcome Questionnaire System 149
and single case research 236
emotions 74
painful 74
empathy 32, 68, 74, 123
empirical imperialism 312
empirical phenomenology 303
empirically supported principles task
force 288
empirically supported relationships
task force 288
empirically supported treatments
(EST) (evidence-based
therapies) 27, 28, 288, 312
enactment of core problems in
microcosm 102, 103, 105
end-results cards 176
enriching (deepening/hermeneutic)
research 94, 95
environmental contingencies 127
epistemology 68, 69, 71
EQ-5D 246
errors, independence of 270
essence 235, 236
ethical issues 39, 84
ethical dilemmas 228
single case quantitative methods
112
theory-building case study
research 99
ethnic minority groups 332
Euclidean distance 236
evidence
as basis of beliefs 5
definition 5
enhancing 337, 338, 342–346
external clinical 4, 5, 22
hierarchy of trustworthiness 5
no, of effectiveness 12, 13
of no effectiveness 12, 13

totality of 22
weight of 22
see also practice-based evidence
evidence-base
inclusive research strategy for
building 22–26
more complete/thorough 346–348
evidence-based medicine (EBM) 4, 5,
22, 347
evidence-based mental health 288
evidence-based practice 330, 334,
338, 347
benefits 12
building a knowledge base for the
psychological therapies 21–53
combined model 50, 52
complementary model 50–52
controversy 4
current view of 3–17
definition 22–24
designs 50–52
key organizations 11
nature 3–6
professional issues 16, 17
scientific issues 12–16, 17
technology of 6–11
tensions 12–17
Evidence-based practice in psychology
(APA report) 24–26
Excel 259, 261
existential therapy 74
Expected Treatment Response (ETR)
approach 258, 273, 274
experiential psychotherapy 290, 297,
298, 300, 304
experiment 6
experimental manipulation 116,
117, 129, 132
as inappropriate 312
versus observation 14

explanatory clinical trials 36
explicit research questions 8, 9
external clinical evidence 4, 5, 22
external validity 13, 14, 22, 53, 115,
    134
    and Practice Research Networks
        312–314
eye movement desensitization and
    reprocessing (EMDR) 258,
    260, 264

fear, pain-related 120, 121
Federal Drug Administration
    research paradigm 234, 235
feedback 257, 268, 269, 271, 278, 320,
    340, 341
    clinical audit 313
    and Continuous Quality
        Improvement 229, 231
    of CORE 205–209, 211, 318, 319
    and the Outcome Questionnaire
        System 145, 146–148,
        147–152
    and practice-based evidence 48,
        49
    for practitioners 339
    and single case quantitative
        methods 130
    therapist 257, 268, 269, 271, 278,
        317
    on therapy training 291
    and the Treatment Outcome
        Package 155, 161
feedback loops 44
first-order characteristics 248
Fisher, Sir Ronald 34, 35
floor effects 164–166, 167
framework analysis 72, 73, 81
framing effects 33, 34
functional analysis 119
funding issues 4, 12

Practice Research Networks
    321–323
single case quantitative methods
    111
see also resource limitations

Galilean approach 235, 236
general practitioners (GPs), and
    CORE Net 210, 214
generality, and theory 94, 100
generalizability 13, 23, 24, 35, 36, 69,
    235–240, 235, 331, 332
    of efficacy research 41
    of single case quantitative methods
        112
    situated 49
generalized anxiety disorder 239
goal consensus 32
good practice 278
GP-CORE (general population) 179,
    181, 193
graded exposure 120, 121
graphical analysis 126
grounded theory 74, 81, 303
    core categories 74, 81
group cohesion 32
group commonality 235, 236
growth curve analysis 269–279
    see also Hierarchical Linear
        Modelling; multi-level
        modelling
Growth Mixture Models (GMMs)
    258, 276–278, 279
    categorical latent variables 276
growth modelling procedures 257,
    269–279
    estimating client change 269–271
    extension using nearest neighbour
        approaches 272–276, 273–275
    Level 1 models 270, 272
    Level 2 models 270

Hamilton Rating Scale for
Depression (HRSD) 185
health insurance 316, 331
Health of the Nation Outcome Scales
for Children and Adolescents
(HoNOSCA) 340
health outcomes
broad range of 37
quantification 44
see also treatment outcomes
measures
Health Plan Employer Data and
Information Set (HEDIS) 248
Hermeneutic Single Case Efficacy
Design (HSCED) 130, 297,
301
Hierarchical Linear Modelling
(HLM) 144, 248
see also growth curve analysis;
multi-level modelling
hierarchies, and randomized
controlled trials (RCTs) 347
history 7, 115, 118
homoscedasticity 270
hope 73, 226
hospital care, benchmarking 233
'hourglass' model 16, 50
hypotheses 38
alternative explanations of the 110,
113, 114, 118, 121, 129, 130,
133, 134, 135
and case studies 100
testing, versus case studies 93, 99,
100
hypothetico-deductive methods 69

IIP-32 273
illnesses, life-threatening 73
Imipramine 26
improvement management 285–323,
332–334, 337–342

organizational and conceptual
framework for practice-based
psychotherapy research
287–305
Practice Research Networks
311–323
and practice-based evidence 42,
43
see also Continuous Quality
Improvement; quality
Improving Access to Psychological
Therapies (IAPT) 41, 48, 52,
343
imputation 270
independence of errors 270
individual differences 332
induction 112
information technology (IT) 46
insight 104, 105
Institute for the Study of Therapeutic
Change 231
instrumentation 115, 130
intake procedures 44, 45
Integra Outpatient Tracking
Assessment (later COMPASS)
226, 227, 230, 232, 240
see also COMPASS-PC
integrative psychotherapy 258, 274
intercept 270
interests
conflicts of 84
issues/questions of 44
internal validity 6, 13, 14, 22, 29, 114,
115
definition 6
and Practice Research Networks
312–314
threats to 6, 7
International Paediatric Nursing
Research Network (IPNRN)
314

International Project on the
    Effectiveness of
    Psychotherapy and
    Psychotherapy Training
    (IPEPPT) 289–291
interpersonal psychotherapy 26,
    100–105, 274
interpersonal style 32
interpretation, theory-building case
    study research 97, 99, 104,
    105
Interpretive Phenomenological
    Analysis (IPA) 74, 75, 81, 303
interviews 71, 83, 84, 301
    narrative 75
    post-treatment (case records) 96
    semi-structured 71, 80, 81, 83, 301
Inventory of Interpersonal Problems
    316
Item Response Theory (IRT) 303

Jacobson plots 199, 200, 201, 268, 268
Japanese business practice 223, 227

knowledge body development 21–53,
    342–344

language, turn-taking 76, 77
language-focused approaches 71, 72,
    75, 76–78, 80, 82
    conversation analysis 76, 77, 82, 84
    discourse analysis 76, 77, 78, 82, 84
    LD-CORE (learning disabilities) 179,
    181
Leeds Community Mental Health
    NHS Trust 177
legitimacy, threats to 16, 17
Life Status Questionnaire (LSQ) 243
'life worlds' 74
life-threatening illnesses 73
Likert frequency scales 162

linear regression, log-linear
    regression line 260, 261–264,
    270, 271
linearity 270
'linguistic turn' 76
lived experience 68
local issues 10, 11, 205–209, 332
log-linear regression 260–264, 270,
    271

mania 164, 168, 171
maturation 115, 118, 131
mean scores 264, 278, 279
    regression to the mean 115
measurement systems 139–215, 343
    Clinical Outcomes in Routine
        Evaluation 175–215
    common 40, 41, 44, 46, 49
    meaningful 336, 337, 338
    non-standardized 124–126, 135
    Outcome Questionnaire System
        141–152
    practice-based evidence 39, 40, 41,
        44, 46, 47, 49
    repeated measures 114, 118, 124,
        128, 129, 131, 336, 337
    single case quantitative methods
        114, 118, 124–126, 128–131,
        135
    standardized 124–126, 135
    system approach to 195
    Treatment Outcome Package
        155–172
median scores 235, 236, 264, 265
Medical Research Council 26
medicine
    evidence-based 4, 5, 22, 347
    practice-based evidence 331
MEDLINE 9
Mental Health Foundation (MHF)
    177

Mental Health Index 230
Mental Health Research Network 314
meta-analysis 9, 10, 27, 28, 244, 347, 348
  researcher allegiance effect 33
methodological pluralism 63–135, 332, 335, 336
  qualitative methods 65–85
  single case quantitative methods 109–135
  theory-building case study research 91–106
mini-interventions 132, 133
monitoring 221–279, 339
  benchmarking 223–250, 257–279
  case tracking 257–279
  ongoing treatment-monitoring 143–152
Mplus 259, 276
multi-level modelling
  benchmarking 241–243
  see also growth curve analysis; Hierarchical Linear Modelling
multiculturalism 25, 332, 333
multiple indicators 341
multiple regression modelling 236, 243
multiple-baseline design 121, 122, 134
multivariate models 236, 248

Nagelkerke R^2 test 168
narrative analysis 75, 76, 81
National Advisory Mental Health Council (NAMHC) 23, 24
National Cancer Research Network 314
National Center for Quality Assurance, Health Plan Employer Data and Information Set (HEDIS) 248

national health service delivery systems 25
National Health Service (NHS) 177, 232, 241, 320, 323
  CORE Net 210–214
  databases 205–207, 257, 258, 259, 272
  primary care psychological therapy and counselling 205–207, 206
National Institute for Health and Clinical Evidence (NICE) 30, 41, 211, 247
  clinical guidelines 10, 11, 15, 27
  cost-effectiveness 11, 15
National Institute of Health Research (NIHR) 314
National Institute of Mental Health (NIMH) 23, 26
  Treatment of Depression Collaborative Research Project 176
National Institutes of Health 23
National Outcomes Management Project (NOMP) 229
National Registry of Evidence-based Programs and Practices (NREPP) 150
natural theory-building 345, 346
naturalistic research
  lack of controls 159
  naturalistic laboratories 41
  and the Treatment Outcome Package 155–172
nearest neighbour (NN) approach 258, 272–276, 273–275, 279
  clinical utility 274
  validity 274
Neck-Focused Flashback Severity Scale (N-FFS) 121
Neck-Focused Panic Attack Severity Scale (N-PASS) 121

negative thoughts, discomfort and
    believability of 124, 125
non-specific treatment effects 7,
    292–297, 294, 295
normality 270
normative data 230, 231, 232
    of the Outcome Questionnaire
    System 142, 151

objectivity 4
observation 312
    permeation of theory 93, 94, 95
    and theory 92–94, 95, 97, 98, 99,
    100, 106
    versus experiment 14
Obsessive-Compulsive Disorder 114,
    123, 124
Ohio Youth Scales 166
ongoing treatment-monitoring
    143–152
    barriers to 150–152
Ophthalmic Research Network 314
OQMeasures 141
organizations, key, of evidence-based
    practice 11
Outcome Questionnaire (OQ)
    System 141–152
    data collection process 150
    feedback 145, 146–148, 147–152
    internal consistency 142
    normative comparisons 142, 151
    ongoing treatment-monitoring
    144–152
    Outcome Questionnaire-10
    (OQ-10) 143
    Outcome Questionnaire-30
    (OQ-30) 142, 144
    Outcome Questionnaire-45
    (OQ-45) 141, 142, 144, 145,
    147–149, 151, 152, 226, 227,
    231, 232, 240, 293–295, 304

and quality assurance 143, 149
    scoring 142
    Severe Outcome Questionnaire
    (SOQ) 142
    as single case measure 143
    software-OQ-Analyst 141, 142, 150
    treatment failure prediction 144,
    145, 147–150, 148
    Youth Outcome Questionnaire
    (YOQ) 142, 144
    Youth Outcome Questionnaire-30
    (YOQ-30) 143, 144
Outcome Rating Scale (ORS) 226,
    227
outcomes
    training 291, 292, 294, 298, 302
    see also health outcomes; treatment
    outcome measures
ownership, research 41, 42, 337

pain
    -related fear 120, 121
    chronic back 120, 121
    emotional 74
panic attacks, neck-focused 121
panic disorder 237, 239
paradigm wars 69
participants *see* clients
Partners for Change Outcome
    Measurement System
    (PCOMS) 231
partnership, research 337
patient reported outcome measures
    (PROMs) 175, 246
patient-centred systems 214
patients *see* clients
peer support, and CORE 207, 209,
    214
Penn Helpline Alliance
    Questionnaire-II 295, 296
Penn State Training PRN 317, 318

Pennsylvania PRN 289, 316–318
Pennsylvania Psychological
    Association (PPA) 316
person-centred therapy 27, 33, 258,
    287, 289, 290, 297, 298
    Interpretive Phenomenological
        Analysis 74, 75
    and Practice Research Networks
        319
    and web-based resources 304
personality, voice metaphor 100–102
pharmacological therapy 315
    see also drug trials
phenomenological psychology 69, 71,
    74, 75, 81
phobia, social 132
PHQ-9 185, 192, 193
physical therapists 225, 226
PICO (Population, Intervention,
    Comparison, Outcome)
    algorithm 8, 9
placebo effects 26, 27, 28, 29, 36
polypharmacy 315
post-session questionnaires 301
post-traumatic stress disorder
    (PTSD) 121, 122, 260–264,
    260–263, 272, 273
practical/pragmatic clinical trials
    35–37
practice improvement *see*
    improvement management
practice research 23, 24
Practice Research Networks (PRNs)
    40, 41, 195, 287, 289, 311–323
    bias 321
    definition 313
    examples 314–320
    funding 321–323
    outcome measures 311–314,
        318–321
    paradigm 312–320

sample issues 320, 321, 322
    strengths 320, 321
    weaknesses 321, 322
practice-based evidence
    benchmarking 43, 223–250,
        257–279
    building a knowledge base for the
        psychological therapies
        21–53
    case tracking 43, 257–279
    change agency support 48, 49
    client selection 40, 49
    Clinical Outcomes in Routine
        Evaluation 175–215
    combined model 50, 52
    complementary model 50–52, 330,
        334, 348
    and the current view of
        evidence-based practice 3–17
    data 42–45, 47–49
    data drilling 341
    definition 22, 23
    designs 38, 42, 50–52, 51
    development 329–348
    differentiation from effectiveness
        research 331
    enhancing evidence 337, 338,
        342–346
    equipoise 335, 336, 343, 344
    ethics 39
    evidence base of 346–348
    features 37–43, 38, 39
    feedback 341
    framework 43–45
    hallmarks 37, 38, 39, 330, 334–337
    history 330, 331
    hypotheses 38
    and improving the client's journey
        through psychological
        services 340, 341
    investigator allegiance 38

knowledge body development
        21–53, 342–344
locations 39
measurement systems 39, 40, 41,
        44, 46, 47, 49, 336, 337, 338
and methodological pluralism 332,
        335, 336
and multiculturalism 332, 333
and a multidisciplinary
        environment 331–333
and multiple indicators 341
organizational and conceptual
        framework 287–305
    expanded protocols 302
    generic/pan-theoretical
        concepts 292–297, 294, 295
    maximum protocols 297
    minimum protocols 297–300,
        301, 305
    priorities 292, 293
    research protocols 297–302
    star design 290, 291, 292
    systematic case study protocols
        297, 300–302, 305
    therapy measurement domains
        291–297, 292, 294, 295
    training protocols 297
    treatment-specific research
        domains 292, 297, 298
Outcome Questionnaire System
        141–152
and ownership 41, 42,
        337
and partnership 337
and patterns of change 341, 342
philosophy and policy 38
and practice improvement 42, 43,
        332, 333, 334, 337–342
and Practice Research Networks
        40, 41, 311–323
and the practitioner 334, 335

principles 290
problem solving 341
and the processes of change 341,
        342
for psychological therapies 333,
        337
qualitative method selection 65–85
quality 42, 43, 47
quality feedback 48, 49
and randomized controlled trials
        50–52, 51, 330, 331, 334, 346,
        347, 348
relation of measurement to sample
        39
relevance 109, 110–113, 135, 346
research questions 41, 42
responsiveness 346
rigorous nature 109, 135
samples 38, 39, 40, 46
single case quantitative methods
        109–135
theory-building case study
        research as 91–106
tools 333, 334
and treatment delivery 47, 48
Treatment Outcome Package
        155–172, 226, 227, 240
treatments 38
vulnerabilities 45–48
practice-based evidence for clinical
        practice improvement
        (PBE-CPI) 42, 333
practice-based evidence national
        databases (PBE-NDs) 205
practice-research gap see
        research-practice gap
PracticeNet 315, 316
practitioner effects 344, 345, 347
    see also therapist effects
practitioner-led research 319
practitioners

and CORE 207–209, 339
effective 25
and missing data 46, 47
and practice-based evidence 334,
    335
process notes 96, 100, 301
and research ownership 41, 42, 337
research-practitioner models 202
and theory-building 345, 346
    see also scientist-practitioner;
        therapists
Pragmatic Case Study 297
pre-post design 118
primary research literature,
    systematic reviews 8–10, 11
principal component analysis (PCA)
    162
problem solving 341
process notes 96, 100, 301
process research 15, 44, 289–291, 292,
    294, 298, 299, 301, 335, 336,
    341, 342
    component evaluation 32
    training processes 291–292, 295,
        298
professional functioning scales 302
professional issues 16, 17
progress
    estimation 257, 258, 260–279
    see also change
protocol-imposed restrictions 31
psychiatrists 77, 315
psychoanalytic therapy 258
psychodynamic therapy 74, 258, 287,
    300, 319
    brief 78
    psychodynamic-interpersonal
        therapy 100–105
psychological expertise 3
psychological helping relationships
    66

psychological services research, and
    Practice Research Networks
    311–323
Psychology Clinic, Department of
    Psychology, Penn State 317
psychometrics, new, powerful 303,
    304
psychosis 77
psychotherapy 26–28
    benchmarking 225–227, 229–232,
        234, 235, 235, 238–241, 243,
        245, 246, 247–249
    empathy 68
    integrative 258, 274
    interpersonal 26, 274
    modelling change 269, 270, 272
    organizational and conceptual
        framework for practice-based
        research on the effectiveness
        of 287–305
    and qualitative methods 68, 75, 85
    and randomized controlled trial
        limitations 32
    and single case quantitative
        methods 112, 113
    as storytelling 75
    and theory-building case study
        research 91, 92, 96, 97, 100
Psychotherapy change measures
    conference (1975) 176
Psychotherapy Research Initiative 177
psychotherapy training,
    organizational and
    conceptual framework for
    practice-based effectiveness
    research 287–305
public health research paradigm 234,
    235

Qualitative European Drug Research
    Network 314

qualitative methods 48, 335, 346
   advantages 67, 68, 79
   'brand names' 70
   and causality 68
   choice of 78–82, 83
   and comparison 68
   computer-assisted analysis 78
   data collection methods 70, 71
   defining qualitative research 67, 68
   families of 71–78, 80–82
   features 70–72
   generic approaches 70
   and 'giving voice' 67, 68
   good practice guidelines 84, 85
   in-depth understanding of 67, 79,
      83, 84
   'insider's view' of 67
   interviews 71, 80, 81, 83, 84
   language-focused approaches 71,
      72, 75, 76–78, 80, 82
   personal preferences for 78, 79
   philosophical background 68, 69
   potential risks 83
   practical factors 78, 79, 80
   presence in psychological literature
      66, 67
   quality assessment 84, 85
   and quantitative methods 15, 68,
      69, 72, 73, 77, 79, 80, 83, 84
   and the research question 72, 79,
      82
   selection 65–85
   self-report 70, 71
   single case 110
   systemic 302, 303
   thematic analysis 71–76, 80, 81
   and theory generation 69, 79
   theory-building case study
      research 96, 97
   therapeutic benefits 83
   therapy transcripts 71, 72
   thick description 67
   treatment outcome measures 301
   using with your own clients 83, 84
   video/audio recordings 71
quality 339
   benchmarking 43, 223–250
   case tracking 43
   and CORE 318, 319
   and practice-based evidence 42,
      43, 47
quality assurance 143, 149, 228, 229
quality of life 168, 170
quantification
   of outcomes 44
   of process 44
quantitative methods 48, 335
   and qualitative methods 15, 68, 69,
      72, 73, 77, 79, 80, 83, 84
   single case 109–135
   theory-building case study
      research 96
   treatment outcome measures 301
questions, research 41, 42

random regression modelling *see*
      growth curve analysis;
      Hierarchical Linear Modelling
randomization 7, 8, 26, 29, 31, 159,
      330
   rejection of the notion of 14
   and single case quantitative
      methods 110, 116–119, 121,
      129, 132, 134
   tests 134
randomized controlled trials (RCTs)
      6, 8, 10, 13, 21–43
   Central Register of Controlled
      Trials 11
   and clinical judgment 16
   combined model 52
   comparison 7, 8

complementary to practice-based
    evidence 50–52, 330, 334, 348
contrast with practice-based
    studies 37–43
control 6, 8
of depression 26, 247
design 38, 42
domination 329
and effectiveness research 331
ethical issues 39
external validity 13, 14, 22
funding issues 12
as gold standard 28, 35
hallmarks 37, 38, 39
and hierarchies 347
hypotheses 38
impractical 290
inclusive research strategy for
    building an evidence-base
    21–26
internal validity 13, 22, 29
and investigator allegiance 38
issues with 26–37, 53
and location 39
measurement systems 39, 40
and methodological pluralism 335
versus observation 14
ongoing treatment-monitoring
    144–150, 146–148, 151
philosophy and policy 38
practical clinical trials 35–37
and practice-based evidence
    50–52, 51, 330, 331, 334,
    346–348
pragmatic 14
and qualitative research 15
randomization 7, 8, 26, 29, 31, 116,
    330
relation of measurement to sample
    39
and responsiveness 31–33
samples 38, 39
and statistical analysis 28, 34
systematic reviews 9
treatments 38, 47
rapport 198
Rasch analysis 303, 304
real-world settings 24, 26, 36, 37
realism, naive 69
reality, nature of 69
recovery rates, and CORE 199, 201,
    203, 204, 211
reflective practice 49
refugees 121, 122
regression models 272
    binary logistic regression 168
    linear regression 260, 261,
        261–263, 264, 270, 271
    multiple regression modelling 236,
        243
    traditional 270
    see also growth curve analysis;
        Hierarchical Linear Modelling
regression to the mean 115
rehabilitation 42
reinforcement 119
reinforcers 123
relevance criterion 109, 110–113,
    126, 129, 132, 135, 346
Reliable Change Index (RCI) 147, 166
replication, single case quantitative
    methods 133, 134
research networks
    single case quantitative methods
        134, 135
    see also Practice Research Networks
research questions 41, 42
research-practice gap 287, 288, 289,
    305, 311, 312, 313, 315, 317,
    319, 329, 337, 338, 343
research-practitioner models 202
researcher allegiance effect 29, 33, 38

residential care, disruptive behaviour
  of children in 119, 127
resource limitations 4
  see also funding issues
responsivity 31–33, 128, 346
reviews 24, 28
  traditional 8
  see also systematic reviews
rigour criterion 109, 110, 126, 129,
    132, 135
risk adjustment
  and the Treatment Outcome
    Package 159
  see also case-mix (risk) adjustment
risk management, and CORE 198,
    211
rituals, cleaning 123, 124
road traffic accidents 260, 272
role reversal 103
root mean square error of
    approximation (RMSEA) 162,
    163
routine service delivery, presenting
    and disseminating outcomes
    data 257–279

sample issues 39, 40, 46
  Practice Research Networks 320,
    321, 322
  randomized controlled trials 38, 39
  relation of measurement to sample
    39
SAS 259
scatter plots 267, 268
SCID 185, 192, 193
SCID I 318
SCID II 318
science, and psychological therapy 3,
    4
scientific issues, and evidence-based
    practice 12–16, 17

scientist-practitioner 12, 337, 338,
    343
scorecard (report card) of outcomes
    226, 227
scree test 162
seasonality 199, 200
second-order characteristics 248
self-disclosure 80–82
self-report measures 70, 71
  Continuous Quality Improvement
    230, 231
  CORE 175, 214
  of improvement 141, 142, 144,
    145, 147–149, 151, 152
service data, simple presentations
    264–268, 265–268
service systems research 23, 24
session-by-session assessments 96
settings
  practice/routine 37, 39, 39, 47, 332
  real-world 24, 26, 36, 37
  recruitment from a range of 36, 37
Severe Outcome Questionnaire
    (SOQ) 142
severity of client problems 293–295,
    299, 300, 303, 304
  recovery benchmarks 241, 242, 243
sexual assault 264
SF-36 164–166, 229
Short Form A and B 179, 180,
    188–190
single case methodology 110, 336,
    342, 346
  and benchmarking 235, 236, 250,
    257–264, 272–275
  and case tracking 257–264,
    260–263, 272–275
  see also single case qualitative
    methods; single case
    quantitative methods
single case qualitative methods 110

single case quantitative methods
109–135
AB design 117, 118, 129–131, 134
ABC design with counterbalancing
119–121
advantages 110–113
alternating treatment design 124,
125, 129, 134
alternative explanations of the
hypothesis 110, 113, 114, 118,
121, 129,130, 133, 134, 135
analysis 124–126, 134
applying behavioural
methodologies to
non-behavioural
interventions 127
baselines 114–118, 121, 122, 123,
129, 131, 134
basic features 114–117
brief 132
changing criterion design 121–124,
123
characteristics of non-behavioural
treatments 127, 128
definition 110
ethical nature 112
and experimental manipulation
116, 117, 129, 132
feedback 130
funding requirements 111
generalizability 112
infrastructure requirements 111
instrumentation 115, 130
journals and 135
measurement 114, 118, 124–126,
128–131, 135
methodology 113–126
mini-interventions as experimental
manipulations 132
mini-interventions and treatment
complexity 133

modifying the research ideal
129–135
multiple-baseline design 121, 122,
134
and non-behavioural treatments
127, 128, 129, 130
practical considerations 128, 129,
134, 135
pre-post design 118
problems applying the research
ideal to clinical practice
126–129
and randomization 110, 116–119,
121, 129, 132, 134
relevance 110–113, 126, 129, 132,
135
and repeated measurement 114,
118, 124, 128, 129, 131
replication 133, 134
research ideal 113–135
research networks 134, 135
retrospective baseline 131
rigorous 126, 129, 132, 135
strong-inference procedure 133,
134
types of design 117–124, 135
and validity 113, 114, 115, 118,
119, 134
and visual analysis of graphed data
126, 128, 134
withdrawal design 118, 119, 127,
128
single-blind trials 29
slope 270, 272
social anxiety 132
social constructionism 69, 71
Society for Psychotherapy Research
160
software-OQ-Analyst 141, 142, 150
specific factors 15, 16, 292, 297, 298
SPlus 259, 265

spontaneous remission 6, 7
SPSS 259, 265
standard deviation 246, 247, 278
'star' design 290, 291, 292
  multi-orientation 291
statistical judgment 16
statistical packages 257, 259
  tracking patterns/exceptions 259
statistical power 28, 34
storytelling 75, 76
stratification 247, 248
Strengths and Difficulties
  Questionnaire (SDQ) 340
streptomycin 26
stroke rehabilitation 42
strong-inference procedure 133, 134
subject positions 78
summaries, CORE 198–200,
  199–201, 201
supervision *see* clinical supervision
Supervision Practitioner Research
  Network 345
SWYT database 262, 263, 265–268,
  271
Symptom Checklist-90-R
  (SCL-90-R) 192, 293–295,
  304
Systat 259, 260, 261, 265
systematic reviews 8–10
  Cochrane Database of Systematic
    Reviews 11
  comprehensive study searches 9
  explicit research questions 8, 9
  quality appraisal 9
  synthesis 9, 10
systemic qualitative research methods
  302, 303
systemic therapies 287, 300

tape-assisted recall 71, 82, 83
task analysis 77

technology transfer study 36, 37, 235,
  235, 237–239
Teen-CORE 193
teleoanalysis 30, 50, 53, 330, 348
Temple study (1975) 26, 27
termination of therapy,
  client-initiated 203, 203, 206,
  207
test-retest reliability, Treatment
  Outcome Package 162–164,
  165
thematic analysis 71–76, 80, 81
  content analysis 72, 73, 81
  framework analysis 72, 73, 81
  grounded theory 74, 81
  Interpretive Phenomenological
    Analysis 74, 75, 81
  narrative analysis 75, 76, 81
theory
  changing through case study
    research 95, 97, 98, 99
  definition 91
  familiarity with 95, 98
  as growing and changing way of
    understanding 94
  importance of 91, 92
  natural 345, 346
  and practice improvement 332
  and qualitative methods 69, 79
  quality control through research
    92–95
theory-building 69, 79, 91, 92, 332
  natural 345, 346
theory-building case study research
  91–106
  analyzing case study materials
    97
  applying the case to the theory 97,
    98
  case selection 95, 96
  case study example 100–105

and conclusions 100
ethical issues 99
and generality 100
interpretation 97, 99, 104, 105
literature 98, 99
process 95–98
qualitative analysis 96, 97
quantitative analysis 96
reporting 98–100
rich case record 96
writing tips 98, 99
therapeutic action, and context 128
therapeutic alliance 30, 32
  and CORE Net 210
  measuring 295–297, 299, 300, 301, 303
  and power differentials 82
  see also common factors
therapeutic change *see* change
therapist effects 28, 34, 35, 37, 292, 294, 298, 299, 301
  masking 35
  see also practitioner effects
therapist-as-research-consumer model 288
therapists
  autonomy 152
  benchmarking 224–226, 241–243, 249
  characteristics 292, 294, 298, 299, 301
  effectiveness 34
  feedback 257, 268, 269, 271, 278, 317
  framework analysis of the competence of 73
  ideal 172
  inability to predict treatment failure 149, 150, 152
  interventions 128
  involvement in research 289

Practice Research Networks 316, 317, 319, 322
responsiveness 31–33, 128
self-disclosure 80–82
self-portrayal 82
therapy of 74
and the Treatment Outcome Package 156–159, 161, 172
see also practitioners
'thick description' 67
thought-control strategies 124, 125
threshold boundaries 271, 273, 273
timelines 131
timing issues
  as confounding variable 6, 7
  and the Treatment Outcome Package 158, 159
top-down approaches 269, 288, 314, 321
top-up strategies 214
Total Quality Management (TQM) 223, 227, 228, 232
trainee/trainer characteristics 292, 295, 298
training
  organizational and conceptual framework for practice-based effectiveness research 287–305
  outcomes 291, 292, 294, 298, 302
  and Practice Research Networks 317, 318
  processes 291, 292, 295, 298
transcripts 71, 72, 96, 97
transferability 94, 95
translational research 312, 315
transparency 4, 17, 152
  of reviews 8
treatment
  complexity 127, 128, 133
  confounding variables 5, 6

treatment (*Cont.*)
　databases 41
　delivery and practice-based
　　evidence 47, 48
　effects 347
　efficacy 5, 6
　evidence-based/empirically
　　supported 16
　funding pressures 4, 12
　homogenous 13
　knowledge base 21–53
　length 6
　professional status 3
　qualitative methods 65–85
　and science 3, 4
　service orientation 3, 4
　see also specific therapies
Treatment of Depression
　　Collaborative Research
　　Program 26
Treatment Evaluation and
　　Management (TEAM) 226,
　　227, 240
treatment failure 341
　estimation 271, 275
　and the Outcome Questionnaire
　　System 144, 145, 147–150, 148
　therapist's judgments of 149, 150,
　　152
　and the Treatment Outcome
　　Package 155
　see also deterioration
treatment outcome measures 25, 335,
　　336
　benchmarking 224–250, 257–279
　case records 96
　case tracking 257–279
　client-directed outcome-informed
　　approach 339
　core 176
　from routine service delivery
　　257–279

organizational and conceptual
　　framework for practice-based
　　psychotherapy research
　　288–291, 290, 292, 294, 298,
　　299, 301
　paradigms of 234–236, 234, 235
　Practice Research Networks
　　311–314, 318–321
　scorecard (report card) of 226,
　　227
　see also change; health outcomes
Treatment Outcome Package (TOP)
　　155–172, 226, 227, 240,
　　293–295, 317, 318
　benchmarking 155, 156, 159, 170,
　　171, 172
　ceiling effects 164–166, 167
　construction 160, 161
　convergent validity 164
　cost 158
　criterion validity 168–170
　current applications 170–172
　data processing 158, 159
　development 159–161
　discriminant validity 164
　enlightening aggregate data 172
　factor structure 161, 162, 163
　feedback 155, 161
　floor effects 164–166, 167
　links to research 171, 172
　modules 161
　outcome questionnaire 172
　outcomes as guide to the therapy
　　process plan 157
　patient reports that inform 170,
　　171
　psychometric overview 161–170
　risk adjustment 159
　royalty fees 158
　sensitivity to change 166–168, 169
　subscales 161, 164, 165, 166–171
　test-retest reliability 162–164, 165

timing 158, 159
and treatment failure 155
utility 157, 158
vision and philosophy 156–159
treatment plans, modification
decisions 315
treatment process *see* process research
treatment session records 71, 72, 96,
97, 301
treatment as usual (TAU) 36
tuberculosis 26
Tucker-Lewis index (TLI) 162, 163
Type 1 translational research 22
Type 2 translational research 22

universalism, limits of 332
utilization management 315

validity
concurrent 192
construct 115, 185
convergent 164, 185, 192
criterion 168–170
discriminant 164
external 13, 14, 22, 53, 115, 134,
312–314
internal 6, 7, 13, 14, 22, 29, 114,
115, 312–314
and the nearest neighbour
approach 274
randomized controlled trials 13,
14, 22, 29
and single case quantitative
methods 113, 114, 115, 118,
119, 134
statistical conclusion 115
and the Treatment Outcome
Package 164, 168–170
variables
case-mix 159
categorical latent 276

confounding 5, 6, 7, 14
dependent 6, 31, 168
independent 6, 7, 31, 127, 168
instrumental (propensity scores)
14
randomization 7
variation 114
within-subject 110, 111, 128
video/audio recordings of therapy
sessions 71, 96, 100, 301
virtual communities 304, 305
visual analysis 126, 128, 134
vulnerability 102–104

waiting times, benchmarking 227,
232, 241
web-based resources 304, 305
withdrawal design 118, 119, 119, 127,
128
within-subject variability 110, 111,
128
Working Alliance Inventory (WAI)
295–297, 296
world-views 74
wraparound process 332

Xerox Corporation 224, 227

young people, depression amongst
238, 239, 248
Youth Life Status Questionnaire
(YLSQ) 240
Youth Outcome Questionnaire
(YOQ) 142, 144
Youth Outcome Questionnaire-30
(YOQ-30) 143, 144
YP-CORE (young persons) 179, 181,
193, 194

zone of proximal development (ZPD)
101, 103–105